Quesadillas . . . Pumpkin Chowder . . .
Mozzarella, Tomato, and Arugula Salad . . .
Creamy Apricot Chicken . . . Pasta
Mediterranean . . . BBQ Beef on a Bun . . .
High-Fiber Apple Muffins . . . Banana
Brown Betty . . . Walnut Marble Cake . . .
Cocoa-Rum Warmer . . .

You'll find recipes for these and many other flavorful dishes
in WEIGHT WATCHERS® QUICK SUCCESS® PROGRAM
COOKBOOK. Delectable enough to please even the most dis-
criminating palates, all the recipes can be prepared in an hour
or less.

WEIGHT WATCHERS®
QUICK SUCCESS®
PROGRAM COOKBOOK

WEIGHT WATCHERS®
QUICK SUCCESS®
PROGRAM COOKBOOK

by Jean Nidetch

Photography by Gus Francisco

A PLUME BOOK

WEIGHT WATCHERS and QUICK SUCCESS are registered trademarks of
WEIGHT WATCHERS INTERNATIONAL, INC.

PLUME
Published by the Penguin Group
Penguin Books USA Inc., 375 Hudson Street, New York, New York 10014, U.S.A.
Penguin Books Ltd, 27 Wrights Lane, London W8 5TZ, England
Penguin Books Australia Ltd, Ringwood, Victoria, Australia
Penguin Books Canada Ltd, 10 Alcorn Avenue, Toronto, Ontario, Canada M4V 3B2
Penguin Books (N.Z.) Ltd, 182–190 Wairau Road, Auckland 10, New Zealand

Penguin Books Ltd, Registered Offices: Harmondsworth, Middlesex, England

Published by Plume, an imprint of Dutton Signet, a division of Penguin Books USA Inc.
Published simultaneously in Canada.

First Printing, July, 1990
11 10 9 8 7 6 5 4 3 2

 REGISTERED TRADEMARK—MARCA REGISTRADA

LIBRARY OF CONGRESS CATALOGING-IN-PUBLICATION DATA
Nidetch, Jean.
  Weight Watchers Quick Success Program cookbook/by Jean Nidetch.
    p.   cm.
  Includes index.
  ISBN 0-452-26428-6 (pbk.)
  1. Reducing diets—Recipes.   I. Weight Watchers International.
II. Title.
RM222.2.N525   1988
613.2'5—dc 19   88-21045
                                                     CIP

Printed in the United States of America
Set in Helvetica
Designed by Julian Hamer

Acknowledgments

Now that our new Program cookbook is a reality, it's time to thank the many dedicated people who contributed their talents to it.

We are grateful to Eileen Pregosin, under whose leadership the Publication Services staff has produced another outstanding cookbook.

Thanks go to our hard-working and talented chefs: Nina Procaccini, Christy Foley-McHale, Susan Haines, and Judi Rettmer. Not only did they develop and test the hundreds of recipes in this book, they also did the food styling for the photographs.

To our skillful editors, Patricia Barnett, Isabel Fleisher, Anne Neiwirth, Elizabeth Resnick-Healy, and April Rozea, we offer our appreciation for the difficult task of researching, writing, editing, and proofreading the manuscript. And thanks to Nancy Castaldo for her fine secretarial skills.

We would also like to thank Barbara Warmflash for her support, as well as for managing the many additional areas so necessary to the publication of this book.

And finally, we would like to express our sorrow at the passing this year of Irene Kask Pink, our editor at New American Library, and to gratefully acknowledge all the support and encouragement we have received from her over the years. Her guidance on this as well as on past cookbooks has been invaluable.

WEIGHT WATCHERS INTERNATIONAL

Contents

A Letter from Jean Nidetch

Dear Friends,

There's a big hit show in town and it's winning rave reviews everywhere. What is it? Why, *Weight Watchers Quick Success Program Cookbook,* as if you didn't already know. It's packed with more than 300 mouth-watering, easy-to-prepare recipes that are so delicious you'll never even realize you're dieting.

And when it comes to dieting, who knows and understands your needs better than Weight Watchers? With over 25 years of experience, we are the world leader in the weight-loss field. Our Programs *work,* and the Quick Success program is our best one yet. Why? Because it's faster, simpler, and healthier than ever before. This cookbook shows you just how flexible and versatile the Quick Success program really is, and how anyone can make it fit their individual life style. There are recipes to please every palate, plus menus to guide you in meal planning, and since they all conform to our Food Plan, there's no guesswork involved. And that's one giant step toward your ultimate goal — permanent weight loss.

But let's get back to our hit show and to the all-star cast waiting in the wings. Begin by reading "Setting the Stage," which contains important information about the Food Plan and how to use it. Next, look over the "Command Performance" section. In it you'll find information about microwave cooking, plus tips on ingredients, cooking methods, convenience equipment, and nutrition. In short, you'll learn what every good cook needs to know to prepare delicious, healthy meals.

And now, the curtain rises on our play in six acts — Fruit, Vegetables, Fat, Protein, Bread, and Milk — the six Exchanges that make up the Food Plan. As each act unfolds, you'll be guided through the Plan step by step, Exchange by Exchange. The grand finale is Options, and it is full of delightful surprises. You'll find helpful hints

1

in every act, as well as nutrition information, Exchange Lists, and, of course, the stars of our show, the recipes.

Imagine dining on Pasta with Veal Sausage Bolognese or Pork with Caraway Cream. Are you a vegetable lover? You'll find so many wonderful ways to serve them, like Buttery Eggplant Stew or Minted Medley. If you're a devotee of dessert—and who isn't—you'll adore Coffee-Nut-Flavored Mousse, Berry-Yogurt Parfait, and Orange-Iced Chiffon Cake. These and the hundreds of other recipes in this book were developed and prepared in the test kitchen of Weight Watchers International by our staff of expert chefs.

So what does dieting have to do with drama? Well, Shakespeare wrote that "all the world's a stage," and he was so right! The best thing about our stage is that *you* get to be the director, the producer, the star, and the audience. With our *Quick Success Program Cookbook* as your script, you'll be getting standing ovations for your culinary productions—and won't that be grand?

Best wishes,
Jean Nidetch
Founder, Weight Watchers International, Inc.

Setting the Stage: The Food Plan

Think of this chapter as your theater program. It's designed to introduce you to our phased Food Plan and to give you some help in building menus based on the recipes in this book. You'll also learn how to use the recipes in conjunction with the Food Plan. In doing this, you'll be setting the stage for successful weight loss and healthy eating.

We've included Menu Planners for Weeks 1 through 8, plus two bonus Menu Planners for Week 5: Vegetarian and Reduced-Sodium. Our Vegetarian Menu Planner is based on the Weight Watchers Vegetarian Plan, a lacto-ovo type of diet. This means that it is designed for those who choose to omit meat, poultry, and fish from their diet, but who wish to include eggs, milk, and milk products.

The Reduced-Sodium Menu Planner is designed to help you lower your sodium intake by restricting daily sodium levels to no more than an average of 2,000 milligrams. We've also included a list of many Program foods that contain less than 100 milligrams of sodium per Exchange. This list can be very useful if you are concerned about your sodium intake and wish to do your own menu planning.

In subsequent chapters of this book we discuss each of the categories (called Exchanges) in our Food Plan, plus a special category called "Options" that shows you how to add variety and interest to the Food Plan. There are tested recipes for each category, as well as tips to help you in cooking and meal planning. You'll find that our Food Plan truly is faster, simpler, and healthier than ever before.

Exchange Lists appear within each chapter. Each list indicates food servings that contain similar nutrients. You may substitute any item on an Exchange List for any other item on that list; however, you may only make these substitutions within the same Exchange List. For example, you may not exchange an item on the Bread list for an item on the Fruit list.

3

Week 1—Begin with our flexible yet balanced Food Plan that allows you to lose weight faster than ever before. You'll also get to select Optional Calories right from the start.

Weeks 2, 3, 4—The number of Optional Calories increases each week you remain on the Food Plan. Plus, you'll find that the Exchange Lists offer a greater variety of foods with each passing week.

Week 5—This is the Plan you will follow until you reach goal weight. With more choices and flexibility—including a Floating Exchange—you can customize the Food Plan to make it just right for you.

The Floating Exchange allows you to add an extra Exchange to your Daily Totals. Each day you can choose *one* Exchange from either the Fruit, Protein, Bread, or Milk Exchanges.

Weeks 6 and 8—Enjoy ethnic cuisines and special-occasion foods you never would have dreamed were possible on the Food Plan.

About the Menu Planners

• The weights indicated on the Menu Planners for poultry, meats, and fish are net cooked (or drained canned) weights (without skin and bones). Refer to the tips in each chapter for explanations of food items and cooking procedures.

• See the chart below for the Total Daily Exchanges for Women for each of the weeks of the Food Plan. (Numbers in parentheses are for Men and Youths, except for Milk figures, which are for Youths only.)

TOTAL DAILY EXCHANGES

	Week 1	Week 2	Week 3	Week 4	Week 5
Fruit	2 to 3 (3 to 4)	2 to 3 (3 to 4)	2 to 3 (3 to 5)	2 to 3 (3 to 5)	2 to 3 (3 to 5)
Vegetables	3 (at least)	3 (at least)	3 (at least)	3 (at least)	3 (at least)
Fat	3 (3)	3 (3)	3 (3)	3 (3)	3 (3)
Protein	5 to 6 (7 to 8)	5 to 6 (7 to 8)	5 to 6 (7 to 8)	5 to 6 (7 to 8)	5 to 6 (7 to 8)
Bread	2 (4)	2 to 3 (4 to 5)	2 to 3 (4 to 5)	3 (5)	3 (5)
Milk	2 (3)	2 (3)	2 (3 to 4)	2 (3 to 4)	2 (3 to 4)
Floating (optional)	0 (0)	0 (0)	0 (0)	0 (0)	1 (1)

We suggest you keep a daily food record to help you keep track of your daily Exchanges and to plan ahead.

Note: To add interest to your menus and to help you individualize the Food Plan, see the Options section (page 371).

• We recommend that you eat three meals a day. Snacks are optional, but if you choose to have any, they should be planned. Exchanges eaten as snacks should be counted toward your daily total. (See Total Daily Exchanges above.)

• Breakfast is required. The morning meal provides essential nutrients as well as the energy you need to perform your daily tasks. Breakfast-skippers tend to experience a mid-morning slump with a decrease in alertness. If you do not select at least 1 Protein Exchange at breakfast, you should eat 1 Bread Exchange with at least ½ Milk Exchange. Although fruit is not required at breakfast, it is recommended.

• Bold type on the Menu Planners indicates that the recipe is included in this book; menus are based on one serving of each recipe.

• You may consume additional vegetables daily, provided you follow the guidelines outlined in the Vegetable Exchange section (page 91).

• To increase the protein quality of dry beans, lentils, or peas, plan to supplement them with grains, poultry, meat, fish, egg, cheese, or milk (such as rice and beans, franks and lentils, etc.).

• We recommend that you eat the following per week:
no more than 3 eggs
no more than 4 ounces of hard or semisoft cheese
between 9 and 15 ounces of fish or shellfish
no more than 12 ounces of limited meats (those marked with an asterisk [*])
no more than 150 Optional Calories (Week 1); no more than 200 Optional Calories (Week 2); no more than 300 Optional Calories (Week 3); no more than 400 Optional Calories (Week 4); no more than 500 Optional Calories (Week 5 and beyond)

• The Menu Planners that follow are designed for Women. Additions for Men and Youths are noted on the Menu Planners.

MENU PLANNER FOR WEEK 1

Men and Youths: Daily add 2 Protein Exchanges, 2 Bread Exchanges, and 1 Fruit Exchange.

Youths only: Daily add 1 Milk Exchange.

Day 1

BREAKFAST
½ cup Peach Slices
½ cup Cooked Cereal
½ cup Skim Milk
Coffee or Tea

LUNCH
Roast Beef Sandwich (2½ ounces sliced roast beef with 3 tomato slices, 2 lettuce leaves, and 1½ teaspoons Russian dressing on 2 slices reduced-calorie wheat bread)

1 serving **Fresh Mushroom Salad** (page 127)
1 small Orange
Coffee, Tea, or Mineral Water

DINNER
3 ounces Broiled Swordfish Steak
½ cup *each* Cooked Chopped Spinach and Sliced Yellow Squash
Romaine-Cauliflower Salad (1 cup torn romaine lettuce with ½ cup cauliflower florets, 3 tomato wedges, ¼ cup sliced radishes, and 1½ teaspoons French dressing mixed with 2 teaspoons lemon juice and ¼ teaspoon Dijon-style mustard)

½ cup Reduced-Calorie Chocolate Pudding
Coffee or Tea

SNACK
Banana Yogurt (½ medium banana, diced, mixed with ¼ cup plain low-fat yogurt and dash nutmeg)

Optional Calories: 0

Day 2

BREAKFAST
½ cup Grapefruit Juice
1 Scrambled Egg
1-ounce Pita, toasted
½ cup Skim Milk
Coffee or Tea

LUNCH
Tuna-Vegetable Combo (2 ounces tuna with 1 cup torn lettuce, ½ cup *each* sliced carrot, celery, and cucumber, and 1 serving **Mustard-Caper Vinaigrette** [page 145])

1 small Apple
Coffee, Tea, or Mineral Water

DINNER
1 serving **Chicken 'n' Biscuits** (page 231)
½ cup *each* Cooked Carrot Sticks and Whole Green Beans
1½ cups Tossed Salad with 1½ teaspoons Italian Dressing mixed with 2 teaspoons Red Wine Vinegar
½ cup Skim Milk
Coffee or Tea

SNACK
1 cup Skim Milk; Gelatin 'n' Fruit (½ cup low-calorie orange-flavored gelatin topped with ½ cup fruit salad)

Optional Calories: 43

Day 3

BREAKFAST
½ cup Pineapple Chunks
⅓ cup Cottage Cheese
½ cup Skim Milk
Coffee or Tea

LUNCH
Chicken 'n' Swiss on Rye (1½ ounces sliced chicken with ½ ounce Swiss cheese, ½ cup shredded lettuce, and 1 teaspoon reduced-calorie mayonnaise on 2 slices reduced-calorie rye bread)

6 Celery Sticks and 3 Cherry Tomatoes
1 cup Watermelon Chunks
Coffee, Tea, or Mineral Water

DINNER
3 ounces Poached Shrimp with Lemon Wedge
1 serving **Tomato-Garlic Toasts** (page 295)
Spinach Salad (1 cup torn spinach with ¼ cup *each* grated carrot and sliced red onion, and 1½ teaspoons French dressing)
Coffee or Tea

SNACK
1 serving Reduced-Calorie Chocolate Dairy Drink; 1 cup Strawberries topped with ¼ cup Plain Low-Fat Yogurt

Optional Calories: 0

6

Day 4

BREAKFAST

1 small Orange
¾ ounce Cold Cereal
1 cup Skim Milk
Coffee or Tea

LUNCH

Cottage Cheese and Peaches (⅔ cup cottage cheese topped with ½ cup peach slices)
6 Melba Rounds
1 teaspoon Margarine
6 Zucchini Sticks and ½ cup Mushrooms
Coffee, Tea, or Mineral Water

DINNER

3 ounces Broiled Lamb Chop with Chopped Mint
¾ cup Cooked Broccoli Florets
½ cup Cooked Red Bell Pepper Strips
1 serving **Leek Salad** (page 122)
Coffee or Tea

SNACK

½ cup Reduced-Calorie Butterscotch Pudding; 1 small Apple

Optional Calories: 3

Day 5

BREAKFAST

1 cup Strawberries
1 ounce Muenster Cheese
1 serving **Cinnamon Monkey Bread** (page 290)
1 cup Skim Milk
Coffee or Tea

LUNCH

Tofu Salad (3 ounces diced tofu with ½ cup broccoli florets, 3 cherry tomatoes, sliced, ¼ cup diced scallions, and ½ teaspoon Chinese sesame oil plus rice vinegar)
1-ounce Roll
1 teaspoon Reduced-Calorie Margarine
Coffee, Tea, or Mineral Water

DINNER

3 ounces Baked Chicken Cutlet sprinkled with Lemon Juice and Chopped Parsley
½ cup each Cooked Sliced Mushrooms and Zucchini
Endive Salad (⅔ cup each torn lettuce and sliced Belgian endive with 1½ teaspoons blue cheese dressing mixed with 2 tablespoons plain low-fat yogurt plus garlic powder)
2-inch wedge Honeydew
½ cup Skim Milk
Coffee or Tea

SNACK

1 serving **Hot Citrus Tea** (page 409); ½ medium Banana, sliced and topped with 2 tablespoons Plain Low-Fat Yogurt

Optional Calories: 55

Day 6

BREAKFAST

Fruit Pizza (⅓ cup cottage cheese with ½ cup pineapple chunks on 1-ounce pita)
½ cup Skim Milk
Coffee or Tea

LUNCH

Turkey on a Roll (2 ounces sliced turkey with 3 tomato slices, 2 lettuce leaves, each 2 teaspoons mayonnaise on 1-ounce roll)
3 Radishes and 6 Celery Sticks
1 small Orange
Coffee, Tea, or Mineral Water

DINNER

2 ounces Broiled Fillet of Sole
½ cup each Cooked Cauliflower Florets and Wax Beans
1 serving **Mozzarella, Tomato, and Arugula Salad** (page 179)
½ cup Skim Milk
Coffee or Tea

SNACK

1 serving Reduced-Calorie Vanilla Dairy Drink

Optional Calories: 0

Day 7

BREAKFAST

1 small Orange
¾ ounce Cold Cereal
½ cup Skim Milk
Coffee or Tea

LUNCH

1 serving **Four-Cheese Omelet** (page 182)
1 cup Mixed Green Salad with 1½ teaspoons Thousand Island Dressing
½ cup Strawberries topped with 2 tablespoons Plain Low-Fat Yogurt
Coffee, Tea, or Mineral Water

DINNER

Steak 'n' Onions (3 ounces broiled steak with ½ cup cooked sliced onions and mushrooms)
1 serving **Zucchini Bake** (page 136)
Bibb Salad (1 cup torn Bibb lettuce with ½ cup sliced mushrooms, 3 red bell pepper rings, and ½ teaspoon olive oil plus red wine vinegar and herbs)
1 serving **Banana Chiffon Pie** (page 67)
Coffee or Tea

SNACK

1 cup Skim Milk; 2 x 3-inch wedge Watermelon

Optional Calories: 45

Total Optional Calories for Week: 146

MENU PLANNER FOR WEEK 1

Men and Youths: Daily add 2 Protein Exchanges, 2 Bread Exchanges, and 1 Fruit Exchange.

Youths only: Daily add 1 Milk Exchange.

Day 1

BREAKFAST
½ cup Orange Sections
1 serving **Buckwheat Pancakes** (page 300)
½ cup Skim Milk
Coffee or Tea

LUNCH
Chicken-Vegetable Salad (2 ounces sliced chicken with ¼ cup *each* broccoli and cauliflower florets, 3 cherry tomatoes, and 1 serving **Mustard-Caper Vinaigrette** [page 145])
1 slice Whole Wheat Bread
1 medium Peach
Coffee, Tea, or Mineral Water

DINNER
1 serving **Blackened Redfish** (page 196)
6 Cooked Asparagus Spears
½ cup Cooked Julienne-Cut Carrots
Bibb-Escarole Salad (¾ cup *each* torn Bibb lettuce and escarole with 2 tablespoons plain low-fat yogurt and ¼ teaspoon Dijon-style mustard)
Coffee or Tea

SNACK
1 serving Reduced-Calorie Vanilla Dairy Drink; 1 cup Strawberries

Optional Calories: 60

Day 2

BREAKFAST
2-inch wedge Honeydew
⅓ cup Cottage Cheese
3 Melba Rounds
½ cup Skim Milk
Coffee or Tea

LUNCH
Roast Beef 'n' Cheese Pita (1 ounce *each* roast beef and American cheese with 2 *each* tomato slices and lettuce leaves and 1 teaspoon mayonnaise in 1-ounce whole wheat pita)
6 *each* Zucchini and Celery Sticks
Coffee, Tea, or Mineral Water

DINNER
3 ounces Broiled Chicken Breasts sprinkled with Lemon Juice
1 serving **Gingered Citrus Carrots** (page 110)
½ cup Cooked Spinach
1½ cups Tossed Salad with 1 serving **Spicy Salad Croutons** (page 295) plus Red Wine Vinegar and Herbs
½ cup Reduced-Calorie Chocolate Pudding
Coffee or Tea

SNACK
½ cup Pineapple Chunks topped with ¼ cup Plain Low-Fat Yogurt

Optional Calories: 20

Day 3

BREAKFAST
½ medium Banana
¾ ounce Cold Cereal
½ cup Skim Milk
Coffee or Tea

LUNCH
Tuna Sandwich (2 ounces tuna with ¼ cup chopped celery, 2 lettuce leaves, and 2 teaspoons reduced-calorie mayonnaise on 2 slices reduced-calorie multi-grain bread)
½ cup *each* Cauliflower Florets and Mushrooms
1 small Orange
Coffee, Tea, or Mineral Water

DINNER
1 serving **Lamb Chops with Minted Honey Marinade** (page 250)
½ cup *each* Cooked Sliced Yellow Squash and Pearl Onions
½ cup Cooked Shredded Red Cabbage
Lettuce Wedge with 1 tablespoon Thousand Island Dressing
½ cup Skim Milk
Coffee or Tea

SNACK
½ cup Fruit Salad; 1 cup Skim Milk

Optional Calories: 15

8

Day 4

BREAKFAST
1 cup Strawberries
1 Scrambled Egg
1 slice Raisin Bread, toasted
1 teaspoon Reduced-Calorie
  Margarine
½ cup Skim Milk
Coffee or Tea

LUNCH
Pita Melt (1 ounce pita topped with
2 each tomato slices, red onion
slices, and 1 ounce Muenster
cheese, grilled)
1 serving **Mediterranean Cucumber
Salad** (page 113)
Coffee, Tea, or Mineral Water

DINNER
1 serving **Poached Salmon with Mint
Vinaigrette** (page 198)
Pimiento 'n' Asparagus (¾ cup
cooked sliced asparagus with
¼ cup pimiento strips and 1 teaspoon reduced-calorie margarine)
Spinach Salad (1 cup torn spinach
leaves with 3 tomato wedges and
¼ cup carrot curls plus balsamic
vinegar)
½ cup Reduced-Calorie Butterscotch
Pudding
Coffee or Tea

SNACK
Peach Yogurt (½ cup diced peach
mixed with ¼ cup plain low-fat
yogurt)

Optional Calories: 0

Day 5

BREAKFAST
1 cup Honeydew Chunks
⅓ cup Cottage Cheese
¾ cup Skim Milk
Coffee or Tea

LUNCH
Turkey Sandwich (2 ounces sliced
turkey with 4 tomato slices, ¼ cup
shredded lettuce, and 1½ teaspoons
Russian dressing on 2 slices
reduced-calorie rye bread)
6 Carrot Sticks and ½ cup Broccoli
Florets
1 small Apple
Coffee, Tea, or Mineral Water

DINNER
3 ounces Broiled Steak
½ cup each Cooked Sliced Onions
and Mushrooms
1½ cups Tossed Salad with 1 serving
Buttermilk-Blue Cheese Dressing
(page 356)
2 x 3-inch wedge Watermelon
Coffee or Tea

SNACK
1 cup Skim Milk; 1 serving **Toasted
Cinnamon Sticks** (page 294)

Optional Calories: 30

Day 6

BREAKFAST
½ cup Orange Sections
1 Sunny-Side-Up Egg
1 slice Whole Wheat Bread, toasted
1 teaspoon Reduced-Calorie Grape
  Spread
½ cup Skim Milk
Coffee or Tea

LUNCH
Ham Sandwich (2 ounces baked
Virginia Ham with 2 lettuce leaves
and 1 teaspoon mayonnaise on
2 slices reduced-calorie rye bread)
6 Celery Sticks and 3 Cherry
Tomatoes
½ medium Banana
Coffee, Tea, or Mineral Water

DINNER
3 ounces Baked Cod sprinkled with
Paprika
1 serving **Spaghetti Squash Florentine**
(page 123)
1½ cups Mixed Green Salad with
1 serving **Salsa Vinaigrette**
(page 148)
½ cup Reduced-Calorie Vanilla
Pudding
Coffee or Tea

SNACK
1 cup Strawberries topped with ¼ cup
Plain Low-Fat Yogurt

Optional Calories: 18

Day 7

BREAKFAST
2-inch wedge Honeydew
Cinnamon-Yogurt Oatmeal (½ cup
cooked oatmeal topped with
2 tablespoons plain low-fat yogurt
plus dash cinnamon)
½ cup Skim Milk
Coffee or Tea

LUNCH
1 serving **Tomato-Cheese Tarts**
(page 173)
Vegetable-Tuna Salad (1 ounce tuna
with 1 cup torn lettuce, 6 tomato
wedges, ¼ cup shredded red
cabbage, and ½ teaspoon olive oil
plus red wine vinegar and herbs)
½ cup Pineapple Chunks
Coffee, Tea, or Mineral Water

DINNER
1 serving **Grilled Chicken with Dijon
Mayonnaise** (page 221)
1 serving **Green Beans Sauté**
(page 119)
Bibb and Pepper Salad (1 cup torn
Bibb lettuce with ¼ cup each red
and yellow bell pepper strips,
2 tablespoons plain low-fat yogurt,
and ¼ teaspoon Dijon-style
mustard)
Coffee or Tea

SNACK
1 serving Reduced-Calorie Chocolate
Dairy Drink; ½ medium Banana

Optional Calories: 0

Total Optional Calories for Week: 143

9

MENU PLANNER FOR WEEK 2

Men and Youths: Daily add 2 Protein Exchanges, 2 Bread Exchanges, and 1 Fruit Exchange.

Youths only: Daily add 1 Milk Exchange.

Day 1

BREAKFAST
2-inch wedge Honeydew
½ cup Cooked Cereal
½ cup Skim Milk
Coffee or Tea

LUNCH
Tuna Sandwich (3 ounces tuna with 3 tomato slices, ¼ cup shredded lettuce, and 2 teaspoons reduced-calorie mayonnaise on 2 slices reduced-calorie multi-grain bread)
6 *each* Carrot Sticks and Cucumber Spears
1 small Apple
Coffee, Tea, or Mineral Water

DINNER
1 serving **Chicken, Prosciutto, and Eggplant Bake** (page 224)
½ cup Cooked Ziti Macaroni sprinkled with 1 teaspoon Grated Parmesan Cheese
½ cup Cooked Sliced Zucchini
1½ cups Tossed Salad with 1½ teaspoons Italian Dressing mixed with Red Wine Vinegar
1 cup Skim Milk
Espresso

SNACK
½ cup Raspberries; ½ cup Skim Milk

Optional Calories: 25

Day 2

BREAKFAST
½ cup Orange-Grapefruit Juice
1 Soft-Cooked Egg
½ Whole Wheat English Muffin, toasted
1 teaspoon Reduced-Calorie Margarine
1 cup Skim Milk
Coffee or Tea

LUNCH
Dijon-Turkey Salad (1 ounce diced turkey with ¼ cup sliced celery and 2 teaspoons *each* Dijon-style mustard and reduced-calorie mayonnaise)
1 slice Pumpernickel Bread
6 *each* Green and Red Bell Pepper Strips
1 medium Peach
Coffee, Tea, or Mineral Water

DINNER
3 ounces Broiled Lamb Chop
1 serving **Carrot and Mushroom Loaf** (page 107)
3 ounces Boiled Red Potato
Spinach-Carrot Salad (1 cup spinach leaves with 3 radishes, sliced, ¼ cup grated carrot, and 1½ teaspoons French dressing mixed with 2 teaspoons lemon juice and ¼ teaspoon mustard)
Coffee or Tea

SNACK
1 serving Reduced-Calorie Vanilla Dairy Drink; ½ cup Blueberries

Optional Calories: 15

Day 3

BREAKFAST
½ cup Pineapple Chunks
⅓ cup Cottage Cheese
1 slice Raisin Bread, toasted
¾ cup Skim Milk
Coffee or Tea

LUNCH
Roast Beef Sandwich (2 ounces sliced roast beef with 2 lettuce leaves, ¼ cup alfalfa sprouts, and 1 teaspoon *each* mayonnaise and horseradish on 1-ounce roll)
3 Cherry Tomatoes and ½ cup Cauliflower Florets
1 small Orange
Coffee, Tea, or Mineral Water

DINNER
2 ounces Broiled Shrimp with Chopped Parsley and Lemon Slices
1 serving **Pasta with Eggplant and Prosciutto Sauce** (page 306)
Tomato-Cucumber Salad (1½ cups torn lettuce with 6 *each* tomato and cucumber slices, and 1½ teaspoons Thousand Island dressing)
Coffee or Tea

SNACK
Strawberry Yogurt (1 cup strawberries, sliced, mixed with ½ cup plain low-fat yogurt and dash cinnamon)

Optional Calories: 10

Day 4

BREAKFAST

½ medium Banana, sliced
¾ ounce Cold Cereal
½ cup Skim Milk
Coffee or Tea

LUNCH

1 serving **Oriental Pork and Rice Salad** (page 251)
6 *each* Carrot and Zucchini Sticks
Coffee, Tea, or Mineral Water

DINNER

4 ounces Baked Chicken Breast with Tarragon Leaves
1 cup Cooked Broccoli Florets
½ cup Cooked Sliced Carrot
1 cup Tossed Salad with 1 serving **Spicy Salad Croutons** (page 295) and 1½ teaspoons Blue Cheese Dressing
2-inch wedge Honeydew
Coffee or Tea

SNACK

½ cup Reduced-Calorie Chocolate Pudding; ½ cup Skim Milk

Optional Calories: 30

Day 5

BREAKFAST

½ cup Orange-Grapefruit Juice
Cheddar Melt (1 ounce Cheddar cheese on 1 slice pumpernickel bread, melted)
¾ cup Skim Milk
Coffee or Tea

LUNCH

Chicken Sandwich (2 ounces sliced chicken with 4 lettuce leaves, 3 tomato slices, and 2 teaspoons reduced-calorie mayonnaise on 2 slices reduced-calorie multi-grain bread)
6 *each* Celery Sticks and Red Bell Pepper Strips
Coffee, Tea, or Mineral Water

DINNER

3 ounces Grilled Halibut Steak
1 cup Cooked French-Style Green Beans with ¼ cup Cooked Button Mushrooms
Iceberg Salad (iceberg lettuce wedge with 4 tomato wedges and 1½ teaspoons Russian dressing mixed with 2 tablespoons plain low-fat yogurt and ¼ teaspoon mustard)
1 serving **Banana Brown Betty** (page 339)
Coffee or Tea

SNACK

Dill Dip (½ cup *each* plain low-fat yogurt and diced cucumber plus dill weed); Assorted Vegetable Sticks

Optional Calories: 40

Day 6

BREAKFAST

Peach-Yogurt Cereal (½ cup plain low-fat yogurt mixed with ¾ ounce cold cereal and ½ cup peach slices)
Café au Lait (½ cup hot coffee and ¼ cup hot skim milk with dash cinnamon)

LUNCH

1 serving **Open-Face Turkey Sandwich with Brie Sauce** (page 234)
½ cup Broccoli Florets and 3 Radishes
Coffee, Tea, or Mineral Water

DINNER

3 ounces Grilled Ham Steak
½ cup *each* Cooked Chopped Spinach and Cauliflower Florets
1½ cups Mixed Green Salad with 1½ teaspoons Olive Oil plus Red Wine Vinegar and Herbs
1 serving **Cottage Fruit 'n' Custard Cake** (page 189)
Coffee or Tea

SNACK

½ cup Skim Milk; 1 cup Strawberries

Optional Calories: 40

Day 7

BREAKFAST

1 small Orange, cut into wedges
1 Scrambled Egg
½ Whole Wheat English Muffin, toasted
1 teaspoon Margarine
½ cup Skim Milk
Coffee or Tea

LUNCH

1 serving **Broccoli, Potato, and Cheese Soup** (page 105)
1 ounce Muenster Cheese
1 Rice Cake
½ medium Banana
Coffee, Tea, or Mineral Water

DINNER

3 ounces Broiled Flounder Fillet sprinkled with Paprika
¾ cup Cooked Sliced Yellow Squash with ¼ cup Cooked Diced Green Bell Pepper
Sprout-Mushroom Salad (½ cup *each* alfalfa sprouts and sliced mushrooms with 1½ teaspoons French dressing on 4 lettuce leaves)
1 serving **Raspberry and Pudding Treat** (page 359)
Coffee or Tea

SNACK

½ cup Skim Milk; ½ cup Honeydew Balls

Optional Calories: 30

Total Optional Calories for Week: 190

MENU PLANNER FOR WEEK 2

Men and Youths: Daily add 2 Protein Exchanges, 2 Bread Exchanges, and 1 Fruit Exchange.

Youths only: Daily add 1 Milk Exchange.

Day 1

BREAKFAST
½ cup Strawberries, sliced
¾ ounce Cold Cereal
¾ cup Skim Milk
Coffee or Tea

LUNCH
Tuna-Pasta Salad (2 ounces tuna with ½ cup each chilled cooked small shell macaroni, broccoli florets, zucchini slices, and 1 tablespoon creamy Italian dressing)
6 each Carrot Sticks and Green Bell Pepper Strips
1 small Orange
Coffee, Tea, or Mineral Water

DINNER
3 ounces Baked Veal Chop
6 Cooked Asparagus Spears
1½ cups Tossed Salad with 1½ teaspoons Buttermilk Dressing mixed with 2 tablespoons Plain Low-Fat Yogurt and ¼ teaspoon Mustard
1 serving **Pineapple Chunks with Raspberry Sauce** (page 88)
Coffee or Tea

SNACK
1 serving Reduced-Calorie Chocolate Dairy Drink

Optional Calories: 25

Day 2

BREAKFAST
½ cup Fruit Salad
⅓ cup Cottage Cheese
½ Raisin English Muffin, toasted
1 teaspoon Reduced-Calorie Margarine
1 cup Skim Milk
Coffee or Tea

LUNCH
Roast Beef Sandwich (2 ounces sliced roast beef with ½ cup alfalfa sprouts, 2 lettuce leaves, and 1 teaspoon mustard on 2 slices reduced-calorie wheat bread)
6 each Cherry Tomatoes and Celery Sticks
1 medium Peach
Coffee, Tea, or Mineral Water

DINNER
1 serving **Bluefish and Potato Casserole** (page 194)
1 cup Cooked Green Beans
½ cup Cooked Sliced Yellow Squash
Romaine Salad (1 cup torn romaine lettuce with ½ cup sliced mushrooms, ¼ cup diced scallions, and 1½ teaspoons French dressing mixed with 2 teaspoons lemon juice and ¼ teaspoon mustard)
Coffee or Tea

SNACK
½ cup Plain Low-Fat Yogurt sprinkled with dash Cinnamon; 1 cup Cantaloupe Chunks

Optional Calories: 10

Day 3

BREAKFAST
½ medium Grapefruit
1 ounce Gouda Cheese
½ small Bagel, toasted
½ cup Skim Milk
Coffee or Tea

LUNCH
Shrimp-Stuffed Pocket (2 ounces tiny shrimp with ¼ cup each diced cucumber and alfalfa sprouts, 3 tomato slices, and 2 teaspoons reduced-calorie mayonnaise in 1-ounce pita)
½ cup each Cauliflower and Broccoli Florets
Coffee, Tea, or Mineral Water

DINNER
3 ounces Baked Chicken
3 ounces Parslied Boiled Potato
1 serving **Gingered Citrus Carrots** (page 110)
1½ cups Mixed Green Salad with 1½ teaspoons Thousand Island Dressing mixed with 2 tablespoons Plain Low-Fat Yogurt and ¼ teaspoon Mustard
½ cup Blueberries topped with 2 tablespoons Plain Low-Fat Yogurt and dash Cinnamon
Coffee or Tea

SNACK
3 ounces Vanilla Dietary Frozen Dessert

Optional Calories: 20

Day 4

BREAKFAST
1 cup Strawberries
Mushroom Omelet (1 egg with ¼ cup sliced mushrooms)
1 Rice Cake
1 teaspoon Reduced-Calorie Margarine
½ cup Skim Milk
Coffee or Tea

LUNCH
Turkey-Swiss Sandwich (1 ounce each sliced turkey and Swiss cheese with 4 lettuce leaves, 3 tomato slices, and 1 tablespoon reduced-calorie mayonnaise on 2 slices reduced-calorie rye bread)
6 each Zucchini Sticks and Red Bell Pepper Strips
½ medium Banana
Coffee, Tea, or Mineral Water

DINNER
1 serving Gingered Salmon (page 197)
½ cup Cooked Fettuccine
½ cup each Cooked Chopped Spinach and Button Mushrooms
Radish-Sprout Salad (¼ cup each sliced radishes and alfalfa sprouts on 4 lettuce leaves with 1 teaspoon olive oil plus red wine vinegar and herbs)
Cappuccino (½ cup each hot espresso and hot skim milk with cinnamon stick stirrer)

SNACK
½ cup Reduced-Calorie Butterscotch Pudding

Optional Calories: 10

Day 5

BREAKFAST
½ cup Orange and Grapefruit Sections
¾ ounce Cold Cereal
1 cup Skim Milk
Coffee or Tea

LUNCH
Fruit 'n' Cheese Platter (⅔ cup cottage cheese with ½ cup each cantaloupe balls and strawberries, sliced, and ¼ cup blueberries on 4 lettuce leaves)
3 Melba Rounds
Coffee, Tea, or Mineral Water

DINNER
1 serving Chicken with Sun-Dried Tomatoes (page 225)
½ cup Cooked Noodles with 1 teaspoon Margarine
½ cup each Cooked Diced Eggplant and Stewed Tomatoes with Basil
1½ cups Tossed Salad with 1½ teaspoons Italian Dressing mixed with 2 teaspoons Red Wine Vinegar
Coffee or Tea

SNACK
Tropical Yogurt (½ cup plain low-fat yogurt mixed with ¼ cup canned crushed pineapple and ¼ teaspoon coconut extract)

Optional Calories: 55

Day 6

BREAKFAST
½ medium Banana, sliced
⅓ cup Cottage Cheese
½ small Bagel
1 cup Skim Milk
Coffee or Tea

LUNCH
1 serving Eggs and Prosciutto Toasts (page 162)
1 cup Mixed Green Salad with Red Wine Vinegar and Herbs
½ cup Skim Milk
Coffee, Tea, or Mineral Water

DINNER
3 ounces Broiled Flank Steak
3 ounces Cooked Red Potato
6 Cooked Broccoli Spears
1½ cups Tossed Salad with 1 serving Raspberry-Nut Vinaigrette (page 147)
1 serving Sparkling Oranges (page 82)
Coffee or Tea

SNACK
3 ounces Chocolate Dietary Frozen Dessert

Optional Calories: 70

Day 7

BREAKFAST
½ cup Orange Sections
1 Poached Egg
½ Raisin English Muffin, toasted
1 teaspoon Reduced-Calorie Margarine
½ cup Skim Milk
Coffee or Tea

LUNCH
1 serving Cheese 'n' Broccoli-Topped Potato (page 174)
1½ cups Tossed Salad with 1½ teaspoons French Dressing mixed with 2 teaspoons Lemon Juice and ¼ teaspoon Mustard
½ cup Skim Milk
Coffee, Tea, or Mineral Water

DINNER
1 serving Eggplant and Tomato Appetizer (page 115)
4 ounces Broiled Halibut with Paprika and Lemon Wedges
½ cup Cooked Carrot Sticks
Pepper-Cucumber Combo (½ cup cucumber slices with 6 red bell pepper strips plus red wine vinegar and herbs on 4 lettuce leaves)
Coffee or Tea

SNACK
¾ cup Skim Milk; ½ cup Fruit Salad

Optional Calories: 3

Total Optional Calories for Week: 193

13

MENU PLANNER FOR WEEK 3

Men and Youths: Daily add 2 Protein Exchanges, 2 Bread Exchanges, and 1 to 2 Fruit Exchanges.

Youths only: Daily add 1 to 2 Milk Exchanges.

Day 1

BREAKFAST
Ricotta-Apple Toast (¼ cup part-skim ricotta cheese with 1 small apple, sliced, and dash cinnamon on 1 slice reduced-calorie wheat bread, toasted)
½ cup Skim Milk
Coffee or Tea

LUNCH
Chick-Pea Salad (2 ounces drained canned chick-peas with 1 ounce shredded Swiss cheese, ¼ cup each sliced mushrooms and carrot, and 1½ teaspoons Italian dressing, mixed with 2 teaspoons red wine vinegar on 4 lettuce leaves)
1 Rice Cake
Coffee, Tea, or Mineral Water

DINNER
3 ounces Grilled Sliced Steak
3 ounces Baked Potato
1 teaspoon Margarine
1 cup Cooked Cauliflower Florets
1½ cups Mixed Green Salad with Lemon Juice and Herbs
1 serving Berry-Yogurt Parfait (page 364)
Coffee or Tea

SNACK
1 serving Reduced-Calorie Chocolate Dairy Drink; 1 small Orange

Optional Calories: 35

Day 2

BREAKFAST
½ cup Orange Juice
Nutmeg-Yogurt Cereal (½ cup cooked cereal topped with 2 tablespoons plain low-fat yogurt and dash nutmeg)
½ cup Skim Milk
Coffee or Tea

LUNCH
Open-Face Turkey Sandwich (2 ounces sliced turkey with ¼ cup alfalfa sprouts, 3 tomato slices, 2 lettuce leaves, and 2 teaspoons mayonnaise on 1 slice reduced-calorie multi-grain bread)
6 each Celery and Carrot Sticks
½ medium Banana
Coffee, Tea, or Mineral Water

DINNER
3 ounces Broiled Flounder Fillet with dash Paprika
1-ounce Roll
1 teaspoon Margarine
6 Cooked Broccoli Spears
1½ cups Tossed Salad with 1 serving Creamy Onion Dressing (page 356)
½ cup Skim Milk
Coffee or Tea

SNACK
20 small Grapes; ½ cup Skim Milk

Optional Calories: 0

Day 3

BREAKFAST
½ medium Grapefruit
1 Poached Egg
½ English Muffin, toasted
1 teaspoon Reduced-Calorie Margarine
1 cup Skim Milk
Coffee or Tea

LUNCH
Ham-Macaroni Salad (2 ounces diced ham with ½ cup each chilled cooked elbow macaroni and broccoli florets, ¼ cup sliced celery, and 1 tablespoon reduced-calorie mayonnaise on 4 lettuce leaves)
1 small Nectarine
Coffee, Tea, or Mineral Water

DINNER
3 ounces Baked Chicken
3 ounces Baked Yam
1 serving Lemon-Sautéed Beets (page 108)
Cucumber-Tomato Salad (½ cup cucumber slices with 6 cherry tomatoes plus red wine vinegar and herbs on 4 lettuce leaves)
Coffee or Tea

SNACK
½ cup Reduced-Calorie Butterscotch Pudding; ½ cup Fruit Salad

Optional Calories: 20

14

Day 4

BREAKFAST
1 cup Strawberries
¾ ounce Cold Cereal
½ cup Skim Milk
Coffee or Tea

LUNCH
Sliced Chicken Platter (2 ounces sliced chicken with 6 tomato slices, 3 radish roses, ½ cup each grated carrot, sliced mushrooms, and green bell pepper strips, and 2 tablespoons reduced-calorie mayonnaise on 4 lettuce leaves)
½ cup each Cauliflower Florets and Mushrooms
1 Rice Cake
Coffee, Tea, or Mineral Water

DINNER
3 ounces Broiled Scallops with Chopped Fresh Parsley
1 serving **Fettuccine with Chick-Peas and Eggplant** (page 307)
2 ounces Baked Chicken
3 ounces Cooked New Potato
¾ cup Cooked Baby Carrots
Cabbage-Scallion Salad (1 cup torn lettuce leaves with ½ cup shredded red cabbage, 2 tablespoons sliced scallion, and 1½ teaspoons French dressing mixed with 2 teaspoons lemon juice and ¼ teaspoon mustard)
Coffee or Tea

SNACK
Peach Yogurt (¾ cup plain low-fat yogurt mixed with 1 medium peach, diced)

Optional Calories: 35

Day 5

BREAKFAST
½ cup Fruit Salad
¼ cup Part-Skim Ricotta Cheese
½ English Muffin, toasted
½ cup Skim Milk
Coffee or Tea

LUNCH
Salmon in a Pita (2 ounces salmon with 2 tablespoons each chopped onion and grated carrot, 4 lettuce leaves, 4 cucumber slices, and 1 tablespoon reduced-calorie mayonnaise in 1-ounce pita)
½ cup each Cauliflower Florets and Broccoli Florets
1 small Orange
Coffee, Tea, or Mineral Water

DINNER
1 serving **Vegetable-Stuffed Mushrooms** (page 126)
2 ounces Baked Chicken
3 ounces Cooked New Potato
Chicory-Sprout Salad (¾ cup each torn chicory and lettuce with ¼ cup each alfalfa sprouts and sliced celery plus red wine vinegar and herbs)
Coffee or Tea

SNACK
½ cup Skim Milk; 1 serving **Nutty Chocolate Pudding** (page 407)

Optional Calories: 95

Day 6

BREAKFAST
½ cup Orange Juice
1 serving **High-Fiber Apple Muffins** (page 64)
¾ cup Skim Milk
Coffee or Tea

LUNCH
Chef's Salad (1 ounce each julienne-cut roast beef and thinly sliced Swiss cheese with 1 cup torn lettuce, 8 tomato wedges, ½ cup each sliced cucumber and celery, and 1 tablespoon Thousand Island dressing mixed with 2 tablespoons plain low-fat yogurt and ¼ teaspoon mustard)
1-ounce Roll
Coffee, Tea, or Mineral Water

DINNER
1 serving **Creole Red Beans and Rice** (page 267)
Cheese-Topped Broccoli (6 broccoli spears topped with 1 ounce Cheddar cheese, melted)
Romaine-Watercress Toss (¾ cup torn romaine lettuce with ¼ cup watercress plus lemon juice and herbs)
½ cup Skim Milk
Coffee or Tea

SNACK
Pineapple Shake (½ cup each skim milk and canned crushed pineapple and 2 ice cubes processed in blender)

Optional Calories: 40

Day 7

BREAKFAST
1 medium Peach
¾ cup Cold Cereal
½ cup Skim Milk
Coffee or Tea

LUNCH
1 serving **Hummus Soup** (page 269)
Deviled Egg (1 hard-cooked egg mixed with 2 teaspoons reduced-calorie mayonnaise, ¼ teaspoon mustard, and dash paprika)
6 Tomato Wedges with ½ cup Cucumber Slices plus Lemon Juice and Herbs on 4 Lettuce Leaves
1 cup Strawberries topped with ¼ cup Plain Low-Fat Yogurt
Coffee, Tea, or Mineral Water

DINNER
3 ounces Grilled Halibut Steak with Lemon Wedge
1 serving **Gratin of Leeks and Gorgonzola** (page 121)
1½ cups Tossed Salad with 1½ teaspoons Russian Dressing mixed with 2 tablespoons Plain Low-Fat Yogurt and ¼ teaspoon Mustard
½ cup Fruit Salad
Coffee or Tea

SNACK
¾ cup Skim Milk; 1 cup Popcorn

Optional Calories: 75

Total Optional Calories for Week: 300

15

MENU PLANNER FOR WEEK 3

Men and Youths: Daily add 2 Protein Exchanges, 2 Bread Exchanges, and 1 to 2 Fruit Exchanges.

Youths only: Daily add 1 to 2 Milk Exchanges.

Day 1

BREAKFAST
1 serving **Banana-Peanut Breakfast Shake** (page 388)
2 Graham Crackers
Coffee or Tea

LUNCH
Ham and Cheese Sandwich (1 ounce *each* baked Virginia ham and American cheese with 2 *each* lettuce leaves and tomato slices and 1 teaspoon reduced-calorie mayonnaise on 2 slices reduced-calorie rye bread)
½ cup *each* Carrot Sticks and Broccoli Florets
Coffee, Tea, or Mineral Water

DINNER
3 ounces Roast Chicken
1 serving **Creamy Minted Potatoes** (page 325)
½ cup Cooked Brussels Sprouts
1½ cups Mixed Green Salad with 1½ teaspoons Caesar Dressing mixed with 2 teaspoons Lemon Juice and ½ teaspoon Mustard
1 large Tangerine
Coffee or Tea

SNACK
1 serving Reduced-Calorie Chocolate Dairy Drink; 1 cup Cantaloupe Chunks

Optional Calories: 60

Day 2

BREAKFAST
1 cup Honeydew Chunks
⅓ cup Cottage Cheese
1 slice Reduced-Calorie Rye Bread, toasted
1 teaspoon Reduced-Calorie Margarine
½ cup Skim Milk
Coffee or Tea

LUNCH
Chicken Salad (2 ounces sliced chicken with 2 tablespoons chopped celery, ¼ cup alfalfa sprouts, and 1 tablespoon reduced-calorie mayonnaise on 2 lettuce leaves)
¾ ounce Breadsticks
6 Cherry Tomatoes
20 small Grapes
Coffee, Tea, or Mineral Water

DINNER
1 serving **Eggplant and Tomato Appetizer** (page 115)
3 ounces Broiled Scrod
½ cup Cooked Brown Rice
½ cup Cooked Sliced Beets
1½ cups Tossed Salad with 1 teaspoon Imitation Bacon Bits plus Balsamic Vinegar and Herbs
½ cup Fruit Salad
½ cup Skim Milk
Coffee or Tea

SNACK
½ cup Reduced-Calorie Vanilla Pudding topped with 1 Maraschino Cherry

Optional Calories: 20

Day 3

BREAKFAST
½ cup Grapefruit Juice
¾ ounce Cold Cereal
½ cup Skim Milk
Coffee or Tea

LUNCH
Salmon Sandwich (2 ounces salmon with 2 tablespoons *each* chopped celery and onion, 2 lettuce leaves, and 2 teaspoons reduced-calorie mayonnaise on 2 slices reduced-calorie wheat bread)
½ cup *each* Zucchini Sticks and Green Bell Pepper Strips
1 medium Peach
Coffee, Tea, or Mineral Water

DINNER
1 serving **Bean Burgers** (page 270)
1 cup Cooked Wax Beans
Greek Salad (1 ounce drained canned chick-peas with ½ ounce crumbled feta cheese, 2 cups torn romaine lettuce, 6 tomato wedges, and ½ cup sliced cucumber plus red wine vinegar and herbs)
Coffee or Tea

SNACK
1 cup Skim Milk; ½ cup Low-Calorie Cherry-Flavored Gelatin topped with ¼ cup Plain Low-Fat Yogurt

Optional Calories: 8

Day 4

BREAKFAST
3 medium Prunes
1/3 cup Cottage Cheese
1 Rice Cake
1/2 cup Skim Milk
Coffee or Tea

LUNCH
Roast Beef on a Roll (2 ounces sliced roast beef with 4 lettuce leaves, 3 tomato slices, 1/4 cup alfalfa sprouts, and 1 tablespoon Russian dressing on 1-ounce roll)
1/2 cup sliced Mushrooms and 3 Radishes
1 small Orange
Coffee, Tea, or Mineral Water

DINNER
3 ounces Grilled Tuna Steak with Lemon Wedge
3 ounces Parslied Boiled Potato
1 cup Cooked Shredded Red Cabbage
1 1/2 cups Tossed Salad with 1 serving **Mustard-Caper Vinaigrette** (page 145)
1/2 cup Skim Milk
Coffee or Tea

SNACK
1 serving Reduced-Calorie Vanilla Dairy Drink

Optional Calories: 0

Day 5

BREAKFAST
1/2 medium Banana
1/2 cup Cooked Cereal
1 cup Skim Milk
Coffee or Tea

LUNCH
1 serving **Chunky Cheese Salad** (page 177)
3/4 ounce Breadsticks
1 cup Cantaloupe Chunks
Coffee, Tea, or Mineral Water

DINNER
1 serving **Italian Cannellini Beans and Sausage** (page 262)
1/2 cup *each* Cooked Sliced Carrots and Spinach Leaves
Lettuce Wedge with 1 tablespoon French Dressing
Coffee or Tea

SNACK
1 cup Skim Milk; 2 Graham Crackers

Optional Calories: 15

Day 6

BREAKFAST
1/2 cup Grapefruit Juice
1 serving **Crunchy Oven-Fried French Toast** (page 287)
1 cup Skim Milk
Coffee or Tea

LUNCH
Turkey in a Pita (2 ounces sliced turkey with 1/4 cup grated carrot, 2 lettuce leaves, and 2 teaspoons reduced-calorie mayonnaise in 1-ounce pita)
6 *each* Cucumber Spears and Cherry Tomatoes
1 large Tangerine
Coffee, Tea, or Mineral Water

DINNER
1 serving **Clams in Red Sauce** (page 207)
1/2 cup Cooked Cauliflower Florets
1/2 cup Cooked Zucchini Sticks with 1/4 cup Pearl Onions
1 1/2 cups Mixed Green Salad with Red Wine Vinegar plus Herbs
Coffee or Tea

SNACK
1/2 cup Reduced-Calorie Butterscotch Pudding

Optional Calories: 105

Day 7

BREAKFAST
1 small Orange, cut into wedges
1 serving **Cheese and Rice Muffins** (page 337)
1/2 cup Skim Milk
Coffee or Tea

LUNCH
1 serving **Greek Lentil Salad** (page 271)
1 slice Pumpernickel Bread
6 Red Bell Pepper Strips and 1/2 cup Cauliflower Florets
Coffee or Tea

DINNER
3 ounces Broiled Veal Chop
1-ounce Roll
1/2 cup *each* Stewed Tomatoes, Cooked Mushroom Caps, and Sliced Onion
1 1/2 cups Tossed Salad with 1 1/2 teaspoons Blue Cheese Dressing mixed with 2 tablespoons Plain Low-Fat Yogurt plus Garlic Powder
1 serving **Berries in Vanilla Sauce** (page 69)
Coffee or Tea

SNACK
1 serving Reduced-Calorie Chocolate Dairy Drink; 20 small Grapes

Optional Calories: 75

Total Optional Calories for Week: 283

17

MENU PLANNER FOR WEEK 4

Men and Youths: Daily add 2 Protein Exchanges, 2 Bread Exchanges, and 1 to 2 Fruit Exchanges.

Youths only: Daily add 1 to 2 Milk Exchanges.

Day 1

BREAKFAST
½ medium Grapefruit sprinkled with ½ teaspoon Sugar
¾ ounce Cold Cereal
½ cup Skim Milk
Coffee or Tea

LUNCH
Shrimp-Spinach Salad (2 ounces tiny shrimp with 1 cup torn spinach, ¼ cup *each* sliced carrot, celery, and mushrooms, 6 tomato wedges, 1 teaspoon imitation bacon bits, and 1½ teaspoons Italian dressing mixed with 2 teaspoons red wine vinegar)
1 slice Whole Wheat Bread
Coffee, Tea, or Mineral Water

DINNER
1 serving **Chicken and Pasta Teriyaki** (page 227)
½ cup *each* Cooked Chinese Pea Pods and Yellow Squash Sticks
Chick-Pea Salad (2 ounces drained canned chick-peas with ½ cup torn lettuce, 2 tablespoons chopped scallion, and 1½ teaspoons French dressing mixed with 2 teaspoons lemon juice and ¼ teaspoon mustard)
1 cup Skim Milk
Coffee or Tea

SNACK
1 small Pear; ½ cup Skim Milk

Optional Calories: 75

Day 2

BREAKFAST
½ cup Orange Sections sprinkled with 1 teaspoon Shredded Coconut
1 Scrambled Egg with 1 tablespoon Chopped Scallion
1 slice Rye Bread, toasted
1 teaspoon Reduced-Calorie Margarine
¾ cup Skim Milk
Coffee or Tea

LUNCH
Turkey in a Pita (2 ounces sliced turkey with 2 *each* tomato slices, lettuce leaves, and onion slices and 2 teaspoons reduced-calorie mayonnaise in 1-ounce whole wheat pita)
½ cup Broccoli Florets and 6 Red Bell Pepper Strips
Coffee, Tea, or Mineral Water

DINNER
2½ ounces Broiled Swordfish with Lime Wedge
1 serving **Carrot-Potato Toss** (page 106)
½ cup Cooked Sliced Beets
1½ cups Mixed Green Salad with 1½ teaspoons Caesar Dressing mixed with 2 teaspoons Lemon Juice and ¼ teaspoon Mustard
Coffee or Tea

SNACK
½ cup Reduced-Calorie Butterscotch Pudding; 10 large Cherries

Optional Calories: 25

Day 3

BREAKFAST
1 cup Cantaloupe Chunks
Lox 'n' Bagel (½ small bagel topped with 2 tablespoons whipped cream cheese and 1 ounce smoked salmon)
1 cup Skim Milk
Coffee or Tea

LUNCH
Peanut Butter-Banana Grahams (2 tablespoons peanut butter and ½ medium banana, sliced, on 4 graham crackers)
6 *each* Carrot and Celery Sticks
Coffee, Tea, or Mineral Water

DINNER
Italian-Style Chicken (3 ounces baked chicken cutlet topped with ½ cup *each* stewed chopped Italian tomatoes and sliced zucchini)
1 cup Cooked Green Beans
Spinach Salad (1½ cups torn spinach with ½ cup sliced mushrooms and 1½ teaspoons Italian dressing mixed with 2 teaspoons red wine vinegar)
1 serving **Apple-Spice Tea** (page 63)

SNACK
1 serving Reduced-Calorie Vanilla Dairy Drink

Optional Calories: 87

18

Day 4

BREAKFAST
½ medium Grapefruit
1 Blueberry Muffin (2 ounces)
¾ cup Skim Milk
Coffee or Tea

LUNCH
Chick-Pea and Cheese Salad (2 ounces drained canned chick-peas with 1 ounce julienne-cut Fontina cheese, 1½ cups torn lettuce, ½ cup *each* sliced cucumber, carrot, and celery, and 1½ teaspoons Thousand Island dressing mixed with 2 tablespoons plain low-fat yogurt and ¼ teaspoon mustard)
1 small Pear
Coffee, Tea, or Mineral Water

DINNER
3 ounces Baked Fillet of Sole
1 serving **Country Corn Pudding** (page 317)
½ cup *each* Cooked Sliced Carrot and Spinach Leaves
1½ cups Tossed Salad with Red Wine Vinegar and Herbs
½ cup Strawberries
Coffee or Tea

SNACK
½ cup Skim Milk; 1 medium Plum

Optional Calories: 20

Day 5

BREAKFAST
½ cup Low-Calorie Cranberry Juice
Bagel Melt (½ small bagel topped with 1 ounce Swiss cheese, melted)
½ cup Skim Milk
Coffee or Tea

LUNCH
Tuna Sandwich (2 ounces tuna with ¼ cup *each* chopped celery and scallions, 2 lettuce leaves, ½ cup alfalfa sprouts, and 1 tablespoon reduced-calorie mayonnaise on 2 slices reduced-calorie rye bread)
½ cup Cauliflower Florets
10 small Grapes
Coffee, Tea or Mineral Water

DINNER
3 ounces Broiled Lamb Chop with Mint Sprig
3 ounces Cooked Sliced Sweet Potato
1 serving **Braised Red Cabbage with Apple and Caraway** (page 104)
Bibb Salad (1 cup torn Bibb lettuce with ¼ cup *each* shredded red cabbage and carrot, and 1½ teaspoons French dressing mixed with 2 teaspoons lemon juice and ¼ teaspoon mustard)
½ cup Reduced-Calorie Chocolate Pudding
Coffee or Tea

SNACK
¼ small Cantaloupe topped with ¼ cup Plain Low-Fat Yogurt

Optional Calories: 15

Day 6

BREAKFAST
1 cup Strawberries
1 serving **Orange Breakfast Loaf** (page 343)
½ cup Skim Milk
Coffee or Tea

LUNCH
1 serving **Grilled Oriental Chicken Salad** (page 220)
1-ounce Roll
1 teaspoon Reduced-Calorie Margarine
½ cup Applesauce sprinkled with dash Cinnamon
Coffee, Tea, or Mineral Water

DINNER
3 ounces Broiled Scallops
½ cup Cooked Long-Grain Rice with 1 tablespoon Diced Pimiento
1 cup Cooked Chinese Pea Pods
Lettuce and Tomato Salad (1½ cups shredded lettuce with 6 cherry tomato halves and 1½ teaspoons Italian dressing mixed with 2 teaspoons red wine vinegar)
1 serving **Grapes Brûlée** (page 77)
½ cup Skim Milk
Coffee or Tea

SNACK
1 serving Reduced-Calorie Vanilla Dairy Drink

Optional Calories: 120

Day 7

BREAKFAST
½ cup Orange Sections
⅓ cup Cottage Cheese sprinkled with dash Cinnamon
1 slice Reduced-Calorie Rye Bread, toasted
¾ cup Skim Milk
Coffee or Tea

LUNCH
1 serving **French Bread Pizza** (page 170)
1 cup Tossed Salad with 1 teaspoon Olive Oil plus Red Wine Vinegar and Herbs
2 medium Plums
Coffee, Tea, or Mineral Water

DINNER
3 ounces Roast Beef
½ cup *each* Cooked Brussels Sprouts and Wax Beans
1½ cups Tossed Salad with 1½ teaspoons Buttermilk Dressing mixed with 2 tablespoons Plain Low-Fat Yogurt and ¼ teaspoon Mustard
1 serving **Apple-Pear Compote** (page 61)
Coffee or Tea

SNACK
1 cup Skim Milk; 1 Graham Cracker

Optional Calories: 55

Total Optional Calories for Week: 397

19

MENU PLANNER FOR WEEK 4

Men and Youths: Daily add 2 Protein Exchanges, 2 Bread Exchanges, and 1 to 2 Fruit Exchanges.

Youths only: Daily add 1 to 2 Milk Exchanges.

Day 1

BREAKFAST
Berries 'n' Cheese (⅓ cup cottage cheese topped with ½ cup blueberries and dash cinnamon)
1 Graham Cracker
1 cup Skim Milk
Coffee or Tea

LUNCH
Tuna-Vegetable Salad (2 ounces tuna with 1 cup torn lettuce, 6 tomato wedges, ¼ cup *each* sliced red onion, sliced celery, and broccoli florets, and 1 serving **Creamy Herb Dressing** [page 143])
5 large Cherries
Coffee, Tea, or Mineral Water

DINNER
Pita Burger (3 ounces grilled hamburger with 2 *each* lettuce leaves and tomato slices, 1 teaspoon mayonnaise, and 2 teaspoons ketchup in 1-ounce pita)
1 serving **Vinaigrette Potato Salad** (page 330)
½ cup *each* Cooked French-Style Green Beans and Sliced Mushrooms
Iced Tea or Coffee

SNACK
1 serving Reduced-Calorie Chocolate Dairy Drink; 1 small Orange

Optional Calories: 55

Day 2

BREAKFAST
½ cup Orange Juice
¾ ounce Cold Cereal
½ cup Skim Milk
Coffee or Tea

LUNCH
Turkey Sandwich (2 ounces sliced turkey with 2 *each* lettuce leaves and tomato slices, ¼ cup alfalfa sprouts, and 1 tablespoon Russian dressing on 2 slices reduced-calorie wheat bread)
6 Green Bell Pepper Strips and ½ cup Cucumber Slices
1 medium Plum
Coffee, Tea, or Mineral Water

DINNER
3 ounces Broiled Red Snapper Fillet
3 ounces Baked Potato topped with 1 tablespoon Sour Cream
½ cup Cooked Cauliflower Florets and Sliced Carrot
1 teaspoon Reduced-Calorie Margarine
1 serving **Fennel Salad** (page 118)
Coffee or Tea

SNACK
¾ cup Plain Low-Fat Yogurt; 1 medium Peach

Optional Calories: 44

Day 3

BREAKFAST
½ cup Grapefruit Sections
1 ounce Cheddar Cheese
½ English Muffin, toasted
1 teaspoon Reduced-Calorie Margarine
¾ cup Skim Milk
Coffee or Tea

LUNCH
Open-Face Egg Salad Sandwich (2 hard-cooked eggs, chopped, with 2 onion slices, 2 tablespoons chopped celery, 4 lettuce leaves, and 2 teaspoons reduced-calorie mayonnaise on 1 slice reduced-calorie rye bread)
3 Cherry Tomatoes and ½ cup Broccoli Florets
Coffee, Tea, or Mineral Water

DINNER
3 ounces Baked Chicken
1 serving **Creamy Herb Potatoes** (page 324)
1 cup Cooked Chinese Pea Pods with ¼ cup Cooked Pearl Onions
Bibb Salad (1½ cups torn Bibb lettuce with ½ cup bean sprouts, 6 red bell pepper rings, and 1½ teaspoons French dressing mixed with 2 tablespoons plain low-fat yogurt and ¼ teaspoon mustard)
Coffee or Tea

SNACK
Blueberry Pudding (½ cup reduced-calorie vanilla pudding topped with ½ cup blueberries and sprinkled with ½ teaspoon confectioners' sugar)

Optional Calories: 70

Day 4

BREAKFAST

1 medium Peach
Cinnamon-Cheese Toast (⅓ cup cottage cheese sprinkled with dash cinnamon on 1 slice reduced-calorie wheat bread, toasted)
½ cup Skim Milk
Coffee or Tea

<u>LUNCH</u>

1 serving **Mexican Chicken Salad** (page 222)
3 Melba Rounds
1 teaspoon Margarine
½ cup Reduced-Calorie Lime Gelatin topped with ¼ cup Plain Low-Fat Yogurt
Coffee, Tea, or Mineral Water

DINNER

2½ ounces Baked Veal Cutlet with
½ cup Stewed Chopped Tomatoes
¼ cup *each* Cooked Red and Green Bell Pepper Strips
1 serving **Minestrone Salad** (page 321)
2-inch wedge Honeydew Melon
½ cup Skim Milk
Coffee or Tea

SNACK

3 ounces Chocolate Dietary Frozen Dessert topped with 1 tablespoon Thawed Frozen Dairy Whipped Topping

Optional Calories: 86

Day 5

BREAKFAST

½ cup Orange Juice
1 Sunny-Side-Up Egg
½ English Muffin, toasted
1 teaspoon Reduced-Calorie Margarine
1 cup Skim Milk
Coffee or Tea

<u>LUNCH</u>

Salmon in a Pita (2 ounces salmon with 3 tomato slices, ¼ cup grated carrot, 2 lettuce leaves, and 1 teaspoon mayonnaise in 1-ounce whole wheat pita)
6 *each* Celery Sticks and Cucumber Spears
10 large Cherries
Coffee, Tea, or Mineral Water

DINNER

3 ounces Baked Ham Steak
1 serving **Glazed Onions with Cranberries** (page 128)
½ cup Cooked Peas with Chopped Mint
½ cup Cooked Sliced Yellow Squash
1½ cups Mixed Green Salad with ½ teaspoon Olive Oil plus Balsamic Vinegar and Herbs
Coffee or Tea

SNACK

1 serving Reduced-Calorie Vanilla Dairy Drink; 2 medium Plums

Optional Calories: 45

Day 6

BREAKFAST

½ cup Blueberries
¾ ounce Cold Cereal
½ cup Skim Milk
Coffee or Tea

<u>LUNCH</u>

Roast Beef on Rye (2 ounces sliced roast beef with ½ cup shredded lettuce, 2 tomato slices, and 2 teaspoons reduced-calorie mayonnaise on 2 slices reduced-calorie rye bread)
Coffee, Tea, or Mineral Water

DINNER

3 ounces Broiled Tuna Steak
½ cup Cooked Whole Kernel Corn
6 Cooked Broccoli Spears
1½ cups Tossed Salad with 1 tablespoon Buttermilk Dressing
1 serving **Black Forest Pudding** (page 74)
Coffee or Tea

SNACK

½ cup Skim Milk; 1 small Orange

Optional Calories: 50

Day 7

BREAKFAST

1 medium Peach, sliced
Peanut Butter 'n' Grahams (1 tablespoon peanut butter on 2 graham crackers)
1 cup Skim Milk
Coffee or Tea

<u>LUNCH</u>

1 serving **Lobster and Pear Salad** (page 210)
6 Melba Rounds
½ cup Reduced-Calorie Chocolate Pudding
Coffee, Tea, or Mineral Water

DINNER

3 ounces Roast Chicken
3 ounces Baked Potato sprinkled with 1 teaspoon Imitation Bacon Bits
½ cup *each* Cooked Brussels Sprouts and Wax Beans
Cabbage-Sprout Salad (½ cup each shredded red cabbage and alfalfa sprouts with 1½ teaspoons Italian dressing on 4 lettuce leaves)
1 serving **Honey-Poached Pear Fans** (page 84)
Coffee or Tea

SNACK

Orange Fizz (½ cup *each* orange juice and club soda with 3 ice cubes)

Optional Calories: 45

Total Optional Calories for Week: 395

MENU PLANNER FOR WEEK 5

Men and Youths: Daily add 2 Protein Exchanges, 2 Bread Exchanges, and 1 to 2 Fruit Exchanges.

Youths only: Daily add 1 to 2 Milk Exchanges.

Day 1

BREAKFAST
½ cup Low-Calorie Cranberry Juice
⅓ cup Cottage Cheese
1 serving **Applesauce-Rye Muffins** (page 335)
1 serving Reduced-Calorie Hot Cocoa

LUNCH
Tuna Roll (3 ounces tuna with 2 tablespoons *each* chopped celery and onion, ¼ cup alfalfa sprouts, 2 lettuce leaves, and 2 teaspoons reduced-calorie mayonnaise on 1-ounce roll)
6 Cucumber Spears and 3 Radishes
1 small Orange
Coffee, Tea, or Mineral Water

DINNER
1 serving **Chicken Niçoise** (page 233)
½ cup Cooked Long-Grain Rice
½ cup *each* Cooked Spinach and Sliced Yellow Squash
Pepper-Carrot Salad (½ cup *each* red bell pepper rings and sliced carrot with ¼ cup sliced red onion and 1½ teaspoons blue cheese dressing mixed with 2 tablespoons plain low-fat yogurt plus garlic powder on 4 lettuce leaves)
Coffee or Tea

SNACK
¾ cup Skim Milk; ½ cup Pear Slices

Optional Calories: 90

Day 2

BREAKFAST
2-inch wedge Honeydew Melon
Onion Omelet (1 egg with 2 tablespoons chopped onion)
1 slice Reduced-Calorie Wheat Bread
1 teaspoon Reduced-Calorie Margarine
½ cup Skim Milk
Coffee or Tea

LUNCH
Turkey Salad (2 ounces sliced turkey with 6 tomato wedges and ¼ cup *each* sliced celery, carrot, cucumber, and broccoli and cauliflower florets, and 1½ teaspoons Russian dressing mixed with 2 tablespoons plain low-fat yogurt and ¼ teaspoon mustard on 4 lettuce leaves)
3 Melba Rounds
Coffee, Tea, or Mineral Water

DINNER
1 serving **Cheese Enchiladas** (page 171)
1 cup Cooked Green Beans
1 serving **Avocado and Roquefort Salad** (page 390)
1 medium Kiwi Fruit, sliced and topped with 2 tablespoons Plain Low-Fat Yogurt
Coffee or Tea

SNACK
½ cup Reduced-Calorie Chocolate Pudding; 2 Graham Crackers

Optional Calories: 90

Day 3

BREAKFAST
2 tablespoons Raisins
¾ ounce Cold Cereal
1 cup Skim Milk
Coffee or Tea

LUNCH
Shrimp Salad in a Pita (2 ounces tiny shrimp with ¼ cup *each* diced celery and alfalfa sprouts, 3 tomato slices, and 1 tablespoon reduced-calorie mayonnaise in 1-ounce whole wheat pita)
6 *each* Carrot Sticks and Red Bell Pepper Strips
1 small Nectarine
Coffee, Tea, or Mineral Water

DINNER
1 serving **Chicken Zaragoza** (page 232)
6 Cooked Asparagus Spears
½ medium Parslied Broiled Tomato
1½ cups Mixed Green Salad with 1½ teaspoons Italian Dressing mixed with 2 teaspoons Red Wine Vinegar
Mimosa (½ cup orange juice mixed with ¼ cup champagne and garnished with mint sprig)

SNACK
1 serving Reduced-Calorie Vanilla Dairy Drink; 1 Rice Cake

Optional Calories: 70

Day 4

BREAKFAST

½ cup Grapefruit and Orange Sections

Peanut Butter Bagel (1 tablespoon peanut butter with 2 teaspoons reduced-calorie grape spread on ½ small bagel)

½ cup Skim Milk

Coffee or Tea

LUNCH

Swiss 'n' Chick-Pea Toss (1 ounce each drained canned chick-peas and julienne-cut Swiss cheese with 1½ cups mixed green salad, 1 teaspoon imitation bacon bits, and 1½ teaspoons Italian dressing)

Coffee, Tea, or Mineral Water

DINNER

Burger in a Pita (3 ounces broiled hamburger patty with ½ cup each cooked sliced onion and mushrooms and 2 teaspoons ketchup in 1-ounce pita)

1½ cups Tossed Salad with 1½ teaspoons Thousand Island Dressing mixed with 2 tablespoons Plain Low-Fat Yogurt and ¼ teaspoon Mustard

1 serving **Banana Bread Pudding** (page 292)

Coffee or Tea

SNACK

1 serving Reduced-Calorie Hot Cocoa; 2 medium Apricots

Optional Calories: 56

Day 5

BREAKFAST

1 small Nectarine, sliced

⅓ cup Cottage Cheese sprinkled with dash Nutmeg

½ Whole Wheat English Muffin, toasted

1 cup Skim Milk

Coffee or Tea

LUNCH

Roast Beef Sandwich (2 ounces sliced roast beef with 3 tomato slices, ¼ cup sliced mushrooms, 2 lettuce leaves, and 2 teaspoons reduced-calorie mayonnaise on 2 slices reduced-calorie wheat bread)

6 each Cucumber Spears and Celery Sticks

Coffee, Tea, or Mineral Water

DINNER

½ medium Pink Grapefruit sprinkled with ½ teaspoon Brown Sugar

3 ounces Sliced Poached Chicken Cutlet

½ cup Cooked Brussels Sprouts

Carrot and Lettuce Salad (½ cup grated carrot with 1½ teaspoons buttermilk dressing on 4 lettuce leaves)

Coffee or Tea

SNACK

1 cup Skim Milk; 1 serving **Buttermilk-Raisin Scones** (page 340)

Optional Calories: 25

Day 6

BREAKFAST

1 small Orange, cut into wedges

1 Sunny-Side-Up Egg

½ small Bagel, toasted

½ cup Skim Milk

Coffee or Tea

LUNCH

1 serving **Double Onion Soup** (page 129)

Special Turkey Sandwich (2 ounces sliced turkey with ½ cup coleslaw on 1-ounce roll)

3 Cherry Tomatoes and 6 Zucchini Sticks

Coffee, Tea, or Mineral Water

DINNER

1 serving **Braised Sole with Basil-Butter Sauce** (page 202)

½ cup Cooked Noodles

½ cup Cooked Baby Carrots

Vegetable Salad (½ cup each cucumber slices and cauliflower florets, 6 red bell pepper strips, and 1½ teaspoons French dressing on 4 lettuce leaves)

Coffee or Tea

SNACK

Spiced Yogurt (¾ cup plain low-fat yogurt mixed with 2 tablespoons dark raisins and dash cinnamon)

Optional Calories: 110

Day 7

BREAKFAST

1 cup Low-Calorie Cranberry Juice

½ cup Cooked Cereal

½ cup Skim Milk

Coffee or Tea

LUNCH

1 serving **California Shrimp Salad** (page 213)

Apricot Yogurt (2 medium apricots, diced, mixed with ¼ cup plain low-fat yogurt)

Coffee, Tea, or Mineral Water

DINNER

3 ounces Broiled Lamb Chops

1 serving **Barley Salad Vinaigrette** (page 297)

6 cooked Broccoli Spears

Lettuce Wedge with 6 Tomato Slices and ½ teaspoon Olive Oil plus Red Wine Vinegar and Herbs

Coffee or Tea

SNACK

1 serving Reduced-Calorie Chocolate Dairy Drink; 1 cup Honeydew Melon Balls

Optional Calories: 25

Total Optional Calories for Week: 466

23

MENU PLANNER FOR WEEK 5

Men and Youths: Daily add 2 Protein Exchanges, 2 Bread Exchanges, and 1 to 2 Fruit Exchanges.

Youths only: Daily add 1 to 2 Milk Exchanges.

Day 1

BREAKFAST
½ cup Orange Sections
1 serving **Autumn Oatmeal** (page 298)
¾ cup Skim Milk
Coffee or Tea

LUNCH
Tuna-Pasta Toss (2 ounces tuna with ½ cup *each* chilled cooked small shell macaroni, broccoli florets, and sliced carrot and 1½ teaspoons buttermilk dressing mixed with 2 tablespoons plain low-fat yogurt and ¼ teaspoon mustard on 4 lettuce leaves)
6 *each* Celery Sticks and Red Bell Pepper Strips
½ cup Strawberries
Coffee, Tea, or Mineral Water

DINNER
4 ounces Baked Chicken
3 ounces Baked Sweet Potato with 1 teaspoon Reduced-Calorie Margarine and dash Cinnamon
1 serving **Asparagus and Mushroom Sauté** (page 103)
1½ cups Mixed Green Salad with Red Wine Vinegar and Herbs
White Wine Spritzer (¼ cup *each* dry white table wine and club soda with lime wedge)

SNACK
½ cup Reduced-Calorie Chocolate Pudding

Optional Calories: 120

Day 2

BREAKFAST
Pineapple Yogurt Crunch (½ cup *each* plain low-fat yogurt and canned crushed pineapple sprinkled with 1 teaspoon wheat germ)
1 slice Whole Wheat Bread, toasted
1 teaspoon Reduced-Calorie Margarine
Coffee or Tea

LUNCH
Turkey-Tomato Pita (3 ounces sliced turkey with 4 tomato slices, ½ cup shredded lettuce, and 2 teaspoons reduced-calorie mayonnaise in 1-ounce whole wheat pita)
½ cup Cauliflower Florets and 6 Carrot Sticks
1 cup Cantaloupe Balls
Coffee, Tea, or Mineral Water

DINNER
3 ounces Broiled Flounder Fillet with Paprika
1 serving **Barley Pilaf** (page 296)
½ cup *each* Cooked Chinese Pea Pods and Bean Sprouts
Tomato-Squash Salad (6 *each* tomato wedges and yellow squash slices with 1½ teaspoons Italian dressing mixed with 2 teaspoons red wine vinegar on 4 lettuce leaves)
Coffee or Tea

SNACK
1 cup Skim Milk; ¾ ounce Mixed Dried Fruit

Optional Calories: 15

Day 3

BREAKFAST
½ cup Grapefruit Juice
1 Corn Muffin (2 ounces), toasted
2 teaspoons Reduced-Calorie Strawberry Spread
1 cup Skim Milk
Coffee or Tea

LUNCH
Tuna Platter (2 ounces tuna with ½ cup *each* sliced zucchini, cucumber, and mushrooms, 6 tomato wedges, ¼ cup *each* shredded red cabbage and sliced scallions plus red wine vinegar and herbs on 4 lettuce leaves)
1-ounce Roll
1 medium Kiwi Fruit
Coffee, Tea, or Mineral Water

DINNER
1 serving **Braised Rosemary Chicken with Olives** (page 229)
½ cup Cooked Long-Grain Rice
½ cup *each* Cooked Baby Carrots and Cut Green Beans
Pepper-Broccoli Salad (½ cup *each* red bell pepper rings and broccoli florets with 1½ teaspoons French dressing mixed with 2 teaspoons lemon juice and ¼ teaspoon mustard on 1 cup shredded lettuce)
Coffee or Tea

SNACK
1 serving **Banana-Buttermilk Shake** (page 367)

Optional Calories: 121

Day 4

BREAKFAST
1 cup Strawberries, sliced and sprinkled with ½ teaspoon Confectioners' Sugar
1 Poached Egg
1 slice Whole Wheat Bread, toasted
1 teaspoon Margarine
½ cup Skim Milk
Coffee or Tea

LUNCH
Chicken Salad Sandwich (2 ounces diced chicken with ¼ cup chopped celery, ½ cup alfalfa sprouts, 3 green bell pepper rings, and 2 teaspoons reduced-calorie mayonnaise on 2 slices reduced-calorie multi-grain bread)
6 each Zucchini Sticks and Cherry Tomatoes
Coffee, Tea, or Mineral Water

DINNER
3 ounces Broiled Ground Veal Patty with 2 teaspoons Ketchup
Sautéed Mushrooms (½ cup sliced mushrooms and ¼ cup sliced onion sautéed in 1 teaspoon margarine)
6 Cooked Asparagus Spears
1 serving **Carrot-Fruit Salad (page 82)**
2 medium Apricots; ½ cup Skim Milk
Coffee or Tea

SNACK
1 serving Reduced-Calorie Vanilla Dairy Drink; 2 cups Plain Popcorn

Optional Calories: 35

Day 5

BREAKFAST
½ cup Orange Sections
¾ ounce Cold Cereal
1 cup Skim Milk
Coffee or Tea

LUNCH
Bologna Sandwich (2 ounces sliced bologna with 2 each tomato slices and lettuce leaves and 1 teaspoon reduced-calorie mayonnaise on 2 slices reduced-calorie rye bread)
6 each Red Bell Pepper Strips and Cucumber Spears
½ medium Banana
1 medium Oatmeal Cookie (½ ounce)
Coffee, Tea, or Mineral Water

DINNER
3 ounces Poached Salmon Fillet
1 serving **Buttered Fettuccine-Spinach Toss (page 303)**
1 cup Cooked Cauliflower Florets
Boston Salad (1 cup torn Boston lettuce with ½ cup each sliced red onion and zucchini and 1 teaspoon olive oil plus red wine vinegar and herbs)
Coffee or Tea

SNACK
Fruity Yogurt (½ cup plain low-fat yogurt mixed with ¾ ounce mixed dried fruit and dash nutmeg)

Optional Calories: 110

Day 6

BREAKFAST
½ cup Canned Crushed Pineapple
⅓ cup Cottage Cheese
½ cup Skim Milk
Coffee or Tea

LUNCH
1 serving **Calzones (page 169)**
1½ cups Tossed Salad with 1½ teaspoons Italian Dressing mixed with 2 teaspoons Red Wine Vinegar plus Herbs
1 medium Kiwi Fruit
Coffee, Tea, or Mineral Water

DINNER
3 ounces Broiled Pork Chops
Honeyed Pumpkin (½ cup cooked mashed pumpkin with 1 teaspoon margarine, ½ teaspoon honey, and dash cinnamon)
¼ cup each Cooked Green and Wax Beans
Lettuce Wedge with 1½ teaspoons Russian Dressing
½ cup Skim Milk
Coffee or Tea

SNACK
½ cup Reduced-Calorie Chocolate Pudding; 2 Rice Cakes

Optional Calories: 10

Day 7

BREAKFAST
½ cup Grapefruit Juice
¾ ounce Cold Cereal
½ cup Skim Milk
Coffee or Tea

LUNCH
Tuna Melt (1 ounce tuna with 2 tablespoons chopped celery and 2 teaspoons mayonnaise on 1-ounce pita topped with 2 tomato slices and 1 ounce American cheese, melted)
½ cup each Sliced Mushrooms and Cauliflower Florets
Coffee, Tea, or Mineral Water

DINNER
3 ounces Roast Chicken with Tarragon Leaves
½ cup each Cooked Carrot Sticks and Shredded Red Cabbage
1 serving **Caesar Salad (page 176)**
1 serving **Apple-Raisin Pandowdy (page 62)**
Coffee or Tea

SNACK
Strawberry Yogurt (¾ cup plain low-fat yogurt mixed with ½ cup strawberries, sliced)

Optional Calories: 65

Total Optional Calories for Week: 476

25

MENU PLANNER FOR WEEK 6

Men and Youths: Daily add 2 Protein Exchanges, 2 Bread Exchanges, and 1 to 2 Fruit Exchanges.

Youths only: Daily add 1 to 2 Milk Exchanges.

Day 1

BREAKFAST
Raisin-Ricotta "Danish" (¼ cup part-skim ricotta cheese with 1 tablespoon golden raisins and dash nutmeg on ½ whole wheat English muffin, toasted)
½ cup Skim Milk
Coffee or Tea

LUNCH
Turkey in a Pita (2 ounces sliced turkey with ½ cup shredded lettuce, ¼ cup grated carrot, 3 tomato slices, and 2 teaspoons reduced-calorie mayonnaise in 1-ounce pita)
6 each Celery Sticks and Cucumber Spears
Coffee, Tea, or Mineral Water

DINNER
4 ounces Broiled Flounder Fillet with 1 serving Tartar Sauce (page 144)
½ cup Cooked Wide Noodles
1 teaspoon Margarine
½ cup each Cooked Sliced Beets and Chinese Pea Pods
⅛ medium Pineapple
Coffee or Tea

SNACK
¾ cup Plain Low-Fat Yogurt; ¼ small Cantaloupe

Optional Calories: 40

Day 2

BREAKFAST
1 serving Granola (page 299)
½ cup Skim Milk
Coffee or Tea

LUNCH
Ham and Swiss Pasta Salad (1 ounce each diced ham and Swiss cheese with ½ cup cooked chilled elbow macaroni, ¼ cup each sliced zucchini, broccoli florets, and sliced carrot, 6 cherry tomato halves, and 1½ teaspoons butter-milk dressing mixed with 2 table-spoons plain low-fat yogurt and ¼ teaspoon mustard)
½ cup Applesauce
Coffee, Tea, or Mineral Water

DINNER
3 ounces Baked Chicken
3 ounces Baked Potato topped with 2 tablespoons Plain Low-Fat Yogurt
1 serving Brussels Sprouts 'n' Bacon Sauté (page 391)
Cucumber-Tomato Salad (½ cup sliced cucumber with 6 tomato wedges plus red wine vinegar and herbs on 4 lettuce leaves)
Coffee or Tea

SNACK
1 serving Reduced-Calorie Vanilla Dairy Drink; 1 cup Strawberries

Optional Calories: 110

Day 3

BREAKFAST
½ cup Grapefruit Sections
1 Scrambled Egg
½ small Bagel, toasted
1 teaspoon Margarine
½ cup Skim Milk
Coffee or Tea

LUNCH
Roast Beef on Rye (2 ounces sliced roast beef with 3 each tomato slices and lettuce leaves, ½ cup alfalfa sprouts, and 1½ teaspoons Russian dressing on 2 slices reduced-calorie rye bread)
6 Carrot Sticks and 3 Radishes
1 small Pear
Coffee, Tea, or Mineral Water

DINNER
1 serving Fillet Rolls with Crab Sauce (page 201)
½ cup Cooked Long-Grain Rice with ¼ cup Cooked Sliced Mushrooms
½ cup each Cooked Spinach Leaves and Yellow Squash Sticks
1½ cups Mixed Green Salad with 1½ teaspoons French Dressing mixed with 2 teaspoons Lemon Juice and ¼ teaspoon Mustard
½ cup Reduced-Calorie Butterscotch Pudding
Coffee or Tea

SNACK
1 serving Tangy Colada Shake (page 369)

Optional Calories: 120

Day 4

BREAKFAST
½ cup Orange Juice
¾ ounce Cold Cereal
1 cup Skim Milk
Coffee or Tea

LUNCH
Tuna Salad (2 ounces *each* tuna with 2 tablespoons *each* chopped celery and onion and 2 teaspoons reduced-calorie mayonnaise on 4 lettuce leaves)
1-ounce Roll
6 Tomato Wedges and ½ cup Cauliflower Florets
Coffee, Tea, or Mineral Water

DINNER
4 ounces Broiled Chicken
¾ cup Cooked Cauliflower Florets
½ cup *each* Cooked Cubed Eggplant and Stewed Chopped Tomatoes with dash Basil Leaves
1½ cups Tossed Salad with 1 teaspoon Olive Oil mixed with 2 teaspoons Tarragon Vinegar plus Herbs
1 serving **Cherry-Apple Cobbler** (page 73)
1 cup Skim Milk
Coffee or Tea

SNACK
⅓ cup Apple Juice; 1 cup Plain Popcorn

Optional Calories: 35

Day 5

BREAKFAST
1 cup Strawberries, sliced
¼ cup Part-Skim Ricotta Cheese
3 Graham Crackers
1 cup Skim Milk
Coffee or Tea

LUNCH
Peanut Butter-Raisin Sandwich (2 tablespoons *each* peanut butter and golden raisins on 2 slices reduced-calorie wheat bread)
6 *each* Zucchini Sticks and Whole Mushrooms
Coffee, Tea, or Mineral Water

DINNER
3 ounces Broiled Shrimp with Lemon Wedge
½ cup Chinese Pea Pods and 1½ ounces Water Chestnuts sautéed in ½ teaspoon Chinese Sesame Oil
½ cup Cooked Baby Carrots
1 serving **Three-Cabbage Salad** (page 103)
Coffee or Tea

SNACK
1 cup Skim Milk; ½ cup Applesauce sprinkled with dash Cinnamon

Optional Calories: 55

Day 6

BREAKFAST
¼ small Cantaloupe
1 Poached Egg
1 slice Rye Bread
1 teaspoon Reduced-Calorie Margarine
¾ cup Skim Milk
Coffee or Tea

LUNCH
1 serving **Cheese 'n' Ham-Topped Biscuits** (page 175)
Mandarin Orange Salad (¼ cup canned mandarin orange sections with ½ cup *each* torn romaine and iceberg lettuce leaves and 1½ teaspoons French dressing mixed with 2 teaspoons lemon juice and ¼ teaspoon mustard)
Coffee, Tea, or Mineral Water

DINNER
3 ounces Grilled Pork Chop
3 ounces Cooked Sweet Potato sprinkled with dash Cinnamon
6 Cooked Broccoli Spears
½ cup Cooked Wax Beans
Lettuce Wedge with 1½ teaspoons Italian Dressing mixed with 2 teaspoons Red Wine Vinegar
⅛ medium Pineapple with Mint Sprig
Coffee or Tea

SNACK
Peach-Spiced Yogurt (½ cup plain low-fat yogurt mixed with ¼ cup peach slices and dash cinnamon)

Optional Calories: 3

Day 7

BREAKFAST
½ cup Grapefruit Sections
½ cup Cooked Cereal
½ cup Skim Milk
Coffee or Tea

LUNCH
1 serving **Pennsylvania Dutch Corn Chowder** (page 318)
6 Saltines
Chicken-Broccoli Salad (2 ounces julienne-cut chicken with ½ cup blanched broccoli florets, 6 cherry tomato halves, ¼ cup sliced red onion, and 1 tablespoon buttermilk dressing on 4 lettuce leaves)
Coffee, Tea, or Mineral Water

DINNER
1 serving **Cheddar-Bacon Puffs** (page 384)
4 ounces Broiled Swordfish Steak sprinkled with dash Paprika
½ cup Sliced Mushrooms sautéed in 1 teaspoon Reduced-Calorie Margarine
6 Cooked Asparagus Spears sprinkled with Grated Orange Peel
½ cup Raspberries topped with ¼ cup Low-Fat Yogurt
Coffee or Tea

SNACK
½ cup Skim Milk; 1 small Pear

Optional Calories: 135
Total Optional Calories for Week: 498

MENU PLANNER FOR WEEK 8

Men and Youths: Daily add 2 Protein Exchanges, 2 Bread Exchanges, and 1 to 2 Fruit Exchanges.

Youths only: Daily add 1 to 2 Milk Exchanges.

Day 1

BREAKFAST
½ cup Blueberries
½ cup Cooked Cereal
1 cup Skim Milk
Coffee or Tea

LUNCH
Tuna-Stuffed Pocket (2 ounces tuna with 6 cucumber slices, ¼ cup shredded lettuce, 2 tablespoons grated carrot, and 2 teaspoons reduced-calorie mayonnaise in 1-ounce whole wheat pita)
1 small Orange
6 each Green Bell Pepper Strips and Celery Sticks
Coffee, Tea, or Mineral Water

DINNER
3 ounces Broiled Steak
1 small ear Corn
1 teaspoon Margarine
Spinach Salad (2 cups torn spinach with ¼ cup each sliced mushrooms and red onion and 1½ teaspoons French dressing mixed with 2 teaspoons lemon juice and ¼ teaspoon mustard)
1 serving **Coffee-Nut-Flavored Mousse** (page 406)
Coffee or Tea

SNACK
½ cup Reduced-Calorie Vanilla Pudding; 20 small Grapes

Optional Calories: 120

Day 2

BREAKFAST
1 cup Strawberries
1 Scrambled Egg sprinkled with 1 teaspoon Grated Parmesan Cheese
½ cup Skim Milk
Coffee or Tea

LUNCH
Chicken-Vegetable Salad (2 ounces diced chicken with ½ cup broccoli florets, ¼ cup each chopped celery and sliced cucumber, and 1 tablespoon Thousand Island dressing on 4 lettuce leaves)
¾ ounce Crispbreads
2 medium Apricots
Coffee, Tea, or Mineral Water

DINNER
1 serving **New Orleans BBQ Shrimp** (page 214)
1-ounce Roll
1 teaspoon Reduced-Calorie Margarine
¾ cup Cooked Chopped Spinach
1½ cups Mixed Green Salad with ½ teaspoon Olive Oil mixed with 2 teaspoons Balsamic Vinegar and ¼ teaspoon Mustard
½ cup Fruit Salad
½ cup Skim Milk
Coffee or Tea

SNACK
1 cup Skim Milk; 2 cups Plain Popcorn

Optional Calories: 35

Day 3

BREAKFAST
½ cup Grapefruit Sections with Mint Sprig
⅓ cup Cottage Cheese
1 slice Pumpernickel Bread
½ cup Skim Milk
Coffee or Tea

LUNCH
Salmon Sandwich (2 ounces salmon with 2 tablespoons each chopped celery and onion, 2 lettuce leaves, 2 tomato slices, and 2 teaspoons reduced-calorie mayonnaise on 2 slices reduced-calorie multi-grain bread)
6 each Cucumber Spears and Carrot Sticks
Cherry Yogurt (½ cup plain low-fat yogurt mixed with 10 large cherries, pitted and diced)
Coffee, Tea, or Mineral Water

DINNER
Chicken Parmesan (3 ounces baked chicken cutlet topped with ¼ cup tomato sauce, ½ ounce shredded mozzarella cheese, and ½ teaspoon grated Parmesan cheese, melted)
½ cup Cooked Spinach Fettuccine
½ cup Cooked Sliced Zucchini
1½ cups Tossed Salad with 1 tablespoon Italian Dressing
Coffee or Tea

SNACK
1 serving **Choc-a-Nut Drink** (page 367)

Optional Calories: 95

Day 4

BREAKFAST
½ medium Banana, sliced
¾ ounce Cold Cereal
1 cup Skim Milk
Coffee or Tea

LUNCH
Turkey 'n' Sprout Pita (2 ounces sliced turkey with ½ cup alfalfa sprouts, 2 green bell pepper rings, and 2 teaspoons reduced-calorie mayonnaise in 1-ounce whole wheat pita)
6 Zucchini Sticks and ½ cup Whole Mushrooms
1 small Apple
Coffee, Tea, or Mineral Water

DINNER
1 cup Tomato Juice with Lime Wedge
3 ounces Baked Fillet of Sole
3 ounces Baked Potato
1 teaspoon Margarine
½ cup Cooked Sliced Asparagus
1 serving **Mediterranean Cucumber Salad** (page 113)
⅛ medium Pineapple
Coffee or Tea

SNACK
1 serving Reduced-Calorie Chocolate Dairy Drink; 1 small Orange

Optional Calories: 0

Day 5

BREAKFAST
Berry Yogurt (1 cup strawberries, sliced, and ¼ cup blueberries topped with ½ cup plain low-fat yogurt)
1 slice Reduced-Calorie Multi-Grain Bread
1 teaspoon Reduced-Calorie Margarine
Coffee or Tea

LUNCH
Tuna Salad (2 ounces tuna with 2 tablespoons each grated carrot and chopped celery, ½ cup each sliced mushrooms and cucumber, ¼ cup sliced radishes, and 1½ teaspoons Thousand Island dressing mixed with 2 tablespoons plain low-fat yogurt and ¼ teaspoon mustard on 4 lettuce leaves)
¾ ounce Breadsticks
1 medium Peach
Coffee, Tea, or Mineral Water

DINNER
3 ounces Broiled Lamb Chop
1 serving **Minted Medley** (page 110)
½ cup Cooked Cauliflower Florets
Tomato-Cabbage Salad (6 tomato wedges with ¼ cup shredded red cabbage plus red wine vinegar and herbs on 4 lettuce leaves)
Coffee or Tea

SNACK
¾ cup Skim Milk; 1 serving **Lemon-Nut Cookies** (page 399)

Optional Calories: 60

Day 6

BREAKFAST
½ cup Grapefruit Sections
¾ ounce Cold Cereal
½ cup Skim Milk
Coffee or Tea

LUNCH
1 serving **Mexican Beans on Rice** (page 264)
1 cup Mixed Green Salad with 2 ounces Drained Canned Chick-Peas plus Lemon Juice and Herbs
10 large Cherries
Iced Tea or Coffee

DINNER
1 serving **Elegant Ham 'n' Cheese Sandwich** (page 392)
6 Cooked Asparagus Spears
Vegetable Salad (6 tomato wedges with ¼ cup each sliced celery and radishes and ½ teaspoon olive oil mixed with 2 teaspoons balsamic vinegar and ¼ teaspoon mustard on 4 lettuce leaves)
½ cup Strawberries sprinkled with ½ teaspoon Confectioners' Sugar
½ cup Skim Milk
Coffee or Tea

SNACK
½ cup Reduced-Calorie Butterscotch Pudding; 1 Graham Cracker

Optional Calories: 70

Day 7

BREAKFAST
1 serving **Fresh Fruit Ambrosia** (page 400)
⅓ cup Cottage Cheese
¾ ounce Crispbreads
1 cup Skim Milk
Coffee or Tea

LUNCH
Chicken Sandwich (2 ounces sliced chicken with 3 tomato slices, 2 lettuce leaves, ¼ cup alfalfa sprouts, and 1½ teaspoons Russian dressing on 2 slices reduced-calorie multi-grain bread)
½ cup Broccoli Florets and 6 Red Bell Pepper Strips
½ cup Grapefruit Sections
Coffee, Tea, or Mineral Water

DINNER
1 serving **Cheese-Filled Cucumber Cups** (page 178)
3 ounces Sliced Roast Beef
1 Baked Potato sprinkled with 1 teaspoon Chopped Chives
½ cup Cooked Cauliflower Florets
Cucumber-Mushroom Salad (½ cup each cucumber slices with ¼ cup each grated carrot and sliced mushrooms and 1 tablespoon buttermilk dressing on 1 cup torn lettuce)
Coffee or Tea

SNACK
1 serving Reduced-Calorie Chocolate Dairy Drink; 2 medium Apricots

Optional Calories: 105

Total Optional Calories for Week: 485

REDUCED-SODIUM MENU PLANNER FOR WEEK 5

Men and Youths: Daily add 2 Protein Exchanges, 2 Bread Exchanges, and 1 to 2 Fruit Exchanges.

Youths only: Daily add 1 to 2 Milk Exchanges.

Day 1

BREAKFAST
½ medium Banana
¾ ounce Cold Cereal
¾ cup Skim Milk
Coffee or Tea

LUNCH
Tuna Sandwich (2 ounces tuna with 2 tablespoons chopped celery, 3 tomato slices, 4 lettuce leaves, and 1 teaspoon reduced-calorie mayonnaise on 2 slices reduced-calorie rye bread)
6 each Carrot and Zucchini Sticks
1 medium Kiwi Fruit
Coffee, Tea, or Mineral Water

DINNER
4 ounces Baked Chicken
1 serving **Buttered Fettuccine-Spinach Toss** (page 303)
6 Cooked Asparagus Spears
1½ cups Tossed Salad with 1½ teaspoons French Dressing mixed with 2 teaspoons Lemon Juice and ¼ teaspoon Mustard
Café au Lait (1 cup hot coffee with ¼ cup hot skim milk)

SNACK
1 serving Reduced-Calorie Chocolate Dairy Drink; 1 cup Honeydew Chunks

Optional Calories: 35

Day 2

BREAKFAST
1 cup Sliced Papaya
2-ounce Corn Muffin, toasted, with 1 teaspoon Reduced-Calorie Grape Spread
½ cup Skim Milk
Coffee or Tea

LUNCH
Cheddar 'n' Tomato-Stuffed Pocket (2 ounces sliced Cheddar cheese with 3 tomato slices, ¼ cup alfalfa sprouts, and 1 teaspoon reduced-calorie margarine in 1-ounce pita)
6 each Green Bell Pepper Strips and Celery Sticks
10 large Cherries
Coffee, Tea, or Mineral Water

DINNER
1 serving **Blackened Redfish** (page 196)
½ cup each Cooked Cauliflower Florets and Baby Carrots
1½ cups Mixed Green Salad with Red Wine Vinegar plus Herbs
2 Chocolate Chip Cookies (1 ounce)
Iced Tea with Lemon Twist

SNACK
½ cup Skim Milk; ½ cup Reduced-Calorie Vanilla Pudding topped with ½ cup Blueberries

Optional Calories: 158

Day 3

BREAKFAST
1 serving **Autumn Oatmeal** (page 298)
1 serving Reduced-Calorie Hot Cocoa

LUNCH
Open-Face Turkey Sandwich (2 ounces sliced turkey with 3 each tomato slices and lettuce leaves and 1 teaspoon reduced-calorie mayonnaise on 1 slice pumpernickel bread)
½ cup Broccoli Florets and 3 Cherry Tomatoes
Coffee, Tea, or Mineral Water

DINNER
3 ounces Broiled Pork Chop
3 ounces Baked Yam with 1 teaspoon Reduced-Calorie Margarine and dash Cinnamon
1 serving **Braised Red Cabbage with Apple and Caraway** (page 104)
½ cup Cooked Cut Green Beans
½ cup Sliced Mushrooms on 1 cup torn Bibb Lettuce Leaves with 1½ teaspoons Thousand Island Dressing mixed with 2 tablespoons Plain Low-Fat Yogurt and ¼ teaspoon Mustard
Coffee or Tea

SNACK
¾ cup Skim Milk; 1 cup Strawberries

Optional Calories: 60

Day 4

BREAKFAST
1 medium Peach
⅓ cup Cottage Cheese
½ small Bagel
1 cup Skim Milk
Coffee or Tea

LUNCH
Shrimp-Spinach Salad (2 ounces diced shrimp with 1 cup spinach leaves, ½ cup *each* sliced celery and carrot, 8 tomato wedges, and 1 tablespoon Italian dressing)
¾ ounce Flatbreads
Coffee, Tea, or Mineral Water

DINNER
½ medium Pink Grapefruit sprinkled with ½ teaspoon Sugar
3 ounces Roast Chicken with Tarragon Leaves
6 Cooked Broccoli Spears
½ cup Cooked Sliced Beets
1 serving **Barley Salad Vinaigrette** (page 297)
Tea with Lemon

SNACK
1 serving Reduced-Calorie Chocolate Dairy Drink; 1 small Orange

Optional Calories: 10

Day 5

BREAKFAST
1 medium Kiwi Fruit
1 Sunny-Side-Up Egg
1 slice Rye Bread, toasted
1 teaspoon Margarine
1 cup Skim Milk
Coffee or Tea

LUNCH
Roast Beef Sandwich (2 ounces sliced roast beef with ¼ cup cole-slaw on 1-ounce roll)
6 *each* Carrot Sticks and Red Bell Pepper Strips
Cherry Yogurt (½ cup plain low-fat yogurt mixed with 10 large cherries, pitted and diced)
Coffee, Tea, or Mineral Water

DINNER
3 ounces Baked Salmon Steak with Lemon Wedge
1 cup Cooked French-Style Green Beans with ¼ cup Pearl Onions
Vegetable Salad (6 tomato slices with ¼ cup *each* sliced scallions and radishes and 1 teaspoon olive oil plus red wine vinegar and herbs on 4 lettuce leaves)
Coffee or Tea

SNACK
1 serving **Apple-Spice Tea** (page 63); 2 cups Plain Popcorn

Optional Calories: 20

Day 6

BREAKFAST
½ cup Blueberries
¾ ounce Cold Cereal
½ cup Skim Milk
Coffee or Tea

LUNCH
Chef's Salad (1 ounce julienne-cut turkey with 1 hard-cooked egg, cut into wedges, 1½ cups torn iceberg lettuce, 8 tomato wedges, 6 cucumber slices, ¼ cup *each* grated carrot and sliced red onion, and 1 tablespoon blue cheese dressing)
¾ ounce Flatbreads
Coffee, Tea, or Mineral Water

DINNER
1 serving **Creamy Apricot Chicken** (page 226)
½ cup Cooked Bow-Tie Noodles
6 Cooked Asparagus Spears
½ cup Cooked Sliced Yellow Squash
2 tablespoons Raisins
½ cup Skim Milk
Coffee or Tea

SNACK
½ cup Plain Low-Fat Yogurt; 1 cup Honeydew Melon Balls

Optional Calories: 100

Day 7

BREAKFAST
½ medium Grapefruit
1 serving **Brown Bread Muffins** (page 336)
1 cup Skim Milk
Coffee or Tea

LUNCH
Tuna-Stuffed Pocket (2 ounces tuna with ½ cup shredded lettuce, 3 *each* cucumber and tomato slices, and 1 teaspoon mayonnaise in 1-ounce pita)
6 Yellow Squash Sticks and ½ cup Cauliflower Florets
Iced Tea or Coffee

DINNER
3 ounces Grilled Sirloin Steak
1 small ear Corn
1 teaspoon Reduced-Calorie Margarine
½ cup Sliced Mushrooms and Onions sautéed with ½ teaspoon Reduced-Calorie Margarine
Lettuce Wedge with Red Wine Vinegar and Herbs
1 serving **Apple-Pear Compote** (page 61)
Coffee or Tea

SNACK
½ cup Reduced-Calorie Butterscotch Pudding; ½ cup Papaya Chunks

Optional Calories: 95
Total Optional Calories for Week: 478

31

Foods Containing Less Than 100 Milligrams of Sodium per Exchange

FOOD ITEM/ AMOUNT	SODIUM CONTENT (mg)

Fruit Exchange

Figures are given for fresh, uncooked items unless otherwise specified.

Apple, 1 small	0
Apple Juice, ⅓ cup	2
Applesauce (no sugar added), ½ cup	2
Apricots	
dried, 4 halves	1
fresh, 2 medium	1
Banana, ½ medium	1
Berries	
Blackberries, ½ cup	0
Blueberries, ½ cup	4
Boysenberries, frozen, ½ cup	1
Cranberries, 1 cup	1
Raspberries, ½ cup	0
Strawberries, 1 cup	2
Cherries, 10 large	0
Cranberry Juice, low-calorie, 1 cup	8
Currants	
dried, 2 tablespoons	1
fresh, ¾ cup	2
Dates, dried, 2	1
Dried Fruit	
Apple, ¾ ounce	19
Apricot, ¾ ounce	2
Mixed, ¾ ounce	4
Fig	
dried, 1 large	2
fresh, 1 large	1
Fruit Juices, combined, ⅓ cup	5
Fruit Salad, canned	
with juice, ½ cup	6
with water, ½ cup	4
Grapefruit, ½ medium	0
Grapefruit Juice, ½ cup	1
Grapefruit Sections (no sugar added), ½ cup	2
Grapes, 12 large	1
Kiwi Fruit, 1 medium	4
Kumquats, 3 medium	3
Mandarin Orange, canned with juice, ½ cup	6
Mango, ½ small	2
Melon	
Cantaloupe, 1 cup	14
Honeydew, 1 cup	17
Nectar, any type, ⅓ cup	4

Fruit Exchange (cont.)

Nectarine, 1 small	0
Orange, 1 small	0
Orange Juice, ½ cup	1
Orange-Grapefruit Juice, ½ cup	5
Orange Sections, ½ cup	0
Papaya, ½ medium	4
Peach, 1 medium	0
Pear, 1 small	0
Persimmon, ½ medium	1
Pineapple Juice, ⅓ cup	1
Pineapple	
canned with juice, ½ cup	1
fresh, ⅛ medium	1
Plums, 2 medium	0
Prune Juice, ⅓ cup	3
Prunes, dried, 2 large	1
Raisins, 2 tablespoons	2
Tangerine, 1 large	1
Watermelon, 1 cup	3

Vegetable Exchange

Figures are given for fresh, uncooked items unless otherwise specified. Cooked items contain no added salt.

Artichoke Hearts, ½ cup	40
Asparagus, ½ cup	2
Beans, green or wax (cooked), ½ cup	2
Beets, cooked, ½ cup	42
Broccoli	
cooked, ½ cup	9
florets, frozen, ½ cup	15
raw, ½ cup	21
Brussels Sprouts, cooked, ½ cup	16
Cabbage	
cooked, ½ cup	14
raw, ½ cup	6
Carrot	
cooked, ½ cup	51
raw, ½ cup	19
Carrot Juice, ½ cup	36
Cauliflower	
cooked, ½ cup	4
raw, ½ cup	8
Celery	
cooked, ½ cup	48
raw, ½ cup	53
Chinese Pea Pods, raw or cooked, ½ cup	3
Cucumber, ½ cup	1
Eggplant	
cooked, ½ cup	1
raw, ½ cup	2

Vegetable Exchange (cont.)

Endive, Belgian, ½ cup	6
Greens	
Beet, raw, ½ cup	38
Chard, raw, ½ cup	38
Kale, raw *or* cooked, ½ cup	15
Mustard, cooked, ½ cup	11
raw, ½ cup	7
Leeks	
cooked, ½ cup	5
raw, ½ cup	10
Lettuce, iceberg, ½ cup	3
Mushrooms	
cooked, ½ cup	2
raw, ½ cup	1
Okra	
cooked (frozen), ½ cup	3
raw, ½ cup	4
Onion	
cooked, ½ cup	8
raw, ½ cup	2
Peppers, bell	
cooked, ½ cup	1
raw, ½ cup	2
Pumpkin, cooked, ½ cup	1
Radishes, raw, ½ cup	14
Rhubarb, raw, ½ cup	2
Scallions, ½ cup	2
Spinach	
cooked, ½ cup	63
raw, ½ cup	22
Sprouts	
Alfalfa, ½ cup	1
Bean, ½ cup	3
Summer Squash,	
raw *or* cooked, ½ cup	1
Tomato	
cooked, ½ cup	13
fresh, chopped, ½ cup	7
fresh, whole, 1 medium	10
Turnip	
cooked, ½ cup	39
raw, ½ cup	44
Watercress, ½ cup	7
Zucchini	
cooked, ½ cup	3
raw, ½ cup	2

Fat Exchange

Margarine, 1 teaspoon	47
reduced-calorie, 2 teaspoons	86
Mayonnaise, 1 teaspoon	28
reduced-calorie, 2 teaspoons	71
Salad Dressings	
Blue Cheese, 1½ teaspoons	88
Italian, 1½ teaspoons	55
Thousand Island,	
1½ teaspoons	56
Vegetable Oil, corn, 1 teaspoon	0

Protein Exchange

Cooked items contain no added salt.

Beef, all lean, broiled	
Round, lean, 1 ounce	18
Sirloin, 1 ounce	18
Cheese, ricotta,	
part-skim, ¼ cup	78
Chicken, roasted, 1 ounce	24
Dried Beans, Lentils, Peas, dry	
Chick-Peas, ¾ ounce	5
Kidney Beans, ¾ ounce	2
Lentils, ¾ ounce	6
Lima Beans, ¾ ounce	1
Pinto Beans, ¾ ounce	2
Split Peas, ¾ ounce	8
Egg, 1 large	69
Egg Substitute, ¼ cup	80
Fish	
Cod, raw, 1 ounce	15
Salmon, raw, 1 ounce	21
Lamb, loin, lean,	
roasted, 1 ounce	19
Liver, chicken, raw, 1 ounce	22
Organ Meats	
Beef Heart, raw, 1 ounce	24
Beef Liver, raw, 1 ounce	39
Calf Liver, raw, 1 ounce	21
Pork, loin center, lean,	
broiled, 1 ounce	22
Shrimp, cooked, 1 ounce	39
Tofu, 3 ounces	6
Tongue, beef, cooked, 1 ounce	17
Turkey, cooked, 1 ounce	21
Veal, loin, roasted, 1 ounce	18

Bread Exchange

Cooked and packaged items contain no added salt.

Barley	
cooked, ½ cup	2
dry, ¾ ounce	1
Cereal, cooked, ½ cup	1
Corn, whole-kernel,	
cooked, ½ cup	14
ear, 1 small	14
Cornmeal, dry, ¾ ounce	0
Crispbreads, ¾ ounce	52
Flour, 3 tablespoons	1
Graham Crackers, 2 squares	94
Hominy Grits, cooked, ½ cup	0
Lima Beans	
cooked (fresh), ½ cup	14
cooked (frozen), ½ cup	45
Matzo, ½ board	1
Parsnip, cooked, ½ cup	8

Bread Exchange (cont.)

Pasta, cooked

Cellophane Noodles, ½ cup	3
Macaroni, ½ cup	1
Noodles, ½ cup	2
Peas, green, cooked, ½ cup	2
Plantain, peeled, 3 ounces	5
Popcorn, plain, popped, 2 cups	0

Potato

Sweet, boiled, 3 ounces	11
White	
baked with skin, 3 ounces	7
boiled, 3 ounces	4
Rice, brown *or* white,	
cooked, ½ cup	0
Rice Cakes, 2	0
Taco Shell, 1 shell	5
Tortilla, corn, 1	53
Water Chestnuts, 3 ounces	12
Winter Squash,	
cooked, 4 ounces	1
Zwieback, 2	32

Milk Exchange

Flavored Milk Pudding,	
reduced-calorie	
(chocolate), ½ cup	65
Yogurt, plain, low-fat, ½ cup	79

Options

10-Calorie Foods

Bacon Bits, imitation,	
1 teaspoon	94
Bread Crumbs, dried,	
1 teaspoon	15
Cheese, Parmesan,	
grated, 1 teaspoon	31
Cocoa, dry, 2 teaspoons	0
Coconut, sweetened,	
1 teaspoon	4
Cornstarch, 1 teaspoon	0
Creamer, nondairy (liquid	
or powder), 1 teaspoon	4
Egg White, ½	25
Flour, 1 teaspoon	0
Honey, ½ teaspoon	0
Olives, black, 2 medium	53
Relish	
sour, 1 teaspoon	68
sweet, 1 teaspoon	36
Seeds, poppy *or* sesame,	
½ teaspoon	0
Sugar, ½ teaspoon	0
Syrup, table, ½ teaspoon	0

50-Calorie Foods

Cream, any type, 1 tablespoon	6
Half-and-Half, 2 tablespoons	12

Options (cont.)

Jam, 1 tablespoon	2
Jelly, 1 tablespoon	3
Marshmallows, 2 medium	
(½ ounce)	8
Tartar Sauce, 2 teaspoons	68
Whipped Topping	
dairy, ¼ cup	20
nondairy, ¼ cup	15

100-Calorie Foods

Avocado, 2 ounces	6
Beer, 8 ounces	12
light, 12 ounces	11
Cream Cheese, 2 tablespoons	84
Gelatin, fruit flavored,	
prepared, ½ cup	61
Liqueurs, any type,	
1 fluid ounce	trace
Sour Cream, 3 tablespoons	23
Wine, 4 ounces	9
Dessert, 2 ounces	5

150-Calorie Foods

Brandy *or* Cognac,	
2 fluid ounces	trace
Chocolate	
bitter *or* semisweet, 1 ounce	1
candy, 1 ounce	27
Cookies	
Oatmeal, 1 ounce	46
Vanilla Wafer, 1 ounce	71
Frozen Tofu, 4 ounces	50
Gin, Rum, *or* Vodka, 2 ounces	0
Whiskey, 2 ounces	1
Sherbet, ½ cup	44
Sorbet, ½ cup	11

Combination Foods

Angel Food Cake, ¹⁄₁₂ of 9″ cake	53
Coleslaw, ½ cup	14
Granola, 1 ounce	25
Nuts, dry roasted	
(without added salt)	
Almonds, ½ ounce shelled	3
Brazil Nuts, ½ ounce shelled	trace
Cashews, ½ ounce shelled	2
Hazelnuts, ½ ounce shelled	0
Macadamia Nuts,	
½ ounce shelled	1
Peanuts, ½ ounce shelled	5
Pecans, ½ ounce shelled	0
Pignolias (pine nuts),	
½ ounce	1
Pistachios, ½ ounce shelled	1
Walnuts, ½ ounce shelled	2
Peanut Butter, with added salt	
chunky, 1 tablespoon	65
smooth, 1 tablespoon	76
Pound Cake, 1 slice (2 ounces)	66

Our seven-day Vegetarian Menu Planner is based on the Weight Watchers Vegetarian Plan, a lacto-ovo plan (one that includes milk products and eggs). The Plan offers a wide variety of foods for you to choose from, as illustrated in the satisfying and nutritious meals and snacks included in this Menu Planner. For some additional menu ideas, you can create your own customized menus by simply omitting the meat, poultry, and fish selections from the other Menu Planners in this book and substituting selections of your choice (eggs, cheese, beans, tofu, etc.) from the list below. Remember that if you are following the Vegetarian Plan, you may have all of the items listed below beginning on Week 1.

Protein Exchange List

SELECTION	ONE EXCHANGE
Cheese	
Cottage	⅓ cup
Hard	1 ounce
Pot	⅓ cup
Ricotta, part-skim	¼ cup
Semisoft	1 ounce
Other	
Dry Beans, Lentils, *or* Peas	2 ounces cooked *or* ¾ ounce dry
Egg	1
Egg Substitutes	¼ cup
Tempeh	1 ounce
Tofu, firm *or* soft	3 ounces

Options List

COMBINATIONS

Peanut Butter, 1 tablespoon	1 Fat Exchange; 1 Protein Exchange

In addition, make the following changes to your Weekly Limits:

FOODS	LIMIT PER WEEK
Eggs	5 Exchanges
Hard *or* Semisoft Cheese	6 Exchanges

Be sure to consult your physician to see if you need an iron supplement.

VEGETARIAN MENU PLANNER FOR WEEK 5

Men and Youths: Daily add 2 Protein Exchanges, 2 Bread Exchanges, and 1 to 2 Fruit Exchanges.

Youths only: Daily add 1 to 2 Milk Exchanges.

Day 1

BREAKFAST
1 cup Strawberries
1/3 cup Cottage Cheese
1 slice Whole Wheat Bread, toasted
3/4 cup Skim Milk
Coffee or Tea

LUNCH
3/4 cup Vegetable Bouillon
Chick-Pea Toss (4 ounces drained canned chick-peas with 1 cup torn lettuce, 6 tomato wedges, 1/2 cup each cauliflower florets and sliced mushrooms, and 1 1/2 teaspoons blue cheese dressing mixed with 2 tablespoons plain low-fat yogurt plus garlic powder)
3/4 ounce Breadsticks
2 medium Plums
Coffee, Tea, or Mineral Water

DINNER
Sautéed Tofu (6 ounces diced tofu with 1/2 cup each sliced onion and green and red bell pepper strips, 1/2 teaspoon each minced garlic and minced pared gingerroot, sautéed in 1 teaspoon vegetable oil)
1/2 cup Cooked Long-Grain Rice
6 Cooked Broccoli Spears
1 serving **Mozzarella, Tomato, and Arugula Salad** (page 179)
Coffee or Tea

SNACK
1/2 cup Reduced-Calorie Chocolate Pudding; 1/2 cup Peach Slices

Optional Calories: 10

Day 2

BREAKFAST
1/2 cup Orange Sections
1/2 cup Cooked Cereal
1 cup Skim Milk
Coffee or Tea

LUNCH
1 serving **Black Beans and Rice with Cumin Vinaigrette** (page 258)
1/2 cup Sliced Zucchini and 6 Carrot Sticks
1/2 cup Pineapple Chunks topped with 1/4 cup Plain Low-Fat Yogurt
Coffee, Tea, or Mineral Water

DINNER
1 serving **White Bean and Cheddar Casserole** (page 261)
1/2 cup each Cooked French-Style Green Beans and Sliced Yellow Squash
1 1/2 cups Tossed Salad with 2 ounces Chilled Cooked White Kidney Beans and 1 1/2 teaspoons French Dressing mixed with 2 teaspoons Lemon Juice and 1/4 teaspoon Mustard
1/4 small Cantaloupe
1/2 cup Skim Milk
Coffee or Tea

SNACK
1 serving **Herb-Cheese Spread** (page 166) with Celery Sticks; 3 Saltine Crackers

Optional Calories: 50

Day 3

BREAKFAST
1/2 cup Grapefruit Juice
1 Poached Egg
1/2 small Bagel, toasted
3/4 cup Skim Milk
Coffee or Tea

LUNCH
Pasta Salad (1/2 cup chilled cooked small shell macaroni with 4 ounces chilled cooked small white beans, 1/4 cup each cut green beans and sliced red onion, 6 cherry tomato halves, 1 tablespoon Italian dressing, and 1 teaspoon grated Parmesan cheese)
1 large Tangerine
Iced Tea or Coffee

DINNER
1 serving **Cheese 'n' Broccoli-Topped Potato** (page 174)
Italian-Style Beans (4 ounces cooked white kidney beans with 1/2 cup stewed chopped tomatoes plus basil and garlic)
1 1/2 cups Mixed Green Salad with 1/2 teaspoon Olive Oil plus Red Wine Vinegar and Herbs
Coffee or Tea

SNACK
1 serving Reduced-Calorie Chocolate Dairy Drink; 20 small Grapes

Optional Calories: 13

Day 4

BREAKFAST
1 serving **High-Fiber Apple Muffins** (page 64)
¾ cup Skim Milk
Coffee or Tea

LUNCH
1 serving **Marinated Black Bean Salad** (page 259)
¾ ounce Breadsticks
1 teaspoon Reduced-Calorie Margarine
Berries 'n' Cream (1 cup strawberries, sliced, topped with 1 tablespoon sour cream and dash cinnamon)
Coffee, Tea, or Mineral Water

DINNER
Pasta 'n' Beans (½ cup cooked spaghetti topped with 4 ounces cooked red kidney beans and ½ cup tomato sauce)
Chick-Pea Salad (2 ounces drained canned chick-peas with 6 red bell pepper rings, ¼ cup grated carrot, and 1½ teaspoons buttermilk dressing mixed with 2 tablespoons plain low-fat yogurt and ¼ teaspoon mustard on 1 cup torn lettuce leaves)
1 cup Skim Milk
Coffee or Tea

SNACK
2 Graham Crackers; 1 medium Peach

Optional Calories: 124

Day 5

BREAKFAST
⅓ cup Pineapple Juice
¾ ounce Cold Cereal
½ cup Skim Milk
Coffee or Tea

LUNCH
Peanut Butter 'n' Preserves (2 tablespoons peanut butter with 1 tablespoon strawberry preserves on 2 slices reduced-calorie multi-grain bread)
2 medium Plums
Coffee, Tea, or Mineral Water

DINNER
1 serving **Quesadillas** (page 172)
Bean 'n' Vegetable Salad (1½ cups tossed salad with 4 ounces chilled cooked white kidney beans and 6 each tomato wedges and red and green bell pepper rings plus red wine vinegar and herbs)
½ cup Orange Sections sprinkled with 1 teaspoon Shredded Coconut
8 fluid ounces Beer

SNACK
½ cup Skim Milk; ½ cup Reduced-Calorie Chocolate Pudding

Optional Calories: 180

Day 6

BREAKFAST
1 serving **Creamy Apple-Raisin Treat** (page 167)
1 cup Skim Milk
Coffee or Tea

LUNCH
1 serving **Mexican Beans on Rice** (page 264)
6 each Carrot and Celery Sticks
1 large Tangerine
Iced Tea with Lemon Wedge

DINNER
Mushroom Pita Pizza (1 ounce pita topped with ¼ cup tomato sauce, 1 ounce shredded mozzarella cheese, ½ cup sliced mushrooms, and 1 teaspoon grated Parmesan cheese, grilled)
1½ cups Mixed Green Salad with 2 ounces Drained Canned Chick-Peas and 1 tablespoon Italian Dressing
Coffee or Tea

SNACK
1 serving Reduced-Calorie Vanilla Dairy Drink; 1 cup Strawberries

Optional Calories: 30

Day 7

BREAKFAST
Pineapple Spritzer (⅓ cup *each* chilled pineapple juice and club soda with mint sprig)
1 serving **Poached Eggs California** (page 164)
½ cup Skim Milk
Coffee or Tea

LUNCH
Fruit 'n' Cheese Platter (⅔ cup cottage cheese with 1 medium plum, pitted and sliced, 10 small grapes, and ½ cup strawberries, sliced, on 4 lettuce leaves)
½ small Bagel
1 teaspoon Margarine
½ cup Reduced-Calorie Butterscotch Pudding
Coffee or Tea

DINNER
Greek Salad (4 ounces chilled cooked red kidney beans with 1 ounce crumbled feta cheese, 2 cups torn lettuce leaves, 6 cherry tomatoes, ½ cup sliced cucumber, ¼ cup *each* broccoli florets and sliced celery, and 1 tablespoon Caesar dressing)
¾ ounce Breadsticks
Coffee or Tea

SNACK
½ cup Skim Milk; ½ cup Orange Sections

Optional Calories: 45

Total Optional Calories for Week: 452

Command Performance:
Tips for Success

Using Recipes with the Food Plan

• The recipes in this book were developed to fit the various stages of the Food Plan and are so noted. As you progress from Week 1 to Week 8 you may, of course, continue to use the recipes developed for the previous weeks.

• Always take time to measure and weigh ingredients carefully; this is vital to both recipe results and weight control. Don't try to judge portions by eye.

To weigh foods, use a scale.

To measure liquids, use a standard glass or clear plastic measuring cup. Place it on a level surface and read markings at eye level. Fill the cup just to the appropriate marking. To measure less than ¼ cup, use standard measuring spoons.

To measure dry ingredients, use metal or plastic measuring cups that come in sets of four: ¼ cup, ⅓ cup, ½ cup, and 1 cup. Spoon the ingredients into the cup, then level with the straight edge of a knife or metal spatula. To measure less than ¼ cup, use standard measuring spoons and, unless otherwise directed, level as for measuring cup.

A dash is measured as approximately ¹⁄₁₆ of a teaspoon (½ of a ⅛-teaspoon measure or ¼ of a ¼-teaspoon measure).

• In any recipe for more than one serving it is important to mix ingredients well and to divide evenly so that each portion will be the same size.

• Recipes that serve two can be doubled or tripled; however, use seasonings cautiously.

39

Insights on Ingredients

- Reading product labels is the best way to determine if the item you are using is what the recipe calls for. This may sound very simple, but the label contains a great deal of important information that will help you succeed on the Food Plan. Some recipes call for items of specific caloric content; some products are permissible on the Food Plan only if they meet certain nutritional guidelines. These facts, as well as other points of interest, can be found on items whose labels contain nutritional information. Get into the habit of reading labels and you'll find that your time, as well as your money, is being well spent.

In addition, the following pointers will help guide you through our ingredient lists:

- Recipes calling for lettuce leaves assume use of either iceberg or romaine; 4 lettuce leaves provide 1 Vegetable Exchange. If any other type of lettuce is used (for example, Boston or Bibb), 8 lettuce leaves provide 1 Vegetable Exchange.

- The herbs used in these recipes are dried unless otherwise indicated. If you are substituting fresh herbs, use approximately four times the amount of dried (for example, 1 teaspoon chopped fresh parsley instead of ¼ teaspoon dried parsley leaves). If fresh herbs are indicated and you wish to substitute dried, use approximately ¼ the amount of fresh (for example, ¼ teaspoon dried basil instead of 1 teaspoon chopped fresh basil). If you are substituting ground (powdered) herbs for dried leaves, use approximately half the amount of dried (¼ teaspoon ground thyme instead of ½ teaspoon dried thyme leaves).

- If you are substituting fresh spices for ground, use approximately eight times the amount of ground (for example, 1 teaspoon minced pared gingerroot instead of ⅛ teaspoon ground ginger).

- Generally, dried herbs and spices should not be kept for more than a year. Date the container at the time of purchase and check periodically for potency. Usually, if the herb or spice is aromatic, it is still potent; if the aroma has diminished, the recipe may require a larger amount of the seasoning.

- We've used fresh vegetables unless otherwise indicated. If you substitute frozen or canned vegetables, it may be necessary to adjust cooking times accordingly.

• When vegetable oil is called for, use safflower, sunflower, soybean, corn, cottonseed, or peanut oil, or any combination of these oils.

• Since olive oil and Chinese sesame oil have distinctive flavors, they have been specifically indicated. There are two types of sesame oil: light and dark. The light oil is relatively flavorless and may be used as a substitute for any other vegetable oil. When sesame oil is specified, use the dark variety. This product, made from toasted sesame seeds, has a rich amber color and a characteristic sesame flavor.

• Some of our recipes make use of certain unusual ingredients, such as wild mushrooms, sun-dried tomatoes, radicchio (red chicory), or balsamic vinegar. Don't be afraid to explore and experiment with foods like these — they'll add exciting new flavors to your cooking. And, if you can't get them, try using the substitutions we have frequently suggested.

• To add interest and excitement to many of the recipes, a variety of vinegars have been indicated such as balsamic, raspberry, and seasoned rice. If you are unable to find these flavors, red wine vinegar may be substituted.

• If a variety of liqueur that is specified in a recipe is unavailable, you may substitute one of your favorites.

• When a recipe calls for butter or whipped butter, use lightly salted butter unless otherwise specified.

• Fresh mussels and clams should be purchased live and should have shells that are tightly closed. Give any slightly open shells a hard tap and they should snap shut, but if they don't, do not use them. Remember that shells will open during cooking; any that remain closed should be discarded. It's a good idea to buy more shellfish than you need for the recipe in case you need to discard some.

Getting the Best Results

• Read through a recipe completely before you begin. Make sure you understand the method and have all the ingredients and utensils on hand. Gather all ingredients and any special utensils needed in one place and make sure that all items are at proper temperature (for example, if you're beating egg whites, you'll want them at room temperature).

- Room temperature means 68° to 72° F.

- Measure and/or weigh all ingredients carefully.

- We do not recommend marinating foods in aluminum containers. Certain foods react with aluminum and this can have an adverse effect. Rather, glass or stainless-steel containers should be used. An alternative method is to use a plastic bag to marinate foods. Place marinade and items to be marinated in a leakproof plastic bag, close bag securely, and let marinate according to recipe directions. After food has been marinated, the bag can be discarded so there's one less pan to clean.

- If a meat mallet is not available for pounding meat, use a saucepan instead. Pound with the bottom of the saucepan and, unless otherwise specified, pound until meat is about ¼ inch thick.

- When using eggs, it's a good idea to break each one into a cup or bowl before combining with other ingredients or additional eggs. This will avoid wasting other items should one egg happen to be spoiled.

- When dissolving flour, cornstarch, or arrowroot in liquid, add the dry ingredient to the liquid, not vice versa. This helps prevent lumps.

- When dissolving unflavored gelatin over direct heat, be sure to keep heat low and stir constantly. This is important since gelatin burns very easily.

- When a recipe calls for the use of custard cups, select items made of heatproof glass or heavy ceramic.

- Some recipes include instructions to preheat the oven. If you decide not to preheat, allow an extra 5 to 10 minutes of cooking time.

- The cooking times on most recipes are approximate and should be used as guides. Remember, not all ovens are alike, so be sure to check for doneness as directed.

- When baking, place the pan in the middle of the center oven rack so that air circulates freely, and food bakes evenly. It's best to use one oven rack at a time. If you're using two racks, place them so that the oven is divided into thirds, then stagger the pans so that one is not directly above the other.

• When baking in a muffin pan and using only some of the cups, it's a good idea to partially fill the empty cups with water. This will prevent the pan from warping or burning. When ready to remove muffins from the pan, drain off the water very carefully; remember, it will be boiling hot.

• When broiling, 4 inches is the standard distance from the heat source and should be used with any recipes that do not specify otherwise. If it is necessary to broil closer to or farther away from the heat, the appropriate distance will be indicated.

• If a dish is to be chilled or frozen after cooking, always allow it to cool slightly before refrigerating or freezing. Placing a very hot item in the refrigerator or freezer can adversely affect the functioning of the appliance. Cover all items that are to be refrigerated; cover or properly wrap all items that are to be placed in the freezer. If a dish is not covered, odors from other foods may permeate it, or vice versa. Drying may also occur, particularly in frost-free refrigerators, or the flavor may be spoiled by the accidental dripping from other foods. Freezer-burn may occur on foods not properly covered or wrapped before being frozen.

• We recommend serving chilled foods on chilled plates and hot foods on warmed plates. Plates and glassware should be chilled in the refrigerator for about 5 minutes prior to serving. Plates and platters can be heated by placing them in a warm oven (no more than 200° F) for 5 to 10 minutes before serving, or in a warmer, or on a warming tray.

• If you want to serve crisp, brightly colored vegetables, try blanching them rather than fully cooking them. Plunge the vegetables into boiling water, then rinse with or plunge into cold water to stop the cooking process. Blanched vegetables are great for snacks or crudités.

Convenience Equipment

Blender

Before the food processor there was the basic blender. If your blender is stashed away in a cabinet, get it out, put it on the counter, and rediscover what it can do for you.

You can use it to
• Whip up shakes and mixed drinks
• Prepare salad dressings and mayonnaise

- Make tomato sauce
- Puree fruits and vegetables

When processing liquids, never fill your blender to the top; always start on low speed, gradually increasing to the desired speed.

Food Processor

The versatile and hard-working food processor can blend, chop, grate, shred, mix, slice, knead, and make crumbs quickly and efficiently. Once considered chefs' specialty equipment, food processors are now widely available and enormously popular. They are available in large-capacity models as well as in new compact ones that take up very little counter space and are perfect for processing small amounts of an ingredient.

The following tips will help you make the most of your food processor:

- Slice or chop salad vegetables in quantity using the processor; store prepared vegetables in covered containers or plastic bags in the refrigerator.

- Chop large quantities of onion, celery, and green pepper; freeze in premeasured amounts for use in cooking.

- Process dry foods before moist ones, even if the dry ones are needed last. You won't have to wash the work bowl as often.

- Rinse blades and bowl immediately after use for easier cleanup.

- If you accidentally overprocess a food, don't throw it out—find another use for it. Fruits can be used as sauces; vegetables can be seasoned, cooked, and served pureed as a side dish.

Pressure Cooker

Pressure cookers have been around for many decades—your mother probably had one and used it often. It's still a time- and energy-saver since foods cook in about one-third of their regular cooking time. That's because the pressure of built-up steam inside the cooker produces higher temperatures than would be produced under regular cooking conditions.

Pressure cookers also preserve valuable nutrients, since foods cook for a short time in a small amount of liquid. Excellent for vegetables, the pressure cooker will also tenderize less-tender cuts of meat.

Microwave Oven

The microwave oven is swiftly becoming the most popular appliance on the market today, and with good reason. It's quick, cool, and clean. A microwave oven does the job of a conventional oven in about one-fourth the time, using much less energy. It doesn't heat up your kitchen—a definite "plus" in warm weather. In fact, cleanup is a breeze if you cook on disposable plastic or paper.

Micro-convection ovens do the quick-cooking job of a microwave oven but, because they use circulating hot air, will also brown food the way a convection oven does.

Convenience Tips for the Microwave

• Always follow the manufacturer's directions regarding use and care of your microwave oven.

• Before buying special microwave-safe cookware, test the cookware you already own to determine if it is safe for the microwave oven (metal and metal-trimmed cookware should never be used in the microwave oven). Suppose you want to test one of your ceramic casseroles. Place it in the oven along with a glass 1-cup liquid measure filled with water. Microwave on High for 1 minute. If the water is warm and the casserole is cool, the casserole is safe for use in the oven. If the casserole is warm or hot, it is absorbing microwaves and should not be used in the oven, as it may break. Microwave absorption by cookware also means less efficient cooking of foods.

• Make after-dinner cleanup easier by micro-cooking and serving in the same dish. Try reheating individual portions right on the dinner plate.

• Many foods cooked in the microwave oven continue to cook after being removed from the oven. For this reason, remove them while they are still slightly undercooked, and allow for "standing time" to complete the cooking process. Use the standing time to finish preparing the rest of the meal or to microwave another food.

How the Microwave Can Make Life Easier

• The microwave oven speeds meal preparation. Did you forget to take out that piece of meat or poultry from the freezer in time for it to thaw? Don't worry—the microwave thaws it in minutes. And cooked dishes can be reheated in the time it takes to set the table.

• Use the microwave oven to increase the amount of juice that can be squeezed from oranges, lemons, limes, and grapefruits. Before cutting and squeezing, microwave on High until the fruit is slightly warm to the touch, 20 to 25 seconds.

• When making flavored vinegars, speed the release of flavors with the microwave oven. Combine the vinegar and herb in a well-washed ketchup or other condiment bottle and microwave until slightly warm *(not hot).*

• To soften and warm tortillas, place 4 tortillas between damp paper towels and microwave on High until warm to the touch, 20 to 40 seconds.

• Use your microwave oven to melt chocolate, butter, or margarine. Because the microwave energy penetrates from all sides rather than just the base, as in range-top cooking, the food will melt faster than it would in a double boiler. You don't even have to wait until the food is completely melted—just stir the last small pieces into the already-melted part until it is completely smooth.

• Use the microwave to toast coconut. Spread a tablespoon of coconut evenly on a microwave-safe plate and microwave on High for 40 to 50 seconds, checking and stirring midway through cooking.

• Plump raisins and other dried fruit in water just to cover in a microwave-safe bowl.

• Start cooking chicken or potatoes in the microwave; for browning and crispness, finish them in a conventional or convection oven, or even on the barbecue.

• Breads and rolls can be defrosted and warmed in seconds in the microwave oven. Wrap bread in paper towels and microwave *just until warm.* (Overheating will toughen the bread.)

• Remember that anything sugary, such as dried fruit, becomes hot very quickly, so time these items carefully to avoid overcooking. Wrap in paper towels to absorb moisture before placing in the microwave oven.

• Top-of-the-range isn't the only way to sauté. When a recipe calls for sautéing, combine the food with the margarine, butter, or oil in a microwave-safe bowl or casserole. Microwave, stirring occasionally, until cooked as desired. Then add other ingredients directly to the bowl and continue cooking. (You can even serve in the same bowl or casserole.) No messy skillet to clean.

• The microwave oven does more than cook. It speeds up some tasks that take more time using conventional appliances. The following chart is a guide to its many uses:

Reheating or Warming	Melting	Softening	Defrosting
Cup of tea or coffee	Butter or margarine	Ice milk or ice cream	Meats
			Poultry
Liqueurs for flaming	Cheeses	Hardened brown sugar	Frozen vegetables
	Chocolate		
Sauces for pancakes or desserts		Frozen whipped topping	Frozen baked goods
		Cream cheese (remove foil wrap first)	
Individual servings of food right on serving plate or in bowl (slice of pie; cup of soup)		Refrigerated peanut butter (for ease in spreading)	
Warming egg whites—if whites need to be at room temperature for beating			

• For people on the move, "no time for breakfast" is no longer an acceptable excuse when a microwave oven is available. Hot cereals are seconds away, as are eggs—yes, eggs. Of course, you may not be able to prepare a skillet-type sunny-side-up egg in the microwave oven, but if you want an egg breakfast in a flash, it's a small sacrifice to make.

For a delicious scrambled egg, break the egg into a small microwave-safe bowl, add 2 tablespoons of skim, low-fat, or whole milk or water, ½ teaspoon of margarine or butter, and a dash of seasoning. Stir as you would for scrambled eggs. Microwave, partially covered, for 1 minute on Medium-High, stir, and continue to cook on Medium-High, partially covered, until almost set, ½ to 1 minute longer. Serve with a slice of toast spread with margarine, butter, or reduced-calorie fruit-flavored spread, and a piece of fruit or a glass of fruit juice. Add a cup of coffee or tea and you have a delicious full meal to start the day, with no skillet to clean.

Never microwave eggs in the shell and *never* microwave a whole egg without pricking the yolk with a toothpick to break the outer membrane. If you forget to do this the egg may explode, making a real mess. (This also applies to such foods as potatoes, eggplant, and winter squash.)

• Microwave ovens without browning units will not give foods the characteristic, appetizing color we have come to expect from conventional ovens. To add some color, try sprinkling food with seasonings or herbs before microwaving.

Freezer Facts

Your freezer is an appliance you probably take for granted, but living without one would certainly be quite inconvenient. Just think back to the days of the "icebox," when people had to buy ice regularly and shop for fresh foods nearly every day. Long-term freezing was virtually unheard of.

Today there are literally thousands of frozen convenience foods in the frozen foods section of large supermarkets. And, for many people, convenience also means preparing home-cooked meals in advance and freezing them.

When wrapping foods (such as meats) for the freezer, be sure to use moisture- and vapor-resistant wrap that molds easily to the shape of the food. Let hot items cool before freezing so you get the most efficient performance from your freezer. Fill freezer containers as close to the top as possible to keep air out. (If filling with liquid, be sure to leave room for expansion that occurs during the freezing process.) A layer of plastic wrap placed directly on the food surface will help prevent ice crystals from forming.

Here are some more tips for turning your freezer into an even greater timesaver.

• Prepare breakfast foods such as pancakes and muffins in advance and freeze. Then just pop them into the microwave oven or toaster-oven to reheat in a flash.

• Casseroles and stews of poultry, fish, or meat with vegetable or pasta freeze well because they are usually coated with sauce.

(Cooked potatoes, however, tend to lose their shape and texture when frozen, so avoid freezing dishes containing potatoes.) And remember, serving-size portions thaw faster.

• Pasta dishes like lasagna or baked ziti are perfect to prepare ahead and freeze. Don't try freezing a pasta salad, though. The vegetables and dressing will not be appetizing when you serve it.

• Soups and sauces freeze well. For faster thawing, freeze in individual portions. Don't freeze creamed soups or sauces—you can always add the milk later.

• Desserts such as cakes, cookies, fruit pies, and cobblers not only freeze well but also enable you to prepare desserts in advance so they are available when guests drop by.

• Pastry and cookie dough can be prepared when you have the time, then frozen, which makes homemade baking a snap!

• Coffee (beans, ground, instant, or freeze-dried) stays fresh for months in the freezer. You can buy it on sale—no more running to the store when you're down to your last potful.

• Flour can also be kept in the freezer for months.

• Don't throw away meat scraps, bones, and pieces of raw vegetables. Freeze them for use in making stock.

• With the aid of your freezer you're no longer limited to enjoying fresh herbs only when you have a garden full. Harvest your herbs when they are plentiful or buy them from the local supermarket or greengrocer, snip off the leaves, and seal them in plastic freezer bags. Freeze them and you'll have them on hand whenever a recipe calls for fresh herbs (don't plan to use them for garnish since the freezing process will leave them looking wilted and less attractive).

Other Helpful Hints

Metric Conversions

If you are converting the recipes in this book to metric measurements, use the chart on the next page as a guide.

Volume		Oven Temperatures	
¼ teaspoon	1 milliliter	250° F	120° C
½ teaspoon	2 milliliters	275° F	140° C
1 teaspoon	5 milliliters	300° F	150° C
1 tablespoon	15 milliliters	325° F	160° C
2 tablespoons	30 milliliters	350° F	180° C
3 tablespoons	45 milliliters	375° F	190° C
¼ cup	50 milliliters	400° F	200° C
⅓ cup	75 milliliters	425° F	220° C
½ cup	125 milliliters	450° F	230° C
⅔ cup	150 milliliters	475° F	250° C
¾ cup	175 milliliters	500° F	260° C
1 cup	250 milliliters	525° F	270° C
1 quart	1 liter		

Weight		Length	
1 ounce	30 grams	1 inch	25 millimeters
¼ pound	120 grams	1 inch	2.5 centimeters
½ pound	240 grams		
¾ pound	360 grams		
1 pound	480 grams		

Pan Substitutions

It's best to use the pan size that's recommended in a recipe; however, if your kitchen isn't equipped with that particular pan, chances are a substitution will work just as well. The pan size is determined by the volume of food it holds. When substituting, use a pan as close to the recommended size as possible. Food cooked in too small a pan may boil over; food cooked in too large a pan may dry out or burn. To determine the dimensions of a baking pan, measure across the top, between the inside edges. To determine the volume, measure the amount of water the pan holds when completely filled.

When you use a pan that is a different size from the one recommended, it may be necessary to adjust the suggested cooking time. Depending on the size of the pan and the depth of the food in it, you may need to add or subtract 5 to 10 minutes. If you substitute glass or glass-ceramic for metal, the oven temperature should be reduced by 25° F.

The following chart provides some common pan substitutions:

Recommended Size	Approximate Volume	Possible Substitutions
8 x 1½-inch round baking pan	1½ quarts	10 x 6 x 2-inch baking dish 9 x 1½-inch round baking pan 8 x 4 x 2-inch loaf pan 9-inch pie plate
8 x 8 x 2-inch baking pan	2 quarts	11 x 7 x 1½-inch baking pan 12 x 7½ x 2-inch baking pan 9 x 5 x 3-inch loaf pan two 8 x 1½-inch round baking pans
13 x 9 x 2-inch baking pan	3 quarts	14 x 11 x 2-inch baking dish two 9 x 1½-inch round baking pans two 8 x 1½-inch round baking pans

Sugar Substitutes

The use of sugar substitutes on the Weight Watchers food plan has always been optional. Natural sweetness is available in the form of fruits and honey. You may also use white and brown sugar, fructose, molasses, syrup, jams, jellies, and preserves. The use of sugar substitutes is completely optional, and we believe the decision about using them should be made by you and your physician.

Nutrition Notes

The foods we eat provide the nutrients we need to stay healthy — about 40 in all, including proteins, fats, carbohydrates, fiber, vitamins, minerals, and water. It is the amount of proteins, fats, and carbohydrates in foods that determines their caloric content. Our bodies use these nutrients for energy, growth, repair of body tissue, and regulation and control of body processes.

• Proteins are necessary for building and maintaining body tissue and are excellent sources of iron and B vitamins. The best sources of protein are fish, poultry, lean meat, eggs, milk, cheese, and legumes.

• Carbohydrates are the body's best source of energy and fiber. Foods high in carbohydrates contain lots of B vitamins, too. Whole grains, breads, cereals, legumes, fruits, and vegetables are excellent sources of carbohydrates.

• Fats are the most concentrated source of energy and supply us with essential fatty acids and fat-soluble vitamins. Margarine and vegetable oils are pure sources of fat; lean meat, fish, poultry, cheese, eggs, and milk also contain fat. We recommend that fats comprise no more than 30 percent of your daily caloric intake, with less than 10 percent being saturated, up to 10 percent polyunsaturated, and the rest monounsaturated.

• Fiber is becoming more important to the diet as we discover that it may help lower blood cholesterol levels and control levels of blood sugar. Bran products, whole grains, legumes, fruits, and vegetables are good fiber sources.

• Vitamins and minerals are also essential for the body's proper functioning. The B vitamins help convert carbohydrate into energy; vitamin C helps give strength to body tissues, and vitamin A is important for good vision.

• Calcium builds and maintains strong bones and teeth, and is essential throughout your life to help prevent osteoporosis in later years. The best sources of calcium are, of course, milk and other dairy products. But calcium is also found in sardines and salmon (canned with bones), tofu and cooked soybeans, and in certain fruits and vegetables such as oranges, cooked collard, turnip, and mustard greens, broccoli, and spinach.

• Iron is one of the toughest minerals to get in ample supply, particularly for women. And it is one of the most vital because it is essential to the formation of red blood cells. Be on the lookout for lean meat (especially red meat), poultry, shellfish, liver, legumes, and enriched grains, which are all good sources.

• Sodium can play a significant role in masking actual weight loss since it affects the body's water balance and causes some people to retain water, adding to weight. Sodium occurs naturally in certain foods, and additional amounts are often added in processing prepared foods. Your daily sodium intake should not exceed 3 grams (3,000 milligrams). Remember, just ¼ teaspoon of salt contains 533 milligrams of sodium!

• Cholesterol is an essential part of all body tissue and is found in foods of animal origin. High blood cholesterol has been associated with an increased risk of heart disease. Because of this risk factor, we recommend that you limit your cholesterol intake to an average of 300 milligrams per day, based on your weekly cholesterol intake. To lower your cholesterol intake choose low-fat dairy products, reduce your intake of eggs and organ meats, and select poultry or fish in place of meats.

The objective of daily menu planning is to provide yourself with basic nutrients while staying within your caloric limit. Remember that no single food supplies all the essential nutrients in the amounts needed, and that variety is the key to success. The greater the variety of food, the less likely you are to develop a deficiency or an excess of any nutrient, and the more interesting and attractive your diet will be.

Using the Exchange and Nutrition Information on the Recipes

Each recipe in this book is followed by an Exchange Information statement. This statement provides information as to how one serving of the item prepared from that recipe fits into the Food Plan. You will find this statement useful when preparing your menus as it will help you keep track of your Exchanges. If you make any changes in the recipes, be sure to adjust the Exchange Information accordingly.

Since many people are concerned about nutrition, on each recipe we have also included the per-serving nutrition analysis for calories, protein, fat, carbohydrate, calcium, sodium, cholesterol, and dietary fiber. These figures were calculated using the most up-to-date data available; they will change if the recipe is altered, even if the substitution in ingredients does not affect the Exchange Information. The nutrition information for recipes containing cooked items such as rice, pasta, or vegetables has been calculated on the assumption that no extra salt or fat has been added during cooking.

A NOTE ON THE RECIPE SYMBOLS

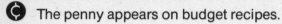 The clock face on recipes indicates that they can be prepared in 30 minutes or less.

The penny appears on budget recipes.

The Fruit Exchange

Act 1: A Feast of Fruit

Our play opens in the garden of earthly delights, where fruits of every description grow in lush abundance. In this best of all possible worlds, sample Strawberry Blossoms, Pear-Raspberry Crisp, or Tropical Fruits with Ginger Cream. The garden is fairly bursting with delectable choices, all performing for you now in Act 1.

Daily Exchanges

	WEEKS 1 AND 2	WEEKS 3, 4, AND 5
Women	2 to 3 Exchanges	2 to 3 Exchanges
Men and Youths	3 to 4 Exchanges	3 to 5 Exchanges

Fruit Exchange Notes

• Fruits supply vitamin A, vitamin C, carbohydrate, potassium, and fiber. Since individual fruits vary widely in the amount of nutrients they supply, it is important that you take advantage of the wide variety supplied by the Exchange Lists.

• Select at least one serving of one of the following vitamin C-rich fruits each day: orange, grapefruit, strawberries, cantaloupe, honeydew melon, papaya, kiwi fruit, guava, and ugli fruit. Tomato juice and mixed vegetable juice, both found in the Vegetable Exchange List, are also excellent sources of vitamin C. You may select one serving of either of these juices instead of the above fruits to fulfill your vitamin C requirement.

• When using canned or frozen fruit, use only those products that have no sugar added.

• Except for pineapple slices and spears, when using canned fruit, 1 Exchange is ½ cup *or* the fresh equivalent with up to 2 tablespoons juice (for example, ½ cup canned sliced peaches *or* 2 canned peach halves). Two slices *or* 4 spears of canned pineapple is 1 Fruit Exchange.

• Measure frozen fruit in its frozen state, never thawed or partially thawed. Exchanges are the same as for fresh fruit.

• When using undiluted frozen concentrated fruit juice, 1 Fruit Exchange is
  2 tablespoons orange, grapefruit, or orange-grapefruit juice
  4 teaspoons apple, grape, pineapple, or combined fruit juice
  (except orange-grapefruit juice)

Fruit Exchange Lists

Week 1

Selections	One Exchange
Apple	1 small (about ¼ pound) *or* ¾ cup
Banana	½ medium (about 3 ounces with peel)
Cantaloupe	¼ small (about 9 ounces with rind) *or* 1 cup
Fruit Salad	½ cup
Grapefruit	½ medium (about ½ pound with rind)
Grapefruit Juice	½ cup
Grapefruit Sections	½ cup
Honeydew *or* Similar Melon	2-inch wedge (about 7 inches long) *or* 1 cup
Orange	1 small (about 6 ounces with rind)
Orange-Grapefruit Juice	½ cup
Orange Juice	½ cup
Orange Sections	½ cup
Peach	1 medium (about ¼ pound with pit) *or* ½ cup
Pineapple	⅛ medium (about 4½ ounces with rind) *or* ½ cup
Strawberries	1 cup whole (about 5 ounces) *or* ¾ cup sliced
Watermelon	2 x 3-inch wedge *or* 1 cup

Week 2

You may use all of the items listed under Week 1 and may add the following to your Exchange List:

Selections	One Exchange
Berries	
Blackberries	½ cup
Blueberries	½ cup
Boysenberries	½ cup
Elderberries	½ cup
Huckleberries	½ cup
Loganberries	½ cup
Mulberries	½ cup
Raspberries	½ cup

Week 3

You may use all of the items listed under Weeks 1 and 2 and may add the following to your Exchange List:

Selections	One Exchange
Grapes	20 small *or* 12 large
Mandarin Orange	1 large (about ¼ pound with rind)
Nectarine	1 small (about 5 ounces with pit)
Prunes	2 large *or* 3 medium
Tangerine	1 large (about ¼ pound with rind)

Week 4

You may use all of the items listed under Weeks 1, 2, and 3 and may add the following to your Exchange List:

Selections	One Exchange
Apple Cider, unfermented (carbonated *or* noncarbonated)	⅓ cup
Apple Juice	⅓ cup
Applesauce, canned *or* homemade (no sugar added)	½ cup
Cherries	10 large
Combined Fruit Juices, any type	⅓ cup
Cranberries	1 cup
Cranberry Juice, low-calorie	1 cup
Cranberry Juice, regular	⅓ cup
Nectar, any type	⅓ cup
Pear	1 small (about 5 ounces) *or* ½ large
Plums	2 medium (about 2½ ounces with pit each)

Week 5

You may use all of the items listed under Weeks 1, 2, 3, and 4 and may add the following to your Exchange List:

Selections	One Exchange
Apricots	
Dried	4 halves
Fresh	2 medium (about 1¼ ounces with pit each)

Selections	One Exchange
Carambola (Star Fruit)	1 medium (about 4½ ounces with rind)
Crab Apples	2
Currants	
Dried	2 tablespoons
Fresh	¾ cup
Dates, dried *or* fresh	2
Dried Fruit, any type	¾ ounce
Fig, dried *or* fresh	1 large
Genips	2
Gooseberries	¾ cup
Grape Juice, carbonated *or* noncarbonated	⅓ cup
Guava	¼ pound (with skin and seeds)
Kiwi Fruit	1 medium (about 3 ounces with rind)
Kumquats	3 medium
Lichees, fresh	8
Loquats	10
Mango	½ small (about 6½ ounces with rind, without pit)
Murcot (Honey Tangerine)	1 medium (about ¼ pound with rind)
Papaya	½ medium (about ½ pound with seeds and skin) *or* 1 cup
Passion Fruit	3 (total of about ¼ pound)
Persimmon	½ medium (about 2 ounces)
Pineapple Juice	⅓ cup
Prickly Pear (Cactus Pear)	1 medium
Prune Juice	⅓ cup
Quince	1 medium
Raisins	2 tablespoons
Soursop (Guanabana)	¼ cup
Sweetsop (Sugar Apple)	⅓ cup
Tamarinds	2
Tangelo	1 large
Tangerine Juice	½ cup
Ugli Fruit	1 medium

Apple-Pear Compote ◑

WEEK 4   MAKES 4 SERVINGS

½ cup dry white table wine
1 teaspoon honey
½ teaspoon vanilla extract
¼ teaspoon ground cinnamon
⅛ teaspoon *each* ground nutmeg
    and ginger
1 small Granny Smith apple (about
    ¼ pound), pared and chopped

1 small McIntosh apple (about
    ¼ pound), pared and chopped
10 ounces pears, pared and chopped
¼ cup thawed frozen dairy whipped
    topping

In 2-quart saucepan combine wine, honey, vanilla, and spices and cook over high heat until mixture comes to a boil; add Granny Smith apple. Reduce heat to medium and cook until liquid is reduced by half, 8 to 10 minutes. Add McIntosh apple and pears and cook until fruit is tender and liquid is almost completely evaporated and syrupy, about 3 minutes.

To serve, into 4 dessert dishes spoon ¼ of the fruit mixture; top each with 1 tablespoon whipped topping.

Each serving provides: 1 Fruit Exchange; 50 Optional Calories
Per serving: 105 calories; 0.3 g protein; 1 g fat; 20 g carbohydrate; 13 mg calcium;
    7 mg sodium; 0 mg cholesterol; 3 g dietary fiber

Apple-Raisin Pandowdy ©

WEEK 5   MAKES 4 SERVINGS

¾ pound Granny Smith apples, cored, pared, and cut into ⅛-inch-thick slices
¼ cup golden *or* dark raisins
½ teaspoon lemon juice
⅓ cup unfermented apple cider (no sugar added)
2 teaspoons cornstarch
¼ teaspoon ground cinnamon

⅛ teaspoon *each* ground cloves, nutmeg, and mace
2 tablespoons whipped butter, softened
4 ready-to-bake refrigerated buttermilk flaky biscuits (1 ounce each)
2 teaspoons granulated sugar
1 tablespoon plus 1 teaspoon maple syrup

Preheat oven to 400° F. In medium mixing bowl combine apple slices, raisins, and lemon juice and toss to combine; set aside. In 1-cup liquid measure combine apple cider, cornstarch, and spices, stirring to dissolve cornstarch; add to apple mixture and mix well. Transfer mixture to 1½-quart casserole; dot top of mixture with butter. Cover and bake until fruit is tender-crisp, 15 to 20 minutes.

Arrange biscuits over fruit mixture in center of casserole with edges touching. Sprinkle ½ teaspoon sugar over each biscuit and bake until biscuits are lightly browned, 10 to 15 minutes longer. Remove from oven; pour 1 teaspoon syrup over each biscuit and serve.

Each serving provides: 1 Bread Exchange; 1½ Fruit Exchanges; 60 Optional Calories
Per serving: 220 calories; 2 g protein; 7 g fat; 41 g carbohydrate; 19 mg calcium;
   328 mg sodium; 8 mg cholesterol; 2 g dietary fiber

Apple-Spice Tea ⊙◑

WEEK 4   MAKES 2 SERVINGS, ABOUT 1 CUP EACH

1½ cups water
⅔ cup unfermented apple cider
   (no sugar added)
2 teaspoons firmly packed dark
   brown sugar
Two 1-inch strips *each* orange
   and lemon peels

1 cinnamon stick
3 whole cloves
1 whole allspice
2 tea bags
Garnish: 2 lemon slices

In 1-quart saucepan combine all ingredients except tea bags; cook over high heat and bring to a boil. Reduce heat to medium-low; add tea bags and let simmer until flavors blend, about 5 minutes. Pour tea through sieve into decorative teapot or directly into tea cups, discarding solids, and serve each portion with a lemon slice.

Each serving provides: 1 Fruit Exchange; 20 Optional Calories
Per serving: 63 calories; 0.1 g protein; 0.1 g fat; 16 g carbohydrate; 27 mg calcium;
   11 mg sodium; 0 mg cholesterol; dietary fiber data not available

High-Fiber Apple Muffins ℂ

WEEK 3   MAKES 12 SERVINGS, 1 MUFFIN EACH

Start the day with one of these satisfying muffins and ½ cup plain low-fat yogurt. Muffins can be frozen; then just thawed at room temperature or heated in a microwave or toaster-oven and served warm.

1½ cups buttermilk
3 ounces ready-to-eat natural
　high-fiber bran cereal
1 egg, lightly beaten
2 tablespoons *each* margarine, melted,
　and honey
1 pound apples, cored, pared,
　and diced
16 large pitted prunes, diced
¾ cup *each* whole wheat flour and
　all-purpose flour

2 tablespoons firmly packed dark
　brown sugar
1½ teaspoons double-acting baking
　powder
½ teaspoon ground cinnamon
¼ teaspoon *each* baking soda and
　ground nutmeg
⅛ teaspoon salt

In large mixing bowl combine buttermilk, cereal, egg, margarine, and honey; stir to combine and let stand until cereal softens, 3 to 4 minutes.

Preheat oven to 375° F. In medium mixing bowl combine remaining ingredients, stirring to combine; add to cereal mixture and stir just until combined. Spray twelve 2½-inch-diameter muffin-pan cups with nonstick cooking spray; fill each cup with an equal amount of batter (each will be about ⅔ full). Bake for 30 minutes (until muffins are browned and a toothpick, inserted in center, comes out dry). Remove muffins to wire rack and let cool for 5 minutes; invert muffins onto wire rack and let cool completely.

Each serving provides: 1 Bread Exchange; ½ Fat Exchange; 1 Fruit Exchange; 40 Optional
　Calories
Per serving: 177 calories; 5 g protein; 3 g fat; 37 g carbohydrate; 87 mg calcium;
　235 mg sodium; 24 mg cholesterol; 6 g dietary fiber

Savory Baked Apples ℂ

WEEK 5   MAKES 2 SERVINGS, 1 APPLE EACH

2 teaspoons margarine
2 tablespoons finely chopped onion
3 ounces cooked ground pork *or* **veal**
¼ cup rinsed and drained sauerkraut*
2 tablespoons dark *or* **golden raisins,**
chopped
1 tablespoon country Dijon-style
mustard

¼ teaspoon caraway seed
⅛ teaspoon salt
Dash pepper
2 Rome Beauty apples (6 ounces each)
2 cups water

Preheat oven to 400° F. In 8-inch nonstick skillet melt margarine; add onion and sauté over medium-high heat, stirring frequently, until tender, about 1 minute. Add remaining ingredients except apples and water and mix well to combine; cook until heated through, 1 to 2 minutes. Set aside.

Core apples, making a cavity about 1½ inches in diameter and 1½ inches deep; set apples upright in 8 x 8 x 2-inch baking pan. Spoon half of meat mixture (about ¼ cup) into each apple. Pour water into pan and bake until apples are tender and filling is browned, 30 to 35 minutes.

Each serving provides: 1½ Protein Exchanges; ¼ Vegetable Exchange; 1 Fat Exchange;
2 Fruit Exchanges; 3 Optional Calories
Per serving with pork: 276 calories; 10 g protein; 16 g fat; 26 g carbohydrate; 24 mg calcium;
506 mg sodium (estimated); 41 mg cholesterol; 3 g dietary fiber
With veal: 239 calories; 13 g protein; 10 g fat; 26 g carbohydrate; 27 mg calcium;
498 mg sodium (estimated); 43 mg cholesterol; 3 g dietary fiber

*Use the sauerkraut that is packaged in plastic bags and stored in the refrigerator section of the supermarket; it is usually crisper and less salty than the canned.

Banana Mousse

WEEK 5   MAKES 4 SERVINGS

For a different taste sensation, after the banana mousse is prepared, spoon it into individual dessert dishes, cover with plastic wrap, and freeze until firm.

**¾ pound ripe bananas, peeled and
   sliced
2 tablespoons dark rum**

**1 teaspoon lemon juice
½ cup thawed frozen dairy whipped
   topping**

In medium bowl (not aluminum*) combine banana slices, rum, and lemon juice; let marinate for 1 hour. Transfer to work bowl of food processor and process until pureed. Transfer to medium bowl; fold in whipped topping. Into each of 4 dessert dishes spoon ¼ of the banana mousse. Serve immediately or cover with plastic wrap and refrigerate until ready to serve.

Each serving provides: 1 Fruit Exchange; 45 Optional Calories
Per serving: 93 calories; 1 g protein; 2 g fat; 15 g carbohydrate; 4 mg calcium;
   11 mg sodium; 0 mg cholesterol; 1 g dietary fiber

*It's best to marinate in glass or stainless-steel containers; acidic ingredients such as lemon juice may react with aluminum, causing color and flavor changes in food.

Banana Chiffon Pie ©

WEEK 1   MAKES 8 SERVINGS

3 ounces ready-to-eat crunchy nut-like
   cereal nuggets
2 tablespoons plus 1 teaspoon
   granulated sugar, divided
2 tablespoons water
¾ pound bananas, peeled and sliced

4 eggs, separated
½ cup plain low-fat yogurt
⅛ teaspoon vanilla extract
Dash *each* salt and cream of tartar

Preheat oven to 400° F. In small mixing bowl combine cereal nuggets, 2 teaspoons sugar, and the water, mixing thoroughly. Spray 10-inch pie pan with nonstick cooking spray and press cereal mixture evenly over bottom of pan; set aside.

In blender container combine bananas, egg yolks, yogurt, and vanilla and process at high speed until smooth, scraping down sides of container as necessary; transfer to large mixing bowl and set aside.

Using electric mixer at medium speed, in medium mixing bowl combine egg whites, salt, and cream of tartar and beat until soft peaks form. Gradually beat in remaining 5 teaspoons sugar, 1 teaspoon at a time, beating until stiff peaks form. Stir half the beaten whites into banana mixture, then fold in remaining whites. Carefully pour into prepared crust and bake for 10 minutes. Reduce heat to 350° F and bake 10 minutes longer (until a knife, inserted in center, comes out clean). Remove pie to wire rack and let cool for 1 hour. Serve immediately or cover with plastic wrap and refrigerate until ready to serve.

Each serving provides: ½ Protein Exchange; ½ Bread Exchange; ½ Fruit Exchange;
   30 Optional Calories
Per serving: 127 calories; 5 g protein; 3 g fat; 20 g carbohydrate; 46 mg calcium;
   135 mg sodium; 138 mg cholesterol; 1 g dietary fiber

Cranberry Relish ◑

Fresh cranberries are usually featured in supermarkets during the autumn months. To enjoy them all year long, freeze them in a plastic freezer bag.

1 small navel orange (about 6 ounces)
2 cups cranberries
1½ ounces mixed dried fruit
⅓ cup unfermented apple cider
  (no sugar added)
3 tablespoons firmly packed light
  brown sugar

¼ teaspoon *each* grated lemon and
  orange peel
⅛ teaspoon *each* ground ginger
  and nutmeg

Over 2-quart saucepan to catch juice, remove skin and membranes from orange; dice orange and add to saucepan with juice. Add remaining ingredients to saucepan and cook over high heat until mixture comes to a boil. Reduce heat to medium-low and cook, stirring frequently, until liquid is reduced and mixture thickens, about 10 minutes. Let cool to room temperature before serving.

Each serving provides: 1½ Fruit Exchanges; 45 Optional Calories
Per serving: 116 calories; 1 g protein; 0.3 g fat; 30 g carbohydrate; 32 mg calcium;
  6 mg sodium; 0 mg cholesterol; 1 g dietary fiber (this figure does not include cranberries;
  nutrition analysis not available)

Variation: Cherry-Berry Relish —Substitute ¾ ounce *each* dried blueberries and dried cherries for the mixed dried fruit.

Per serving: 112 calories; 1 g protein; 0.4 g fat; 28 g carbohydrate; 32 mg calcium;
  5 mg sodium; 0 mg cholesterol; 1 g dietary fiber (this figure does not include cranberries;
  nutrition analysis not available)

Berries in Vanilla Sauce ◑

WEEK 3   MAKES 4 SERVINGS

Perfect for Independence Day, this spectacular dessert of strawberries, blueberries, and creamy vanilla sauce takes only ten minutes to prepare. Enjoy the holiday festivities knowing dessert is chilling in the refrigerator.

½ cup low-fat milk (1% milk fat)
2 tablespoons plus 2 teaspoons nonfat
   dry milk powder
1 tablespoon *each* cornstarch and
   granulated sugar
1 teaspoon vanilla extract

⅛ teaspoon ground nutmeg
3 tablespoons half-and-half (blend
   of milk and cream)
1 egg
2 cups strawberries
1 cup blueberries

In 1-quart saucepan combine milk and milk powder, cornstarch, sugar, vanilla, and nutmeg, stirring to dissolve cornstarch; cook over medium heat, stirring constantly, until mixture thickens slightly, 2 to 3 minutes.

In small mixing bowl beat together half-and-half and egg; slowly stir ¼ cup milk mixture into egg mixture; stir egg mixture into remaining milk mixture in saucepan. Reduce heat to low and cook, stirring constantly, until mixture thickens, 2 to 3 minutes. Transfer to bowl; cover with plastic wrap and refrigerate until chilled, about 30 minutes.

To serve, into each of 4 dessert dishes combine ½ cup strawberries and ¼ cup blueberries; top each with ¼ of the sauce (about ¼ cup).

Each serving provides: 1 Fruit Exchange; ¼ Milk Exchange; 60 Optional Calories
Per serving. 124 calories; 5 g protein; 3 g fat; 19 g carbohydrate; 104 mg calcium;
   56 mg sodium; 74 mg cholesterol; 3 g dietary fiber

Mixed Fruit with Apricot-Rum Puree ◑

WEEK 5   MAKES 4 SERVINGS

6 dried apricot halves
¼ cup water
2 tablespoons dark rum
1 tablespoon granulated sugar
Dash ground cinnamon
1 medium kiwi fruit (about 3 ounces),
    pared and sliced

½ medium banana (about 3 ounces),
    peeled and sliced
½ cup strawberries, sliced
1 tablespoon lemon juice

In small saucepan combine apricots, water, rum, sugar, and cinnamon and bring to a boil. Reduce heat and let simmer until apricots are softened, about 10 minutes. Remove from heat and let cool. Transfer mixture to blender container and process until pureed, scraping down sides of container as necessary; set aside. In small mixing bowl combine remaining ingredients, tossing to combine.

To serve, into each of 4 dessert dishes spoon ¼ of the apricot mixture; top each portion with ¼ of the fruit mixture.

Each serving provides: 1 Fruit Exchange; 35 Optional Calories
Per serving: 72 calories; 1 g protein; 0.2 g fat; 14 g carbohydrate; 12 mg calcium;
    3 mg sodium; 0 mg cholesterol; 1 g dietary fiber (this figure does not include kiwi fruit;
    nutrition analysis not available)

Meringues with Raspberry Sauce

WEEK 2   MAKES 4 SERVINGS, 2 MERINGUES EACH

This elegant dessert can be prepared up to 1 hour in advance.

2 cups raspberries (reserve ½ cup
  berries for garnish)
⅓ cup granulated sugar, divided
2 teaspoons lemon juice
2 cups water

2 egg whites (at room temperature)
1 teaspoon vanilla, almond, *or* maple
  extract
Garnish: 4 mint sprigs

In work bowl of food processor process raspberries until pureed. Set sieve over small bowl and press puree through sieve into bowl. Stir in 2 teaspoons sugar and lemon juice; set aside.

In 10-inch nonstick skillet heat water until barely simmering. Using electric mixer on medium speed, in medium mixing bowl beat egg whites until frothy; gradually add remaining sugar and extract and beat until stiff, not dry. On a plate, using a pastry bag fitted with a star tip,* pipe ⅛ of the beaten whites into a ring about 2 inches in diameter. Using a pancake turner carefully transfer egg white ring into simmering water. Repeat procedure 7 more times, making 7 more meringues and sliding each into water. Cook meringues for 10 minutes; carefully turn each meringue over and cook 10 minutes longer.

Cover a wire rack with sheet of paper towel. Using a slotted spoon, remove meringues from skillet and arrange on rack to drain.

To serve, onto each of 4 serving plates spoon ¼ of the raspberry puree; top puree with 2 meringues and ¼ of the reserved berries. Garnish each portion with a mint sprig.

Each serving provides: 1 Fruit Exchange; 90 Optional Calories
Per serving: 106 calories; 2 g protein; 0.3 g fat; 24 g carbohydrate; 16 mg calcium;
  26 mg sodium; 0 mg cholesterol; 3 g dietary fiber

*If pastry bag is not available, using 2 soup spoons, shape ⅛ of the beaten whites into a large round or oval and slide into simmering water. Repeat procedure as recipe directs.

Strawberry Blossoms ◐◑

WEEK 4	MAKES 2 SERVINGS

1 cup strawberries
¼ cup thawed frozen dairy whipped topping
2 tablespoons cream cheese, softened
½ teaspoon confectioners' sugar

2 teaspoons reduced-calorie strawberry spread (16 calories per 2 teaspoons), melted

Set each berry on stem end. Using a sharp knife, cut each in half lengthwise, *just to but not through* base of berry; then, following same procedure, cut each half lengthwise, making four quarters. Gently press strawberry quarters apart, forming a flower; set aside. In small bowl combine whipped topping, cream cheese, and sugar, mixing until smooth. Using a pastry bag filled with a small star tip, or a small spoon, fill each strawberry with an equal amount of the cheese mixture. Divide strawberries evenly onto 2 dessert plates and drizzle each with an equal amount of strawberry spread.

Each serving provides: ½ Fruit Exchange; 90 Optional Calories
Per serving: 107 calories; 2 g protein; 7 g fat; 10 g carbohydrate; 22 mg calcium; 53 mg sodium; 16 mg cholesterol; 1 g dietary fiber

Cherry-Apple Cobbler

WEEK 5	MAKES 8 SERVINGS

¾ cup plus 1 tablespoon all-purpose flour, divided
2 tablespoons granulated sugar, divided
1 teaspoon double-acting baking powder
¼ teaspoon baking soda
2 tablespoons plus 2 teaspoons margarine

3 tablespoons buttermilk
50 large pitted cherries
¾ pound apples, cored, pared, and chopped
1 tablespoon butter, cut into small pieces

In medium mixing bowl combine ¾ cup flour, 1 tablespoon sugar, the baking powder, and baking soda; using a pastry blender or 2 knives used scissors-fashion cut in margarine until mixture resembles coarse meal. Stir in buttermilk, stirring until mixture is combined and forms dough. Let stand for 5 minutes.

Preheat oven to 425° F. Spray an 8-inch pie pan with nonstick cooking spray; add cherries and apples and stir to combine. Sprinkle remaining tablespoon flour and sugar over fruit mixture and stir slightly to combine. Dot with butter; set aside.

Between 2 sheets of wax paper roll dough, forming a 9-inch circle about ⅛-inch thick.* Place dough over filling in pie pan and fold edges under. Gently pierce dough to allow steam to escape. Bake until crust is golden brown, about 30 minutes. Remove from oven and let cool slightly.

Each serving provides: ½ Bread Exchange; 1 Fat Exchange; 1 Fruit Exchange; 35 Optional Calories
Per serving: 174 calories; 2 g protein; 6 g fat; 29 g carbohydrate; 48 mg calcium; 144 mg sodium; 4 mg cholesterol; 2 g dietary fiber

*Dough can be broken into small pieces and sprinkled over filling rather than rolled into a crust.

Black Forest Pudding ❷❿

WEEK 4   MAKES 4 SERVINGS, 1 PUDDING EACH

20 large fresh *or* thawed frozen pitted cherries (no sugar added)
¾ cup thawed frozen nondairy whipped topping, divided
2 cups skim *or* nonfat milk

1 envelope (four ½-cup servings) reduced-calorie instant chocolate pudding mix
4 maraschino cherries with stems

In small mixing bowl combine the fresh (or frozen) cherries and ½ cup whipped topping; set aside. Using 2 cups milk, prepare pudding according to package directions but do not chill.

Into each of four dessert dishes spoon ⅛ of the pudding; top with ¼ of the cherry mixture and the remaining pudding. Top each portion with 1 tablespoon of the remaining whipped topping and a maraschino cherry. Serve immediately.

Each serving provides: ½ Fruit Exchange; 1 Milk Exchange; 50 Optional Calories
Per serving: 152 calories; 5 g protein; 4 g fat; 26 g carbohydrate; 163 mg calcium;
  425 mg sodium; 2 mg cholesterol; 1 g dietary fiber

Figs with Mint Cream ◑

WEEK 5   MAKES 2 SERVINGS, 1 FIG EACH

Honey, mint, and sour cream combine to make a refreshing topping for figs or any fresh fruit, such as oranges, pears, or peaches.

2 large fresh figs
1 tablespoon plus 1½ teaspoons *each*
    sour cream and thawed frozen dairy
    whipped topping

1½ teaspoons chopped fresh mint
⅛ teaspoon grated orange peel
1 teaspoon honey
Garnish: 2 mint sprigs

Using sharp knife, cut each fig lengthwise, ¾ of the way down, being sure not to cut through base of fig, making 2 halves; cut each fig half lengthwise, making 4 quarters. Arrange figs on serving platter and set aside.

In small mixing bowl combine sour cream, whipped topping, mint, and orange peel and stir until thoroughly combined. Pour half of mint mixture over each fig and then drizzle each portion with ½ teaspoon honey. Garnish with mint sprigs.

Each serving provides: 1 Fruit Exchange; 45 Optional Calories
Per serving: 91 calories; 1 g protein; 3 g fat; 16 g carbohydrate; 36 mg calcium;
    10 mg sodium; 5 mg cholesterol; dietary fiber data not available

Compote of Spiced Fresh Fruit ◑

WEEK 8   MAKES 10 SERVINGS, ABOUT 1 CUP EACH

Two 2-inch cinnamon sticks
2-inch piece pared gingerroot, sliced
6 whole cloves
2 cups water
½ cup *each* granulated sugar and
   freshly squeezed lemon juice
¼ cup pear-flavored brandy *or* regular
   brandy

2 cups *each* cantaloupe and honeydew
   chunks
10 ounces pears, cored and cut into
   chunks
½ pound Granny Smith apples, cored
   and cut into chunks
20 large cherries, pitted

On small piece of cheesecloth place cinnamon sticks, gingerroot, and cloves. Tie ends of cloth together forming a bag. Place spice bag in small saucepan; add water, sugar, and lemon juice and cook over high heat, stirring frequently, until sugar is dissolved and mixture comes to a boil. Boil mixture without stirring for 5 minutes. Remove from heat; stir brandy into liquid and let cool slightly. Remove and discard spice bag.

In large glass or stainless-steel bowl (not aluminum*) combine fruits; add brandy mixture and stir to combine. Cover with plastic wrap and refrigerate until thoroughly chilled, about 2 hours.

Each serving provides: 1 Fruit Exchange; 65 Optional Calories
Per serving with pear-flavored brandy: 124 calories; 1 g protein; 0.5 g fat; 29 g carbohydrate;
   19 mg calcium; 7 mg sodium; 0 mg cholesterol; 2 g dietary fiber
With regular brandy: 122 calories; 1 g protein; 0.5 g fat; 27 g carbohydrate; 19 mg calcium;
   7 mg sodium; 0 mg cholesterol; 2 g dietary fiber

*It's best to marinate in glass or stainless-steel containers; acidic ingredients such as lemon juice may react with aluminum, causing color and flavor changes in food.

Grapes Brûlée ☾ ◐

WEEK 4   MAKES 2 SERVINGS

Red or green grapes are both equally wonderful in this recipe. For an especially attractive presentation, try combining both varieties.

40 small seedless grapes   **2 teaspoons granulated brown sugar**
2 tablespoons sour cream

Rinse grapes with cold water and pat dry with paper towels. Into each of 2 individual flameproof serving dishes arrange 20 grapes; spread half of the sour cream over each portion of grapes and then sift half of the sugar over sour cream in each dish. Set dishes on sheet pan and broil 3 inches from heat source until sugar melts and is caramelized, about 1 minute. Remove dishes from broiler and let cool slightly.

Each serving provides: 1 Fruit Exchange; 55 Optional Calories
Per serving: 94 calories; 1 g protein; 3 g fat; 17 g carbohydrate; 28 mg calcium;
   10 mg sodium; 6 mg cholesterol; 1 g dietary fiber

Citrus Sauce ⒸⒹ

WEEK 5	MAKES 4 SERVINGS

Brighten your breakfast with French toast or pancakes topped with this wonderful sauce or try it over angel food cake for a colorful dessert.

¾ pound navel oranges
1 medium grapefruit (about 1 pound)
½ cup orange juice (no sugar added)
2 tablespoons *each* granulated sugar
   and whipped butter

1 tablespoon cornstarch
½ teaspoon grated lemon peel

Over 1-quart saucepan to catch juice, remove skin and membranes from oranges; section oranges and set aside. Over saucepan remove skin and membranes from grapefruit; section half of the fruit* and set aside. Add orange juice, sugar, butter, cornstarch, and lemon peel to saucepan, stirring to dissolve cornstarch; cook over medium-high heat, stirring constantly, until mixture comes to a boil. Reduce heat to low and cook, stirring frequently, until mixture thickens, 2 to 3 minutes. Add orange and grapefruit sections and cook until fruit is heated through and flavors blend, 1 to 2 minutes. Remove from heat and let cool to room temperature.

Each serving provides: 1 Fruit Exchange; 65 Optional Calories
Per serving: 119 calories; 1 g protein; 3 g fat; 23 g carbohydrate; 38 mg calcium;
   30 mg sodium; 8 mg cholesterol; 1 g dietary fiber (this figure does not include grapefruit;
   nutrition analysis not available)

*Remaining half of grapefruit can be sectioned, stored in a covered container, and refrigerated for use at another time.

Melon 'n' Tonic ◐

WEEK 6	MAKES 2 SERVINGS, ABOUT 1 CUP EACH

1 cup chilled pitted watermelon chunks (reserve 4 chunks for garnish)
2 tablespoons vodka
1 cup plus 2 tablespoons tonic water, chilled

Ice cubes
Garnish: 2 mint sprigs

Chill two 12-ounce glasses. In blender container process fruit until pureed; stir in vodka. Pour in tonic water; stir once to combine. Fill each chilled glass with ice cubes; pour half of the melon mixture into each glass. Insert a decorative skewer or toothpick into 1 reserved watermelon chunk, top with a mint sprig, and then 1 additional watermelon chunk. Repeat procedure using remaining reserved watermelon chunks and a mint sprig. Set 1 skewer (or toothpick) on each glass.

Each serving provides: ½ Fruit Exchange; 95 Optional Calories
Per serving: 105 calories; 0.5 g protein; 0.3 g fat; 18 g carbohydrate; 8 mg calcium;
    7 mg sodium; 0 mg cholesterol; 0.2 g dietary fiber

Citrus-Spritzer Punch ◐

WEEK 5	MAKES 4 SERVINGS, ABOUT ¾ CUP EACH

1⅓ cups pineapple-orange juice (no sugar added), chilled
1 cup dry white table wine, chilled
2 tablespoons each freshly squeezed lemon and lime juice

1 cup lemon-lime flavored seltzer, chilled
4 lemon or lime slices
Ice cubes
Garnish: 4 mint sprigs

In punch bowl combine pineapple-orange juice, wine, lemon and lime juices; stir well. Pour in seltzer. Add lemon (or lime) slices to punch.

To serve, fill each punch glass with ice; pour ¼ of punch into each glass and garnish with a mint sprig.

Each serving provides: 1 Fruit Exchange; 50 Optional Calories
Per serving: 87 calories; 1 g protein; 0.1 g fat; 13 g carbohydrate; 23 mg calcium;
    4 mg sodium; 0 mg cholesterol; dietary fiber data not available

Quince Sauté ◑

Serve as an accompaniment to roast pork or chicken.

2 tablespoons whipped butter
2 teaspoons vegetable oil
3 medium quinces, pared, cored, sliced,
   and sprinkled with 1 tablespoon
   lemon juice

½ cup *each* diced onion and celery
2 tablespoons dried currants
½ teaspoon salt
Dash ground allspice

In 9-inch nonstick skillet combine butter and oil and heat until butter is melted; add quinces, onion, and celery and sauté over medium heat, stirring occasionally, until vegetables are tender-crisp, about 5 minutes. Stir in currants and seasonings; cover and cook over medium heat until quinces are soft, about 20 minutes.

Each serving provides: ½ Vegetable Exchange; ½ Fat Exchange; 1 Fruit Exchange;
   25 Optional Calories
Per serving: 108 calories; 1 g protein; 5 g fat; 16 g carbohydrate; 25 mg calcium;
   320 mg sodium; 8 mg cholesterol; 0.3 g dietary fiber (this figure does not include quince;
   nutrition analysis not available)

Variation: Pear Sauté—Substitute 15 ounces pears, pared, cored, and sliced for the quinces.

Per serving: 124 calories; 1 g protein; 6 g fat; 20 g carbohydrate; 28 mg calcium;
   317 mg sodium; 8 mg cholesterol; 3 g dietary fiber

Marsala Oranges

WEEK 4   MAKES 4 SERVINGS

1½ pounds navel oranges   2 tablespoons sour cream
¼ cup *each* granulated sugar,
    dry marsala wine, water, and thawed
    frozen dairy whipped topping

Using a zester or vegetable peeler, remove zest* from oranges and cut into 1-inch-long strips. Measure 2 tablespoons zest and reserve; discard any extra zest. Slice oranges crosswise and arrange on serving platter; set aside.

In small saucepan combine sugar, wine, and water and cook over high heat until mixture comes to a boil; add orange zest and cook until mixture is reduced by half and zest is lightly caramelized, about 5 minutes. Pour syrup through sieve evenly over orange slices, reserving zest. Turn oranges to coat both sides with syrup and decoratively arrange on platter. Cover with plastic wrap and refrigerate until flavors blend, overnight or at least 30 minutes.

To serve, in small bowl combine whipped topping and sour cream and spoon onto center of platter. Garnish with reserved orange zest.

Each serving provides: 1 Fruit Exchange; 105 Optional Calories
Per serving: 155 calories; 1 g protein; 3 g fat, 30 g carbohydrate; 63 mg calcium;
    10 mg sodium; 3 mg cholesterol; 2 g dietary fiber

*The zest of the orange is the peel without any of the pith (white membrane).

Sparkling Oranges ◑

WEEK 2   MAKES 2 SERVINGS

¾ pound oranges
⅓ cup champagne *or* sparkling dry
   white wine
2 teaspoons *each* granulated sugar and
   freshly squeezed lime juice

1 teaspoon julienne-cut lime peel
   (matchstick pieces), blanched
½ teaspoon fresh chopped mint

Over medium bowl to catch juice, remove skin and membrane from oranges; section oranges. Add remaining ingredients except mint, stir to combine, and let stand for 5 minutes.

To serve, into each of 2 saucer champagne glasses arrange half of orange mixture and sprinkle each portion with half of the mint.

Each serving provides: 1 Fruit Exchange; 60 Optional Calories
Per serving: 102 calories; 1 g protein; 0.3 g fat; 19 g carbohydrate; 59 mg calcium;
   2 mg sodium; 0 mg cholesterol; 2 g dietary fiber

Carrot-Fruit Salad ◑

WEEK 5   MAKES 2 SERVINGS

½ medium banana (about 3 ounces),
   peeled and sliced
2 teaspoons rice vinegar
1 small apple (about 4 ounces), grated

½ cup grated carrot
1 tablespoon *each* dried currants and
   sliced scallion (green onion)

In blender container combine banana and vinegar and process at medium speed until smooth, about 30 seconds. Transfer to glass or stainless-steel bowl (not aluminum*); add remaining ingredients and toss to combine. Serve immediately.

Each serving provides: ½ Vegetable Exchange; 1 Fruit Exchange; 15 Optional Calories
Per serving: 83 calories; 1 g protein; 0.4 g fat; 21 g carbohydrate; 19 mg calcium;
   11 mg sodium; 0 mg cholesterol; 2 g dietary fiber

*It's best to marinate in glass or stainless-steel containers; acidic ingredients such as vinegar may react with aluminum, causing color and flavor changes in food.

Peaches and Cream Muffins ⒸⓄ

WEEK 4   MAKES 12 SERVINGS, 1 MUFFIN EACH

Lining muffin pans with paper baking cups makes cleanup a cinch.

2¼ cups all-purpose flour
2 tablespoons granulated sugar
2 teaspoons double-acting baking
   powder
1 teaspoon baking soda

¼ cup margarine
3 cups drained canned sliced peaches
   (no sugar added), diced
⅓ cup plus 2 teaspoons sour cream
1 egg, beaten

Preheat oven to 400°F. Line twelve 2½-inch-diameter muffin-pan cups with paper baking cups and set aside.

In medium mixing bowl combine flour, sugar, baking powder, and baking soda; with pastry blender or 2 knives used scissors-fashion cut in margarine until mixture resembles coarse meal. In separate medium mixing bowl combine remaining ingredients; add to flour mixture and stir to combine *(do not overmix)*. Fill each baking cup with an equal amount of batter (each will be about ⅔ full). Bake for 15 minutes (until muffins are golden brown and a toothpick, inserted in center, comes out dry). Remove muffins to wire rack and let cool for 5 minutes; invert muffins onto wire rack and let cool completely.

Each serving provides: 1 Bread Exchange; 1 Fat Exchange; ½ Fruit Exchange;
   35 Optional Calories
Per serving: 164 calories; 3 g protein; 6 g fat; 24 g carbohydrate; 52 mg calcium;
   196 mg sodium; 26 mg cholesterol, 2 g dietary fiber

3.5

Honey-Poached Pear Fans ⊙ ◐

WEEK 4	MAKES 2 SERVINGS, 1 PEAR HALF EACH

1 small ripe pear (about 5 ounces), cut in half lengthwise, cored, and pared
¼ cup water
1 tablespoon *each* very thin strips lemon and lime peel and honey *or* light corn syrup

1½ teaspoons *each* lemon juice and freshly squeezed lime juice
1 cinnamon stick (2 inches)
Garnish: 1 mint sprig

Place pear halves cut-side down on work surface; using a sharp paring knife, and starting 1 inch from stem end, cut each pear half lengthwise making 5 slices that radiate out from stem like a fan; set aside.

In 9-inch nonstick skillet combine remaining ingredients except garnish and cook over medium heat until mixture comes to a boil. Using a spatula, carefully place each pear half in skillet. Reduce heat to low, cover, and let simmer until pear halves are tender and flavors blend, 10 to 15 minutes. Carefully transfer pear halves to serving platter. Remove and discard cinnamon stick, top with poaching liquid, and garnish with a mint sprig. Serve immediately or cover with plastic wrap and refrigerate until chilled.

Each serving provides: ½ Fruit Exchange; 30 Optional Calories
Per serving with honey: 73 calories; 0.3 g protein; 0.3 g fat; 19 g carbohydrate;
    16 mg calcium; 1 mg sodium; 0 mg cholesterol; 2 g dietary fiber
With corn syrup: 71 calories; 0.3 g protein; 0.3 g fat; 18 g carbohydrate; 20 mg calcium;
    7 mg sodium; 0 mg cholesterol; 2 g dietary fiber

Pear-Raspberry Crisp

WEEK 8   MAKES 4 SERVINGS

10 ounces pears, cored, pared, and cut into ⅛-inch-thick slices
1 teaspoon *each* granulated sugar and lemon juice
1 cup fresh *or* thawed frozen raspberries (no sugar added)
6 gingersnap cookies (1 ounce), made into crumbs
¼ ounce chopped pecans
1 tablespoon firmly packed light brown sugar
1 tablespoon plus 1 teaspoon margarine, melted
1 tablespoon butter, melted

Preheat oven to 425°F. In 8 x 8 x 2-inch baking dish arrange pear slices; add granulated sugar and lemon juice and toss well to coat. Add raspberries and toss to combine; set aside.

In small mixing bowl combine cookie crumbs, pecans, and brown sugar; add margarine and butter and mix well until thoroughly combined. Sprinkle crumb mixture evenly over fruit mixture and bake until pears are tender and topping is crisp and lightly browned, 25 to 30 minutes.

Each serving provides: 1 Fat Exchange; 1 Fruit Exchange; 95 Optional Calories
Per serving: 170 calories; 1 g protein; 9 g fat; 23 g carbohydrate; 25 mg calcium;
  116 mg sodium; 11 mg cholesterol; 3 g dietary fiber

Pears with Gorgonzola and Port

WEEK 5	MAKES 2 SERVINGS, 2 PEAR HALVES EACH

1 cup plus 2 tablespoons water, divided
½ teaspoon lemon juice
2 small Bartlett pears (about 5 ounces each), cut lengthwise into halves, cored, and pared
2 tablespoons port wine
1 tablespoon granulated sugar
½ teaspoon vanilla extract
2 teaspoons whipped butter, softened
1 ounce Gorgonzola cheese, crumbled

Preheat oven to 375°F. In medium mixing bowl combine 1 cup water and the lemon juice; add pear halves and turn to coat. Using a slotted spoon, remove pears from water mixture, discarding water, and arrange cored-side up in shallow flameproof 1-quart casserole. In small saucepan combine remaining 2 tablespoons water, the wine, sugar, and vanilla and cook over medium heat until sugar is dissolved, about 1 minute. Pour wine mixture evenly over pear halves and place ½ teaspoon butter into cored section of each pear half. Cover and bake until pears are tender and heated through, 20 to 25 minutes. Remove from oven and turn oven control to broil. Place ¼ ounce cheese into cored section of each pear half and broil until cheese melts, 1 to 2 minutes.

To serve, into each of 2 dessert dishes arrange 2 pear halves and top with half of the pan juices.

Each serving provides: ½ Protein Exchange; 1 Fruit Exchange; 70 Optional Calories
Per serving: 193 calories; 4 g protein; 6 g fat; 28 g carbohydrate; 90 mg calcium;
219 mg sodium; 16 mg cholesterol; 3 g dietary fiber

Stuffed Pears
with Pecan Sauce

WEEK 8   MAKES 2 SERVINGS, 1 PEAR EACH

2 small pears (about 5 ounces each),
  cut lengthwise into halves, cored,
  and pared
½ cup water
1½ teaspoons granulated sugar
4 orange zests*
½ ounce shelled pecans, divided

1½ teaspoons *each* firmly packed dark
  brown sugar, butter, and dark corn
  syrup
1 tablespoon plus 1½ teaspoons
  whipped cream cheese
Dash grated orange peel

In 9-inch skillet arrange pears cut-side down; add water, granulated sugar, and zests and bring mixture to a boil. Reduce heat, cover, and let simmer until pears are softened, about 10 minutes, turning pears halfway through cooking time. Using a slotted spoon, transfer pears to plate, reserving poaching liquid; set pears aside and let cool.

Grind ¼ of the pecans; set aside. In same skillet combine remaining pecans, the brown sugar, butter, corn syrup, and reserved poaching liquid and, stirring constantly, bring mixture to full boil. Reduce heat and let simmer until mixture thickens slightly, about 3 minutes.

In small bowl combine ground pecans, cream cheese, and grated orange peel; stir to combine. Spread half of the cheese mixture over cored section of each of 2 pear halves; gently press a remaining pear half over each filled half, forming 2 whole pears. Set pears upright on serving platter and top with pecan mixture.

Each serving provides: ½ Protein Exchange; ½ Fat Exchange; 1 Fruit Exchange;
  95 Optional Calories
Per serving: 211 calories; 2 g protein; 11 g fat; 31 g carbohydrate; 29 mg calcium;
  60 mg sodium; 15 mg cholesterol; 4 g dietary fiber

*The zest of the orange is the peel without any of the pith (white membrane). To remove zest from orange, use a zester or vegetable peeler; wrap orange in plastic wrap and refrigerate for use at another time.

Pineapple Chunks with Raspberry Sauce ◑

WEEK 2   MAKES 2 SERVINGS

The delicious raspberry sauce that accompanies the fresh pineapple can be whipped up in only one minute.

½ cup fresh *or* thawed frozen
   raspberries (no sugar added)
1 tablespoon plus 1 teaspoon dry white
   table wine

1½ teaspoons granulated sugar
1 cup pared fresh pineapple chunks

In blender container combine raspberries, wine, and sugar and process at high speed until pureed, about 1 minute. Set sieve over medium mixing bowl; using a rubber scraper press puree through sieve into bowl, discarding seeds. Cover with plastic wrap and refrigerate until ready to serve.

To serve, into each of 2 dessert dishes arrange ½ cup pineapple and top each with ½ of the raspberry mixture.

Each serving provides: 1½ Fruit Exchanges; 25 Optional Calories
Per serving: 72 calories; 1 g protein; 0.5 g fat; 16 g carbohydrate; 13 mg calcium;
   1 mg sodium; 0 mg cholesterol; 3 g dietary fiber

Tropical Fruits with Ginger Cream ◐

WEEK 5   MAKES 4 SERVINGS

½ cup plain low-fat yogurt
¼ cup thawed frozen dairy whipped
   topping
1 teaspoon minced pared gingerroot
¼ teaspoon grated orange peel

1 cup *each* cubed pared seeded papaya
   and cubed pared pineapple
6 ounces banana, peeled and sliced
1 tablespoon plus 1 teaspoon shredded
   coconut

In small mixing bowl combine yogurt, whipped topping, gingerroot, and orange peel; stir well until thoroughly combined. Cover and refrigerate until flavors blend, 20 to 30 minutes.

In medium mixing bowl combine papaya, pineapple, and banana.

To serve, spoon ¼ of fruit mixture into each of 4 dessert dishes. Top each portion with ¼ of the yogurt mixture and sprinkle each with 1 teaspoon coconut.

Each serving provides: 1 Fruit Exchange; ¼ Milk Exchange; 40 Optional Calories
Per serving: 96 calories; 2 g protein; 2 g fat; 19 g carbohydrate; 65 mg calcium;
   31 mg sodium; 2 mg cholesterol; 1 g dietary fiber

Frisco Salad ◐

WEEK 5   MAKES 2 SERVINGS

Boston or red-leaf lettuce is perfect for this salad. Or, for that extra-special touch, use radicchio.

1 small navel orange (about 6 ounces)
1 small McIntosh apple (about
    ¼ pound), cored and diced
¼ avocado (2 ounces), pared and diced
1 tablespoon freshly squeezed lemon
    juice
2 cups shredded lettuce leaves

½ cup chopped fennel
2 tablespoons freshly squeezed
    lime juice
1 tablespoon chopped fresh mint
2 teaspoons olive oil
⅛ teaspoon salt
Dash pepper

Over small bowl to catch juice, remove skin and membranes from orange; reserve juice. Dice orange and set aside. In medium mixing bowl combine apple, avocado, and lemon juice, tossing to coat; add diced orange, lettuce, and fennel and set aside.

Add remaining ingredients to reserved orange juice, stirring well to combine. Pour dressing over salad and toss well to coat. Transfer to serving bowl and serve immediately.

Each serving provides: 2½ Vegetable Exchanges; 1 Fat Exchange; 1 Fruit Exchange;
    50 Optional Calories
Per serving: 157 calories; 2 g protein; 9 g fat; 22 g carbohydrate; 88 mg calcium;
    173 mg sodium; 0 mg cholesterol; 3 g dietary fiber

The Vegetable Exchange

Act 2: The Versatile Vegetable

These talented performers can do just about anything: in Act 2 they star in appetizers, soups, salads, sauces, main dishes, and side dishes. Variety is the theme, with everything from Spicy Eggplant Oriental to crunchy Three-Cabbage Slaw to Zucchini Bake. With the versatile stars of the Vegetable Exchange, you are never at a loss for interesting and flavorful combinations.

Daily Exchanges

	WEEKS 1, 2, 3, 4, AND 5
Women, Men, and Youths	3 Exchanges (at least)

Vegetable Exchange Notes

- Vegetables supply calcium, fiber, folic acid, iron, and vitamin A. In addition, because of their high bulk and water content, vegetables are an excellent way to satisfy hunger. Remember, variety is the key to both satisfaction and good nutrition.

- One Vegetable Exchange is ½ cup (raw or cooked) or ½ medium (tomato, cucumber, zucchini, etc.), unless otherwise specified. (See chart on pages 98–101.) Although 3 Exchanges (1½ cups) daily are the minimum, more is preferable.

- Canned or frozen vegetables that contain butter, sugar, cornstarch, sauces, etc., are not permitted.

- Mixed vegetables that contain a starchy vegetable such as corn, peas, water chestnuts, or parsnips should be considered a Bread Exchange; ½ cup is 1 Bread Exchange.

- The liquid that vegetables have been cooked in contains water-soluble nutrients; save this to use in soups, sauces, etc.

Vegetable Exchange Lists

Week 1

Selections	One Exchange
Arugula	½ cup
Asparagus	½ cup or 6 spears
Bamboo Shoots	½ cup
Beans, green or wax	½ cup
Broccoli	½ cup or 2 spears
Cabbage (all varieties including Chinese)	½ cup
Carrots	½ cup or ½ medium
Cauliflower	½ cup

Selections	One Exchange
Celery	½ cup *or* 2 medium ribs
Chicory (Curly Endive)	½ cup
Cucumbers	½ cup, ½ medium, *or* 1 small
Endive, Belgian (French)	½ cup *or* 1 medium head (about 3 ounces)
Escarole	½ cup
Gherkins, fresh	½ cup *or* ½ medium
Kirbies	½ cup *or* ½ medium
Leeks	½ cup
Lettuce	½ cup
Mushrooms	
Dried	½ cup reconstituted *or* 2 large *or* 8 small
Fresh	½ cup
Onions	½ cup *or* 1 medium (about 2 ounces)
Peppers	
Banana	½ cup
Bell	½ cup *or* ½ medium
Chili	½ cup *or* 1 medium
Jalapeño	2 small
Pimientos	½ cup *or* 3 whole
Radishes	½ cup *or* 12 whole
Scallions (Green Onions)	½ cup *or* 8 medium (about 1¾ ounces)
Shallots	½ cup
Spinach	½ cup *or* 8 leaves
Squash Leaves	½ cup
Squash, summer	
Caserta	½ cup
Chayote	½ cup
Cocozelle	½ cup
Mirleton	½ cup
Scallop (Cymling, Pattypan)	½ cup *or* ½ of 5-ounce squash
Spaghetti	½ cup
Vegetable Marrow	½ cup
Yellow (Crookneck and Straightneck)	½ cup *or* ½ medium
Zucchini	½ cup *or* ½ medium

Tomatoes
  Blanched, peeled, seeded,
    and chopped   3 medium (about ½ cup)
  Canned, all varieties
    (packed in their own
    juice *or* tomato puree)   ½ cup
  Cherry   6 small, medium, *or* large
  Plum   1 large (about 1¾ to 2½ ounces)
                        or 2 small (about 1 ounce each)
  Regular, fresh   ½ cup *or* ½ medium
  Stewed   ½ cup
  Sun-Dried (not packed
    in oil)   2 halves
Truffles   ½ cup
Watercress   ½ cup

Week 2

You may use all of the vegetables listed under Week 1 and may add the following to your Exchange List:

Selections	One Exchange
Cardoon	½ cup
Eggplant	½ cup
Sprouts, alfalfa *or* bean	½ cup

Week 3

You may use all of the vegetables listed under Weeks 1 and 2 and may add the following to your Exchange List:

Selections	One Exchange
Beets	½ cup
Brussels Sprouts	½ cup
Fennel (Anise, Sweet Anise, or Finocchio)	½ cup
Kohlrabi	½ cup *or* 1 medium
Pickles, unsweetened	½ cup *or* ½ medium
Pumpkin	½ cup

Week 4

You may use all of the vegetables listed under Weeks 1, 2, and 3 and may add the following to your Exchange List:

Selections	One Exchange
Chinese Pea Pods (Snow Peas)	½ cup *or* 1½ ounces
Juices (limit to a total of 1 Exchange per day)	
Tomato *or* Mixed Vegetable	1 cup
Carrot	½ cup
Sauerkraut	½ cup
Tomato Products (limit to 1 Exchange per day)	
Tomato Paste	¼ cup
Tomato Puree *or* Sauce	½ cup

Week 5

You may use all of the vegetables listed under Weeks 1, 2, 3, and 4 and may add the following to your Exchange List:

Selections	One Exchange
Artichokes	
Whole, small	½ pound
Hearts	3 (about ¼ pound) *or* ½ cup
Bottle Gourd	½ cup
Cactus Leaves	½ cup
Celeriac	½ cup
Chinese Chard (Bok Choy)	½ cup
Chinese Winter Melon	½ cup
Comfrey Leaves	½ cup
Fiddlefern (Fiddlehead Greens)	½ cup
Grape Leaves	½ cup *or* 12 leaves
Greens	
Beet	½ cup
Chard	½ cup
Collard	½ cup
Dandelion	½ cup
Kale	½ cup
Mustard	½ cup
Rutabaga	½ cup
Turnip	½ cup

Hearts of Palm (Palmetto)	½ cup
Jerusalem Artichokes (Sunchokes)	½ cup
Jicama	½ cup
Lamb's-Quarters	½ cup
Lotus Root	½ cup
Nasturtium Leaves	½ cup
Okra	½ cup
Peppergrass	½ cup
Rhubarb	½ cup
Rutabagas	½ cup
Salsify (Oyster Plant)	½ cup
Sourgrass (Sorrel)	½ cup
Turnips	½ cup

Average Approximate Size/Dimensions and Weight for Vegetables (fresh, including seeds and skin, unless otherwise specified)

Vegetables	Number	Approx. Size/ Dimensions	Approx. Weight	Number of Exchanges
Asparagus Spears	6		3 to 5 ounces	1
Broccoli, bunch	1	medium	1 pound	8
Cabbage, head:				
Chinese (celery)	1		¾ pound	8
green	1	small	1 pound	12
red	1	medium	1½ pounds	18
Cabbage, leaves:				
green	2	medium/large	3¾ ounces	1
	3	small	3 ounces	1
red	1	medium/large	2½ ounces	1
	2	small	3 ounces	1
Carrots, whole	1	medium (1⅛-inch diameter at top x 7½ inches long)	3 to 4 ounces	2
sticks	6	3½ inches x ½ inch each		1
Cauliflower	1	medium (6- to 7-inch diameter)	1½ pounds	12
	1	small	1 pound	8
Celery, ribs	1	large (8 x 1½ inches)		1
	2	medium (6 inches x 1 inch each)		1
	3	small (5 inches x ¾ inch each)		1
sticks	6	3½ inches x ½ inch each		½
Cucumbers, whole	1	large (6½-inch circumference at widest part x 8¼ inches long)	9½ ounces	2¼

Vegetables	Number	Approx. Size/ Dimensions	Approx. Weight	Number of Exchanges
Cucumbers (cont.)				
	1	medium (6-inch circumference at widest part x 7 inches long)	½ pound	2
	1	small (5¼-inch circumference at widest part x 6¼ inches long)	6 ounces	1
spears	6			1
Eggplants, whole	1	large	1½ pounds	8
	1	medium	1 to 1¼ pounds	6
	1	small	¾ pound	4
	1	tiny	½ pound	3
slices, round	6	thin (¼ inch thick each)		1½
Endives (Belgian or French)	1	medium	3 ounces	1
Grape Leaves	12			1
Leeks				
green and white portion	1	medium		1
white portion only	2	medium		1
Lettuce, head:				
Boston and Bibb	1	16-inch circumference at widest part	½ pound	2½
iceberg	1	medium to large	2½ pounds	8
	1	small	1¼ pounds	4
romaine (cos) and	1	medium	1¼ pounds	12
loose-leafed	1	small	10 ounces	8
Lettuce, leaves:				
Boston, Bibb, and radicchio (red chicory)	8			1
iceberg	4	small, medium, and large		1
romaine (cos) and loose-leafed	4	small, medium, and large		1

Vegetables	Number	Approx. Size/ Dimensions	Approx. Weight	Number of Exchanges
Mushrooms, whole	3	large (2-inch diameter)	3¼ ounces	2
	7	medium (1½-inch diameter)	3 ounces	2
	18	small (1-inch diameter)	3½ ounces	2
caps	4	large	3 ounces	2
	8	medium	3 ounces	2
	16	small	3¼ ounces	2
Onions				
slices	1	large		½
	4	medium		1
Peppers:				
chili, whole,	1	medium		1
fresh *or* canned	1	small		½
green *or* red bell, whole	1	large (3-inch diameter x 3¾ inches high)	7 ounces	4
	1	medium (2½-inch diameter x 2¾ inches high)	3¼ ounces	2
rings	4			1
strips	6			1
Pickles, whole	1	large (5½-inch circumference at widest part x 4 inches long)	4¾ ounces	4
	1	medium (4-inch circumference at widest part x 3¾ inches long)	2¼ ounces	2
slices	3	large	1½ ounces	1
	5	medium	1⅛ ounces	1
spears	3			1
Radishes	12	medium to large (2- to 4-inch circumference each at widest part)	2 to 3½ ounces	1

Vegetables	Number	Approx. Size/ Dimensions	Approx. Weight	Number of Exchanges
Squash:				
scallop (pattypan, cymling)	1	4-inch diameter	5 ounces	2
spaghetti	1		2½ to 3 pounds	8
zucchini	1	medium	5 ounces	2
yellow *or* zucchini sticks	6			1
Tomatoes, whole	1	large (3-inch diameter x 2⅛ inches high)	7 ounces	3
	1	medium (2½-inch diameter x 2 inches high)	4¾ ounces	2
	1	small (2¼-inch diameter)	3½ ounces	1½
slices:				
regular	3			1
thin	5	⅛ inch thick each		1
wedges	8			2
Turnips	1	medium	2 ounces	1

Asparagus and Mushroom Sauté ◐

WEEK 5	MAKES 2 SERVINGS

2 teaspoons vegetable oil
2 cups diagonally sliced asparagus
    spears (1-inch pieces)
1 cup sliced shiitake mushrooms*
¼ cup sliced scallions (green onions),
    green and white portion
½ garlic clove, minced
½ teaspoon minced pared gingerroot

¼ cup water
1 tablespoon black bean sauce
1½ teaspoons teriyaki sauce
1 teaspoon dry sherry
½ packet (about ½ teaspoon) instant
    chicken broth and seasoning mix
½ teaspoon cornstarch

In 10-inch nonstick skillet heat oil; add asparagus and sauté, stirring constantly, for 3 to 4 minutes. Add mushrooms, scallions, garlic, and gingerroot and cook, stirring constantly, until liquid is almost evaporated, 3 to 4 minutes longer. In small bowl combine remaining ingredients, stirring to dissolve cornstarch; add to skillet and, stirring constantly, cook over medium heat until mixture thickens, about 1 minute.

Each serving provides: 3¼ Vegetable Exchanges; 1 Fat Exchange; 25 Optional Calories
Per serving: 110 calories; 6 g protein; 5 g fat; 13 g carbohydrate; 41 mg calcium;
    425 mg sodium (this figure does not include black bean sauce; nutrition analysis not
    available); 0 mg cholesterol; 3 g dietary fiber

*Crimini, oyster, or regular mushrooms may be substituted for the shiitake mushrooms.

Braised Red Cabbage with Apple and Caraway ◐

WEEK 4	MAKES 4 SERVINGS

The tartness of the Granny Smith apple complements the cabbage in this colorful side dish.

2 teaspoons margarine
4 cups shredded red cabbage
1 cup sliced thoroughly washed leeks
   (white portion with some green)
1 tablespoon all-purpose flour
1 small Granny Smith apple (about
   ¼ pound), pared, cored, and diced
⅓ cup unfermented apple cider
   (no sugar added)

¼ cup canned ready-to-serve chicken
   broth
1 teaspoon caraway seed
⅛ teaspoon salt
Dash pepper

In 12-inch nonstick skillet melt margarine; add cabbage and leeks and sauté over high heat, until cabbage is tender-crisp, 7 to 8 minutes. Sprinkle flour over vegetables and stir quickly to combine; stir in remaining ingredients. Reduce heat to medium, cover, and cook until apple is fork-tender, 3 to 4 minutes longer.

Each serving provides: 2½ Vegetable Exchanges; ½ Fat Exchange; ½ Fruit Exchange;
   15 Optional Calories
Per serving: 86 calories; 2 g protein; 2 g fat; 16 g carbohydrate; 59 mg calcium;
   168 mg sodium; 0 mg cholesterol; 2 g dietary fiber

Broccoli, Potato, and Cheese Soup

WEEK 2	MAKES 4 SERVINGS, ABOUT 1¼ CUPS EACH

2 teaspoons *each* olive *or* vegetable oil and margarine
1 cup chopped onions
1 small garlic clove
1 quart water
4 cups chopped broccoli (florets and spears)
¾ pound pared all-purpose potatoes, cut into chunks
3 packets instant chicken broth and seasoning mix
2 ounces Gorgonzola *or* blue cheese, crumbled
⅛ teaspoon white pepper

In 3-quart saucepan combine oil and margarine and heat until margarine is melted; add onions and garlic and sauté until onions are translucent, 1 to 2 minutes. Add water, broccoli, potatoes, and broth mix; stir to combine and bring mixture to a full boil. Reduce heat and let simmer until potatoes are tender, about 15 minutes. Remove from heat and let cool slightly.

Pour 2 cups broccoli mixture into blender container and process until smooth. Transfer soup to 2-quart bowl and repeat procedure with remaining broccoli mixture; return to saucepan. Stir cheese* and pepper into soup and cook, stirring occasionally, over low heat, until soup is heated and cheese is melted, 4 to 5 minutes.

Each serving provides: ½ Protein Exchange; 1 Bread Exchange; 2½ Vegetable Exchanges; 1 Fat Exchange; 10 Optional Calories
Per serving: 199 calories; 9 g protein; 9 g fat; 24 g carbohydrate; 135 mg calcium; 992 mg sodium; 11 mg cholesterol; 3 g dietary fiber

*If desired, crumble ½ ounce cheese over each portion of soup rather than stirring into saucepan.

Carrot-Potato Toss ⊙◐

WEEK 4   MAKES 2 SERVINGS

If you plan ahead and cook the potato and egg for this recipe in advance, you can put the dish together in minutes.

1 cup diced carrots, blanched
3 ounces pared cooked all-purpose
   potato, diced
½ cup frozen peas, blanched
2 tablespoons chopped dill pickle
1 tablespoon minced onion
¼ cup plain low-fat yogurt
1 hard-cooked egg, sliced

1 tablespoon reduced-calorie
   mayonnaise
2 teaspoons cottage cheese
1 teaspoon *each* cider vinegar and
   Dijon-style mustard
¼ teaspoon white pepper

In medium bowl combine carrots, potato, peas, pickle, and onion; toss to combine and set aside.

In blender container combine remaining ingredients and process at high speed until smooth, scraping down sides of container as necessary; pour over vegetable mixture and toss to coat. Serve immediately or cover with plastic wrap and refrigerate until ready to serve.

Each serving provides: ½ Protein Exchange; 1 Bread Exchange; 1⅛ Vegetable Exchanges;
   ½ Fat Exchange; ¼ Milk Exchange; 15 Optional Calories
Per serving: 184 calories; 9 g protein; 6 g fat; 25 g carbohydrate; 104 mg calcium;
   409 mg sodium; 142 mg cholesterol; 3 g dietary fiber

Carrot and Mushroom Loaf ⊙

WEEK 2   MAKES 4 SERVINGS

2 teaspoons margarine
1 cup finely diced onions
3 cups grated carrots
2½ cups sliced mushrooms
½ cup low-fat milk (2% milk fat)
2 eggs

2 tablespoons chopped fresh Italian
  (flat-leaf) parsley
¼ teaspoon *each* salt and ground
  nutmeg
Dash white pepper
2 ounces mozzarella cheese, shredded

In 10-inch nonstick skillet melt margarine; add onions and sauté over high heat until translucent, about 1 minute. Reduce heat to medium; add carrots and sauté for 3 minutes. Add mushrooms and sauté until carrots are tender, about 5 minutes. Remove from heat and let cool for 5 minutes.

Preheat oven to 350° F. Using a wire whisk, in medium mixing bowl combine milk, eggs, parsley, salt, nutmeg, and pepper and beat until combined; add vegetable mixture and cheese and stir to combine. Spray 9 x 5-inch loaf pan with nonstick cooking spray; add vegetable-cheese mixture to pan. Place loaf pan in 13 x 9-inch baking pan and fill with hot water to a depth of about 2 inches. Bake for 40 minutes (until a knife, inserted in center, comes out clean). Remove baking pan from oven and loaf pan from water bath; let cool slightly. Invert loaf onto serving platter.

Each serving provides: 1 Protein Exchange; 3¼ Vegetable Exchanges; ½ Fat Exchange;
  15 Optional Calories
Per serving: 173 calories; 9 g protein; 9 g fat; 16 g carbohydrate; 163 mg calcium;
  292 mg sodium; 150 mg cholesterol; 3 g dietary fiber

Lemon-Sautéed Beets ©◐

WEEK 3   MAKES 2 SERVINGS

2 teaspoons margarine
2 cups grated pared beets
1 tablespoon minced onion
½ teaspoon salt

Dash pepper
1 tablespoon lemon juice
2 teaspoons light corn syrup

In 9-inch nonstick skillet melt margarine; add beets, onion, salt, and pepper and sauté until onion is translucent, 2 to 3 minutes. Stir in remaining ingredients. Reduce heat to low, cover, and cook until flavors blend and beets are tender, 3 to 5 minutes.

Each serving provides: 2 Vegetable Exchanges; 1 Fat Exchange; 20 Optional Calories
Per serving: 117 calories; 2 g protein; 4 g fat; 20 g carbohydrate; 32 mg calcium;
   696 mg sodium; 0 mg cholesterol; 1 g dietary fiber

Three-Cabbage Salad ©◐

WEEK 6   MAKES 8 SERVINGS, ABOUT 1 CUP EACH

3 cups *each* shredded green and savoy
   cabbage
2 cups shredded red cabbage
1½ cups grated carrots
½ cup minced onion
⅓ cup sour cream
6 slices crisp bacon, crumbled

2 tablespoons plus 2 teaspoons
   reduced-calorie mayonnaise
2 tablespoons *each* chopped fresh dill
   and lemon juice
1 tablespoon Dijon-style mustard
Dash pepper

In medium mixing bowl combine cabbages, carrots, and onion; set aside. In small mixing bowl combine remaining ingredients, mixing well. Pour sour cream mixture over cabbage mixture; toss to combine. Cover bowl with plastic wrap and refrigerate until flavors blend, about 30 minutes.

Each serving provides: 2½ Vegetable Exchanges; ½ Fat Exchange; 55 Optional Calories
Per serving: 95 calories; 3 g protein; 6 g fat; 8 g carbohydrate; 54 mg calcium;
   197 mg sodium; 10 mg cholesterol; 1 g dietary fiber

Oriental Coleslaw ⊖◑

WEEK 5   MAKES 4 SERVINGS

If you own a food processor, you can save time by using it to grate the carrot and shred the cabbage for this tangy coleslaw.

2 tablespoons rice vinegar
1 tablespoon teriyaki sauce
2 teaspoons *each* dark corn syrup,
   Chinese sesame oil, and peanut oil
1 garlic clove, minced
½ teaspoon minced pared gingerroot
4 cups shredded Chinese cabbage

6 ounces drained canned water
   chestnuts, thinly sliced
½ cup grated carrot
¼ cup diagonally sliced scallions
   (green onions)
1 tablespoon sesame seed, toasted

In small mixing bowl combine vinegar, teriyaki sauce, corn syrup, oils, garlic, and gingerroot; mix well to combine

In large bowl combine remaining ingredients except sesame seed; add dressing and toss well to coat. Cover with plastic wrap and refrigerate until flavors blend, about 30 minutes.

To serve, toss salad again and then sprinkle with sesame seed.

Each serving provides: ½ Bread Exchange; 2¼ Vegetable Exchanges; 1 Fat Exchange;
  25 Optional Calories
Per serving: 108 calories; 2 g protein; 6 g fat; 14 g carbohydrate; 74 mg calcium;
  192 mg sodium; 0 mg cholesterol; 5 g dietary fiber

Gingered Citrus Carrots

2 teaspoons margarine
2 cups julienne-cut carrots (matchstick pieces)
½ cup thinly sliced scallions (green onions), green and white portion
½ teaspoon grated pared gingerroot
1 tablespoon *each* lemon and orange juice (no sugar added)

2 teaspoons reduced-calorie orange marmalade (16 calories per 2 teaspoons)
1 teaspoon firmly packed light brown sugar

In 1-quart saucepan melt margarine; add carrots, scallions, and gingerroot and cook over medium heat, stirring occasionally, until carrots are tender-crisp, 4 to 5 minutes. Add remaining ingredients and stir to combine. Reduce heat to low, cover, and let simmer until flavors blend, about 5 minutes.

Each serving provides: 2½ Vegetable Exchanges; 1 Fat Exchange; 20 Optional Calories
Per serving: 123 calories; 2 g protein; 4 g fat; 21 g carbohydrate; 58 mg calcium;
   98 mg sodium; 0 mg cholesterol; 3 g dietary fiber

Minted Medley ©①

1 teaspoon olive *or* vegetable oil
1 cup *each* diagonally sliced parsnips and carrots, blanched
¼ cup canned ready-to-serve chicken broth

1 tablespoon *each* chopped fresh mint and lemon juice
1 teaspoon Dijon-style mustard
Dash pepper

In 8-inch nonstick skillet heat oil; add parsnips and carrots and sauté over medium heat until heated through, 1 to 2 minutes. Add remaining ingredients and stir well to combine; cook until flavors blend and vegetables are tender-crisp, 2 to 3 minutes.

Each serving provides: 1 Bread Exchange; 1 Vegetable Exchange; ½ Fat Exchange;
   5 Optional Calories
Per serving: 110 calories; 2 g protein; 3 g fat; 20 g carbohydrate; 45 mg calcium;
   234 mg sodium; 0 mg cholesterol; 4 g dietary fiber

Oriental Vegetables ☯

1½ teaspoons vegetable oil
½ teaspoon Chinese sesame oil
½ cup cubed red bell pepper (1-inch pieces)
2 tablespoons diagonally sliced scallion (green onion)
1½ teaspoons minced pared gingerroot
½ garlic clove, minced
1 cup diagonally sliced carrots, blanched

½ cup *each* shiitake *or* regular mushrooms and frozen baby corn ears
¼ cup canned ready-to-serve chicken broth
1 tablespoon *each* rice vinegar and teriyaki sauce
1 teaspoon cornstarch
½ teaspoon crushed red pepper
¼ teaspoon Worcestershire sauce

In 10-inch skillet heat oils over high heat; add bell pepper, scallion, gingerroot, and garlic and sauté for 1 minute. Add carrots, mushrooms, and corn and sauté until vegetables are tender-crisp, 2 to 3 minutes. In 1-cup liquid measure combine remaining ingredients, stirring to dissolve cornstarch. Add to vegetable mixture and cook, stirring constantly, until mixture thickens, 3 to 4 minutes.

Each serving provides: 2⅛ Vegetable Exchanges; 1 Fat Exchange; 30 Optional Calories
Per serving: 138 calories; 5 g protein; 5 g fat; 19 g carbohydrate; 41 mg calcium;
   539 mg sodium; 0 mg cholesterol; 2 g dietary fiber

Buttery Chayote and Vegetable Sauté ⒸⒹ

Chayote squash, also referred to as mirleton, is a ribbed pear-shaped green summer squash. If chayote is not available, any variety of summer squash may be substituted.

2 tablespoons whipped butter
1 tablespoon plus 1 teaspoon olive
 or vegetable oil
4 cups shredded pared chayote
 (remove and discard center fibers)
2 cups grated carrots
1 cup *each* diced onions and celery

2 tablespoons *each* chopped fresh basil
 and Italian (flat-leaf parsley)
1 to 2 garlic cloves, minced
1 teaspoon salt
½ teaspoon white pepper

In 10-inch nonstick skillet combine butter and oil and heat until butter is melted; add chayote and carrots and cook, stirring constantly, until vegetables are softened, about 5 minutes. Add remaining ingredients; stir to combine and cook until flavors blend, about 10 minutes.

Each serving provides: 4 Vegetable Exchanges; 1 Fat Exchange; 25 Optional Calories
Per serving: 143 calories; 3 g protein; 8 g fat; 18 g carbohydrate; 82 mg calcium;
 632 mg sodium; 8 mg cholesterol; 1 g dietary fiber

Variation: Chayote and Vegetable Sauté (Week 1)—Omit butter. Omit Optional Calories from Exchange Information.

Per serving: 118 calories; 3 g protein; 6 g fat; 18 g carbohydrate; 81 mg calcium;
 603 mg sodium; 0 mg cholesterol; 1 g dietary fiber

Mediterranean Cucumber Salad

WEEK 1   MAKES 2 SERVINGS

1 medium red bell pepper
8 lettuce leaves
1 cup thinly sliced cucumber
¼ cup thinly sliced red onion
2 ounces feta *or* goat cheese, crumbled
2 tablespoons *each* chopped fresh dill,
   balsamic *or* red wine vinegar,
   and water

2 teaspoons olive oil
⅛ teaspoon salt
Dash pepper

Preheat broiler. On baking sheet lined with heavy-duty foil broil pepper 3 inches from heat source, turning frequently, until charred on all sides; let stand until cool enough to handle, 15 to 20 minutes.

Peel pepper; remove and discard stem ends and seeds. Cut pepper into matchstick pieces and set aside.

Line serving platter with lettuce leaves. Decoratively arrange cucumber slices and roasted pepper over lettuce; top with onion slices and cheese. In small bowl combine remaining ingredients and stir well to combine; pour evenly over salad.

Each serving provides: 1 Protein Exchange; 3¼ Vegetable Exchanges; 1 Fat Exchange
Per serving with feta cheese: 147 calories; 5 g protein, 11 g fat; 8 g carbohydrate;
   191 mg calcium; 462 mg sodium; 25 mg cholesterol; 1 g dietary fiber
With goat cheese: 175 calories; 7 g protein; 13 g fat; 9 g carbohydrate; 94 mg calcium;
   320 mg sodium; 26 mg cholesterol; 1 g dietary fiber

Buttery Eggplant Stew ©

WEEK 5   MAKES 4 SERVINGS, ABOUT 1 CUP EACH

2 tablespoons whipped butter
2 teaspoons olive *or* vegetable oil
2 cups *each* cubed pared eggplant
   and sliced onions
½ cup *each* chopped red and green
   bell pepper
1 small garlic clove, mashed
1 tablespoon all-purpose flour
1 packet *each* instant beef and chicken
   broth and seasoning mix

2 cups canned Italian tomatoes (with
   liquid); drain, seed, and chop
   tomatoes, reserving liquid
2 tablespoons chopped Italian
   (flat-leaf) parsley
½ teaspoon oregano leaves

In 2-quart saucepan combine butter and oil and heat until butter is melted; add eggplant and cook over medium heat, stirring constantly, for 5 minutes. Add onions, bell peppers, and garlic and stir to combine; cover and cook until tender, about 10 minutes. Sprinkle flour and broth mixes over vegetables and stir quickly to combine; cook, stirring constantly, for 1 minute. Add water to reserved tomato liquid to measure 2 cups. Add tomato liquid, tomatoes, parsley, and oregano to vegetable mixture and, stirring constantly, bring mixture to a boil. Reduce heat and let simmer until flavors blend, about 15 minutes.

Each serving provides: 3½ Vegetable Exchanges; ½ Fat Exchange; 40 Optional Calories
Per serving: 126 calories; 4 g protein; 6 g fat; 17 g carbohydrate; 75 mg calcium;
   710 mg sodium; 8 mg cholesterol; 3 g dietary fiber

Variation: Eggplant Stew (Week 2)—Substitute 2 teaspoons margarine for the butter. Increase Fat Exchange to 1 and decrease Optional Calories to 15.

Per serving: 118 calories; 3 g protein; 5 g fat; 17 g carbohydrate; 75 mg calcium;
   703 mg sodium; 0 mg cholesterol; 3 g dietary fiber

Eggplant and Tomato Appetizer ◉

WEEK 2   MAKES 4 SERVINGS

1 small eggplant (about ¾ pound), cut
  lengthwise into ¼-inch-thick slices
1 tablespoon plus 1 teaspoon olive oil,
  divided
3 tablespoons balsamic or red wine
  vinegar, divided
2 garlic cloves, minced, divided

¼ teaspoon salt, divided
⅛ teaspoon pepper, divided
2 tablespoons chopped fresh basil,
  divided
1 medium tomato, chopped

On nonstick baking sheet arrange eggplant slices in a single layer; using a pastry brush, lightly brush half of the oil over eggplant and broil until lightly browned and tender-crisp, 2 to 3 minutes. Turn eggplant over; brush with remaining oil and broil 2 to 3 minutes longer.

In 8-inch glass pie plate drizzle half of the vinegar. Arrange half of the eggplant slices over bottom of plate, overlapping edges slightly; sprinkle with half of the garlic, salt, pepper, and basil. Top with the tomato and drizzle remaining vinegar over tomato. Top with remaining eggplant slices and sprinkle with remaining garlic, salt, pepper, and basil. Set a 6- or 7-inch plate over pie plate and set a 2-pound weight on plate. Let marinate at room temperature for 30 minutes or refrigerate overnight.

To serve, remove weight and plate and cut into 4 equal wedges.

Each serving provides: 1½ Vegetable Exchanges; 1 Fat Exchange
Per serving: 73 calories; 1 g protein; 5 g fat; 8 g carbohydrate; 49 mg calcium;
   141 mg sodium; 0 mg cholesterol; 2 g dietary fiber

Spicy Eggplant Oriental ◐

WEEK 2   MAKES 2 SERVINGS

1 teaspoon peanut *or* vegetable oil
¾ teaspoon Chinese sesame oil
¼ teaspoon chili oil
4 cups cubed eggplant (½-inch cubes)
½ cup sliced scallions (green onions)
1 teaspoon minced pared gingerroot
2 garlic cloves, minced

½ cup canned ready-to-serve chicken broth
1 tablespoon *each* soy sauce and rice vinegar
1 teaspoon granulated sugar

In 10-inch nonstick skillet heat oils; add eggplant, scallions, ginger-root, and garlic and cook over medium-high heat, stirring occasionally, until vegetables are softened, 1 to 2 minutes. In 1-cup liquid measure or small mixing bowl combine remaining ingredients, stirring until sugar is dissolved. Stir into skillet; increase heat to high and continue cooking, stirring occasionally, until eggplant is cooked through, 4 to 5 minutes.

Each serving provides: 4½ Vegetable Exchanges; 1 Fat Exchange; 20 Optional Calories
Per serving: 116 calories; 3 g protein; 5 g fat; 16 g carbohydrate; 81 mg calcium;
 776 mg sodium; 0 mg cholesterol; 3 g dietary fiber

Spicy Eggplant Soup ☻

WEEK 5   MAKES 4 SERVINGS

1 teaspoon olive *or* vegetable oil
½ cup finely diced onion
1 garlic clove, minced
4 cups chopped pared eggplant
3 cups water
6 ounces pared all-purpose potato,
   cut into 1-inch pieces
1 packet instant chicken broth and
   seasoning mix

½ cup evaporated skimmed milk
1 teaspoon curry powder
½ teaspoon *each* salt and ground
   cumin
¼ teaspoon ground turmeric

In 4-quart saucepan heat oil; add onion and garlic and cook over medium-high heat, stirring occasionally, until onion is translucent, about 2 minutes. Add eggplant, water, potato, and broth mix and stir to combine; cook over high heat until mixture comes to a boil. Reduce heat to medium and let simmer until potato is tender, about 20 minutes. Let cool slightly, about 5 minutes.

In work bowl of food processor process eggplant mixture until pureed. Set food mill over 4-quart saucepan; process eggplant mixture in food mill, discarding eggplant seeds. Return eggplant mixture to saucepan and place over medium heat; gradually stir in milk. Cook, stirring constantly, until heated through *(do not boil)*. Stir in seasonings and serve immediately.

Each serving provides: ½ Bread Exchange; 2¼ Vegetable Exchanges; ¼ Milk Exchange;
   15 Optional Calories
Per serving: 103 calories; 5 g protein; 1 g fat; 19 g carbohydrate; 138 mg calcium;
   565 mg sodium; 1 mg cholesterol; 2 g dietary fiber

Fennel Salad ◑

WEEK 4   MAKES 2 SERVINGS

1 small Granny Smith apple (about
    ¼ pound), cored, pared, and grated
1 teaspoon lemon juice
2 cups sliced fennel (¼-inch-thick
    slices)
¼ cup thinly sliced scallions (green
    onions)
1 ounce Gruyère *or* Swiss cheese,
    shredded

1½ teaspoons sour cream
1 teaspoon olive oil
½ teaspoon *each* country Dijon-style
    mustard and champagne *or* red wine
    vinegar

In large mixing bowl combine apple and lemon juice and toss to combine; add fennel, scallions, and cheese and set aside. In small bowl combine remaining ingredients; pour over apple mixture and toss well to coat.

Each serving provides: ½ Protein Exchange; 2¼ Vegetable Exchanges; ½ Fat Exchange;
    ½ Fruit Exchange; 10 Optional Calories
Per serving with Gruyère cheese: 137 calories; 6 g protein; 8 g fat; 12 g carbohydrate;
    210 mg calcium; 196 mg sodium; 17 mg cholesterol; 3 g dietary fiber
With Swiss cheese: 132 calories; 6 g protein; 7 g fat; 12 g carbohydrate; 203 mg calcium;
    185 mg sodium; 15 mg cholesterol; 3 g dietary fiber

Variation: Fennel Salad with Yogurt Dressing (Week 3)—Substitute 1½ teaspoons plain low-fat yogurt for the sour cream. Reduce Optional Calories to 3.

Per serving with Gruyère cheese: 132 calories; 6 g protein; 7 g fat; 12 g carbohydrate;
    212 mg calcium; 196 mg sodium; 16 mg cholesterol; 3 g dietary fiber
With Swiss cheese: 127 calories; 6 g protein; 7 g fat; 12 g carbohydrate; 205 mg calcium;
    186 mg sodium; 13 mg cholesterol; 3 g dietary fiber

Green Beans Sauté ⊖⦿

WEEK 1   MAKES 2 SERVINGS

Balsamic vinegar lends a unique touch to this side dish as well as to any tossed salad.

2 teaspoons olive *or* vegetable oil
½ cup cooked pearl onions
1 garlic clove, minced
2 cups cooked green beans, cut in half
1 small plum tomato, blanched, peeled,
    seeded, and chopped

1 tablespoon balsamic *or* red wine
    vinegar
Dash pepper

In 10-inch nonstick skillet heat oil; add onions and garlic and sauté over high heat, stirring frequently, until onions are browned, about 2 minutes. Add remaining ingredients and stir to combine; cook, stirring frequently, until flavors blend and vegetables are heated through, 2 to 3 minutes.

Each serving provides: 2¾ Vegetable Exchanges; 1 Fat Exchange
Per serving: 106 calories; 3 g protein; 5 g fat; 15 g carbohydrate; 78 mg calcium;
   10 mg sodium; 0 mg cholesterol; 2 g dietary fiber

Green Bean and Mushroom Salad ⊙ ◑

WEEK 1   MAKES 2 SERVINGS

1½ cups green beans, blanched
½ cup sliced mushrooms
¼ cup plain low-fat yogurt
2 tablespoons *each* minced scallion
   (green onion), reduced-calorie
   mayonnaise, and cottage cheese

1 tablespoon minced fresh parsley
1 teaspoon *each* lemon juice and
   Dijon-style mustard
Dash *each* salt and pepper

In medium bowl combine green beans and mushrooms, tossing to combine; set aside.

In blender container combine remaining ingredients and process until pureed, scraping down sides of container as necessary; pour over green bean-mushroom mixture and toss to coat. Serve immediately or cover and refrigerate until ready to serve.

Each serving provides: 2⅛ Vegetable Exchanges; 1½ Fat Exchanges; ¼ Milk Exchange,
   15 Optional Calories
Per serving: 108 calories; 5 g protein; 5 g fat; 11 g carbohydrate; 98 mg calcium;
   334 mg sodium; 9 mg cholesterol; 2 g dietary fiber

Mozzarella, Tomato,
and Arugula Salad

Kale Stew

Hominy Chowder

Cream of Wild Mushroom Soup

Cheese Enchiladas

Portuguese Clams
and Sausage

Chilled Mussels with Seasoned Mayonnaise

Pasta Mediterranean

Black Forest Pudding

Gratin of Leeks and Gorgonzola ◑

WEEK 3   MAKES 2 SERVINGS

1 quart water
3 to 4 peppercorns
1 bay leaf
1 garlic clove, crushed
4 medium leeks, thoroughly washed and cut in half lengthwise (white portion with some green)

¼ cup half-and-half (blend of milk and cream)
1 teaspoon cornstarch
1 ounce Gorgonzola cheese

In 10-inch skillet combine water, peppercorns, bay leaf, and garlic; cover and cook over high heat until mixture comes to a boil. Add leeks and cook covered until tender, 4 to 5 minutes.

While leeks are cooking prepare sauce. In small saucepan combine half-and-half and cornstarch, stirring to dissolve cornstarch; cook over medium heat, stirring occasionally, until mixture thickens, 2 to 3 minutes. Stir in cheese and continue cooking, stirring constantly, until cheese melts, about 1 minute longer.

Drain leeks, discarding cooking liquid and seasonings, and arrange in 12-ounce flameproof au gratin dish or shallow 1-quart flameproof casserole. Pour cheese mixture evenly over leeks; broil until sauce is lightly browned, 3 to 4 minutes.

Each serving provides: ½ Protein Exchange; 1 Vegetable Exchange; 55 Optional Calories
Per serving: 159 calories; 6 g protein; 8 g fat; 18 g carbohydrate; 172 mg calcium;
  230 mg sodium; 22 mg cholesterol; 1 g dietary fiber

Leek Salad ◑

WEEK 1   MAKES 2 SERVINGS

2 cups water
2 cups thoroughly washed sliced leeks,
    separated into rings (white portion
    and some green)
1 medium tomato, chopped
½ cup sliced mushrooms
1 tablespoon plus 1 teaspoon *each*
    olive oil and raspberry *or* red wine
    vinegar

1 tablespoon Dijon-style mustard
1½ teaspoons *each* minced shallot
    or onion and water
¼ teaspoon granulated sugar
Dash pepper
2 lettuce leaves

In 1-quart saucepan bring water to a boil; add leeks and cook until tender, about 10 minutes. Drain leeks and soak in bowl of ice water to stop cooking process; drain well.

In large mixing bowl combine leeks, tomato, and mushrooms, tossing to combine. Cover with plastic wrap and refrigerate until ready to serve. In small bowl combine remaining ingredients, except lettuce, and, using a wire whisk, beat until combined. Cover with plastic wrap and refrigerate until ready to serve.

To serve, pour dressing over leek mixture and toss to coat. Line serving platter or bowl with lettuce leaves; toss salad again and spoon over lettuce.

Each serving provides: 3¾ Vegetable Exchanges; 2 Fat Exchanges; 3 Optional Calories
Per serving: 175 calories; 3 g protein; 10 g fat; 21 g carbohydrate; 73 mg calcium;
    252 mg sodium; 0 mg cholesterol; 2 g dietary fiber

Kale Stew ☾

WEEK 5   MAKES 4 SERVINGS

2 teaspoons olive *or* vegetable oil
1 cup *each* diced onions and carrots
2 bay leaves
2 cups shredded green cabbage
6 ounces cubed pared all-purpose
  potato
¼ pound smoked turkey sausage links,
  sliced
1½ quarts water

3 packets instant beef broth and
  seasoning mix
6 cups chopped kale, thoroughly
  washed and drained, stems removed
6 ounces drained canned white kidney
  beans
1 ounce Cheddar cheese, shredded

In 4-quart saucepan heat oil; add onions, carrots, and bay leaves and sauté until carrots are tender-crisp, 4 to 5 minutes. Add cabbage, potato, and sausage and stir to combine; cook until cabbage is wilted, about 5 minutes. Add water and broth mix; stir to combine and bring mixture to a full boil. Add kale and stir to combine; cook until potato and kale are tender, about 20 minutes. Stir in beans and cook until heated through, about 5 minutes. Remove and discard bay leaves.

To serve, transfer stew to soup tureen or serving bowl and sprinkle with cheese.

Each serving provides: 2 Protein Exchanges, ½ Bread Exchange; 5 Vegetable Exchanges;
  ½ Fat Exchange; 10 Optional Calories
Per serving: 277 calories; 16 g protein; 10 g fat; 35 g carbohydrate; 255 mg calcium;
  1,173 mg sodium (estimated); 27 mg cholesterol; 10 g dietary fiber

Multi-Layered Salad ☉

WEEK 6   MAKES 4 SERVINGS

Save precious time by cooking the eggs and bacon for this colorful salad in advance.

⅔ cup cottage cheese
½ cup plain low-fat yogurt
¼ cup *each* chopped scallions (green onions), divided, and reduced-calorie mayonnaise
1 tablespoon white wine vinegar
1 teaspoon Dijon-style mustard
¼ teaspoon salt
⅛ teaspoon pepper

6 cups torn lettuce leaves
½ cup grated carrot
4 ounces shredded Jarlsberg *or* Swiss cheese, divided
4 hard-cooked eggs, sliced
1 cup frozen peas, blanched
4 slices crisp bacon, crumbled
6 cherry tomatoes, halved

In blender container combine cottage cheese, yogurt, 2 tablespoons scallion, the mayonnaise, vinegar, mustard, salt, and pepper and process on medium speed until pureed, about 1½ minutes, scraping down sides of container as necessary. Set aside.

In medium mixing bowl combine lettuce, carrot, and remaining 2 tablespoons scallion, tossing to combine. In bottom of 2-quart bowl arrange half of the lettuce mixture; sprinkle with half of the cheese and then top with egg slices. Top with the peas, then with remaining lettuce mixture, the bacon, and remaining cheese. Spread cottage cheese mixture completely over cheese. Arrange tomato halves over salad. Cover salad with plastic wrap and refrigerate for at least 1 hour or overnight.

To serve, toss salad to combine.

Each serving provides: 2½ Protein Exchanges; ½ Bread Exchange; 3½ Vegetable Exchanges; 1½ Fat Exchanges; ¼ Milk Exchange; 45 Optional Calories
Per serving with Jarlsberg cheese: 365 calories; 24 g protein; 21 g fat; 16 g carbohydrate; 376 mg calcium; 796 mg sodium; 300 mg cholesterol; 3 g dietary fiber
With Swiss cheese: 372 calories; 25 g protein; 23 g fat; 16 g carbohydrate; 449 mg calcium; 745 mg sodium; 317 mg cholesterol; 3 g dietary fiber

Romaine Toss ◑

This simple salad is packed full of flavor and can be prepared in a matter of minutes.

1 tablespoon lemon juice
2 drained canned anchovy fillets
2 teaspoons drained capers
1 small garlic clove
¼ cup plain low-fat yogurt

2 tablespoons reduced-calorie
  mayonnaise
4 cups torn romaine lettuce leaves
6 *each* cherry tomatoes and pitted
  black olives, halved

In work bowl of food processor combine lemon juice, anchovies, capers, and garlic and process until pureed, about 30 seconds; add yogurt and mayonnaise and process until thoroughly mixed, about 30 seconds longer. Set aside.

In medium bowl combine lettuce, tomatoes, and olives; add dressing and toss to coat. Serve immediately.

Each serving provides: 4½ Vegetable Exchanges; 1½ Fat Exchanges; ¼ Milk Exchange;
  20 Optional Calories
Per serving: 113 calories; 5 g protein; 7 g fat; 8 g carbohydrate; 118 mg calcium;
  446 mg sodium; 9 mg cholesterol; 3 g dietary fiber

Vegetable-Stuffed Mushrooms

WEEK 2   MAKES 4 SERVINGS, 6 MUSHROOMS EACH

24 small mushrooms
1 tablespoon lemon juice
½ cup *each* chopped onion, red bell
  pepper, celery, and carrot
1 small garlic clove
2 teaspoons *each* olive *or* vegetable oil
  and dry white table wine

3 tablespoons seasoned dried bread
  crumbs
2 teaspoons *each* margarine, melted,
  and grated Parmesan cheese

Remove stems from mushrooms and reserve for another use. Rinse mushroom caps and, using paper towels, gently dry. In large bowl combine mushroom caps and lemon juice; toss to combine and set aside. In work bowl of food processor combine vegetables and garlic and, using an on-off motion, process until minced *(do not puree)*.

Preheat oven to 400°F. In 9-inch nonstick skillet heat oil; add vegetable mixture and cook over medium heat, stirring occasionally, until vegetables are softened, 2 to 3 minutes. Stir in wine; cook over medium-low heat until moisture has evaporated and flavors blend, 1 to 2 minutes. Remove from heat; stir in bread crumbs.

Into each mushroom cap spoon an equal amount of vegetable mixture. Arrange mushrooms on nonstick baking sheet and bake for 10 minutes. Turn oven control to broil. Brush each mushroom with an equal amount of margarine and sprinkle with cheese. Broil 3 inches from heat source until vegetable mixture is browned, 1 to 2 minutes.

Each serving provides: 1¾ Vegetable Exchanges; 1 Fat Exchange; 30 Optional Calories
Per serving: 90 calories; 2 g protein; 5 g fat; 10 g carbohydrate; 35 mg calcium;
  208 mg sodium; 1 mg cholesterol; 1 g dietary fiber

Fresh Mushroom Salad

WEEK 1   MAKES 2 SERVINGS, ABOUT 1 CUP EACH

This salad will receive rave reviews from mushroom lovers. It can be made in minutes and then marinated in your refrigerator.

2 cups sliced mushrooms
¼ cup sliced scallions (green onions),
   white portion only
5 sun-dried tomato halves (not packed
   in oil)
2 tablespoons chopped fresh Italian
   (flat-leaf) parsley
1 tablespoon *each* chopped fresh basil
   and drained capers
½ small garlic clove, minced

2 tablespoons raspberry *or* seasoned
   rice vinegar
1 tablespoon freshly squeezed lemon
   juice
2 teaspoons olive oil
¼ teaspoon salt
Dash pepper
1 ounce mozzarella cheese, shredded
4 lettuce leaves

In medium mixing bowl combine mushrooms, scallions, tomatoes, parsley, basil, capers, and garlic; set aside.

In small jar that has a tight-fitting cover or small bowl combine vinegar, lemon juice, oil, salt, and pepper; cover and shake or stir well. Pour dressing over mushroom mixture and toss to combine. Cover with plastic wrap and refrigerate until flavors blend, overnight or at least 30 minutes.

To serve, sprinkle cheese over mushroom mixture and toss to combine. Arrange lettuce leaves on serving platter and top with mushroom mixture.

Each serving provides: ½ Protein Exchange; 4 Vegetable Exchanges; 1 Fat Exchange
Per serving: 140 calories; 6 g protein; 8 g fat; 13 g carbohydrate; 126 mg calcium;
   452 mg sodium; 11 mg cholesterol; 4 g dietary fiber

Glazed Onions with Cranberries ⊕◑

WEEK 4   MAKES 4 SERVINGS

1 tablespoon plus 1 teaspoon
   margarine
2 cups frozen pearl onions
1 tablespoon *each* granulated sugar
   and firmly packed light brown sugar

1 cup cranberries
1 tablespoon grated orange peel
⅛ teaspoon ground ginger (optional)

In 10-inch nonstick skillet melt margarine; add onions and sauté over medium-high heat, stirring frequently, until lightly browned, 1 to 2 minutes. Reduce heat to low and stir in sugars; cover and cook until onions are tender-crisp, 5 to 7 minutes. Add remaining ingredients and mix well to thoroughly combine. Cook uncovered until cranberries are cooked through, 2 to 3 minutes.

Each serving provides: 1 Vegetable Exchange; 1 Fat Exchange; 45 Optional Calories
Per serving: 107 calories; 1 g protein; 4 g fat; 18 g carbohydrate; 42 mg calcium;
  55 mg sodium; 0 mg cholesterol; dietary fiber data not available

Double Onion Soup

This flavorful soup, which blends both onions and leeks, is ready to be served in about half an hour.

2 tablespoons whipped butter
2 cups *each* sliced onions and
   thoroughly washed leeks (white
   portion only)
1 quart water
½ cup *each* diced red and yellow bell
   pepper

2 tablespoons chopped Italian
   (flat-leaf) parsley
2 packets instant beef broth and
   seasoning mix

In 2-quart saucepan melt butter; add onions and leeks and cook, stirring occasionally, until softened, about 5 minutes. Add remaining ingredients; stir to combine and bring to a boil. Reduce heat and let simmer until flavors blend, about 15 minutes.

Each serving provides: 2½ Vegetable Exchanges; 30 Optional Calories
Per serving: 95 calories; 2 g protein; 3 g fat; 15 g carbohydrate; 55 mg calcium;
   508 mg sodium; 8 mg cholesterol; 2 g dietary fiber

Variation: Double Onion Soup with Cheese (Week 1) — Substitute 4 teaspoons margarine for the whipped butter. When ready to serve soup, top each portion with 1 teaspoon grated Parmesan cheese. Add 1 Fat Exchange to Exchange Information and reduce Optional Calories to 15.

Per serving: 111 calories; 3 g protein; 5 g fat; 15 g carbohydrate; 79 mg calcium;
   554 mg sodium; 1 mg cholesterol; 2 g dietary fiber

Three-Pepper Salad ◑

WEEK 4   MAKES 2 SERVINGS

A minimum of ingredients produces a colorful salad with a maximum of flavor and appeal.

½ cup *each* julienne-cut green, red, and yellow bell pepper (matchstick pieces), blanched
2 tablespoons rice vinegar

1 teaspoon *each* sesame seed, toasted, Dijon-style mustard, and honey
½ teaspoon reduced-sodium soy sauce

In medium mixing bowl combine bell peppers; set aside. Using a wire whisk, in small mixing bowl combine remaining ingredients and beat until combined; pour over bell peppers and toss to coat. Cover with plastic wrap and refrigerate until flavors blend, about 30 minutes.

Each serving provides: 1½ Vegetable Exchanges; 20 Optional Calories
Per serving: 43 calories; 1 g protein; 1 g fat; 8 g carbohydrate; 7 mg calcium;
  130 mg sodium; 0 mg cholesterol; 1 g dietary fiber

Pickled Cocktail Onions ◐◑

WEEK 1   MAKES 8 SERVINGS, ABOUT ¼ CUP EACH

These onions can be stored in the refrigerator for about 1 month.

1 cup *each* apple cider vinegar and water
2 tablespoons salt
1½ teaspoons granulated sugar
½ medium chili pepper, seeded and quartered

1 garlic clove, sliced
2 bay leaves
1 teaspoon mustard seed
2 cups frozen pearl onions, thawed

In 2-quart saucepan combine all ingredients except onions and bring to a boil. Reduce heat to low and let simmer for 5 minutes. Remove from heat and let cool slightly. Spoon onions into large wide-mouth jar with tight-fitting cover; pour in vinegar mixture. Cover and refrigerate overnight for flavors to blend. Use a slotted spoon for portioning.

Each serving provides: ½ Vegetable Exchange; 4 Optional Calories
Per serving: 25 calories; 1 g protein; 0.2 g fat; 6 g carbohydrate; 29 mg calcium;
  829 mg sodium; 0 mg cholesterol; trace dietary fiber

Pumpkin Chowder

WEEK 5   MAKES 4 SERVINGS, ABOUT 1 CUP EACH

Pumpkins aren't just for carving into jack-o'-lanterns; cook fresh pumpkin for this creamy soup rather than using canned.

1 tablespoon plus 1 teaspoon
   margarine
¼ pound Canadian-style bacon, minced
1 cup chopped thoroughly washed
   leeks (white portion only)
3 cups water
2 cups canned *or* cooked and pureed
   fresh pumpkin
2 packets instant chicken broth and
   seasoning mix

6 ounces cubed pared all-purpose
   potato
¼ teaspoon *each* crumbled sage and
   thyme leaves
Dash *each* pepper and ground nutmeg
¼ cup half-and-half (blend of milk
   and cream)

In 3-quart saucepan melt margarine; add bacon and leeks and cook, stirring frequently, until leeks are tender-crisp, about 2 minutes. Add water, pumpkin, and broth mix and stir until thoroughly combined; bring mixture to a boil. Reduce heat to low; add potato and seasonings and let simmer until potato is tender and flavors blend, about 20 minutes. Remove from heat and stir in half-and-half.

Each serving provides: 1 Protein Exchange; ½ Bread Exchange; 1½ Vegetable Exchanges;
   1 Fat Exchange; 30 Optional Calories
Per serving with canned pumpkin: 193 calories; 9 g protein; 8 g fat; 23 g carbohydrate;
   72 mg calcium; 959 mg sodium; 20 mg cholesterol; 3 g dietary fiber
With cooked fresh pumpkin: 176 calories; 9 g protein; 8 g fat; 19 g carbohydrate;
   59 mg calcium; 954 mg sodium; 20 mg cholesterol; 1 g dietary fiber (this figure does not
   include cooked fresh pumpkin; nutrition analysis not available)

Variation: Pumpkin Chowder with Ham (Week 3)—Substitute cooked smoked ham for the Canadian-style bacon.

Per serving with canned pumpkin: 190 calories; 10 g protein; 8 g fat; 23 g carbohydrate;
   72 mg calcium; 901 mg sodium; 21 mg cholesterol; 3 g dietary fiber
With cooked fresh pumpkin: 173 calories; 9 g protein; 7 g fat; 19 g carbohydrate;
   59 mg calcium; 896 mg sodium; 21 mg cholesterol; 1 g dietary fiber (this figure does not
   include cooked fresh pumpkin; nutrition analysis not available)

Spaghetti Squash Alfredo-Style

WEEK 5   MAKES 4 SERVINGS

Although it takes about an hour to bake spaghetti squash, once the squash is baked, the final preparation of this recipe takes only about 5 minutes.

1 spaghetti squash (2½ to 3 pounds)
2 tablespoons whipped butter
2 ounces grated Parmesan cheese
¼ cup half-and-half (blend of milk and cream)

¼ teaspoon salt
Dash pepper
2 tablespoons minced fresh Italian (flat-leaf) parsley

Preheat oven to 350° F. Using tines of a fork, pierce squash in several places; place whole squash on baking sheet and bake until tender, about 1 hour. Cut squash in half lengthwise and remove and discard seeds. Into medium mixing bowl scoop out pulp; add butter and toss until butter is melted. Add cheese, half-and-half, salt, and pepper and toss to combine. Transfer to serving platter and sprinkle with parsley.

Each serving provides: ½ Protein Exchange; 2 Vegetable Exchanges; 50 Optional Calories
Per serving: 183 calories; 8 g protein; 10 g fat; 17 g carbohydrate; 266 mg calcium;
    473 mg sodium; 25 mg cholesterol; 0.1 g dietary fiber (this figure does not include
    spaghetti squash; nutrition analysis not available)

Spaghetti Squash Florentine ©

WEEK 1   MAKES 4 SERVINGS

To save time, bake the squash in advance and store the pulp in a resealable plastic container. To keep the shell halves from getting soggy, fill them with paper towels, place in a resealable plastic bag, and set on a shelf in the refrigerator cut-side down.

1 spaghetti squash (2½ to 3 pounds)
2 teaspoons *each* olive *or* vegetable oil
    and margarine
1 cup *each* red bell pepper strips, sliced
    onions, and mushrooms
1 small garlic clove, minced
4 cups spinach leaves, thoroughly
    washed, drained, and torn into
    pieces

½ teaspoon *each* oregano leaves, salt,
    and white pepper
1 tablespoon plus 1 teaspoon grated
    Parmesan cheese

Preheat oven to 350° F. Using tines of a fork, pierce squash in several places; place whole squash on baking sheet and bake until tender, about 1 hour.

Cut squash in half lengthwise and remove and discard seeds; scoop out pulp, reserving shells. Set aside shells and pulp.

In 10-inch nonstick skillet combine oil and margarine and heat until margarine is melted; add bell pepper, onions, mushrooms, and garlic and sauté until tender crisp, about 5 minutes. Add spinach and stir to combine; cook until spinach is wilted and thoroughly cooked, about 3 minutes. Add reserved squash pulp and seasonings and stir to combine. Spoon half of squash-vegetable mixture into each reserved shell. Sprinkle each filled shell with 2 teaspoons Parmesan cheese.

Each serving provides: 5½ Vegetable Exchanges; 1 Fat Exchange; 10 Optional Calories
Per serving: 156 calories; 5 g protein; 6 g fat; 23 g carbohydrate; 149 mg calcium;
    411 mg sodium; 1 mg cholesterol; 3 g dietary fiber (this figure does not include spaghetti
    squash; nutrition analysis not available)

Spinach in Garlic-Cream Sauce ◑

WEEK 4	MAKES 2 SERVINGS

1 teaspoon *each* olive oil and margarine
2 small garlic cloves, minced
6 cups spinach leaves, trimmed,
   thoroughly washed, and drained

3 tablespoons whipped cream cheese
½ teaspoon salt
Dash ground nutmeg

In 10-inch nonstick skillet combine oil and margarine and heat until margarine is melted; add garlic and cook, stirring constantly, for ½ minute *(do not burn).* Add spinach and stir to combine; cook over medium heat, stirring occasionally, until spinach is wilted and tender, about 5 minutes. Pour off any excess liquid from skillet; add cream cheese, salt, and nutmeg, and cook, stirring constantly, until cheese is melted and mixture is heated through, about 2 minutes.

Each serving provides: 6 Vegetable Exchanges; 1 Fat Exchange; 50 Optional Calories
Per serving: 125 calories; 6 g protein; 10 g fat; 7 g carbohydrate; 184 mg calcium;
  755 mg sodium; 14 mg cholesterol; 5 g dietary fiber

Red Vegetable Pesto ◐

Serve warm as a sauce over cooked pasta or chilled as a salad dressing. This can be stored in a covered container in the refrigerator for about 2 weeks.

1 large Spanish onion (about ¼ pound), cut in half
1 large red bell pepper (about 7 ounces)
2 garlic cloves
18 sun-dried tomato halves (not packed in oil)

2 tablespoons plus 2 teaspoons olive oil
2 tablespoons lemon juice
1 tablespoon balsamic *or* red wine vinegar
2 teaspoons Dijon-style mustard
1 teaspoon fennel seed

Preheat broiler. On baking sheet lined with heavy-duty foil arrange onion cut-side down, the bell pepper, and garlic cloves and broil 3 inches from heat source, turning bell pepper frequently, until all vegetables are charred; let stand until cool enough to handle, 15 to 20 minutes. Peel onion, bell pepper, and garlic; remove and discard stem ends and seeds from pepper.

In work bowl of food processor combine onion, bell pepper, garlic, and remaining ingredients and process until smooth. Transfer to medium bowl (not aluminum*), cover with plastic wrap, and refrigerate until ready to use.

Each serving provides: 1¾ Vegetable Exchanges; 1 Fat Exchange
Per serving: 81 calories; 2 g protein; 5 g fat; 9 g carbohydrate; 19 mg calcium; 51 mg sodium; 0 mg cholesterol; 1 g dietary fiber

*It's best to marinate in glass or stainless-steel containers; ingredients such as lemon juice and vinegar may react with aluminum, causing color and flavor changes in food.

Zucchini Bake ©

WEEK 1   MAKES 4 SERVINGS

3 cups sliced zucchini (⅛-inch-thick
   slices)
2 teaspoons salt
⅓ cup plus 2 teaspoons plain dried
   bread crumbs

2 tablespoons grated Parmesan cheese
1 tablespoon plus 1 teaspoon reduced-
   calorie margarine (tub)
2 teaspoons Italian seasoning

Set colander in medium mixing bowl; arrange zucchini in colander, sprinkle with salt, and let stand for 10 minutes.

Preheat oven to 350°F. Using a fork, in small mixing bowl combine remaining ingredients, mixing well. Using paper towel wipe zucchini slices dry. Spray 8 x 8 x 2-inch baking dish with nonstick cooking spray and arrange zucchini in dish, overlapping slices slightly. Sprinkle crumb mixture over zucchini and bake until zucchini is tender, about 30 minutes.

Each serving provides: ½ Bread Exchange; 1½ Vegetable Exchanges; ½ Fat Exchange; 15 Optional Calories
Per serving: 81 calories; 3 g protein; 3 g fat; 10 g carbohydrate; 64 mg calcium; 717 mg sodium; 2 mg cholesterol; 1 g dietary fiber

The Fat Exchange

Act 3: Fat — Friend or Foe

Fat has always been cast as the villain, but not in our production! Why, without its assistance we wouldn't have Creamy Herb Dressing, Blue Cheese Dip, or Rémoulade Sauce. So relax and enjoy Act 3 — you have nothing to fear from the Fat Exchange.

Daily Exchanges

	WEEKS 1, 2, 3, 4, AND 5
Women, Men, and Youths	3 Exchanges

Fat Exchange Notes

- Fats supply polyunsaturated fatty acids and vitamin E.

- When measuring fats, be sure your measurements are level.

- You may use any of the following vegetable oils, alone or in combination: safflower, sunflower, walnut, soybean, corn, wheat germ, cottonseed, sorghum, sesame, rice, bran, peanut, rapeseed (canola), and olive.

- Chili oil, because of its nature, is generally used only in very small amounts. It may be combined with another vegetable oil to obtain a measurable amount of oil.

- Check the label on margarine to determine if it is permitted. Use margarine that lists liquid vegetable oil as the first ingredient in the ingredient listing.

- You may use your Fat Exchanges to broil, pan-broil, bake, roast, sauté, or stir-fry all foods except poultry and game with the skin and raw beef, ham, lamb, pork, and tongue.

- You may use Fat Exchanges as part of a marinade (do not use with poultry and game that have not been skinned, or with the raw meats listed above); all of the marinade must be consumed and counted toward the Food Plan. Therefore, all pan juices that accumulate while cooking foods that have been marinated in Fat Exchanges must be consumed.

Fat Exchange List

Weeks 1-5

Selections	One Exchange
Margarine, liquid vegetable oil	1 teaspoon
Margarine, reduced-calorie (stick)	1½ teaspoons
Margarine, reduced-calorie (tub)	2 teaspoons
Mayonnaise, commercial and homemade	1 teaspoon
Mayonnaise, reduced-calorie	2 teaspoons
Salad Dressing, any type	1½ teaspoons
Vegetable Oil	1 teaspoon

Blue Cheese Dip ◑

WEEK 4   MAKES 8 SERVINGS, 2 TABLESPOONS EACH

Guests will rave when you serve this dip with assorted vegetables as an hors d'oeuvre.

½ cup sour cream
⅓ cup reduced-calorie mayonnaise
2 tablespoons lemon juice
¼ cup half-and-half (blend of milk
   and cream)

2 ounces blue cheese, crumbled
2 tablespoons chopped scallion
   (green onion)
Dash white pepper

In small mixing bowl combine sour cream, mayonnaise, and lemon juice, mixing well; stir in remaining ingredients. Cover with plastic wrap and refrigerate until flavors blend, about 30 minutes.

Each serving provides: 1 Fat Exchange; 65 Optional Calories
Per serving: 93 calories; 2 g protein; 9 g fat; 2 g carbohydrate; 63 mg calcium;
   185 mg sodium; 18 mg cholesterol; trace dietary fiber

Russian Dressing ◐◑

WEEK 5   MAKES 8 SERVINGS, ABOUT 2½ TABLESPOONS EACH

A favorite with young and old, this dressing is made extra-rich with sour cream. It will keep for about 1 week in the refrigerator.

½ cup sour cream
⅓ cup reduced-calorie mayonnaise
¼ cup *each* chili sauce and pickle relish

In small mixing bowl combine all ingredients, mixing well. Cover with plastic wrap or transfer to jar with tight-fitting cover; refrigerate until flavors blend, about 30 minutes. Just before serving, stir or shake well.

Each serving provides: 1 Fat Exchange; 55 Optional Calories
Per serving: 77 calories; 0.8 g protein; 6 g fat; 6 g carbohydrate; 20 mg calcium;
   250 mg sodium; 10 mg cholesterol; dietary fiber data not available

Avocado Dressing ◑

This creamy dressing can double as a dip for crudités. It will keep for about 1 week in the refrigerator.

¾ cup buttermilk
3 ounces pitted very ripe avocado,
    pared and chopped
⅓ cup reduced-calorie mayonnaise
¼ cup sour cream

1 tablespoon lemon juice
1 garlic clove, minced
¼ teaspoon salt
⅛ teaspoon white pepper

In blender container or work bowl of food processor combine all ingredients and process until smooth, scraping down sides of container as necessary. Transfer to bowl or jar with tight-fitting cover; cover and refrigerate until flavors blend, about 30 minutes. Just before serving, stir well.

Each serving provides: 1 Fat Exchange; 45 Optional Calories
Per serving: 66 calories; 1 g protein; 6 g fat; 3 g carbohydrate; 37 mg calcium;
    171 mg sodium; 7 mg cholesterol; 0.2 g dietary fiber

Roasted Red Pepper Dressing ◑

WEEK 1 MAKES 12 SERVINGS, ABOUT 2 TABLESPOONS PLUS 1½ TEASPOONS EACH

Roasted red bell peppers make this dressing one you'll savor. It will keep for about 2 weeks in the refrigerator.

14 ounces red bell peppers
¼ cup olive oil
3 tablespoons *each* lemon juice and
    red wine vinegar
2 tablespoons fresh basil

1 tablespoon chopped onion
1 small garlic clove
2 teaspoons salt
Dash pepper

Preheat broiler. On baking sheet lined with heavy-duty foil broil bell peppers 3 inches from heat source, turning frequently, until charred on all sides; let stand until cool enough to handle. Over small bowl to catch juice, peel bell peppers; reserve juice. Remove and discard stem ends and seeds.

In blender container combine bell peppers, reserved bell pepper juice, and remaining ingredients and process until smooth, scraping down sides of container as necessary. Transfer to bowl or jar with tight-fitting cover; cover and refrigerate until ready to use. Just before serving, stir or shake well.

Each serving provides: ¾ Vegetable Exchange; 1 Fat Exchange
Per serving: 50 calories; 0.3 g protein; 5 g fat; 2 g carbohydrate; 9 mg calcium;
    369 mg sodium; 0 mg cholesterol; 0.4 g dietary fiber

Creamy Herb Dressing ⊖⦿

WEEK 4	MAKES 8 SERVINGS, 3 TABLESPOONS EACH

This dressing will keep for about 1 week in the refrigerator.

½ cup *each* sour cream and low-fat milk (1% milk fat)
⅓ cup reduced-calorie mayonnaise
3 tablespoons chopped scallion (green onion)

2 teaspoons *each* chopped fresh parsley, basil, dill, and grated Parmesan cheese
½ teaspoon thyme leaves
⅛ teaspoon white pepper

In blender container combine sour cream, milk, and mayonnaise and process until thoroughly combined, scraping down sides of container as necessary; stir in remaining ingredients. Transfer to bowl or jar with tight-fitting cover; cover and refrigerate until ready to use. Just before serving, stir well.

Each serving provides: 1 Fat Exchange; 45 Optional Calories
Per serving: 67 calories; 1 g protein; 6 g fat; 2 g carbohydrate; 48 mg calcium;
    98 mg sodium; 11 mg cholesterol; 0.1 g dietary fiber

"Tomatonaise" ⊖⦿

WEEK 4	MAKES 12 SERVINGS, ABOUT 2 TEASPOONS EACH

Try this spicy mayo as a dip or as a spread on sandwiches.

½ cup reduced-calorie mayonnaise
1 tablespoon tomato paste

¼ teaspoon granulated sugar
Dash *each* salt and white pepper

In small mixing bowl combine all ingredients until thoroughly blended. Cover with plastic wrap or transfer to jar with tight-fitting cover and refrigerate until ready to use. Just before serving, stir well.

Each serving provides: 1 Fat Exchange; 1 Optional Calorie
Per serving: 28 calories; 0.1 g protein; 3 g fat; 1 g carbohydrate; 0.6 mg calcium;
    97 mg sodium; 3 mg cholesterol; dietary fiber data not available

Rémoulade Sauce ◑

WEEK 5   MAKES 8 SERVINGS, ABOUT 2 TABLESPOONS EACH

This rich-tasting sauce will keep for about 1 week in your refrigerator. Try it over broiled fish or seafood, poached chicken, or hard-cooked eggs.

½ cup sour cream
⅓ cup reduced-calorie mayonnaise
1 tablespoon *each* drained capers,
  chopped, and pickle relish

2 teaspoons mashed anchovy fillets
1 teaspoon *each* tarragon and chervil
  leaves

In small mixing bowl combine all ingredients, mixing well. Cover with plastic wrap or transfer to jar with tight-fitting cover; refrigerate until flavors blend, at least 30 minutes. Just before serving, stir well.

Each serving provides: 1 Fat Exchange; 40 Optional Calories
Per serving: 64 calories; 1 g protein; 6 g fat; 2 g carbohydrate; 24 mg calcium;
  178 mg sodium; 10 mg cholesterol; dietary fiber data not available

Tartar Sauce ◐ ◑

WEEK 4   MAKES 4 SERVINGS, ABOUT 2½ TABLESPOONS EACH

The perfect accompaniment for baked, broiled, or poached fish, this sauce will keep for about 1 week in the refrigerator.

¼ cup sour cream
2 tablespoons plus 2 teaspoons
  reduced-calorie mayonnaise
1 tablespoon *each* lemon juice and
  pickle relish

1 teaspoon *each* drained capers,
  chopped, and Dijon-style mustard
¼ teaspoon *each* hot sauce and
  prepared horseradish

In small mixing bowl combine all ingredients, mixing well. Cover with plastic wrap or transfer to jar with tight-fitting cover; refrigerate until flavors blend, at least 30 minutes. Just before serving, stir well.

Each serving provides: 1 Fat Exchange; 40 Optional Calories
Per serving: 66 calories; 0.6 g protein; 6 g fat; 3 g carbohydrate; 18 mg calcium;
  175 mg sodium; 10 mg cholesterol; dietary fiber data not available

Mustard-Caper Vinaigrette ◐

WEEK 1 MAKES 12 SERVINGS, ABOUT 2 TABLESPOONS PLUS 1½ TEASPOONS EACH

This dressing will keep for about 2 weeks in the refrigerator. Its flavor complements any vegetable salad.

½ cup *each* champagne *or* rice vinegar
   and water
¼ cup drained capers, crushed
2 tablespoons *each* minced shallot
   or onion and Dijon-style mustard

½ teaspoon salt
⅛ teaspoon white pepper
¼ cup olive oil

Using a wire whisk, in small mixing bowl combine all ingredients except oil; gradually beat in oil. Cover with plastic wrap or transfer to jar with tight-fitting cover and refrigerate until ready to use. Just before serving, stir or shake well.

Each serving provides: 1 Fat Exchange
Per serving: 45 calories; trace protein; 5 g fat; 1 g carbohydrate; 1 mg calcium;
   240 mg sodium; 0 mg cholesterol; trace dietary fiber

Oriental Citrus Vinaigrette ⊙◑

WEEK 1 MAKES 12 SERVINGS, ABOUT 2 TABLESPOONS PLUS 1½ TEASPOONS EACH

This tangy salad dressing will keep for about 2 weeks in the refrigerator.

½ cup rice vinegar
⅓ cup plus 2 teaspoons thawed frozen
  concentrated orange juice (no sugar
  added)
2 tablespoons *each* Chinese sesame
  oil, peanut oil, and teriyaki sauce

1 tablespoon *each* lemon juice and
  dark corn syrup
2 teaspoons grated pared gingerroot
1 small garlic clove
¼ cup minced scallions (green onions)

In blender container combine all ingredients except scallions and process until combined; stir in scallions. Transfer to bowl or jar with tight-fitting cover; cover and refrigerate until ready to use. Just before serving, stir or shake well.

Each serving provides: 1 Fat Exchange; 20 Optional Calories
Per serving: 64 calories; 0.4 g protein; 5 g fat; 6 g carbohydrate; 6 mg calcium;
  117 mg sodium; 0 mg cholesterol; 0.7 g dietary fiber

Raspberry-Nut Vinaigrette ◑

WEEK 1 MAKES 12 SERVINGS, ABOUT 2 TABLESPOONS PLUS 1½ TEASPOONS EACH

Raspberry vinegar is the basis for this sweet, fruity dressing. It is available in the gourmet section of most supermarkets and can be used in any recipe calling for vinegar, such as a vinaigrette, a meat or poultry sauce, or a fruit salad dressing. This dressing will keep for about 2 weeks in the refrigerator.

1 cup water
½ cup raspberry vinegar
¼ cup walnut *or* peanut oil
2 tablespoons *each* white wine Worcestershire sauce and Dijon-style mustard

1 tablespoon *each* granulated sugar, lemon juice, and light corn syrup *or* honey
1 small garlic clove
¼ teaspoon *each* salt and white pepper

In blender container combine all ingredients and process until combined. Transfer to bowl or jar with tight-fitting cover; cover and refrigerate until ready to use. Just before serving, stir or shake well.

Each serving provides: 1 Fat Exchange; 10 Optional Calories
Per serving: 56 calories; trace protein; 5 g fat; 4 g carbohydrate; 2 mg calcium;
143 mg sodium; 0 mg cholesterol; dietary fiber data not available

Salsa Vinaigrette ◑

WEEK 1   YIELDS 3 CUPS

This dressing will keep for about 2 weeks in the refrigerator.

1 cup canned Italian tomatoes (with liquid)

½ cup *each* chopped scallions (green onions), white portion only, chopped green bell pepper, and chopped red bell pepper

4 small garlic cloves

1 small chili *or* jalapeño pepper, seeded

1 medium tomato, blanched, peeled, seeded, and diced

¼ cup *each* olive oil, freshly squeezed lime juice, and minced fresh cilantro (Chinese parsley) *or* parsley

2 tablespoons cider vinegar

1 teaspoon salt

Dash pepper

In blender container combine canned tomatoes, scallions, bell peppers, garlic, and chili (or jalapeño pepper) and, using on-off motion, process until mixture is finely chopped *(do not puree).* Add remaining ingredients and stir until combined. Transfer to bowl or jar with tight-fitting cover; cover and refrigerate until ready to use. Just before serving, stir or shake well.

Each ¼-cup serving provides: ½ Vegetable Exchange; 1 Fat Exchange
Per serving: 52 calories; 0.5 g protein; 5 g fat; 3 g carbohydrate; 12 mg calcium;
    218 mg sodium; 0 mg cholesterol; 0.5 g dietary fiber
Each 2-tablespoon serving provides: ¼ Vegetable Exchange; ½ Fat Exchange
Per serving: 26 calories; 0.3 g protein; 3 g fat; 2 g carbohydrate; 6 mg calcium;
    109 mg sodium; 0 mg cholesterol; 0.3 g dietary fiber

Vegetable Vinaigrette ◑

WEEK 5   MAKES 6 SERVINGS, ABOUT 3 TABLESPOONS EACH

Balsamic vinegar, an aged vinegar made from wine, adds a hearty flavor to this delightful dressing, which will keep for about 1 week in the refrigerator.

¾ cup mixed vegetable juice
2 tablespoons balsamic *or* red wine
    vinegar
1 tablespoon olive oil
2 teaspoons Dijon-style mustard
6 pitted black olives, minced, divided
1 tablespoon chopped drained
    pimiento, divided

1 teaspoon *each* drained capers,
    divided, and chopped fresh basil
    or ¼ teaspoon dried
¼ teaspoon *each* salt and pepper

In blender container combine vegetable juice, vinegar, oil, mustard, half of the olives, pimiento, and capers, and all of the seasonings; process at high speed for 2 minutes. Stir in remaining olives, pimiento, and capers. Transfer to bowl or jar with tight-fitting cover; cover and refrigerate until ready to use. Just before serving, stir or shake well.

Each serving provides: ½ Fat Exchange; 5 Optional Calories
Per serving: 36 calories; 0.2 g protein; 3 g fat; 2 g carbohydrate; 10 mg calcium;
    290 mg sodium; 0 mg cholesterol, 0.2 g dietary fiber

The Protein Exchange

Act 4: A Passion for Protein

If it's drama, intrigue, and passion you're after, stick around for Act 4, where the largest cast ever assembled will lead you through twists and turns of plot. Eggs and Cheese, Fish, Poultry, Meat and Veal, and Legumes, are part of an ever-changing scene, different every time you see it. Come join us now as we reveal the secrets of the Protein Exchange.

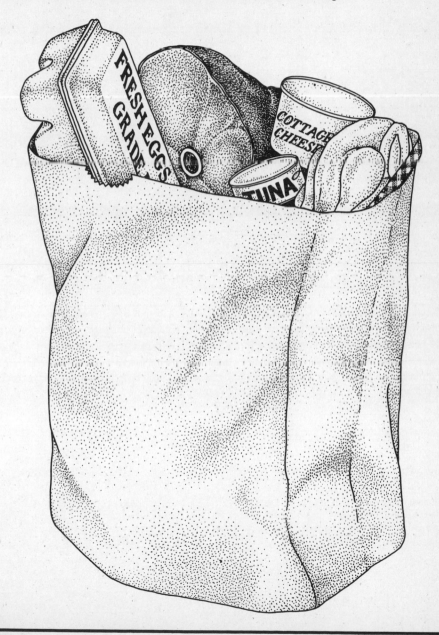

Daily Exchanges

	WEEKS 1, 2, 3, 4, AND 5
Women	5 to 6 Exchanges
Men and Youths	7 to 8 Exchanges

Protein Exchange Notes

• The Protein Exchange supplies B vitamins, calcium, iron, and protein.

• You may select up to 3 eggs a week; they may be small, medium, large, or extra-large in size, white or brown in color. If you are going to consume raw eggs, inspect shells carefully for cracks; cracked eggs may contain salmonella, a type of bacteria that causes intestinal upset.

• You may select up to 4 ounces of hard or semisoft cheese a week.

• Three-quarters of an ounce of uncooked dry beans, lentils, or peas will yield about 2 ounces cooked. You may also use canned and frozen products packed without sugar.

• To determine the amount of boneless raw meat and fish or skinned and boned poultry needed, as a rule of thumb, take the total cooked weight desired, divide by 4, and add this number to the desired cooked weight. For raw meat and fish with bone, take the total skinned and boned cooked weight desired, divide by 2, and add this number to the desired cooked weight (see chart on page 154). If a fraction results from these calculations, round up to the nearest whole number.

As a rule of thumb, raw whole chicken or cut-up parts will yield about 33 percent skinned cooked meat; raw chicken breasts (bone in) will yield about 50 percent skinned cooked meat; and raw Cornish hen will yield about 40 percent skinned cooked meat. Use the charts on page 154 as a guide to purchasing birds of the appropriate size.

Meat, Fish, and Poultry	Desired Skinned and Boned Cooked Weight	Divided by	Equals (ounces)	Start with (raw weight)
Boneless Meat	1 pound	4	4	1¼ pounds
or Fish or	¾ pound	4	3	15 ounces
Skinned and Boned Poultry	9 ounces	4	2¼	¾ pound
Meat or Fish	1 pound	2	8	1½ pounds
with Bone	¾ pound	2	6	1 pound 2 ounces
	9 ounces	2	4½	14 ounces

Whole or Cut-Up Poultry (raw with skin and bone)	Approx. Yield (skinned and boned cooked meat)
Chicken	
6 pounds	2 pounds
5 pounds	1 pound 11 ounces
4½ pounds	1½ pounds
4 pounds	1 pound 5 ounces
3½ pounds	1 pound 3 ounces
3 pounds	1 pound
Cornish Hen	
1½ pounds	10 ounces
1¼ pounds	½ pound

Chicken Breasts (raw with skin and bone)	Approx. Yield (skinned and boned cooked meat)
2 pounds	1 pound
1½ pounds	¾ pound
½ pound	¼ pound
6 ounces	3 ounces

• Clams, lobsters, mussels, oysters, and shrimp are exceptions to the rule of thumb.

—Count 3 medium clams, mussels, oysters, or shrimp as 1 Protein Exchange.

—A 1½-pound lobster will yield about 6 ounces cooked lobster meat; a 6-ounce lobster tail will yield about 3 ounces cooked lobster meat.

• Poultry, veal, game, fish, organ meats, and liver may be boiled, poached, stewed, broiled, pan-broiled, roasted, sautéed, or stir-fried. Since skin is a concentrated source of fat, you should remove skin of poultry and game before pan-broiling, sautéing, stir-frying, or stewing. If you bake, broil, roast, boil, or poach poultry or game with the skin on, remove and discard skin and any additional ingredients (such as vegetables, liquid, etc.) after cooking.

• Use lean meat and remove all visible fat. Raw beef, ham, lamb, pork, and tongue should be cooked on a rack (baked, roasted, or broiled) or boiled; discard fat that cooks out of the meat.

• Uncooked whole poultry and game and raw meats marked with an asterisk (*) may not be stuffed prior to cooking.

• Frankfurters, knockwurst, sausages, bologna, and luncheon meat may be made from beef, chicken, turkey, veal, or a combination of these items; with the exception of luncheon meat, pork may be used in combination with these items, but all-pork products are not permitted. If made from chicken, turkey, veal, or a combination of these, count as a poultry/veal selection; if made in combination with beef or pork, count as a beef/pork selection.

• We recommend that you have 9 to 15 ounces of fish each week. Canned fish should be well drained; do not consume the liquid.

Protein Exchange Lists

The weights indicated for dry beans, lentils, peas, poultry, meats, and fish are net cooked (or drained canned) weights (without skin and bones).

Week 1

You may select up to 12 Exchanges weekly from the meats marked with an asterisk (*), except for organ meats (including liver) which are limited to 4 Exchanges weekly.

Selections	One Exchange
*Beef, lean	1 ounce
Capon	1 ounce
Cheese, cottage (1% fat, 2% fat, 4% fat) or pot	⅓ cup
Cheese, hard or semisoft	1 ounce
Chicken	1 ounce
Cornish Hen	1 ounce
Egg	1
Egg Substitutes	¼ cup
Fish	1 ounce

Selections	One Exchange
Frankfurter and Knockwurst, made from chicken, turkey, *or* veal	1 ounce
*Lamb, lean	1 ounce
Liver	1 ounce
Luncheon Meat, made from chicken, turkey, *or* veal	1 ounce
*Pork, lean	1 ounce
Sausage, made from chicken, turkey, *or* veal	1 ounce
Shellfish	1 ounce
Tofu (soybean curd), firm *or* soft	3 ounces
Turkey	1 ounce
Veal, lean	1 ounce

Week 2

You may use all of the items listed under Week 1 and may add the following to your Exchange List:

Selections	One Exchange
*Ham, lean	1 ounce

Week 3

You may use all of the items listed under Weeks 1 and 2 and may add the following to your Exchange List:

Selections	One Exchange
Cheese, ricotta, part-skin	¼ cup
Dry beans, lentils, peas	¾ ounce dry *or* 2 ounces cooked

Week 4

You may use all of the items listed under Weeks 1, 2, and 3 and may add the following to your Exchange List:

Selections	One Exchange
*Bologna	1 ounce
*Bratwurst	1 ounce
*Frankfurter and Knockwurst, made from beef *or* beef and pork combined	1 ounce

*Luncheon Meat, made from beef	1 ounce
*Sausage, made from beef *or*	
beef and pork combined	1 ounce
Tempeh	
(fermented soybean cake)	1 ounce

Week 5

You may use all of the items listed under Weeks 1, 2, 3, and 4 and may add the following to your Exchange List:

Selections	One Exchange
*Bacon, Canadian-style	1 ounce
*Beefalo	1 ounce
Game	1 ounce
*Liverwurst	1 ounce
*Organ Meats	1 ounce
*Tongue	1 ounce

Eggs and Cheese

Poached Eggs California, Four-Cheese Omelet, and Cheese Enchiladas are just a few of our tempting Protein players. Whether it's breakfast, lunch, brunch, or dinner, you'll find dozens of delicious and satisfying dishes in our Eggs and Cheese section.

Buttery Scrambled Egg in a Pita ☉◐

WEEK 6   MAKES 2 SERVINGS, 2 PITA HALVES EACH

The trick to making this delicious breakfast in just 15 minutes is to let the bacon cook in the microwave while you're preparing the eggs. If you don't have a microwave oven, just prepare the bacon in advance, crumble it, then wrap and refrigerate it until needed.

2 eggs
Dash *each* **salt and pepper**
2 teaspoons whipped butter
½ cup thinly sliced mushrooms
1 tablespoon diced onion

1 slice crisp bacon, crumbled
2 whole wheat pitas (1 ounce each),
toasted and cut into halves crosswise,
forming 4 pockets

In small bowl beat together eggs and seasonings; set aside. In 8-inch nonstick skillet melt butter; add mushrooms and onion and sauté until mushrooms are lightly browned, 1 to 2 minutes. Pour in egg mixture and cook, stirring frequently with a wooden spoon to allow uncooked portions to flow to bottom of pan, until eggs are almost set and slightly creamy; stir in bacon. Continue cooking, stirring frequently, until eggs are set and form large, soft curds. Fill each pita pocket with ¼ of the egg mixture.

Each serving provides: 1 Protein Exchange; 1 Bread Exchange; ½ Vegetable Exchange;
    40 Optional Calories
Per serving: 204 calories; 10 g protein; 9 g fat; 10 g carbohydrate; 40 mg calcium;
    388 mg sodium; 282 mg cholesterol; 0.5 g dietary fiber

Variation: Scrambled Egg in a Pita — 2 teaspoons margarine may be substituted for the butter. Decrease Optional Calories to 20 and add 1 Fat Exchange to Exchange Information.

Per serving: 221 calories; 10 g protein; 11 g fat; 19 g carbohydrate; 41 mg calcium;
    413 mg sodium; 277 mg cholesterol; 0.5 g dietary fiber

Eggs and Prosciutto Toasts

WEEK 2   MAKES 2 SERVINGS

2 diagonally cut slices Italian bread
   (1 ounce each), toasted
1 tablespoon plus 1 teaspoon
   margarine, melted, divided
12 cooked asparagus spears
1½ ounces sliced prosciutto
   (Italian-style ham)

2 poached eggs (hot)
½ ounce grated Parmesan cheese
½ teaspoon oregano leaves

Spray 2 individual flameproof dishes with nonstick cooking spray. Place 1 slice of toast in each dish, cut-side down, and, using 1 tablespoon melted margarine, brush top of each with an equal amount of margarine. Top each slice of toast with 6 asparagus spears, half of the prosciutto, and 1 egg. In small bowl combine cheese, oregano, and remaining melted margarine and sprinkle half of mixture over each egg. Transfer dishes to baking sheet and broil until cheese melts, 1 to 2 minutes.

Each serving provides: 2 Protein Exchanges; 1 Bread Exchange; 1 Vegetable Exchange;
   2 Fat Exchanges
Per serving: 311 calories; 18 g protein; 17 g fat; 21 g carbohydrate; 163 mg calcium;
   793 mg sodium; 290 mg cholesterol; 4 g dietary fiber

Variation: Buttery Eggs and Prosciutto Toasts (Week 5)—Substitute 1 tablespoon whipped butter for the margarine. In method, use 2 teaspoons butter to brush on toast; proceed as directed. Omit 1 Fat Exchange and add 25 Optional Calories to Exchange Information.

Per serving: 269 calories; 18 g protein; 12 g fat; 21 g carbohydrate; 161 mg calcium;
   733 mg sodium; 297 mg cholesterol; 4 g dietary fiber

Open-Face Spiced Egg Salad Sandwiches ◐◑

WEEK 6   MAKES 2 SERVINGS

This special egg salad is a snap to make if you cook the eggs and bacon in advance.

2 eggs, hard-cooked and diced
2 tablespoons *each* diced onion
   and celery
1 slice crisp bacon, crumbled
1 tablespoon plus 1 teaspoon
   reduced-calorie mayonnaise
1½ teaspoons minced fresh Italian
   (flat-leaf) parsley

½ teaspoon Dijon-style mustard
¼ teaspoon prepared horseradish
2 diagonally cut slices Italian bread
   (1 ounce each), toasted
2 lettuce leaves
¼ medium tomato, cut into 2 wedges

In small mixing bowl combine eggs, onion, celery, bacon, mayonnaise, parsley, mustard, and horseradish. Cover and refrigerate until ready to serve.

To serve, top each slice of bread with 1 lettuce leaf, ½ of the egg mixture, and 1 tomato wedge.

Each serving provides: 1 Protein Exchange; 1 Bread Exchange; ¾ Vegetable Exchange;
   1 Fat Exchange; 20 Optional Calories
Per serving: 213 calories; 10 g protein; 10 g fat; 19 g carbohydrate; 46 mg calcium;
   407 mg sodium; 280 mg cholesterol; 1 g dietary fiber

Poached Eggs California

WEEK 5 · MAKES 4 SERVINGS

Use the freshest eggs you can find for this recipe. The white of a very fresh egg adheres to the yolk better than the white of an older egg, making it perfect for poaching.

½ cup *each* alfalfa sprouts and shredded carrot
¼ cup dark raisins, plumped in warm water and drained
2 teaspoons sunflower seed
2 English muffins (2 ounces each), split into halves and toasted
4 lettuce leaves
½ medium tomato, cut into 4 slices
¼ cup red onion slices (separated into rings)
4 eggs, poached (hot)
1 tablespoon plus 1 teaspoon shredded sharp Cheddar cheese, divided
¼ avocado (2 ounces), pared and cut into 4 wedges

In small mixing bowl combine alfalfa sprouts, carrot, raisins, and sunflower seed; set aside. On flameproof serving platter arrange muffin halves, cut-side up; top each muffin half with 1 lettuce leaf, 1 tomato slice, ¼ of the onion, ¼ of sprout mixture, and 1 poached egg. Sprinkle 1 teaspoon cheese over each egg and broil just until cheese melts; remove from broiler and top each portion with 1 avocado wedge. Serve immediately.

Each serving provides: 1 Protein Exchange; 1 Bread Exchange; 1⅛ Vegetable Exchanges; ½ Fruit Exchange; 45 Optional Calories
Per serving: 223 calories; 10 g protein; 9 g fat; 25 g carbohydrate; 67 mg calcium; 317 mg sodium; 275 mg cholesterol; 1 g dietary fiber

Scotch Eggs

WEEK 5   MAKES 2 SERVINGS

This dish is good served warm or chilled.

3 ounces ground veal
⅓ cup plus 2 teaspoons plain dried
    bread crumbs
1 egg white
2 tablespoons minced onion
1 tablespoon chopped fresh parsley
¼ teaspoon salt
⅛ teaspoon *each* rubbed sage and
    thyme leaves

Dash pepper
2 hard-cooked eggs
1 tablespoon uncooked yellow
    cornmeal
1 teaspoon vegetable oil

In medium mixing bowl combine veal, bread crumbs, egg white, onion, parsley, and seasonings, mixing well. Cover each egg with half of the veal mixture, shaping each into a ball; roll balls in cornmeal to coat.

Preheat oven to 350°F. In 8-inch nonstick skillet heat oil; add eggs and cook over medium-high heat, turning frequently, until cornmeal coating is lightly browned, about 5 minutes. Transfer eggs to 1-quart casserole and bake until golden brown, about 20 minutes.

Each serving provides: 2 Protein Exchanges; 1 Bread Exchange; ⅛ Vegetable Exchange;
    ½ Fat Exchange; 30 Optional Calories
Per serving: 276 calories; 19 g protein; 13 g fat; 19 g carbohydrate; 67 mg calcium;
    532 mg sodium; 305 mg cholesterol; 0.5 g dietary fiber

Herb-Cheese Spread ◐

WEEK 4   MAKES 8 SERVINGS, ABOUT ¼ CUP EACH

It takes only about 10 minutes to create this wonderful spread. Use as an accompaniment to melba rounds or rice cakes, or as a stuffing for celery. Prepare it the night before you serve it to enhance the flavor.

1 cup part-skim ricotta cheese
⅓ cup plus 2 teaspoons whipped
  cream cheese
2 tablespoons half-and-half (blend
  of milk and cream)

1 small garlic clove
¼ cup minced fresh dill*
1 teaspoon salt
Dash pepper

In work bowl of food processor or blender container combine ricotta cheese, cream cheese, half-and-half, and garlic and process until combined, scraping down sides of container as necessary. Transfer to small mixing bowl; stir in remaining ingredients. Cover and refrigerate overnight to allow flavors to blend.

Each serving provides: ½ Protein Exchange; 30 Optional Calories
Per serving: 73 calories; 4 g protein; 5 g fat; 2 g carbohydrate; 102 mg calcium;
   342 mg sodium; 18 mg cholesterol; 0 g dietary fiber

*Fresh basil or Italian (flat-leaf) parsley may be substituted for the dill.

Creamy Apple-Raisin Treat

WEEK 5	MAKES 2 SERVINGS

Apples, raisins, and cinnamon are a perfect combination in this very special 15-minute brunch dish. Don't want to fuss in the morning? You can prepare the cheese mixture and even mix the sugars and cinnamon the night before. The rest can be done in about 5 minutes in the morning.

1 small apple (about ¼ pound), cored, pared, and shredded
½ teaspoon lemon juice
⅓ cup cottage cheese
¼ cup part-skim ricotta cheese
2 tablespoons golden raisins

4 slices cinnamon-raisin bread, lightly toasted
1 teaspoon *each* granulated sugar and firmly packed light brown sugar
¼ teaspoon ground cinnamon

In small mixing bowl combine apple and lemon juice and toss lightly to coat; add cheeses and raisins and stir to combine. On baking sheet arrange toast slices and spread ¼ of apple mixture evenly over each slice of toast. In cup or small bowl combine sugars and cinnamon; sprinkle ¼ of mixture (about ½ teaspoon) over each portion of apple mixture. Broil until cheese mixture is heated through and sugar is melted. Serve immediately.

Each serving provides: 1 Protein Exchange; 2 Bread Exchanges; 1 Fruit Exchange; 20 Optional Calories
Per serving: 282 calories; 12 g protein; 6 g fat; 48 g carbohydrate; 152 mg calcium; 363 mg sodium; 16 mg cholesterol; 2 g dietary fiber (this figure does not include raisin bread; nutrition analysis not available)

Broccoli-Cheese Soup

WEEK 2   MAKES 2 SERVINGS

2 teaspoons margarine
¼ cup *each* chopped onion and red
   bell pepper
1 tablespoon plus 1½ teaspoons
   all-purpose flour
1½ cups water
1 cup low-fat milk (1% milk fat)
1 packet instant chicken broth and
   seasoning mix

1 cup broccoli florets
2 tablespoons dry white table wine
1½ teaspoons chopped fresh parsley
⅛ teaspoon *each* thyme leaves and
   white pepper
Dash ground nutmeg
1 ounce Swiss *or* Gruyère cheese,
   shredded

In 1½- or 2-quart saucepan melt margarine; add onion and bell pepper and sauté over high heat until tender-crisp, about 1 minute. Sprinkle flour over vegetables and stir quickly to combine; cook, stirring constantly, for 1 minute. Continuing to stir, gradually add water. Add milk and broth mix, stirring to dissolve broth mix; add remaining ingredients except cheese and stir to combine. Reduce heat to low and cook until broccoli is tender and mixture thickens, 10 to 15 minutes. Stir in cheese and cook until cheese melts, about 1 minute.

Each serving provides: ½ Protein Exchange; 1½ Vegetable Exchanges; 1 Fat Exchange;
   ½ Milk Exchange; 55 Optional Calories
Per serving with Swiss cheese: 205 calories; 12 g protein; 9 g fat; 17 g carbohydrate;
   327 mg calcium; 655 mg sodium; 18 mg cholesterol; 1 g dietary fiber (this figure does not
   include broccoli; nutrition analysis not available)
With Gruyère cheese: 210 calories; 12 g protein; 10 g fat; 17 g carbohydrate;
   334 mg calcium; 666 mg sodium; 20 mg cholesterol; 1 g dietary fiber (this figure does not
   include broccoli; nutrition analysis not available)

Calzones

This popular Italian specialty is made easy by using prepared pizza crust dough.

1 cup part-skim ricotta cheese
3½ ounces mozzarella cheese, shredded
2 ounces Canadian-style bacon, diced
½ ounce grated Parmesan cheese
1 tablespoon *each* chopped fresh
   parsley and basil

¼ teaspoon oregano leaves
Dash pepper
1 refrigerated all-ready pizza crust
   dough (10 ounces)

Preheat oven to 450° F. In medium mixing bowl combine all ingredients except dough and mix until thoroughly combined; set aside.

Divide dough into 5 equal portions (each portion should weigh 2 ounces). Using a rolling pin, roll each portion of dough into an 8 x 6-inch rectangle, about ⅛ inch thick. Spoon ⅕ of cheese mixture (about ⅓ cup) onto center of each portion of dough; enclose filling by folding each rectangle in half, bringing one 6-inch side over to meet the other. Using the tines of a fork, press edges to seal. Using sharp knife, cut a slit in top of each calzone to allow steam to escape while baking. Transfer calzones to nonstick baking sheet and bake until lightly browned, 15 to 20 minutes.

Each serving provides: 2 Protein Exchanges; 2 Bread Exchanges
Per serving: 299 calories; 18 g protein; 11 g fat; 29 g carbohydrate; 283 mg calcium;
   621 mg sodium; 39 mg cholesterol; trace dietary fiber

Variation: Smoked Ham Calzones (Week 2) —Substitute 2 ounces cooked smoked ham for the Canadian-style bacon.

Per serving: 296 calories; 18 g protein; 11 g fat; 29 g carbohydrate; 283 mg calcium;
   623 mg sodium; 38 mg cholesterol; trace dietary fiber

French Bread Pizza

2 teaspoons olive *or* vegetable oil
½ cup *each* sliced mushrooms
 and onion
1 garlic clove, minced
½ cup *each* tomato sauce and drained
 canned Italian tomatoes, seeded and
 diced

1 tablespoon *each* chopped fresh basil
 and parsley
⅛ teaspoon pepper
¼ pound French bread
3 ounces mozzarella cheese, shredded
1 teaspoon grated Parmesan cheese

In 10-inch nonstick skillet heat oil; add mushrooms, onion, and garlic and sauté over medium heat, stirring frequently, until vegetables are tender-crisp, 1 to 2 minutes. Add tomato sauce, tomatoes, basil, parsley, and pepper; stir well to combine and cook until vegetables are tender and flavors blend, 3 to 4 minutes. Using a serrated knife, cut bread in half lengthwise. Spoon half of the tomato mixture onto cut side of each bread half; top each portion with half of the mozzarella cheese and sprinkle each with ½ teaspoon Parmesan cheese. Arrange bread halves on baking sheet and broil until cheese is melted and lightly browned.

Each serving provides: 1½ Protein Exchanges; 2 Bread Exchanges; 1 Fat Exchange;
 2 Vegetable Exchanges; 5 Optional Calories
Per serving: 381 calories; 16 g protein; 16 g fat; 44 g carbohydrate; 308 mg calcium;
 973 mg sodium; 36 mg cholesterol; 3 g dietary fiber

Cheese Enchiladas ⓒ

WEEK 5   MAKES 2 SERVINGS

1 teaspoon olive *or* vegetable oil
1 garlic clove, minced
1 cup canned Italian tomatoes (with
   liquid), pureed in blender
½ cup tomato sauce
1 teaspoon sliced hot *or* mild green
   chili *or* jalapeño pepper
½ teaspoon oregano leaves
¼ teaspoon ground cumin

⅛ teaspoon ground cloves
4 corn tortillas (6-inch diameter each)
¼ pound Colby cheese, shredded
2 pitted black olives, sliced
2 tablespoons sour cream
Garnish: Italian (flat-leaf) parsley sprig
2 chili peppers (optional)

Preheat oven to 350°F. In 1-quart saucepan heat oil; add garlic and sauté over medium heat for 1 minute *(do not brown)*. Stir in pureed tomatoes, tomato sauce, sliced chili (or jalapeño) pepper, and seasonings and cook, stirring frequently, until flavors blend, 4 to 5 minutes.

Spread 1 tablespoon tomato mixture over 1 tortilla, then arrange ¼ of cheese along center of tortilla and roll to enclose; set seam-side down in 8 x 8 x 2-inch baking pan. Repeat procedure 3 more times, using 1 tablespoon sauce mixture and an equal amount of cheese for each tortilla. Pour remaining sauce over rolled tortillas. Bake until cheese is melted and tortillas and sauce are heated through, 15 to 20 minutes.

To serve, transfer enchiladas to serving platter and top with olive slices. Serve with sour cream on the side. Garnish platter with parsley sprig and, if desired, chili peppers.

Each serving provides: 2 Protein Exchanges; 2 Bread Exchanges; 1½ Vegetable Exchanges;
   ½ Fat Exchange; 40 Optional Calories
Per serving: 462 calories; 20 g protein; 27 g fat; 38 g carbohydrate; 545 mg calcium;
   1,049 mg sodium; 60 mg cholesterol; 4 g dietary fiber

Quesadillas ⊂◑

WEEK 5   MAKES 2 SERVINGS

A classic Mexican specialty you can make in just 15 minutes. Serve it as an appetizer for a South-of-the-Border dinner, or enjoy it with a crisp green salad as a light lunch.

1 ounce *each* Monterey Jack cheese and Colby cheese, shredded

4 *each* pitted green and black olives, sliced

2 tablespoons chopped scallion (green onion)

1 tablespoon seeded and chopped hot *or* mild green chili pepper (optional)

2 flour tortillas (6-inch diameter each)

2 teaspoons vegetable oil

In small bowl combine cheeses; set aside. In separate small bowl combine olives, scallion, and, if desired, chili pepper; set aside.

Set 10-inch nonstick skillet over medium heat; add 1 tortilla and heat, turning once, just until tortilla becomes flexible, about 30 seconds on each side *(do not overcook)*. Carefully remove tortilla from pan and lay flat; sprinkle half of the cheese mixture over half of the tortilla, top cheese with half of the olive mixture, and fold tortilla in half to enclose. Repeat procedure with remaining tortilla, cheese mixture, and olive mixture.

In same skillet heat oil; add filled tortillas and cook over medium heat, turning once, until lightly browned and cheese is melted, 1 to 2 minutes on each side. Cut each tortilla in half and serve immediately.

Each serving provides: 1 Protein Exchange; 1 Bread Exchange; ⅛ Vegetable Exchange; 1 Fat Exchange; 20 Optional Calories
Per serving: 242 calories; 9 g protein; 18 g fat; 13 g carbohydrate; 258 mg calcium; 524 mg sodium; 26 mg cholesterol; 1 g dietary fiber

Tomato-Cheese Tarts ◑

WEEK 1   MAKES 2 SERVINGS, 2 TARTS EACH

Prepare these super-easy tarts in practically no time. The secret?
Use biscuit dough from the supermarket dairy case for the crust.

2 ready-to-serve refrigerated buttermilk flaky biscuits (1 ounce each)*
1 egg, beaten
1 ounce Swiss *or* Gruyère cheese, shredded

8 sun-dried tomato halves (not packed in oil), chopped

Preheat oven to 400°F. Spray four 2½-inch-diameter muffin pan cups with nonstick cooking spray. Carefully separate each biscuit into 2 equal layers of dough. Into each sprayed cup place 1 layer of biscuit dough; press into bottom and up sides of cup to form crust. In small mixing bowl combine remaining ingredients; spoon ¼ of mixture into each cup and partially fill remaining cups with water (this will prevent pan from burning and/or warping). Bake until filling is puffed and golden brown, 8 to 10 minutes. Remove pan from oven and carefully drain off water (remember, it will be boiling hot). Set pan on wire rack and allow tarts to cool slightly; remove from pan and serve warm.

Each serving provides: 1 Protein Exchange; 1 Bread Exchange; 2 Vegetable Exchanges
Per serving with Swiss cheese: 225 calories; 11 g protein; 11 g fat; 24 g carbohydrate;
   167 mg calcium; 387 mg sodium; 150 mg cholesterol; 2 g dietary fiber
With Gruyère cheese: 230 calories; 11 g protein; 11 g fat; 24 g carbohydrate;
   175 mg calcium; 397 mg sodium; 153 mg cholesterol; 2 g dietary fiber

*Keep biscuits refrigerated until ready to use. Separate dough into layers as soon as biscuits are removed from refrigerator; they will be difficult to work with if allowed to come to room temperature.

Cheese 'n' Broccoli- Topped Potato ●

WEEK 2   MAKES 2 SERVINGS, 1 POTATO HALF EACH

1 teaspoon margarine
¼ cup *each* diced onion and red bell pepper
½ teaspoon all-purpose flour
½ cup skim *or* nonfat milk
1 cup broccoli florets, blanched

2 ounces sharp Cheddar cheese, shredded
1 baking potato (6 ounces), baked and cut in half lengthwise (hot)

In 9-inch nonstick skillet melt margarine; add onion and pepper and sauté over medium heat until tender-crisp, about 2 minutes. Sprinkle flour over vegetables and stir quickly to combine; cook, stirring constantly, for 1 minute. Reduce heat to low and gradually stir in milk; continuing to stir, cook until mixture thickens slightly, about 1 minute. Stir in broccoli and cheese and cook, stirring constantly, until cheese is melted.

To serve, onto each of 2 plates set 1 potato half, cut-side up; score pulp in each potato half by making several cuts about ⅛ inch deep in one direction, then several cuts in the opposite direction to form a diamond pattern. Top each potato half with half of the vegetable-cheese mixture; serve immediately.

Each serving provides: 1 Protein Exchange; 1 Bread Exchange; 1½ Vegetable Exchanges; ½ Fat Exchange; ¼ Milk Exchange; 3 Optional Calories
Per serving: 247 calories; 14 g protein; 12 g fat; 24 g carbohydrate; 325 mg calcium; 252 mg sodium; 31 mg cholesterol; 0.3 g dietary fiber (this figure does not include broccoli florets; nutrition analysis not available)

Cheese 'n' Ham-Topped Biscuits ⊖◑

WEEK 2   MAKES 2 SERVINGS

A lovely luncheon dish that is ready in less than 30 minutes!

2 ready-to-bake refrigerated buttermilk flaky biscuits (1 ounce each)
1 teaspoon margarine
¼ cup *each* thinly sliced scallions (green onions) and thinly sliced mushrooms

1½ ounces finely diced boiled ham
½ teaspoon all-purpose flour
½ cup skim *or* nonfat milk
2½ ounces Swiss cheese, shredded

Preheat oven to 400° F. Place biscuits on nonstick baking sheet and, using a 1½-inch-diameter round cookie cutter or a knife, cut a circle in center of each biscuit, being careful not to cut through bottom of biscuit. Bake until biscuits are puffed and browned, 8 to 10 minutes. Remove biscuits from oven and, using a fork, carefully remove top of center circle from each biscuit; set large biscuit "rings" and center circles aside.

In 9-inch nonstick skillet melt margarine; add scallions, mushrooms, and ham and sauté over medium heat until vegetables are tender-crisp, about 2 minutes. Sprinkle flour over vegetable mixture and stir quickly to combine; cook, stirring constantly, for 1 minute. Reduce heat to low and gradually stir in milk; continuing to stir, cook until mixture thickens slightly, about 1 minute. Stir in cheese and cook, stirring constantly, until cheese is melted.

To serve, onto each of 2 plates place 1 large biscuit "ring"; top each with half of the cheese mixture, then 1 center biscuit circle.

Each serving provides: 2 Protein Exchanges; 1 Bread Exchange; ½ Vegetable Exchange; ½ Fat Exchange; ¼ Milk Exchange; 3 Optional Calories
Per serving: 295 calories; 19 g protein; 16 g fat; 19 g carbohydrate; 426 mg calcium; 698 mg sodium; 45 mg cholesterol; 1 g dietary fiber

Caesar Salad ◑

WEEK 5 \ MAKES 2 SERVINGS

1 garlic clove, slightly crushed
4 cups torn romaine lettuce leaves
Dash pepper
2 tablespoons water
2 anchovy fillets, chopped
1 tablespoon *each* lemon juice and
  red wine vinegar
2 teaspoons *each* Dijon-style mustard
  and olive oil

½ teaspoon Worcestershire sauce
1 egg, unshelled
Boiling water
2 slices Italian bread (½ ounce each),
  toasted and cut into cubes
1 ounce grated Parmesan cheese

In large salad bowl rub garlic over inside surface of bowl; discard garlic. Add lettuce and pepper and toss to combine; set aside.

In small mixing bowl combine water, anchovies, lemon juice, vinegar, mustard, oil, and Worcestershire sauce and mix until thoroughly combined; set aside.

Place egg into small heatproof bowl; slowly pour in boiling water to cover. Let stand 3 minutes; drain off water. Crack egg into small bowl and beat lightly. Add to lettuce mixture along with anchovy mixture and toss to thoroughly coat. Top salad with bread cubes; sprinkle with cheese and serve immediately.

Each serving provides: 1 Protein Exchange; ½ Bread Exchange; 4 Vegetable Exchanges;
  1 Fat Exchange; 5 Optional Calories
Per serving: 222 calories; 13 g protein; 13 g fat; 14 g carbohydrate; 265 mg calcium;
  703 mg sodium; 151 mg cholesterol; 3 g dietary fiber

Chunky Cheese Salad

WEEK 2   MAKES 2 SERVINGS

A unique salad that uses the creamy smoothness of buttermilk rather than mayonnaise in the dressing. You'll love this sweet and tangy taste combination.

1 small apple (about ¼ pound), cored, pared, and diced
½ cup *each* grated carrot and diced celery
2 ounces Jarlsberg *or* Swiss cheese, diced
1½ ounces *each* diced baked ham and roast turkey breast

¼ cup buttermilk
2 teaspoons Dijon-style mustard
8 lettuce leaves
Dash pepper

In medium mixing bowl combine all ingredients except lettuce and pepper, tossing to combine. Line serving bowl with lettuce leaves; top with cheese mixture and sprinkle with pepper. Serve immediately or cover with plastic wrap and refrigerate until chilled.

Each serving provides: 2½ Protein Exchanges; 2 Vegetable Exchanges; ½ Fruit Exchange; 15 Optional Calories
Per serving with Jarlsberg cheese: 232 calories; 20 g protein; 9 g fat; 16 g carbohydrate; 283 mg calcium; 617 mg sodium; 36 mg cholesterol; 2 g dietary fiber
With Swiss cheese: 239 calories; 21 g protein; 10 g fat; 16 g carbohydrate; 356 mg calcium; 565 mg sodium; 53 mg cholesterol; 2 g dietary fiber

Cheese-Filled Cucumber Cups ◐

WEEK 8   MAKES 2 SERVINGS, 4 FILLED CUCUMBER CUPS EACH

1 medium cucumber
  (about 7 x 2 inches)
1 ounce Gorgonzola cheese
  (at room temperature)

1 tablespoon whipped butter
¼ ounce ground walnuts

Trim ends of cucumber. Using tines of fork, score cucumber; cut crosswise into 8 slices, about ¾ inch thick each. Using a melon baller or teaspoon, scoop out a small amount of seeds from center of each slice, being careful not to go all the way through; set aside. Using a fork, in small bowl mash cheese; add butter and mix until smooth. Stir in nuts. Spoon ⅛ of the nut mixture into center of each cucumber slice. Arrange on serving platter; cover with plastic wrap and refrigerate until ready to serve.

Each serving provides: ½ Protein Exchange; 1 Vegetable Exchange; 55 Optional Calories
Per serving: 109 calories; 4 g protein; 9 g fat; 3 g carbohydrate; 91 mg calcium;
  229 mg sodium; 18 mg cholesterol; 1 g dietary fiber

Mozzarella, Tomato, and Arugula Salad

WEEK 1   MAKES 2 SERVINGS

1 medium red bell pepper
1 tablespoon *each* water and red wine
    vinegar *or* balsamic vinegar
2 teaspoons olive oil
Dash *each* salt and pepper
1 cup arugula leaves*

2 ounces mozzarella cheese, cut into
    10 equal slices
2 large plum tomatoes, cut lengthwise
    into 10 equal slices
Garnish: small basil leaves

Preheat broiler. On baking sheet lined with heavy-duty foil broil pepper 3 inches from heat source, turning frequently, until charred on all sides; let stand until cool enough to handle, 15 to 20 minutes.

Peel pepper; remove and discard stem ends and seeds. Cut pepper into thin strips and set aside.

In small bowl or a jar with tight-fitting cover combine remaining ingredients except arugula, cheese, tomato slices, and garnish; mix or cover and shake well.

Line outside edge of serving platter with arugula; alternately arrange cheese and tomato slices in a circle over arugula, overlapping slices slightly. Arrange roasted pepper strips in center of platter. Pour dressing over cheese, tomato, and pepper strips; garnish salad with basil leaves and serve immediately.

Each serving provides: 1 Protein Exchange; 3 Vegetable Exchanges; 1 Fat Exchange
Per serving: 141 calories; 7 g protein; 11 g fat, 5 g carbohydrate; 173 mg calcium;
    184 mg sodium; 22 mg cholesterol; 1 g dietary fiber

*Lettuce leaves can be substituted for the arugula.

Cheese Crisps

WEEK 5   MAKES 8 SERVINGS, 5 CRACKERS EACH

These thin cheese-flavored crackers are wonderful served with drinks, or try them for a crunchy afternoon or evening snack. Store leftovers in an airtight container.

½ pound Swiss *or* Gruyère cheese, shredded
½ cup whipped butter
¾ cup all-purpose flour

⅛ teaspoon *each* ground red pepper and powdered mustard
16 pimiento-stuffed green olives, minced

Using electric mixer at low speed, in medium mixing bowl combine cheese and butter and beat until combined; add flour and seasonings and continue beating until mixture is thoroughly combined and sticks together. Add olives and stir to combine. Turn dough out onto work surface and shape into a log about 10 inches long and 1½ inches in diameter; wrap in plastic wrap and freeze for 1 hour or refrigerate overnight.

Preheat oven to 400° F. Using a sharp knife, cut half of the dough crosswise into twenty ¼-inch-thick slices. Arrange slices on non-stick cookie sheet and bake until golden, 10 to 12 minutes. Remove cookie sheet from oven and let crackers cool slightly, 1 to 2 minutes. Using a spatula, transfer crackers to wire rack and let cool completely. Repeat procedure, using remaining dough and making 20 more crackers.

Each serving provides: 1 Protein Exchange; ½ Bread Exchange; 60 Optional Calories
Per serving with Swiss cheese: 209 calories; 9 g protein; 15 g fat; 10 g carbohydrate;
    281 mg calcium; 301 mg sodium; 42 mg cholesterol; 1 g dietary fiber
With Gruyère cheese: 219 calories; 10 g protein; 16 g fat; 9 g carbohydrate; 295 mg calcium;
    322 mg sodium; 47 mg cholesterol; 1 g dietary fiber

Cobb Club Sandwich

WEEK 5   MAKES 1 SERVING

3 slices reduced-calorie white, wheat,
   or rye bread (40 calories per slice),
   lightly toasted
2 teaspoons reduced-calorie
   mayonnaise
1 ounce thinly sliced cooked turkey
   breast

1 egg, hard-cooked and sliced
1 lettuce leaf
2 tomato slices
⅛ avocado (1 ounce), pared and sliced
½ ounce blue cheese, crumbled

Spread 1 slice of bread with mayonnaise and set aside. Arrange turkey on second slice of bread; top with egg slices and third slice of bread, then top third slice of bread with lettuce leaf, tomato slices, avocado, and cheese. Set reserved bread slice over cheese, mayonnaise-side down. Secure sandwich with two frilled toothpicks and cut diagonally in half.

Each serving provides: 2½ Protein Exchanges; 1½ Bread Exchanges; 1 Vegetable
   Exchange; 1 Fat Exchange; 50 Optional Calories
Per serving: 327 calories; 24 g protein; 13 g fat; 30 g carbohydrate; 175 mg calcium;
   648 mg sodium; 308 mg cholesterol; 0.3 g dietary fiber

Four-Cheese Omelet

Omelets aren't just for breakfast anymore. This savory mixture can be served with a salad, a glass of mineral water, and fresh fruit for a light but elegant dinner.

2 teaspoons margarine
1 cup quartered mushrooms
½ cup sliced thoroughly washed leeks
   (white portion only)
1½ teaspoons minced shallot *or* onion
2 eggs
½ cup skim *or* nonfat milk
¾ ounce Gruyère cheese, shredded

½ ounce *each* Gorgonzola and
   mozzarella cheese, shredded
¼ ounce grated Parmesan cheese
Dash *each* salt, white pepper, and
   ground nutmeg
Garnish: 2 teaspoons chopped fresh
   Italian (flat-leaf) parsley

Preheat oven to 400° F. In 9-inch nonstick skillet that has a metal or removable handle melt margarine; add mushrooms, leeks, and shallot (or onion) and sauté until tender-crisp, 3 to 4 minutes. In small mixing bowl beat together eggs and milk; stir in cheeses and seasonings. Pour egg mixture over vegetable mixture in skillet and cook, tilting pan, until bottom of egg mixture is set and lightly browned, about 1 minute. Transfer skillet to oven and bake until top of omelet is set, about 5 minutes. Transfer omelet to serving platter and cut in half; serve garnished with parsley.

Each serving provides: 2 Protein Exchanges; 1½ Vegetable Exchanges; 1 Fat Exchange;
   ¼ Milk Exchange
Per serving: 266 calories; 17 g protein; 18 g fat; 10 g carbohydrate; 354 mg calcium;
   445 mg sodium; 301 mg cholesterol; 1 g dietary fiber

Southwest Scramble

WEEK 5   MAKES 2 SERVINGS

2 eggs
2 tablespoons sour cream
1 tablespoon minced fresh cilantro
  (Chinese parsley) *or* parsley
2 teaspoons olive *or* vegetable oil
¼ cup diced onion
1 teaspoon seeded and minced
  jalapeño pepper
1 small garlic clove, mashed

½ medium tomato, blanched, peeled,
  seeded, and chopped
⅛ avocado (1 ounce), pared and diced
Dash *each* salt and pepper
2 flour tortillas (6-inch diameter each),
  heated
1 ounce Monterey Jack *or* Cheddar
  cheese, shredded

Using a fork, in small mixing bowl beat together eggs, sour cream, and cilantro (or parsley) until combined; set aside. In 8-inch nonstick skillet heat oil; add onion, jalapeño pepper, and garlic and sauté until onion is translucent, 1 to 2 minutes. Stir in tomato and cook, stirring occasionally, for 1 minute. Pour in egg mixture and cook, stirring frequently with a wooden spoon to allow uncooked portions to flow to bottom of pan, until eggs are almost set and slightly creamy; stir in avocado, salt, and pepper. Continue cooking until eggs are set and form large soft curds.

To serve, spoon ½ of egg mixture onto center of each tortilla; sprinkle each with ½ ounce cheese and roll to enclose. Secure each tortilla with a toothpick.

Each serving provides: 1½ Protein Exchanges; 1 Bread Exchange; ¾ Vegetable Exchange;
  1 Fat Exchange; 60 Optional Calories
Per serving with Monterey Jack cheese: 306 calories; 13 g protein; 21 g fat;
  18 g carbohydrate; 204 mg calcium; 303 mg sodium; 293 mg cholesterol; 1 g dietary fiber
With Cheddar cheese: 311 calories; 13 g protein; 22 g fat; 18 g carbohydrate;
  200 mg calcium; 375 mg sodium; 295 mg cholesterol; 1 g dietary fiber

Variation: Yogurt Scramble — Substitute 2 tablespoons plain low-fat yogurt for the sour cream. Decrease Optional Calories to 35.

Per serving with Monterey Jack cheese: 285 calories; 13 g protein; 18 g fat;
  18 g carbohydrate; 213 mg calcium; 366 mg sodium; 287 mg cholesterol; 1 g dietary fiber
With Cheddar cheese: 289 calories; 13 g protein; 19 g fat; 18 g carbohydrate;
  210 mg calcium; 378 mg sodium; 290 mg cholesterol; 1 g dietary fiber

Italian Semolina Bake

WEEK 5   MAKES 4 SERVINGS

1 tablespoon whipped butter
1 cup *each* chopped mushrooms and
   well-drained thawed frozen chopped
   spinach
½ cup seeded and chopped tomato
2 tablespoons chopped fresh basil
1 cup low-fat milk (1% milk fat)
½ cup part-skim ricotta cheese

2 eggs
⅓ cup nonfat dry milk powder
¼ teaspoon salt
⅛ teaspoon white pepper
1 cup cooked couscous (semolina)
2 ounces mozzarella cheese, shredded
1 tablespoon grated Parmesan cheese

Preheat oven to 350° F. In 10-inch nonstick skillet melt butter; add mushrooms and sauté over high heat, stirring frequently, until lightly browned, 1 to 2 minutes. Add spinach, tomato, and basil, and cook, continuing to stir, until heated through, 1 to 2 minutes longer; set aside. In medium mixing bowl beat together low-fat milk, ricotta cheese, eggs, milk powder, salt, and pepper until milk powder is dissolved; add spinach mixture and remaining ingredients and stir until thoroughly combined.

Spray 12 x 8-inch baking dish with nonstick cooking spray; transfer semolina mixture to dish and bake for 40 to 45 minutes (until top is lightly browned and a knife, inserted in center, comes out clean).

Each serving provides: 1½ Protein Exchanges; ½ Bread Exchange; 1¼ Vegetable
   Exchanges; ½ Milk Exchange; 25 Optional Calories
Per serving: 246 calories; 17 g protein; 11 g fat; 20 g carbohydrate; 411 mg calcium;
   402 mg sodium; 166 mg cholesterol; 2 g dietary fiber

Swiss Chard Bake ⓒ

WEEK 5   MAKES 4 SERVINGS

This marvelous meatless entrée takes less than a half hour to prepare. While it bakes, you can make a salad, set the table, and relax a bit.

1 tablespoon plus 1 teaspoon olive
   or vegetable oil
1 cup diced onions
1 tablespoon minced fresh chili
   or jalapeño pepper
1 small garlic clove, minced
4 cups thoroughly washed and drained
   Swiss chard, chopped

Dash *each* salt and white pepper
4 eggs
½ cup plain low-fat yogurt
4 ounces Monterey Jack *or* sharp
   Cheddar cheese, shredded

Preheat oven to 350°F. In 10-inch nonstick skillet heat oil; add onions, chili (or jalapeño) pepper, and garlic and sauté until onions are lightly browned, 2 to 3 minutes. Add Swiss chard and sprinkle with salt and pepper; cover skillet and cook over medium-high heat until wilted, 3 to 5 minutes. Remove skillet from heat and let cool slightly.

In large mixing bowl beat together eggs and yogurt; stir in Swiss chard mixture and cheese. Spray 8 x 8 x 2-inch baking pan with nonstick cooking spray; add Swiss chard mixture and bake until mixture is set and golden, 25 to 30 minutes. Remove from oven and let stand 5 minutes before cutting.

Each serving provides: 2 Protein Exchanges; 2½ Vegetable Exchanges; 1 Fat Exchange;
   ¼ Milk Exchange
Per serving with Monterey Jack cheese: 264 calories; 16 g protein; 19 g fat;
   7 g carbohydrate; 321 mg calcium; 351 mg sodium; 301 mg cholesterol; 0.3 g dietary fiber
   (this figure does not include Swiss chard; nutrition analysis not available)
With Cheddar cheese: 273 calories; 16 g protein; 20 g fat; 8 g carbohydrate; 314 mg calcium;
   375 mg sodium; 305 mg cholesterol; 0.3 g dietary fiber (this figure does not include
   Swiss chard; nutrition analysis not available)

Western Potato Pie ☻

WEEK 2   MAKES 4 SERVINGS

A wonderful way to use leftover potato.

1 tablespoon plus 1 teaspoon vegetable
  oil
6 ounces pared cooked potato, diced
½ cup *each* diced green bell pepper
  and chopped onion
4 eggs
¾ cup buttermilk

¼ teaspoon salt
⅛ teaspoon white pepper
¼ pound Swiss *or* Muenster cheese,
  shredded
1 medium tomato, sliced
1 tablespoon grated Parmesan cheese

Preheat oven to 350°F. In 10-inch nonstick skillet heat oil; add potato, bell pepper, and onion and sauté over medium-high heat, stirring frequently, until vegetables are tender and potato is lightly browned, 2 to 3 minutes. Spray 9-inch pie plate with nonstick cooking spray; spread potato mixture in bottom of pie plate.

In medium mixing bowl beat together eggs, buttermilk, salt, and pepper; pour over potato mixture and sprinkle with Swiss (or Muenster) cheese. Arrange tomato slices over cheese, overlapping slices slightly if necessary; sprinkle with Parmesan cheese. Bake 35 to 40 minutes (until lightly browned and a knife, inserted in center, comes out clean). Remove from oven and let stand 10 minutes before slicing.

Each serving provides: 2 Protein Exchanges; ½ Bread Exchange; 1 Vegetable Exchange;
  1 Fat Exchange; ¼ Milk Exchange; 10 Optional Calories
Per serving with Swiss cheese: 302 calories; 17 g protein; 19 g fat; 16 g carbohydrate;
  384 mg calcium; 355 mg sodium; 303 mg cholesterol; 1 g dietary fiber
With Muenster cheese: 300 calories; 16 g protein; 20 g fat; 15 g carbohydrate;
  314 mg calcium; 459 mg sodium; 304 mg cholesterol; 1 g dietary fiber

Rum-Raisin Cheesecake

WEEK 5   MAKES 8 SERVINGS

Microwave tip: Measure the rum in a microwave-safe liquid 1-cup measure. Add the raisins, then microwave on High (100% power) for about 10 seconds. Remove from the oven and let stand until the raisins are plumped. No need to dirty a saucepan!

¼ cup dark rum
½ cup dark raisins
16 graham crackers (2½-inch squares), made into fine crumbs
2 tablespoons plus 2 teaspoons margarine, softened
⅛ teaspoon ground cinnamon
2 cups cottage cheese, pressed through sieve

2 eggs
⅓ cup granulated sugar
3 tablespoons sour cream
2 tablespoons *each* all-purpose flour and half-and-half (blend of milk and cream)
1 teaspoon *each* grated orange peel and vanilla extract

In small saucepan heat rum over low heat until mixture simmers; add raisins, remove from heat, and let stand until raisins plump.

While raisins are plumping, prepare crust. Preheat oven to 400° F. Spray an 8-inch springform pan with nonstick cooking spray. In small mixing bowl combine crumbs, margarine, and cinnamon, mixing thoroughly; using the back of a spoon, press crumb mixture over bottom and 1 inch up sides of sprayed pan. Bake until crust is crisp and brown, 3 to 5 minutes. Remove from oven and let cool.

In large mixing bowl combine remaining ingredients except raisin mixture, stirring until blended; add raisin mixture and stir to combine. Transfer cheese mixture to cooled crust and bake until mixture is just set and golden, 40 to 45 minutes. Transfer pan to wire rack and let cool completely; serve immediately or cover with plastic wrap and refrigerate until ready to serve. To serve, carefully remove sides of pan and cut cake into 8 equal wedges.

Each serving provides: 1 Protein Exchange; 1 Bread Exchange; 1 Fat Exchange; ½ Fruit Exchange; 85 Optional Calories
Per serving: 263 calories; 10 g protein; 10 g fat; 29 g carbohydrate; 61 mg calcium; 375 mg sodium; 80 mg cholesterol; 2 g dietary fiber

Strawberry, Chocolate, and Cheese Parfait ◐

WEEK 8	MAKES 2 SERVINGS

1 cup strawberries, sliced
1 tablespoon strawberry* liqueur
½ cup part-skim ricotta cheese

1½ teaspoons *each* granulated sugar
and whipping cream
½ ounce mini chocolate chips

In small mixing bowl combine strawberries and liqueur; set aside. Using a fork, in separate small mixing bowl combine cheese, sugar, and cream; fold in chips. Into each of 2 long-stemmed glasses or individual dessert dishes spoon half of the cheese mixture, then top each with half of the strawberry mixture. Serve immediately or cover and refrigerate until chilled.

Each serving provides: 1 Protein Exchange; ½ Fruit Exchange; 90 Optional Calories
Per serving: 189 calories; 8 g protein; 9 g fat; 18 g carbohydrate; 195 mg calcium;
    84 mg sodium; 24 mg cholesterol; 1 g dietary fiber

*Raspberry or cherry liqueur may be substituted for the strawberry liqueur.

Cottage Fruit 'n' Custard Cake ⓒ

WEEK 1   MAKES 8 SERVINGS

6 ounces (2½ cups) cornflake crumbs
2 tablespoons plus 2 teaspoons
   margarine
Dash ground cinnamon
1⅓ cups cottage cheese
4 eggs

3 tablespoons all-purpose flour
2 tablespoons granulated sugar
1 teaspoon vanilla extract
½ teaspoon grated orange peel
1½ pounds oranges, peeled and
   sectioned

Preheat oven to 350° F. In small mixing bowl combine crumbs, margarine, and cinnamon, mixing thoroughly. Spray 9 inch springform pan with nonstick cooking spray; press crumb mixture over bottom and 1 inch up sides of pan. Bake until golden, about 5 minutes. Remove pan from oven and let cool slightly.

Using electric mixer at medium speed, in medium mixing bowl combine remaining ingredients except oranges and beat until combined. Arrange orange sections evenly over cooled crust; carefully pour cheese mixture over orange sections. Bake until cheese mixture is set and golden brown, 40 to 45 minutes. Transfer pan to wire rack and let cool completely; serve immediately or cover lightly and refrigerate until ready to serve. To serve, carefully remove sides of pan and cut cake into 8 equal wedges.

Each serving provides: 1 Protein Exchange; 1 Bread Exchange; 1 Fat Exchange;
   ½ Fruit Exchange; 25 Optional Calories
Per serving: 245 calories; 10 g protein; 8 g fat; 32 g carbohydrate; 65 mg calcium;
   484 mg sodium; 142 mg cholesterol; 1 g dietary fiber

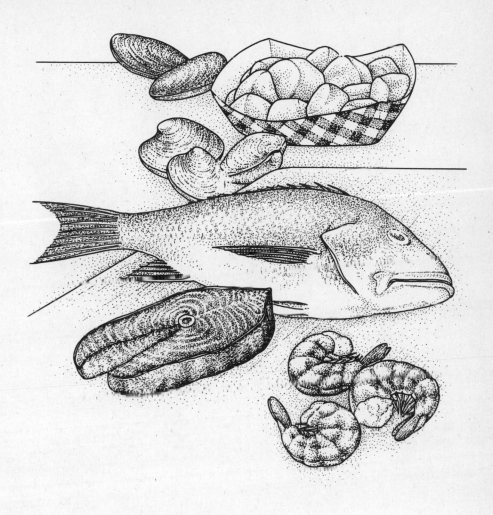

Fish

From the briny deep come flavorful seafood creations you'll savor time and time again. Who can resist the lure of Poached Salmon with Mint Vinaigrette or Scallop and Crab Gratin? Even confirmed landlubbers will rave about our creative cast of seafood sensations.

191

Southwest Skillet Fillets ◐

Avocado, olives, and chili pepper add spice to the mild flavor of fish.

3 tablespoons all-purpose flour
Dash *each* salt and pepper
2 fish fillets (¼ pound each)
2 teaspoons olive *or* vegetable oil
1 teaspoon whipped butter
½ cup *each* thinly sliced onion and
   mushrooms
1 tablespoon minced fresh chili pepper
1 small garlic clove, minced
2 large plum tomatoes, blanched,
   peeled, seeded, and chopped

⅛ very ripe avocado (about 1 ounce),
   pared and diced
4 pimiento-stuffed green olives, sliced
1 tablespoon *each* chopped fresh
   cilantro (Chinese parsley) *or* parsley,
   drained capers, and dry vermouth
Garnish: 2 lime wedges

On sheet of wax paper or a paper plate combine flour, salt, and pepper. Pat fillets dry and dredge in flour mixture, coating both sides and being sure to use all of mixture.

In 9-inch nonstick skillet heat oil; add fish and cook over medium-high heat, turning once, until browned on both sides, about 2 minutes on each side. Transfer to serving platter and keep warm.

In same skillet melt butter; add onion, mushrooms, chili pepper, and garlic and sauté until vegetables are tender-crisp, 2 to 3 minutes. Add remaining ingredients except garnish, stir to combine, and cook until flavors blend and mixture is heated through, about 5 minutes. Spoon over fish fillets and garnish with lime.

Each serving provides: 3 Protein Exchanges; ½ Bread Exchange; 2 Vegetable Exchanges;
   1 Fat Exchange; 50 Optional Calories
Per serving: 264 calories; 24 g protein; 10 g fat; 18 g carbohydrate; 49 mg calcium;
   454 mg sodium; 57 mg cholesterol; 2 g dietary fiber

Bluefish and
Potato Casserole ☺◑

WEEK 2   MAKES 2 SERVINGS

A hearty casserole that is out of the oven in less than half an hour.

2 teaspoons olive *or* vegetable oil
1½ teaspoons margarine
2 garlic cloves, minced
2 tablespoons chopped fresh parsley
1 tablespoon lemon juice
6 ounces very thinly sliced all-purpose
   potato

½ cup very thinly sliced red onion
   (separated into rings)
¼ teaspoon salt
⅛ teaspoon pepper
2 bluefish fillets (¼ pound each)

Preheat oven to 450° F. In small saucepan combine oil and margarine and heat until margarine is melted; add garlic and sauté briefly, just until garlic is lightly browned. Remove from heat and add parsley and lemon juice; stir to combine. In medium mixing bowl combine potato, onion, salt, and pepper; add half of the oil mixture and toss to coat.

Spray 8-inch pie plate with nonstick cooking spray and arrange potato mixture evenly in bottom of plate. Bake for 15 minutes. Arrange bluefish fillets over potato mixture; brush fillets with remaining oil mixture, using half of mixture for each fillet, and bake until fish flakes easily when tested with a fork, about 10 minutes longer.

Each serving provides: 3 Protein Exchanges; 1 Bread Exchange; ½ Vegetable Exchange;
   1½ Fat Exchanges; 10 Optional Calories
Per serving: 294 calories; 25 g protein; 12 g fat; 20 g carbohydrate; 38 mg calcium;
  381 mg sodium; 67 mg cholesterol; 2 g dietary fiber

Halibut Steaks in Vegetable-Wine Sauce

WEEK 5   MAKES 2 SERVINGS

½ cup *each* diced onion, diced yellow
    bell pepper, and bottled clam juice
¼ cup *each* thinly sliced celery and dry
    white table wine
½ small garlic clove, minced
½ teaspoon thyme leaves
1 bay leaf
2 boneless halibut steaks (5 ounces
    each)

1 tablespoon margarine
1½ teaspoons all-purpose flour
1 large plum tomato, blanched, peeled,
    seeded, and chopped
Dash *each* salt and pepper
Garnish: Italian (flat-leaf) parsley sprig

In 10-inch nonstick skillet combine onion, bell pepper, clam juice, celery, wine, garlic, and seasonings and cook over high heat until mixture comes to a full boil; add halibut. Reduce heat to low, cover, and let simmer until fish flakes easily when tested with a fork, about 10 minutes. Using a spatula, carefully transfer fish to serving platter; cover and keep warm. Reserve ½ cup poaching liquid.

In same skillet melt margarine over medium heat; sprinkle with flour and stir quickly to combine; cook, stirring constantly, for 1 minute. Gradually stir in reserved poaching liquid. Reduce heat to medium-low and cook, stirring constantly, until mixture thickens slightly, 1 to 2 minutes. Add tomato, salt, and pepper and let simmer until flavors blend, about 5 minutes; pour sauce over halibut and garnish with parsley. Serve immediately.

Each serving provides: 4 Protein Exchanges; 1¾ Vegetable Exchanges; 1½ Fat Exchanges;
    50 Optional Calories
Per serving: 266 calories; 31 g protein; 9 g fat; 8 g carbohydrate; 111 mg calcium;
    357 mg sodium; 45 mg cholesterol; 1 g dietary fiber

Blackened Redfish

WEEK 1   MAKES 2 SERVINGS

1 tablespoon paprika
1 teaspoon *each* garlic and onion
  powder
½ teaspoon *each* thyme leaves,
  oregano leaves, pepper, and ground
  red pepper

1 tablespoon vegetable oil
1 redfish *or* red snapper fillet (½ pound)
Garnish: 2 lemon wedges

On sheet of wax paper or a paper plate combine seasonings and mix thoroughly; set aside. In 10-inch skillet heat oil over high heat until oil begins to smoke, 3 to 4 minutes. While oil is heating, dredge fish in paprika mixture, coating both sides evenly; carefully place fish in skillet and cook until bottom is charred, 2 to 3 minutes; using a spatula, carefully turn fish over and cook until charred and cooked through, 2 to 3 minutes longer (depending on thickness of fillet). Transfer fish to serving platter and garnish with lemon wedges.

Each serving provides: 3 Protein Exchanges; 1½ Fat Exchanges
Per serving with redfish: 190 calories; 22 g protein; 9 g fat; 5 g carbohydrate;
  148 mg calcium; 88 mg sodium; 48 mg cholesterol; dietary fiber data not available
With red snapper: 197 calories; 24 g protein; 9 g fat; 5 g carbohydrate; 63 mg calcium;
  75 mg sodium; 42 mg cholesterol; dietary fiber data not available

Gingered Salmon

WEEK 2   MAKES 2 SERVINGS

1 tablespoon *each* teriyaki sauce
   and dry sherry
1½ teaspoons lemon juice
½ teaspoon grated pared gingerroot

2 salmon steaks (5 ounces each)
6 chives
½ *each* lemon and lime, thinly sliced

In glass or stainless-steel shallow bowl large enough to hold salmon steaks in a single layer combine teriyaki sauce, sherry, lemon juice, and gingerroot; add salmon and turn to coat with marinade. Cover with plastic wrap and refrigerate at least 1 hour or overnight, turning fish occasionally.

Preheat grill or broiler. Remove salmon from marinade, strain marinade mixture, discarding solids. Spray rack with nonstick cooking spray and grill salmon over hot coals (or broil) basting with marinade and turning once, until fish flakes easily when tested with a fork, 6 to 8 minutes on each side (exact timing will depend upon thickness of steaks).

To serve, transfer salmon to serving platter; top each steak with 3 chives and garnish platter with lemon and lime slices.

Each serving provides: 3 Protein Exchanges; 10 Optional Calories
Per serving: 233 calories; 29 g protein; 9 g fat; 7 g carbohydrate; 45 mg calcium;
   410 mg sodium; 78 mg cholesterol; 0.1 g dietary fiber

Poached Salmon with Mint Vinaigrette

WEEK 1   MAKES 2 SERVINGS

2 salmon steaks (5 ounces each)
1 small very ripe plum tomato,
    blanched, peeled, seeded, and
    chopped
2 tablespoons chopped fresh mint
1 tablespoon *each* chopped shallot
    (or onion), freshly squeezed lime
    juice, and raspberry vinegar

2 teaspoons olive *or* vegetable oil
1 garlic clove, minced
¼ cup water

Set fish in single layer in shallow container (not aluminum*); set aside. In small mixing bowl combine remaining ingredients except water, stirring well; pour over fish and turn once to coat. Cover with plastic wrap and refrigerate overnight or at least 30 minutes.

Drain salmon, reserving marinade. In 10-inch skillet combine marinade mixture and water and cook over medium heat until mixture begins to simmer. Reduce heat to low, add salmon, cover skillet, and cook until fish flakes easily when tested with a fork, 6 to 8 minutes (depending on thickness of steaks). Transfer salmon to serving platter and top with pan juices.

Each serving provides: 3 Protein Exchanges; ¼ Vegetable Exchange; 1 Fat Exchange
Per serving: 213 calories; 23 g protein; 12 g fat; 3 g carbohydrate; 22 mg calcium;
    52 mg sodium; 62 mg cholesterol; 0.2 g dietary fiber

*It's best to marinate in glass or stainless-steel containers; acidic ingredients such as lime juice and vinegar may react with aluminum, causing color and flavor changes in food.

Stacked Salmon Hors d'Oeuvres ◑

WEEK 4	MAKES 4 SERVINGS, 1 HORS D'OEUVRE EACH

These hors d'oeuvres are so easy to prepare, and while they are chilling in the refrigerator you're free to get ready for your guests.

2 ounces cooked *or* drained canned
  salmon
2 tablespoons whipped cream cheese
2 teaspoons chopped red onion
1 teaspoon *each* drained capers and
  lemon juice

Dash *each* hot sauce, salt, and pepper
4 slices reduced-calorie white *or* wheat
  bread (40 calories per slice)

In work bowl of food processor, combine all ingredients except bread and process until thoroughly combined.

Onto 1 slice of bread spread ⅓ of salmon mixture, then top with second slice of bread; repeat procedure 2 more times, ending with a slice of bread. Wrap sandwich in plastic wrap and refrigerate for at least 30 minutes.

To serve, using a serrated knife, cut sandwich into quarters.

Each serving provides: ½ Protein Exchange; ½ Bread Exchange; 15 Optional Calories
Per serving with fresh salmon: 87 calories; 7 g protein; 3 g fat; 9 g carbohydrate;
  27 mg calcium; 175 mg sodium; 16 mg cholesterol; trace dietary fiber
With canned salmon: 77 calories; 5 g protein; 2 g fat; 9 g carbohydrate; 59 mg calcium;
  235 mg sodium; 10 mg cholesterol; trace dietary fiber

Seafood-Rice Salad

Make last-minute preparation easy by cooking the rice and shrimp for this attractive salad in advance.

1½ cups cooked long-grain rice
1 cup sliced pared cucumber
½ cup *each* shredded carrot and
   shredded pared daikon (Japanese
   radish) *or* red radish
¼ avocado (2 ounces), pared and diced
2 ounces *each* smoked salmon (lox),
   cut into thin strips, and shelled and
   deveined cooked small shrimp

¼ cup rice vinegar
2 teaspoons Chinese sesame oil
1 teaspoon *each* honey, warmed, and
   prepared horseradish
Dash *each* salt and pepper
1 cup thoroughly washed and drained
   spinach leaves

In medium mixing bowl combine rice, cucumber, carrot, daikon (or red radish), avocado, salmon, and shrimp. In 1-cup liquid measure combine remaining ingredients except spinach, stirring well; pour vinegar mixture over rice mixture and toss to thoroughly coat.

   To serve, line a serving platter with spinach and top with salad.

Each serving provides: 2 Protein Exchanges; 1½ Bread Exchanges;
   3 Vegetable Exchanges; 1 Fat Exchange; 60 Optional Calories
Per serving: 354 calories; 16 g protein; 10 g fat; 50 g carbohydrate; 87 mg calcium;
   402 mg sodium; 62 mg cholesterol; 3 g dietary fiber

Fillet Rolls with Crab Sauce

WEEK 5   MAKES 2 SERVINGS

½ cup chopped onion, divided
2 tablespoons *each* bottled clam juice
   and water
1½ teaspoons *each* dry white table wine
   and lemon juice
3 black peppercorns
1 small bay leaf
2 sole *or* flounder fillets (3 ounces each)

Dash *each* salt and pepper
1 tablespoon whipped butter
1½ teaspoons all-purpose flour
2 tablespoons half-and-half (blend of
   milk and cream)
2 ounces thawed and thoroughly
   drained frozen crabmeat, flaked

In 9-inch skillet combine ¼ cup onion, the clam juice, water, wine, lemon juice, peppercorns, and bay leaf and bring to a boil. Sprinkle each fillet with salt and pepper; roll up jelly-roll fashion and secure each with a toothpick. Transfer fillets to boiling liquid; cover, reduce heat to low, and let simmer until fish is opaque and flakes easily when tested with a fork, 5 to 10 minutes. Using a slotted spoon, transfer fillets to warm plate; cover and keep warm. Strain liquid through sieve into bowl, discarding solids. Return liquid to skillet and cook over high heat until reduced by half its volume; set aside.

In 1-quart saucepan melt butter; add remaining ¼ cup onion and sauté until softened, 1 to 2 minutes. Sprinkle flour over onion and stir quickly to combine; cook, stirring constantly, for 1 minute. Remove from heat; stir in half-and-half and reduced cooking liquid. Return to medium-low heat and cook, stirring constantly, until mixture thickens, 1 to 2 minutes. Stir in crabmeat and cook until heated through, about 1 minute longer.

To serve, spoon crab mixture onto serving platter; remove and discard toothpicks from fillets and arrange fillets over crab mixture.

Each serving provides: 3 Protein Exchanges; ¼ Vegetable Exchange; 65 Optional Calories
Per serving: 177 calories; 23 g protein; 6 g fat; 6 g carbohydrate; 78 mg calcium;
   283 mg sodium; 82 mg cholesterol; 0.4 g dietary fiber

Braided Sole with Basil-Butter Sauce

WEEK 5   MAKES 2 SERVINGS

2 sole fillets (¼ pound each)
¼ cup dry white table wine
2 tablespoons minced shallot *or* onion
1 garlic clove, minced
1-inch strip lemon peel
2 tablespoons whipped butter
Dash white pepper

2 tablespoons water
1 tablespoon lemon juice
1 cup cooked spinach leaves (hot)
1 large plum tomato, blanched, peeled, seeded, and diced
2 tablespoons thinly sliced basil leaves

Cut each fillet lengthwise into 3 equal strips, stopping about 1 inch from opposite end of fillet. Starting from the center strip of 1 fillet, lap the strips one over the other to braid fillet; fold strips under and repeat procedure with remaining fillet; set aside.

In small saucepan combine wine, shallot (or onion), garlic, and lemon peel and cook over high heat until mixture comes to a boil; continue cooking until liquid is reduced by half (about 2 table-spoons), 2 to 3 minutes. Pour mixture through sieve into bowl, discarding solids. Return mixture to saucepan and set over low heat; using a wire whisk, stir in butter 1 tablespoon at a time, con-tinuing to stir until mixture is smooth and thick. Stir in pepper. Reduce heat to lowest possible setting and keep sauce warm (do not allow mixture to become too hot or it will separate).

Preheat broiler. Spray baking sheet with nonstick cooking spray; arrange fillets on baking sheet and drizzle with water and lemon juice. Broil until fish flakes easily when tested with a fork, 3 to 4 minutes (depending on thickness of fillets).

To serve, onto each of 2 serving plates arrange ½ cup spinach leaves in a single layer in center of plate. Set 1 fillet on center of each spinach-lined plate. Arrange half of the tomato pieces around each fillet, then sprinkle half of the basil over the tomato. Top each fillet with half of the butter mixture.

Each serving provides: 3 Protein Exchanges; 1½ Vegetable Exchanges; 80 Optional Calories
Per serving: 214 calories; 25 g protein; 7 g fat; 8 g carbohydrate; 181 mg calcium;
   220 mg sodium; 70 mg cholesterol; 2 g dietary fiber

Spinach and Rice-Stuffed Fish Rolls ©

WEEK 4   MAKES 4 SERVINGS

Speed preparation by cooking the spinach and rice in advance.

1 package frozen chopped spinach
  (10 ounces), cooked according to
  package directions and drained well
1 cup cooked long-grain rice
½ teaspoon salt
⅓ cup plus 2 teaspoons sour cream

2 tablespoons lemon juice
1 tablespoon chopped fresh dill
4 sole fillets (¼ pound each)
2 teaspoons margarine, melted

Preheat oven to 375° F. In medium mixing bowl combine spinach, rice, and salt; set aside. In small bowl combine remaining ingredients except fish and margarine; add half of the sour cream mixture to spinach mixture and stir to combine. Cover remaining sour cream mixture with plastic wrap and refrigerate until shortly before ready to serve.

Pat fillets dry and place on work surface, skin-side down; spoon ¼ of spinach mixture onto center of each fillet and roll fish to enclose filling. Transfer rolls, seam-side down, to 1-quart casserole and brush each with ½ teaspoon margarine. Bake until fish flakes easily when tested with a fork and is lightly browned, 20 to 25 minutes.

To serve, arrange fillets on serving platter and top each with ¼ of the remaining sour cream mixture.

Each serving provides: 3 Protein Exchanges; ½ Bread Exchange; 1 Vegetable Exchange;
  ½ Fat Exchange; 50 Optional Calories
Per serving: 241 calories; 25 g protein; 8 g fat; 17 g carbohydrate; 136 mg calcium;
  454 mg sodium; 64 mg cholesterol; 2 g dietary fiber

Tuna Oriental with Snow Peas

WEEK 5   MAKES 2 SERVINGS

Chinese pea pods are also referred to as snow peas.

1 boneless tuna steak (½ pound)
2 teaspoons Chinese sesame oil
1 teaspoon whipped butter
1 cup Chinese pea pods (snow peas),
   stem ends and strings removed
¼ cup chopped scallions (green onions)
1 teaspoon minced pared gingerroot
1 small garlic clove, minced

½ cup canned ready-to-serve chicken
   broth
2 tablespoons reduced-sodium soy
   sauce
1 tablespoon hoisin sauce
1 teaspoon cornstarch
1 tablespoon sesame seed, toasted

Preheat broiler. Brush each side of tuna with 1 teaspoon oil; set fish on nonstick baking sheet. Broil 5 inches from heat source, turning once, until fish is cooked through and flakes easily when tested with a fork, 3 to 4 minutes on each side.

While fish is cooking, prepare vegetables. In 10-inch skillet melt butter; add pea pods, scallions, gingerroot, and garlic and sauté over medium-high heat, stirring frequently, until pea pods are tender-crisp, about 1 minute. In 1-cup liquid measure or small mixing bowl combine broth, soy sauce, hoisin sauce, and cornstarch, stirring to dissolve cornstarch; add to skillet. Reduce heat to low and let simmer, stirring occasionally, until mixture thickens, 4 to 5 minutes.

To serve, transfer fish to serving platter and pour any juices from baking sheet over tuna; using a slotted spoon, arrange pea pods around tuna, then top fish with hoisin mixture and sprinkle with sesame seed.

Each serving provides: 3 Protein Exchanges; 1¼ Vegetable Exchanges; 1 Fat Exchange;
   70 Optional Calories
Per serving: 307 calories; 31 g protein; 14 g fat; 13 g carbohydrate; 90 mg calcium;
   1,164 mg sodium; 46 mg cholesterol; 2 g dietary fiber

Portuguese Clams and Sausage

WEEK 5   MAKES 2 SERVINGS

To thoroughly remove sand from clams, refer to Clams Casino recipe (page 206).

2 teaspoons olive *or* vegetable oil
2 ounces diced smoked beef sausage
¼ cup *each* diced onion, red bell
 pepper, and green bell pepper
1 ounce Canadian-style bacon, cut into
 matchstick pieces
½ teaspoon minced hot chili pepper
½ cup seeded and chopped drained
 canned Italian tomatoes

¼ cup *each* dry white table wine
 and water
Dash pepper
1 dozen littleneck clams,* scrubbed
1 teaspoon chopped fresh Italian
 (flat-leaf) parsley

In 12-inch nonstick skillet heat oil; add sausage and cook over medium-high heat, turning occasionally, until sausage is browned, 1 to 2 minutes. Transfer sausage to plate and set aside.

In same skillet combine onion, bell peppers, bacon, and chili pepper and sauté until vegetables are softened, about 1 minute; add remaining ingredients except clams and parsley and cook until flavors blend, 2 to 3 minutes. Add clams and reserved sausage to skillet; cover and cook until clam shells open, about 5 minutes. Transfer to serving dish and sprinkle with parsley.

Each serving provides: 2½ Protein Exchanges; 1¼ Vegetable Exchanges; 1 Fat Exchange; 30 Optional Calories
Per serving: 246 calories; 16 g protein; 15 g fat; 9 g carbohydrate; 57 mg calcium;
 613 mg sodium; 35 mg cholesterol; 1 g dietary fiber

Variation: Portuguese Clams with Sausage and Ham (Week 4)— Substitute 1 ounce cooked smoked ham for the Canadian-style bacon.

Per serving: 242 calories; 15 g protein; 14 g fat; 8 g carbohydrate; 57 mg calcium;
 616 mg sodium; 35 mg cholesterol; 1 g dietary fiber

*One dozen littleneck clams will yield about 2 ounces cooked seafood.

Clams Casino Ⓒ

WEEK 6   MAKES 4 SERVINGS, 6 CLAMS EACH

To ensure that clams are free of sand, the night before preparing this dish, place them in a large bowl and cover with uncooked cornmeal and some water; refrigerate overnight. Before preparing, discard the cornmeal mixture and thoroughly scrub the clams, rinsing them under running cold water.

Coarse salt (optional)
2 dozen cherrystone clams*
2 teaspoons olive *or* vegetable oil
½ cup *each* diced scallions (green
   onions), celery, and green bell pepper
2 tablespoons chopped fresh Italian
   (flat-leaf) parsley

1 tablespoon lemon juice
1 teaspoon Worcestershire sauce
1 to 2 drops hot sauce
2 slices crisp bacon, crumbled
Garnish: 4 lemon wedges

In bottom of 13 x 10½ x 1-inch jelly-roll pan spread coarse salt (if salt is not used, line pan with crumpled foil); set aside. Remove and discard top shell from each clam. Loosen meat in remaining shell halves and set shells on salt (or foil) in jelly-roll pan; set aside.

Preheat oven to 450° F. In small nonstick skillet heat oil; add vegetables and cook over medium heat until softened, 2 to 3 minutes. Stir in remaining ingredients except bacon and garnish. Spoon an equal amount of vegetable mixture over each clam, then sprinkle each with an equal amount of bacon. Bake for 5 minutes *(do not overbake or clams will toughen).* Serve each portion of clams garnished with a lemon wedge.

Each serving provides: 2 Protein Exchanges; ¾ Vegetable Exchange; ½ Fat Exchange;
   20 Optional Calories
Per serving: 133 calories; 16 g protein; 5 g fat; 5 g carbohydrate; 69 mg calcium;
   144 mg sodium; 41 mg cholesterol; 1 g dietary fiber

*Two dozen cherrystone clams will yield about ½ pound cooked seafood.

Clams in Red Sauce

To thoroughly remove sand from clams, refer to Clams Casino recipe (page 206).

1 tablespoon plus 1 teaspoon olive *or* vegetable oil
1 cup diced onion
2 small garlic cloves, minced
8 large plum tomatoes, blanched, peeled, seeded, and chopped
½ cup dry red table wine

2 tablespoons chopped fresh cilantro (Chinese parsley) *or* parsley
1 bay leaf
Dash *each* crushed red pepper, salt, and pepper
4 dozen littleneck clams,* scrubbed

In 5-quart saucepot or Dutch oven heat oil; add onions and garlic and sauté until translucent, 2 to 3 minutes. Stir in tomatoes and cook 1 minute longer. Add wine and seasonings, stir to combine, and bring to a boil. Reduce heat to low and let simmer until flavors blend, about 10 minutes. Arrange clams on tomato mixture; cover and cook until clam shells open, about 10 minutes.

Each serving provides: 2 Protein Exchanges; 2½ Vegetable Exchanges; 1 Fat Exchange; 30 Optional Calories
Per serving: 181 calories; 16 g protein; 6 g fat; 11 g carbohydrate; 78 mg calcium; 108 mg sodium; 38 mg cholesterol; 1 g dietary fiber

*Four dozen littleneck clams will yield about ½ pound cooked seafood.

Steamed Clams
with Julienne Vegetables

WEEK 5   MAKES 2 SERVINGS

To thoroughly remove sand from clams, refer to Clams Casino recipe (page 206).

1 medium carrot, trimmed, pared, and cut into matchstick pieces
1 medium leek (white portion and some green), thoroughly washed and cut into matchstick pieces
1 small celery rib, cut into matchstick pieces

¼ cup *each* dry white table wine, bottled clam juice, and water
1 garlic clove, crushed
1 dozen littleneck clams,* scrubbed

In 12-inch nonstick skillet combine vegetables, wine, clam juice, water, and garlic; cover and bring to a boil. Continue cooking over high heat until vegetables are tender-crisp, 1 to 2 minutes. Arrange clams over vegetable mixture in skillet; cover and let cook until clam shells open, 4 to 5 minutes. To serve, divide clams, vegetables, and cooking liquid into 2 bowls.

Each serving provides: 1 Protein Exchange; 1½ Vegetable Exchanges; 35 Optional Calories
Per serving: 100 calories; 9 g protein; 1 g fat; 10 g carbohydrate; 66 mg calcium; 130 mg sodium; 20 mg cholesterol; 1 g dietary fiber

Variation: Buttery Clams with Julienne Vegetables — Melt 2 tablespoons butter and serve as dipping sauce with clams. Increase Optional Calories to 135.

Per serving: 201 calories; 9 g protein; 12 g fat; 10 g carbohydrate; 70 mg calcium; 247 mg sodium; 51 mg cholesterol; 1 g dietary fiber

*One dozen littleneck clams will yield about 2 ounces cooked seafood.

Dilly Open-Face Crab Sandwiches ◐

WEEK 4   MAKES 2 SERVINGS

2 ounces thawed and drained frozen
  crabmeat
1 tablespoon plus 1 teaspoon
  reduced-calorie mayonnaise
1 tablespoon sour cream
1 teaspoon chopped fresh dill
½ teaspoon *each* lemon juice and
  Dijon-style mustard

¼ teaspoon grated lemon peel
2 slices reduced-calorie pumpernickel
  bread (40 calories per slice)
2 lettuce leaves
2 lemon slices, cut into halves
4 dill sprigs

In small mixing bowl combine crabmeat, mayonnaise, sour cream, dill, lemon juice, mustard, and lemon peel; stir until thoroughly combined. Top each slice of bread with 1 lettuce leaf, then spread half of the crab mixture over each leaf. Cut each slice of bread in half diagonally; garnish each half with half of a lemon slice and 1 dill sprig.

Each serving provides: 1 Protein Exchange; ½ Bread Exchange; ¼ Vegetable Exchange;
  1 Fat Exchange; 15 Optional Calories
Per serving: 118 calories; 8 g protein; 5 g fat; 12 g carbohydrate; 74 mg calcium;
  292 mg sodium; 35 mg cholesterol; 0.1 g dietary fiber

Lobster and Pear Salad ◐

A lovely salad for a special luncheon.

3 tablespoons buttermilk
1 tablespoon plus 1 teaspoon
   mayonnaise
1 tablespoon lemon juice, divided
2 teaspoons chopped, fresh basil *or*
   ½ teaspoon dried
1 teaspoon Dijon-style mustard
½ pound cooked lobster meat,*
   chopped

¼ cup *each* diced scallions (green
   onions) and celery
Dash *each* salt and pepper
20 lettuce leaves
2 small pears (about 5 ounces each),
   pared, cut lengthwise into halves,
   and cored

In medium mixing bowl combine buttermilk, mayonnaise, 2 teaspoons lemon juice, the basil, and mustard, stirring to combine; add lobster, scallions, celery, salt, and pepper and stir to coat.

To serve, line serving platter with lettuce. Brush pears with remaining teaspoon lemon juice and arrange cut-side up on lettuce leaves; top each pear half with ¼ of the lobster mixture.

Each serving provides: 2 Protein Exchanges; 1½ Vegetable Exchanges; 1 Fat Exchange;
   ½ Fruit Exchange; 5 Optional Calories
Per serving: 143 calories; 13 g protein; 5 g fat; 13 g carbohydrate; 94 mg calcium;
   335 mg sodium; 44 mg cholesterol; 2 g dietary fiber

*Cooked lobster meat can be purchased fresh or frozen; if frozen, allow to thaw before using in salad.

Variation: Shrimp and Pear Salad—Substitute shelled and deveined cooked shrimp for the lobster.

Per serving: 143 calories; 13 g protein; 5 g fat; 13 g carbohydrate; 81 mg calcium;
   247 mg sodium; 114 mg cholesterol; 2 g dietary fiber

Chilled Mussels with Seasoned Mayonnaise ⊖

WEEK 1   MAKES 2 SERVINGS

2 tablespoons minced fresh Italian (flat-leaf) parsley
1 tablespoon plus 1 teaspoon reduced-calorie mayonnaise
1 tablespoon *each* minced fresh basil and lemon juice
1 small garlic clove, mashed
Dash *each* salt and pepper

2 cups water
1 lemon, cut in half
1 bay leaf
½ teaspoon black peppercorns, cracked
1½ dozen medium mussels,* scrubbed
4 lemon wedges
6 Italian (flat-leaf) parsley sprigs

In small bowl combine parsley, mayonnaise, basil, lemon juice, garlic, salt, and pepper; cover and refrigerate until serving time.

In 3-quart saucepan combine water, lemon, bay leaf, and peppercorns and bring to a boil; add mussels, cover, and cook until mussels open, 8 to 10 minutes. Using a slotted spoon remove mussels from cooking liquid, discarding liquid. Remove and discard top shell from each mussel. Loosen meat in remaining shell and arrange 9 mussels on each of 2 serving plates. Cover with plastic wrap and refrigerate until chilled, at least 30 minutes.

To serve, top each mussel with an equal amount of mayonnaise mixture and garnish each plate with 2 lemon wedges and 3 parsley sprigs.

Each serving provides: 3 Protein Exchanges; 1 Fat Exchange
Per serving. 144 calories; 15 g protein; 5 g fat; 13 g carbohydrate; 89 mg calcium; 469 mg sodium; 35 mg cholesterol; 0.2 g dietary fiber

*1½ dozen medium mussels will yield about 6 ounces cooked seafood.

Scallop and Crab Gratin

WEEK 5   MAKES 2 SERVINGS

1 tablespoon whipped butter, divided
¼ pound bay *or* sea scallops (cut into halves)
1½ teaspoons lemon juice
1 cup sliced mushrooms
1 tablespoon minced shallot *or* onion
1½ teaspoons all-purpose flour
½ cup whole milk

1 ounce Gruyère *or* Swiss cheese, shredded
2 ounces well-drained thawed frozen crabmeat, flaked
Dash white pepper
3 tablespoons plain dried bread crumbs
Garnish: lemon slice and dill sprig

In 8-inch nonstick skillet melt 1½ teaspoons butter; add scallops and sauté until opaque, 2 to 3 minutes. Sprinkle with lemon juice. Using a slotted spoon, transfer scallops to plate and set aside.

Preheat oven to 450° F. In same skillet melt remaining 1½ teaspoons butter; add mushrooms and shallot (or onion) and sauté over medium-high heat until softened, about 5 minutes. Sprinkle flour over mushroom mixture and stir quickly to combine; cook, stirring constantly, for 1 minute. Continuing to stir, gradually add milk. Reduce heat to medium; stir in cheese and cook, continuing to stir, until cheese is melted. Remove from heat; stir in scallops, crabmeat, and pepper.

Spray 2-cup shallow casserole with nonstick cooking spray; add scallop mixture and sprinkle with bread crumbs. Bake until mixture is bubbly and golden brown, about 25 minutes. Serve garnished with lemon and dill.

Each serving provides: 3 Protein Exchanges; ½ Bread Exchange; 1 Vegetable Exchange; ¼ Milk Exchange; 50 Optional Calories
Per serving with Gruyère cheese: 257 calories; 24 g protein; 11 g fat; 15 g carbohydrate; 276 mg calcium; 349 mg sodium; 79 mg cholesterol; 1 g dietary fiber
With Swiss cheese: 252 calories; 24 g protein; 10 g fat; 16 g carbohydrate; 269 mg calcium; 338 mg sodium; 77 mg cholesterol; 1 g dietary fiber

California Shrimp Salad

WEEK 5   MAKES 4 SERVINGS

Once an avocado has been cut, the pulp has a tendency to turn brown from exposure to the air. To keep this from happening, sprinkle the cut portion with some fresh lemon or lime juice.

2 cups cooked spinach shell *or* rotelle macaroni
2 medium tomatoes, diced
5 ounces shelled and deveined cooked small shrimp
4 ounces drained canned red kidney beans
½ cup *each* thinly sliced red onion (separated into rings) and sliced celery
⅓ cup freshly squeezed lime juice

2 tablespoons *each* chopped fresh Italian (flat-leaf) parsley and olive *or* vegetable oil
1 ounce Monterey Jack cheese, shredded
1 small garlic clove, minced
Dash *each* salt and pepper
8 lettuce leaves
¼ avocado (2 ounces), pared and diced
¼ cup alfalfa sprouts

In large mixing bowl combine all ingredients except lettuce, avocado, and sprouts, and toss to thoroughly combine.

To serve, line serving platter with lettuce leaves; spoon pasta mixture over lettuce and top with avocado and sprouts.

Each serving provides: 2 Protein Exchanges; 1 Bread Exchange; 2½ Vegetable Exchanges; 1½ Fat Exchanges; 25 Optional Calories
Per serving: 280 calories; 15 g protein; 12 g fat; 30 g carbohydrate; 119 mg calcium; 176 mg sodium; 75 mg cholesterol; 3 g dietary fiber

New Orleans BBQ Shrimp ◑

¼ cup water
2 tablespoons tomato paste
1 tablespoon whipped butter
1½ teaspoons Dijon-style mustard
1 teaspoon lemon juice
1 small garlic clove, minced
½ teaspoon Worcestershire sauce
¼ teaspoon ground red pepper

⅛ teaspoon *each* thyme and oregano
   leaves
Dash pepper
½ pound shelled and deveined large
   shrimp (tail feathers left on)
1 cup cooked long-grain rice (hot)

In small saucepan combine all ingredients except shrimp and rice; cook over medium heat, stirring frequently, until mixture is heated through and flavors blend, 2 to 3 minutes.

Preheat broiler. Line baking sheet with heavy-duty foil and arrange shrimp on foil; brush with half of the butter mixture. Broil for 2 to 3 minutes; turn shrimp over, brush with remaining butter mixture, and broil until shrimp turn pink, 2 to 3 minutes longer.

To serve, spread rice onto serving platter; top with shrimp and any butter mixture remaining on baking sheet.

Each serving provides: 3 Protein Exchanges; 1 Bread Exchange; ¼ Vegetable Exchange;
   25 Optional Calories
Per serving: 280 calories; 26 g protein; 5 g fat; 30 g carbohydrate; 82 mg calcium;
   453 mg sodium; 180 mg cholesterol; 1 g dietary fiber

Open-Face
Shrimp Sandwiches ◑

WEEK 4	MAKES 2 SERVINGS

Plan to cook the shrimp in advance so they will have time to chill.

2 ounces shelled and deveined cooked
   small shrimp
1 tablespoon plus 1 teaspoon
   reduced-calorie mayonnaise
1 tablespoon sour cream
½ teaspoon *each* freshly squeezed lime
   juice and Dijon-style mustard

¼ teaspoon grated lime peel
2 slices reduced-calorie wheat bread
   (40 calories per slice)
2 lettuce leaves
Garnish: 2 lime slices, cut into halves

Chop shrimp, reserving 4 for garnish. In small mixing bowl combine chopped shrimp, mayonnaise, sour cream, lime juice, mustard, and lime peel and mix thoroughly. Top each slice of bread with 1 lettuce leaf and half of the shrimp mixture. Cut each slice of bread in half diagonally and garnish each half with half of a lime slice and 1 reserved shrimp.

Each serving provides: 1 Protein Exchange; ½ Bread Exchange; ¼ Vegetable Exchange;
   1 Fat Exchange; 15 Optional Calories
Per serving: 114 calories; 8 g protein; 5 g fat; 11 g carbohydrate; 45 mg calcium;
   275 mg sodium; 62 mg cholesterol; 0.1 g dietary fiber

Brochettes of Squid and Bell Pepper ◑

WEEK 5   MAKES 2 SERVINGS, 2 SKEWERS EACH

¼ cup *each* diced onion and celery
½ pound cleaned squid (discard head,
    tentacles, and ink sac)
1 medium red bell pepper, seeded and
    cut into 1-inch squares
1 tablespoon *each* whipped butter,
    melted, and freshly squeezed lime
    juice

2 teaspoons olive *or* vegetable oil
1 small garlic clove, minced
Dash *each* salt and pepper

Preheat broiler. Spray broiling pan with nonstick cooking spray;
arrange onion and celery in bottom of pan and set aside. Using a
sharp knife, cut squid into 2-inch pieces. Onto each of four 8-inch
wooden skewers alternately thread ¼ of the bell pepper squares
and squid pieces; arrange skewers over vegetables in broiling pan.
In small bowl combine remaining ingredients except salt and
pepper; brush half of mixture over skewers, then sprinkle with salt
and pepper. Broil for 2 minutes; turn skewers over and brush with
remaining butter mixture. Broil until squid is opaque and turns
white in color, about 2 minutes longer *(do not overcook or squid
will toughen)*.

   To serve, transfer vegetable mixture, along with pan juices, to
serving platter; set skewers over vegetable mixture.

Each serving provides: 3 Protein Exchanges; 1½ Vegetable Exchanges; 1 Fat Exchange;
    25 Optional Calories
Per serving: 192 calories; 18 g protein; 9 g fat; 9 g carbohydrate; 53 mg calcium;
    160 mg sodium; 272 mg cholesterol; 1 g dietary fiber

Turkey-Cranberry Salad

Braided Sole with Basil-Butter Sauce

Asparagus and
Mushroom Sauté
Creamy Apricot
Chicken

Oriental Vegetables

Pasta with Salmon Cream Sauce

Orange-Iced Chiffon Cake
Lemon-Nut Cookies
Peanut-Cocoa Cookies

Quick Strawberry Shortcake

Melon 'n' Tonic

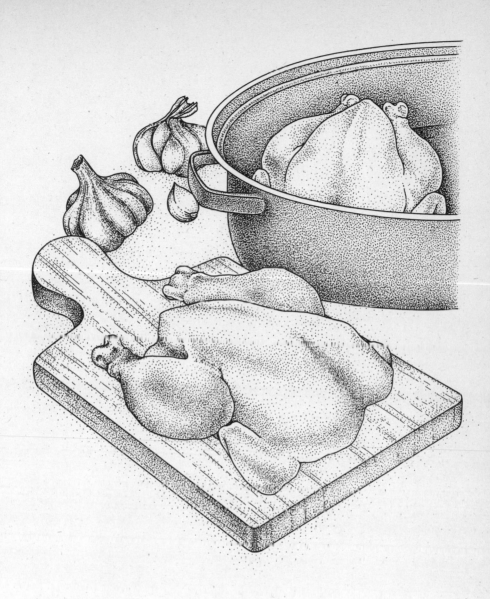

Poultry

The poultry parade is here, starring chicken and turkey in creative concert with so many kinds of foods. So let's hear it for Grilled Chicken with Dijon Mayonnaise, Turkey-Cranberry Salad, and Braised Rosemary Chicken with Olives, to name just a few special features.

217

Grilled Chicken with Tomato Butter ◐

WEEK 5   MAKES 2 SERVINGS

This is a good recipe to remember when the weather permits outdoor grilling.

½ cup boiling water
4 sun-dried tomato halves (not packed
    in oil)
2 tablespoons whipped butter, softened
2 teaspoons margarine, softened
½ teaspoon *each* lemon juice and
    Dijon-style mustard

Dash crushed red pepper
2 chicken cutlets (¼ pound each),
    pounded to ¼-inch thickness

In small bowl combine water and tomatoes and let stand until tomatoes are plumped, about 5 minutes. Drain tomatoes; mince and set aside.

Using a fork, in small mixing bowl combine butter, margarine, lemon juice, mustard, and pepper, mixing until fluffy and thoroughly combined. Stir in tomatoes. Cover with plastic wrap and refrigerate until ready to use.

Arrange chicken on nonstick baking sheet or grill and broil (or cook over hot coals) until browned on 1 side, 3 to 4 minutes. Turn cutlets over and cook until chicken is cooked through, 3 to 4 minutes longer. Transfer chicken to serving plate and top each cutlet with half of the tomato mixture.

Each serving provides: 3 Protein Exchanges; 1 Vegetable Exchange; 1 Fat Exchange;
    50 Optional Calories
Per serving: 235 calories; 27 g protein; 11 g fat; 6 g carbohydrate; 24 mg calcium;
    224 mg sodium; 81 mg cholesterol; 1 g dietary fiber

Grilled Oriental Chicken Salad ◐

WEEK 4   MAKES 2 SERVINGS

2 tablespoons *each* rice vinegar
  and water
2 teaspoons reduced-sodium soy sauce
1 teaspoon *each* Chinese sesame oil,
  vegetable oil, and prepared hot
  Chinese mustard
Dash pepper
5 ounces chicken cutlets, pounded
  to ¼-inch thickness

1 cup *each* shredded Chinese
  cabbage* and lettuce
½ cup Chinese pea pods (stem ends
  and strings removed), blanched
¼ cup carrot curls
1 tablespoon sesame seed, toasted

In small bowl combine vinegar, water, soy sauce, oils, mustard, and pepper; mix until thoroughly combined. Set aside.

Spray baking sheet with nonstick cooking spray. Arrange chicken on baking sheet and broil, turning once, until cooked through, 2 to 3 minutes on each side.

To serve, line serving platter with cabbage and lettuce. Diagonally slice chicken and arrange on cabbage mixture. Decoratively arrange pea pods and carrot curls around chicken and sprinkle with sesame seed. Stir dressing again and pour over salad.

Each serving provides: 2 Protein Exchanges; 2¾ Vegetable Exchanges; 1 Fat Exchange;
  30 Optional Calories
Per serving: 186 calories; 20 g protein; 8 g fat; 9 g carbohydrate; 123 mg calcium;
  296 mg sodium; 41 mg cholesterol; 3 g dietary fiber

*Shredded lettuce may be substituted for the Chinese cabbage.

Grilled Chicken with Dijon Mayonnaise Ⓒ

WEEK 1   MAKES 2 SERVINGS

2 tablespoons reduced-calorie mayonnaise
1 tablespoon Dijon-style mustard
½ teaspoon *each* tarragon and thyme leaves

Dash crushed red pepper
2 chicken cutlets (¼ pound each), pounded to ¼-inch thickness

In medium mixing bowl combine all ingredients except chicken and stir until thoroughly combined; add chicken and turn to coat with mayonnaise mixture. Cover with plastic wrap and refrigerate overnight or at least 4 hours.

Spray nonstick baking sheet with nonstick cooking spray; arrange chicken on baking sheet and, using a rubber scraper, spread mayonnaise mixture over chicken. Broil 5 to 6 inches from heat source until chicken is lightly browned and cooked through, 8 to 10 minutes.

Each serving provides: 3 Protein Exchanges; 1½ Fat Exchanges
Per serving: 177 calories; 26 g protein; 6 g fat; 2 g carbohydrate; 24 mg calcium;
   412 mg sodium; 71 mg cholesterol; dietary fiber data not available

Mexican Chicken Salad

Jalapeño pepper, sour cream, and corn give this chicken salad a taste of Mexico. Plan to cook the chicken in advance or use leftover chicken.

¼ pound skinned and boned cooked chicken, diced
1 medium tomato, seeded and diced
½ cup drained canned whole-kernel corn
¼ cup *each* chopped scallions (green onions) and diced green bell pepper
3 tablespoons sour cream
½ small jalapeño pepper, seeded and minced
1 tablespoon plus 1 teaspoon reduced-calorie mayonnaise
1 tablespoon *each* chopped fresh cilantro (Chinese parsley) *or* parsley and freshly squeezed lime juice
⅛ teaspoon salt
2 cups shredded lettuce
1 corn tortilla (6-inch diameter), toasted and cut in half

In medium mixing bowl combine all ingredients except lettuce and tortilla and mix well. Line a chilled serving plate with lettuce; spoon chicken mixture onto center of lettuce and serve with tortilla.

Each serving provides: 2 Protein Exchanges; 1 Bread Exchange; 3½ Vegetable Exchanges; 1 Fat Exchange; 50 Optional Calories
Per serving: 280 calories; 21 g protein; 13 g fat; 23 g carbohydrate; 110 mg calcium; 312 mg sodium; 63 mg cholesterol; 3 g dietary fiber

Chicken à la Grecque

WEEK 5   MAKES 4 SERVINGS

Feta cheese and fresh mint add a Grecian flair to this dish.

4 chicken cutlets (¼ pound each)
¼ cup lemon juice
2 tablespoons all-purpose flour
2 teaspoons oregano leaves
1 tablespoon plus 1 teaspoon olive oil
1 tablespoon whipped butter
1 cup *each* sliced onions, quartered mushroom caps, and julienne-cut red *or* green bell pepper (matchstick pieces)

2 small garlic cloves, minced
¼ cup *each* dry white table wine *or* vermouth and water
1 packet instant chicken broth and seasoning mix
2 tablespoons minced fresh mint
2 ounces feta cheese, crumbled
Garnish: mint sprigs

In medium bowl (not aluminum*) combine chicken and lemon juice and turn to coat with juice. Let marinate for 10 minutes.

On sheet of wax paper or a paper plate combine flour and oregano. Remove chicken from lemon juice allowing juice to drip into bowl; reserve juice. Dredge chicken in flour mixture, coating both sides.

In 10-inch nonstick skillet that has a metal or removable handle heat oil; add chicken and cook, turning once, until browned on both sides, about 2 minutes on each side. Using tongs, transfer chicken to plate and set aside.

In same skillet melt butter, stirring into pan drippings; add vegetables and garlic and cook over medium heat, stirring constantly, until tender-crisp, about 5 minutes. Add wine (or vermouth), water, broth mix, reserved lemon juice, and minced mint; stir to combine and bring mixture to a boil. Return chicken to skillet. Reduce heat to low, cover, and let simmer until chicken is cooked through, 5 to 10 minutes.

Preheat broiler. Remove skillet from heat; sprinkle feta cheese over chicken and broil until cheese is softened, 2 to 3 minutes. Serve garnished with mint sprigs.

Each serving provides: 3½ Protein Exchanges; 1½ Vegetable Exchanges; 1 Fat Exchange; 45 Optional Calories
Per serving: 272 calories; 30 g protein; 11 g fat; 11 g carbohydrate; 113 mg calcium; 501 mg sodium; 82 mg cholesterol; 1 g dietary fiber

*It's best to marinate in glass or stainless-steel containers; ingredients such as lemon juice may react with aluminum, causing color and flavor changes in food.

Chicken, Prosciutto, and Eggplant Bake

WEEK 2   MAKES 4 SERVINGS

1 tablespoon plus 1 teaspoon olive *or* vegetable oil, divided
¼ cup chopped onion
2 garlic cloves, minced
1 cup canned crushed tomatoes
¾ cup canned ready-to-serve chicken broth
2 tablespoons chopped fresh basil
1 tablespoon chopped fresh parsley
⅛ teaspoon salt
Dash pepper
4 thin chicken cutlets (2 ounces each)
1 baby eggplant (about ¼ pound), cut lengthwise into 4 equal slices
4 slices prosciutto (Italian-style ham), ½ ounce each
2 ounces mozzarella cheese, shredded
1 tablespoon grated Parmesan cheese

In 10-inch nonstick skillet heat 1 teaspoon oil; add onion and garlic and sauté over high heat, stirring frequently, until onion is softened, about 1 minute. Add tomatoes, broth, and seasonings and stir well to combine. Reduce heat to low and let simmer, stirring occasionally, until flavors blend, 20 to 25 minutes.

While tomato mixture simmers, prepare chicken. In 12-inch nonstick skillet heat 1 teaspoon oil; add chicken and cook over high heat, turning once, until both sides are lightly browned and chicken is cooked through, 2 to 3 minutes on each side. Remove chicken from skillet and set aside.

Preheat oven to 450° F. In same skillet heat remaining 2 teaspoons oil; add eggplant slices and cook over high heat, turning once, until both sides are lightly browned and eggplant is cooked through, 1 to 2 minutes on each side.

Spoon half of the tomato mixture (about ½ cup) over bottom of 9 x 9-inch baking dish. Arrange chicken in a single layer over sauce; top each portion of chicken with 1 eggplant slice, then with 1 slice of prosciutto. Spoon remaining sauce over prosciutto and sprinkle evenly with cheeses. Bake until cheeses are melted and prosciutto is heated through, 10 to 15 minutes.

Each serving provides: 2½ Protein Exchanges; 1 Vegetable Exchange; 1 Fat Exchange; 15 Optional Calories
Per serving: 203 calories; 21 g protein; 10 g fat; 7 g carbohydrate; 143 mg calcium; 643 mg sodium; 52 mg cholesterol; 1 g dietary fiber

Chicken with Sun-Dried Tomatoes

WEEK 2   MAKES 2 SERVINGS

1 teaspoon *each* margarine and olive *or* vegetable oil
2 chicken cutlets (¼ pound each), pounded to ¼-inch thickness
1 tablespoon chopped shallot *or* onion
1 garlic clove, minced
1 tablespoon all-purpose flour

½ cup canned ready-to-serve chicken broth
¼ cup dry white table wine
8 sun-dried tomato halves (not packed in oil), cut into matchstick pieces
1 tablespoon *each* chopped fresh basil and lemon juice

In 12-inch nonstick skillet combine margarine and oil and heat until margarine is melted; add chicken and cook over medium-high heat, turning once, until both sides are lightly browned and chicken is cooked through, 2 to 3 minutes on each side. Remove chicken from skillet and set aside.

In same skillet combine shallot (or onion) and garlic and sauté over medium heat until softened, about 1 minute. Sprinkle flour over garlic mixture and stir quickly to combine; cook, stirring constantly, for 1 minute. Continuing to stir, gradually add broth; add remaining ingredients and stir to combine. Reduce heat to low and cook, stirring frequently, until flavors blend and mixture thickens, 5 to 7 minutes. Return chicken to skillet and cook until heated through, 1 to 2 minutes.

Each serving provides: 3 Protein Exchanges; 2 Vegetable Exchanges; 1 Fat Exchange; 55 Optional Calories
Per serving: 260 calories; 30 g protein; 7 g fat; 17 g carbohydrate; 51 mg calcium; 821 mg sodium; 66 mg cholesterol; 2 g dietary fiber

Variation: Chicken with Plum Tomatoes — Substitute 4 large plum tomatoes, seeded and chopped, for the sun-dried tomato halves.

Per serving: Reduce sodium to 371 mg

Creamy Apricot Chicken

WEEK 5   MAKES 2 SERVINGS

1 teaspoon *each* margarine and olive *or* vegetable oil
2 chicken cutlets (¼ pound each), pounded to ¼-inch thickness
1 tablespoon chopped shallot *or* onion
1 tablespoon all-purpose flour
¼ cup sweet vermouth

½ cup canned ready-to-serve chicken broth
1 tablespoon whipping cream
8 dried apricot halves, blanched (hot)
1 teaspoon chopped fresh Italian (flat-leaf) parsley

In 10-inch nonstick skillet combine margarine and oil and heat until margarine is melted; add chicken and cook, turning once, until both sides are lightly browned and chicken is cooked through, 2 to 3 minutes on each side. Remove chicken from skillet; set aside and keep warm.

To same skillet add shallot (or onion) and sauté over medium heat until softened, about 1 minute. Sprinkle flour over shallot and stir quickly to combine; cook, stirring constantly, for 1 minute. Continuing to stir, gradually add vermouth; stir in broth and cook over low heat until mixture is slightly thickened, 4 to 5 minutes. Stir in cream.

To serve, arrange chicken on serving platter; top with sauce and apricot halves and sprinkle with parsley.

Each serving provides: 3 Protein Exchanges; 1 Fat Exchange; 1 Fruit Exchange; 100 Optional Calories
Per serving: 289 calories; 28 g protein; 8 g fat; 17 g carbohydrate; 30 mg calcium; 355 mg sodium; 74 mg cholesterol; 2 g dietary fiber

Chicken and Pasta Teriyaki

WEEK 4   MAKES 4 SERVINGS

¼ cup rice vinegar
2 tablespoons *each* teriyaki sauce,
   dry sherry, and firmly packed
   brown sugar
1 tablespoon minced pared gingerroot
2 garlic cloves, minced
10 ounces skinned and boned chicken
   breasts, cut into thin strips
1 tablespoon plus 1 teaspoon peanut
   or vegetable oil

2 cups cooked cellophane noodles (hot)
2 cups shredded Chinese cabbage
1 cup *each* sliced green *or* red bell
   pepper, diagonally sliced scallions
   (green onions), and drained canned
   straw *or* regular mushrooms
1 tablespoon sesame seed, toasted

In small bowl (not aluminum*) combine vinegar, teriyaki sauce, sherry, sugar, gingerroot, and garlic; add chicken and turn to coat. Cover and refrigerate for 20 minutes.

Using a slotted spoon, remove chicken from marinade, reserving marinade. In 9-inch nonstick skillet heat oil; add chicken and sauté over medium-high heat until chicken is lightly browned, 5 to 6 minutes. Pour in reserved marinade mixture. Reduce heat to medium-low and cook until flavors blend and chicken is tender, 4 to 5 minutes longer. In serving bowl combine remaining ingredients except sesame seed; add chicken mixture and toss to combine. Sprinkle with sesame seed and serve immediately or cover with plastic wrap and refrigerate until ready to serve.

Each serving provides: 2 Protein Exchanges; 1 Bread Exchange; 2½ Vegetable Exchanges;
   1 Fat Exchange; 55 Optional Calories
Per serving: 284 calories; 19 g protein; 7 g fat; 35 g carbohydrate; 95 mg calcium;
   512 mg sodium; 41 mg cholesterol; 3 g dietary fiber (this figure does not include
   cellophane noodles; nutrition analysis not available)

*It's best to marinate in glass or stainless-steel containers; ingredients such as teriyaki
sauce may react with aluminum, causing color and flavor changes in food.

6 points
+
4 cellophane noodles

10
1.5

Sweet and Sour Chicken with Vegetables

WEEK 4	MAKES 4 SERVINGS

You can create an authentic Chinese taste in your own kitchen with this recipe.

15 ounces skinned and boned chicken breasts, cut into thin strips, divided
1 tablespoon cornstarch
1 tablespoon peanut *or* vegetable oil, divided
¼ cup rice vinegar
1 packet instant chicken broth and seasoning mix, dissolved in ¼ cup hot water
1 tablespoon *each* dark corn syrup and dry sherry
1 teaspoon Chinese sesame oil

1 cup quartered mushrooms
½ cup *each* diagonally sliced scallions (green onions) and red *or* green bell pepper strips (2 x ¼-inch strips)
1 tablespoon minced pared gingerroot
2 small garlic cloves, minced
1 cup *each* Chinese pea pods (stem ends and strings removed) and frozen whole baby corn ears
2 tablespoons minced fresh cilantro (Chinese parsley) *or* parsley

In 1-quart bowl combine chicken and cornstarch, tossing to coat. In 12-inch nonstick skillet heat 1½ teaspoons peanut oil; add half of the chicken and cook over high heat, stirring constantly, until golden brown, about 2 minutes. Using a slotted spoon, remove chicken from skillet and set aside. Repeat procedure using remaining peanut oil and chicken and set aside.

In small bowl combine vinegar, dissolved broth mix, corn syrup, sherry, and sesame oil; stir to combine and set aside. To same skillet add mushrooms and sauté until moisture has evaporated, about 2 minutes. Stir in scallions, bell pepper, gingerroot, and garlic and sauté until vegetables are tender-crisp, about 1 minute. Add pea pods and corn and stir to combine. Pour vinegar-broth mixture into skillet; return chicken to skillet and cook over high heat, stirring occasionally, until chicken is heated through and liquid is slightly thickened, about 1 minute. Serve sprinkled with cilantro (or parsley).

Each serving provides: 3 Protein Exchanges; 1½ Vegetable Exchanges; 1 Fat Exchange; 50 Optional Calories
Per serving: 242 calories; 28 g protein; 6 g fat; 16 g carbohydrate; 43 mg calcium; 337 mg sodium; 62 mg cholesterol; 3 g dietary fiber

Braised Rosemary Chicken with Olives

WEEK 5   MAKES 2 SERVINGS

This recipe is especially good prepared with Calamata (Greek) or Gaeta (Italian) olives which lend a distinctive flavor.

2 teaspoons olive *or* vegetable oil
¾ pound chicken breasts, skinned and cut into halves
½ cup frozen pearl onions
¼ cup *each* dry white table wine and water
8 pitted black olives
1 tablespoon *each* drained capers and lemon juice

1 teaspoon *each* rosemary leaves and chopped fresh parsley
½ packet (about ½ teaspoon) instant chicken broth and seasoning mix
⅛ teaspoon pepper
Dash salt

In 3-quart saucepan heat oil over medium-high heat; place chicken skinned-side down in saucepan and cook, turning occasionally, until browned, 2 to 3 minutes. Transfer chicken to plate and set aside. To same saucepan add onions and sauté, stirring occasionally, until onions are lightly browned, 1 to 2 minutes; add remaining ingredients except chicken and stir to thoroughly combine. Return chicken to saucepan. Reduce heat to low, cover, and let simmer until chicken is tender and onions are cooked through, 15 to 20 minutes.

Each serving provides: 3 Protein Exchanges; ½ Vegetable Exchange; 1 Fat Exchange; 55 Optional Calories
Per serving: 234 calories; 27 g protein; 9 g fat; 6 g carbohydrate; 57 mg calcium; 613 mg sodium; 66 mg cholesterol; 1 g dietary fiber

Skillet Chicken Waldorf

This fruity chicken is ready to be served in less than half an hour.

1 tablespoon plus 1 teaspoon olive *or* vegetable oil
10 ounces skinned and boned chicken breasts, cut into cubes
1 cup *each* sliced red onion and celery
1 small Golden Delicious apple (about ¼ pound), cored, pared, and sliced
2 tablespoons golden raisins
½ ounce chopped walnuts
¼ cup water
1 packet instant chicken broth and seasoning mix
8 lettuce leaves

In 10-inch nonstick skillet heat oil; add chicken and sauté over medium heat until browned, about 3 minutes. Add remaining ingredients except water, broth mix, and lettuce; cook, stirring frequently, until vegetables and apple are tender-crisp, 2 to 3 minutes. Add water and broth mix and, stirring frequently, bring to a boil. Reduce heat to low and let simmer for 5 minutes.

To serve, line serving platter with lettuce leaves and top with chicken mixture.

Each serving provides: 2 Protein Exchanges; 1½ Vegetable Exchanges; 1 Fat Exchange; ½ Fruit Exchange; 30 Optional Calories
Per serving: 191 calories; 18 g protein; 8 g fat; 13 g carbohydrate; 46 mg calcium; 323 mg sodium; 41 mg cholesterol; 1 g dietary fiber

Chicken 'n' Biscuits ©

WEEK 1   MAKES 4 SERVINGS

1 tablespoon plus 1 teaspoon margarine
2 cups diced carrots
½ cup *each* diced onion, diced celery,
   and quartered mushrooms
3 tablespoons all-purpose flour
1 cup canned ready-to-serve chicken
   broth
15 ounces skinned and boned chicken
   breasts, cut into cubes

1 tablespoon chopped fresh parsley
1 teaspoon chopped fresh dill
⅛ teaspoon white pepper
4 ready-to-bake refrigerated buttermilk
   flaky biscuits (1 ounce each)

In 3-quart saucepan melt margarine; add carrots, onion, celery, and mushrooms and cook over medium heat, stirring frequently, until vegetables are softened, 2 to 3 minutes. Sprinkle flour over vegetables and stir quickly to combine; cook, stirring constantly, for 1 minute. Gradually stir in broth. Add remaining ingredients except biscuits and stir to combine. Reduce heat to low and cook, stirring occasionally, until mixture thickens, about 5 minutes.

Preheat oven to 425° F. Transfer mixture to 2-quart casserole and bake until carrots are tender-crisp, 10 to 15 minutes. Arrange biscuits over chicken mixture and continue baking until biscuits are golden, 10 to 15 minutes.

Each serving provides: 3 Protein Exchanges; 1 Bread Exchange; 1¾ Vegetable Exchanges;
   1 Fat Exchange; 35 Optional Calories
Per serving: 308 calories; 28 g protein; 9 g fat; 27 g carbohydrate; 47 mg calcium;
   699 mg sodium; 62 mg cholesterol; 2 g dietary fiber

Chicken Zaragoza ◑

WEEK 5   MAKES 4 SERVINGS

2 teaspoons vegetable oil
1¼ pounds chicken breasts, skinned
   and cut into halves
1 cup frozen artichoke hearts
½ cup frozen peas
2 ounces Canadian-style bacon
   or cooked smoked ham, diced
¼ cup diced drained pimiento

2 garlic cloves, minced
3 tablespoons all-purpose flour
1 cup canned ready-to-serve chicken
   broth
2 tablespoons dry sherry
¼ teaspoon thyme leaves
Dash pepper

In 12-inch nonstick skillet heat oil; add chicken and cook over medium-high heat, turning when necessary, until browned, 4 to 5 minutes. Transfer chicken to plate and set aside.

In same pan combine artichoke hearts, peas, bacon (or ham), pimiento, and garlic and sauté for 1 minute. Sprinkle flour over vegetable mixture and stir quickly to combine. Continuing to stir, gradually add broth; add remaining ingredients, stirring until thoroughly combined. Return chicken to pan. Reduce heat to low, cover, and cook until mixture thickens and chicken is cooked through, 15 to 20 minutes.

Each serving provides: 3 Protein Exchanges; ½ Bread Exchange; ½ Vegetable Exchange;
  ½ Fat Exchange; 20 Optional Calories
Per serving with bacon: 244 calories; 32 g protein; 6 g fat; 13 g carbohydrate;
  32 mg calcium; 569 mg sodium; 73 mg cholesterol; 3 g dietary fiber
With ham: 242 calories; 33 g protein; 5 g fat; 13 g carbohydrate; 32 mg calcium;
  539 mg sodium; 73 mg cholesterol; 3 g dietary fiber

Chicken Niçoise ①

For added flavor, try preparing this recipe with Gaeta olives — the olives of Italy.

1 pound 2 ounces chicken parts, skinned
1 teaspoon all-purpose flour
1 teaspoon vegetable oil
½ cup *each* sliced onion, red bell pepper strips, and yellow bell pepper strips*
½ cup canned ready-to-serve chicken broth

¼ cup *each* dry white table wine and tomato puree
6 pitted black olives
1 tablespoon chopped fresh parsley
2 teaspoons chopped fresh rosemary
⅛ teaspoon salt
Dash pepper

Preheat oven to 450° F. Sprinkle chicken with flour to lightly coat. In 10-inch skillet that has a metal or removable handle heat oil; add chicken and cook over high heat, turning occasionally, until chicken is lightly browned, 3 to 5 minutes. Remove chicken from skillet and set aside.

To same skillet add onion and bell peppers and sauté until tender-crisp, about 1 minute. Add remaining ingredients and stir until thoroughly combined. Return chicken to skillet, turning to coat with liquid. Transfer skillet to oven and bake until chicken is cooked through and mixture thickens, 10 to 15 minutes.

Each serving provides: 3 Protein Exchanges; 1½ Vegetable Exchanges; ½ Fat Exchange; 60 Optional Calories
Per serving: 249 calories; 27 g protein; 9 g fat; 11 g carbohydrate, 50 mg calcium; 687 mg sodium; 79 mg cholesterol; 1 g dietary fiber

*One-half cup of green bell pepper strips may be substituted for either the red or yellow bell pepper strips.

Open-Face Turkey Sandwich with Brie Sauce

WEEK 2   MAKES 2 SERVINGS

1 teaspoon margarine
2 teaspoons minced shallot or onion
1½ teaspoons all-purpose flour
½ cup skim or nonfat milk
1 ounce Brie cheese (rind removed), cut into cubes
1 tablespoon Dijon-style mustard, divided
Dash ground nutmeg

2 slices Italian bread (1 ounce each), toasted
1 ounce sliced baked ham
2 ounces sliced roast turkey breast
½ cup sliced asparagus spears (2-inch pieces), blanched
1 teaspoon grated Parmesan cheese

Preheat oven to 350° F. In small saucepan melt margarine; add shallot (or onion) and sauté over medium heat until translucent, about 2½ minutes. Sprinkle with flour and stir quickly to combine; cook, stirring constantly, for 1 minute. Continuing to stir, gradually add milk; cook, stirring, until mixture thickens, 1 to 2 minutes. Add Brie cheese, 1 teaspoon mustard, and the nutmeg and cook over low heat, stirring constantly, until mixture thickens, about 5 minutes. Set aside.

Onto each slice of bread spread 1 teaspoon of the remaining mustard; top each with ½ ounce ham, 1 ounce turkey, and half of the asparagus. Spray 8 x 8 x 2-inch baking dish with nonstick cooking spray; stir sauce again and pour evenly over sandwiches. Sprinkle each portion with ½ teaspoon Parmesan cheese and bake until lightly browned, about 10 minutes.

Each serving provides: 2 Protein Exchanges; 1 Bread Exchange; ½ Vegetable Exchange; ½ Fat Exchange; ¼ Milk Exchange; 15 Optional Calories
Per serving: 258 calories; 21 g protein; 9 g fat; 24 g carbohydrate; 134 mg calcium; 741 mg sodium; 43 mg cholesterol; 1 g dietary fiber

Grilled Cheese and
Turkey Club Sandwich

WEEK 6   MAKES 2 SERVINGS

This sandwich is just as tasty if it isn't grilled, and it can then be part of a brown bag lunch.

6 slices reduced-calorie whole wheat bread (40 calories per slice), lightly toasted

2 teaspoons reduced-calorie mayonnaise

3 ounces thinly sliced roast turkey breast

4 lettuce leaves

½ medium tomato, cut into 4 equal slices

4 slices crisp bacon

1 ounce thinly sliced Muenster *or* Monterey Jack cheese

Spread 2 slices of toast with 1 teaspoon mayonnaise each, then top each with 1½ ounces turkey and another slice of toast. Top each sandwich with 2 lettuce leaves, 2 tomato slices, and 2 bacon slices and set aside.

On each remaining slice of toast arrange ½ ounce cheese; broil or bake in toaster oven until cheese melts, about 1 minute. Top each sandwich with a slice of toast, cheese-side down. Cut each sandwich diagonally in half making 2 triangles, then cut each half again, making 4 small triangles. Insert a toothpick into each triangle.

Each serving provides: 2 Protein Exchanges; 1½ Bread Exchanges; 1 Vegetable Exchange; ½ Fat Exchange; 85 Optional Calories

Per serving with Muenster cheese: 333 calories; 26 g protein; 13 g fat; 29 g carbohydrate; 184 mg calcium; 646 mg sodium; 55 mg cholesterol; 0.4 g dietary fiber

With Monterey Jack cheese: 333 calories; 27 g protein; 13 g fat; 29 g carbohydrate; 188 mg calcium; 633 mg sodium; 54 mg cholesterol; 0.4 g dietary fiber

Turkey-Cranberry Salad

WEEK 4   MAKES 2 SERVINGS

Here's a way to turn leftover Thanksgiving Day turkey and cranberries into a refreshing salad.

¾ pound oranges
1 tablespoon raspberry *or* seasoned
    rice vinegar
2 teaspoons *each* olive oil and honey
¼ teaspoon Dijon-style mustard
8 green leaf lettuce leaves

¼ pound skinned and boned cooked
    turkey, thinly sliced
¼ cup *each* red onion slices (separated
    into rings) and cranberries

Over small bowl to catch juice, remove skin and membranes from oranges and reserve juice; section oranges and set aside. Add vinegar, oil, honey, and mustard to reserved orange juice and, using a wire whisk, beat until thoroughly combined.

Line center of serving platter with lettuce leaves; arrange turkey slices over lettuce, overlapping slices slightly. Decoratively arrange orange sections on platter alongside edge of lettuce. Top turkey with onion slices. Top salad with cranberries and then with dressing.

Each serving provides: 2 Protein Exchanges; 1¼ Vegetable Exchanges; 1 Fat Exchange;
    1 Fruit Exchange; 30 Optional Calories
Per serving: 235 calories; 18 g protein; 8 g fat; 25 g carbohydrate; 96 mg calcium;
    65 mg sodium; 44 mg cholesterol; 3 g dietary fiber

Turkey-Chestnut Sauté

WEEK 5	MAKES 4 SERVINGS

Turkey leftovers never tasted so good!

10 ounces pears, cored, pared,
   and sliced
2 tablespoons lemon juice
2 teaspoons *each* margarine and olive
   or vegetable oil
2 cups sliced mushroom caps
1 cup sliced scallions (green onions),
   white portion only
1 teaspoon all-purpose flour
⅓ cup unfermented apple cider
   or apple juice (no sugar added)

½ cup water
1 packet instant chicken broth and
   seasoning mix
¼ teaspoon thyme leaves
½ pound skinned and boned cooked
   turkey, cut into strips
12 small chestnuts, roasted, peeled,
   and chopped
Garnish: 1 tablespoon chopped fresh
   Italian (flat-leaf) parsley

In small mixing bowl combine pears and lemon juice, tossing slices with juice to prevent browning; set aside.

In 10-inch nonstick skillet combine margarine and oil and heat until margarine is melted; add mushrooms and scallions and sauté until mushrooms are lightly browned, about 2 minutes. Add pear mixture and stir to combine; cook, stirring occasionally, until pears are softened, about 2 minutes. Sprinkle flour evenly over pear mixture and stir quickly to combine; cook, stirring constantly, for 1 minute. Continuing to stir, gradually add cider (or juice); add water, broth mix, and thyme and stir to combine. Bring mixture to a boil. Reduce heat to low, stir in turkey and chestnuts, and let simmer until heated through, 5 to 10 minutes. Serve sprinkled with parsley.

Each serving provides: 2 Protein Exchanges; ½ Bread Exchange; 1½ Vegetable Exchanges; 1 Fat Exchange; ½ Fruit Exchange; 20 Optional Calories
Per serving: 251 calories; 19 g protein; 8 g fat; 28 g carbohydrate; 52 mg calcium; 320 mg sodium; 44 mg cholesterol; 4 g dietary fiber

Turkey Reuben Canapés

WEEK 4   MAKES 4 SERVINGS, 2 CANAPÉS EACH

8 slices thin-sliced party-style
  pumpernickel bread (¾ ounce per
  2 slices), lightly toasted
2 tablespoons Russian dressing
2 ounces thinly sliced roast turkey
  breast (eight ¼-ounce slices)

¼ cup rinsed and drained sauerkraut*
2 ounces thinly sliced Swiss cheese
  (eight ¼-ounce slices)

On nonstick baking sheet arrange bread slices in a single layer; spread each with ¾ teaspoon Russian dressing. Top each with 1 slice turkey, then 1½ teaspoons sauerkraut, and 1 slice cheese. Broil until canapés are heated through and cheese is melted, 1 to 2 minutes.

Each serving provides: 1 Protein Exchange; 1 Bread Exchange; ⅛ Vegetable Exchange;
  1 Fat Exchange
Per serving: 167 calories; 10 g protein; 8 g fat; 13 g carbohydrate; 160 mg calcium;
  268 mg sodium; 23 mg cholesterol; 3 g dietary fiber

*Use the sauerkraut that is packaged in plastic bags and stored in the refrigerator section of the supermarket; it is usually crisper and less salty than the canned.

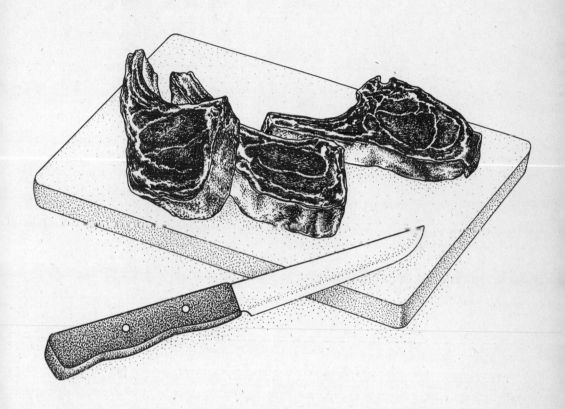

Meat and Veal

Make main-course magic with meats. Whether it's beef, lamb, ham, pork, or veal, you'll love our creative — yet slimming — recipe ideas. Check out Veal Chili or BBQ Beef on a Bun, our Fruited Lamb or Steak au Poivre Vert. Any way you slice it, our meat dishes are "m-m-marvelous."

Steak au Poivre Vert ◑

WEEK 8   MAKES 2 SERVINGS

10 ounces filet mignon*
2 teaspoons margarine
1 teaspoon all-purpose flour
1 tablespoon green peppercorns
2 tablespoons brandy *or* cognac

¼ cup canned ready-to-serve beef broth
2 tablespoons half-and-half (blend
   of milk and cream)
⅛ teaspoon *each* salt and pepper

On rack in broiling pan broil filet mignon 6 inches from heat source, turning once, until medium-rare, 3 to 4 minutes on each side, or until done to taste.

While filet mignon is broiling prepare sauce. In 8-inch nonstick skillet melt margarine; sprinkle with flour and stir quickly to combine; add peppercorns and stir to combine. Gradually add brandy (or cognac) and, stirring constantly, cook 1 minute longer. Stir in broth and cook, stirring occasionally, until mixture thickens and flavors blend, 3 to 4 minutes. Stir in half-and-half, salt, and pepper and remove from heat.

To serve, cut filet mignon into 4 equal slices. Arrange on serving platter and top with sauce.

Each serving provides: 4 Protein Exchanges; 1 Fat Exchange; 75 Optional Calories
Per serving: 335 calories; 33 g protein; 16 g fat; 3 g carbohydrate; 33 mg calcium;
   370 mg sodium; 92 mg cholesterol; trace dietary fiber

*Boneless top round steak may be substituted for the filet mignon. Broil 4 to 5 minutes on each side or until done to taste. To serve, slice steak diagonally across the grain into thin slices. Arrange on serving platter and top with sauce.

Per serving: 321 calories; 37 g protein; 13 g fat; 3 g carbohydrate; 30 mg calcium;
   362 mg sodium, 101 mg cholesterol; trace dietary fiber

Steak with Stroganoff Sauce

WEEK 4   MAKES 2 SERVINGS

½ pound top round *or* boneless
  top loin steak
1 teaspoon *each* margarine and olive
  or vegetable oil
1 cup sliced mushrooms
2 tablespoons chopped shallot
  (or onion)
¼ cup *each* dry white table wine and
  canned ready-to-serve beef broth

½ teaspoon *each* Worcestershire sauce,
  prepared horseradish, and
  cornstarch
Dash white pepper
3 tablespoons sour cream

On rack in broiling pan broil steak 6 inches from heat source, turning once, until medium-rare, 4 to 5 minutes on each side or until done to taste.

While steak is broiling, prepare sauce. In 10-inch nonstick skillet combine margarine and oil and heat until margarine is melted; add mushrooms and shallot (or onion) and sauté over medium-high heat until mushrooms are lightly browned, about 2 minutes. In 1-cup liquid measure combine wine, broth, Worcestershire sauce, horseradish, cornstarch, and pepper, stirring to dissolve cornstarch; add to mushroom mixture and cook over low heat, stirring constantly, until mixture thickens, 2 to 3 minutes. Stir in sour cream and cook, stirring occasionally, until mixture is heated through, 2 to 3 minutes longer.

To serve, slice steak across the grain and top with hot sauce.

Each serving provides: 3 Protein Exchanges; 1⅛ Vegetable Exchanges; 1 Fat Exchange;
  90 Optional Calories
Per serving with top round steak: 291 calories; 29 g protein; 14 g fat; 6 g carbohydrate;
  40 mg calcium; 208 mg sodium; 81 mg cholesterol; 1 g dietary fiber
With boneless top loin steak: 302 calories; 26 g protein; 17 g fat; 6 g carbohydrate;
  42 mg calcium; 214 mg sodium; 74 mg cholesterol; 1 g dietary fiber

Beef and Barley Salad

If you own a microwave oven, you can speed preparation by using it to heat the dressing for this salad.

1 cup cooked pearl barley
¼ pound roast beef, cut into strips
¼ cup thinly sliced scallions
   (green onions)
3 cherry tomatoes, cut into quarters
2 tablespoons *each* chopped fresh
   Italian (flat-leaf) parsley and golden
   raisins

1 tablespoon *each* red wine vinegar
   and Dijon-style mustard
2 teaspoons vegetable oil
1½ teaspoons *each* firmly packed
   brown sugar, lemon juice, and water
Dash *each* salt and pepper

In medium mixing bowl combine barley, roast beef, scallions, cherry tomatoes, and parsley; set aside. In small saucepan combine remaining ingredients; cook over medium heat, stirring occasionally, until mixture comes just to a boil and sugar is dissolved and raisins are plumped. Remove from heat and pour over salad ingredients, tossing to coat. Serve immediately or cover with plastic wrap and refrigerate until chilled.

Each serving provides: 2 Protein Exchanges; 1 Bread Exchange; ½ Vegetable Exchange;
  1 Fat Exchange; ½ Fruit Exchange; 15 Optional Calories
Per serving: 309 calories, 20 g protein, 10 g fat, 35 g carbohydrate, 31 mg calcium,
  336 mg sodium; 46 mg cholesterol; 4 g dietary fiber

Tangy Beef Canapés ⊙ ◑

WEEK 4	MAKES 2 SERVINGS, 2 CANAPÉS EACH

2 tablespoons whipped cream cheese
1 teaspoon prepared horseradish
4 slices thin-sliced party-style
  pumpernickel bread (¾ ounce per
  2 slices)

1 ounce roast beef (cut into four
  ¼-ounce pieces)
1 large plum tomato, cut into 4 slices

In small mixing bowl combine cream cheese and horseradish, mixing well. Spread each slice of bread with ¼ of the cream cheese mixture (about 2 teaspoons); top each with ¼ ounce roast beef and 1 tomato slice.

Each serving provides: ½ Protein Exchange; 1 Bread Exchange; ½ Vegetable Exchange;
  35 Optional Calories
Per serving: 117 calories; 7 g protein; 5 g fat; 13 g carbohydrate; 28 mg calcium;
  170 mg sodium; 21 mg cholesterol; 3 g dietary fiber

BBQ Beef on a Bun ❶❶

A quick recipe that offers a good way to use up leftover roast beef.

⅓ cup plus 2 teaspoons ketchup
1 tablespoon water
2 teaspoons firmly packed brown sugar
1 teaspoon *each* chili powder, honey,
   Dijon-style mustard, cider vinegar,
   Worcestershire sauce, and lemon
   juice

Dash hot sauce
¼ pound roast beef, cut into matchstick
   pieces
2 hamburger rolls (2 ounces each), cut
   into halves and lightly toasted
2 red onion slices

In 8-inch nonstick skillet combine ketchup, water, sugar, chili powder, honey, mustard, vinegar, Worcestershire sauce, lemon juice, and hot sauce; stir to combine and cook over medium heat until heated through, about 1 minute. Add roast beef and stir to combine; cook, stirring occasionally, until beef is heated through and flavors blend, 3 to 4 minutes.

To serve, on each of 2 individual serving plates place bottom half of each roll; top each half with half of the meat mixture, 1 onion slice, and top half of roll.

Each serving provides: 2 Protein Exchanges; 2 Bread Exchanges; ¼ Vegetable Exchange;
   75 Optional Calories
Per serving: 376 calories; 22 g protein; 8 g fat; 52 g carbohydrate; 77 mg calcium;
   905 mg sodium; 49 mg cholesterol; 0.1 g dietary fiber

Smoky Beef Hors d'Oeuvres with Honey-Mustard Sauce ☉◑

WEEK 4	MAKES 4 SERVINGS, 3 HORS D'OEUVRES EACH

4 ready-to-bake refrigerated buttermilk flaky biscuits (1 ounce each)*
2 ounces Cheddar cheese, shredded
6 ounces smoked beef sausage
2 tablespoons honey

1 tablespoon *each* country Dijon-style mustard and prepared hot Chinese mustard

Preheat oven to 375° F. Separate each biscuit into 2 layers; on sheet of wax paper arrange biscuits in 2 lines (4 biscuit layers in each line), with edges touching so that they form 1 rectangle. Cover with separate sheet of wax paper and, using a rolling pin, roll rectangle so that it is about 9 x 5 inches and press edges of biscuit layers together to seal. Sprinkle cheese over entire surface of dough; arrange sausage along wide side of dough. Starting from wide side, roll dough jelly-roll fashion to enclose filling; press seam and ends to seal. Transfer to baking sheet and bake until lightly browned and sausage is heated through, 12 to 15 minutes.

While sausage is baking, prepare sauce. In small bowl combine remaining ingredients and stir well. Remove sausage from oven and, using a serrated knife, cut crosswise into 12 equal pieces. Serve each portion with ¼ of the mustard mixture (about 1 tablespoon).

Each serving provides: 2 Protein Exchanges; 1 Bread Exchange; 30 Optional Calories
Per serving: 323 calories; 11 g protein; 21 g fat; 24 g carbohydrate; 108 mg calcium;
964 mg sodium; 27 mg cholesterol; dietary fiber data not available

*Keep biscuits refrigerated until ready to use. Separate dough into layers as soon as it is removed from the refrigerator; it will be difficult to work with if allowed to come to room temperature.

Veal Chili ℂ

WEEK 4   MAKES 2 SERVINGS

½ cup diced onion
½ jalapeño pepper, seeded and minced
½ pound ground veal
1½ cups canned Italian tomatoes (with liquid); drain, seed, and chop tomatoes, reserving liquid
½ cup tomato sauce
1 tablespoon chili powder
1 teaspoon powdered mustard
½ teaspoon pepper
¼ teaspoon *each* basil and oregano leaves
⅛ teaspoon salt
4 ounces drained canned red kidney beans
2 tablespoons *each* chopped fresh Italian (flat-leaf) parsley and dry white table wine
1 teaspoon lemon juice

Spray 4-quart saucepan with nonstick cooking spray; add onion and jalapeño pepper and sauté over medium heat, stirring frequently, until onion is translucent, about 2 minutes. Add veal and cook until veal is no longer pink, 5 to 7 minutes. Add tomatoes and reserved liquid, tomato sauce, and seasonings and stir to combine. Reduce heat to low and let simmer until flavors blend, about 5 minutes. Add remaining ingredients and stir to combine; cook 15 minutes longer.

Each serving provides: 3 Protein Exchanges; 1 Bread Exchange; 2½ Vegetable Exchanges; 15 Optional Calories
Per serving: 359 calories; 30 g protein; 13 g fat; 30 g carbohydrate; 135 mg calcium; 1,114 mg sodium (estimated); 81 mg cholesterol; 4 g dietary fiber

Veal España ◐

WEEK 2   MAKES 2 SERVINGS

2 veal cutlets (¼ pound each)
1 tablespoon plus 1 teaspoon
  all-purpose flour, divided
2 teaspoons olive *or* vegetable oil
1 ounce cooked smoked ham, finely
  chopped
½ cup finely chopped mushrooms
¼ cup finely chopped drained pimientos

1 garlic clove, minced
¼ cup *each* canned ready-to-serve
  chicken broth and dry white table
  wine
⅛ teaspoon thyme leaves
Dash pepper
1 bay leaf

Dredge cutlets in 1 tablespoon flour, coating both sides. In 10-inch nonstick skillet heat oil; add veal and cook over medium-high heat, turning once, until browned on both sides and tender, 1 to 2 minutes on each side. Transfer veal to plate; set aside.

In same skillet combine ham, mushrooms, pimientos, and garlic and sauté over medium heat, stirring frequently, until mushrooms are tender, about 2 minutes. Sprinkle remaining teaspoon flour over mixture and stir quickly to combine; continuing to stir, gradually add broth. Stir in remaining ingredients. Reduce heat to low and let simmer until sauce has thickened and flavors blend, 5 to 7 minutes. Return veal to skillet and cook until heated through, 1 to 2 minutes. Remove and discard bay leaf before serving.

Each serving provides: 3½ Protein Exchanges; ¾ Vegetable Exchange; 1 Fat Exchange;
  55 Optional Calories
Per serving: 293 calories; 27 g protein; 15 g fat; 8 g carbohydrate; 28 mg calcium;
  415 mg sodium; 87 mg cholesterol; 1 g dietary fiber

Fruited Lamb 🌀 🌑

An excellent way to transform leftover cooked lamb into a delicious entrée.

2 tablespoons reduced-calorie
   soy sauce
1 tablespoon lemon juice
1½ teaspoons *each* honey, hoisin
   sauce, Dijon-style mustard, and olive
   or vegetable oil
½ teaspoon Chinese sesame oil
½ teaspoon chopped fresh rosemary *or*
   ¼ teaspoon dried
2 cups sliced onions

½ cup *each* diced red bell pepper and
   canned crushed pineapple (no sugar
   added), drain and reserve juice
1½ teaspoons cornstarch
6 ounces boned cooked lamb, cut into
   cubes
1 large mandarin orange (about
   4 ounces), peeled and sectioned

In small mixing bowl combine soy sauce, lemon juice, honey, hoisin sauce, mustard, oils, and rosemary. Transfer soy sauce mixture to 9-inch skillet and cook over medium heat, stirring constantly, until mixture comes to a boil. Stir in onions and bell pepper; cover and cook until onions are tender-crisp, about 5 minutes.

In small bowl combine reserved pineapple juice and the cornstarch, stirring to dissolve cornstarch; pour into skillet, add lamb, and let simmer, stirring occasionally, until lamb is heated through. Stir in crushed pineapple and orange sections and cook until heated through, 2 to 3 minutes longer.

Each serving provides: 3 Protein Exchanges; 2½ Vegetable Exchanges; 1 Fat Exchange;
  1 Fruit Exchange; 30 Optional Calories
Per serving: 379 calories; 28 g protein; 14 g fat; 38 g carbohydrate; 63 mg calcium;
  911 mg sodium; 78 mg cholesterol; 2 g dietary fiber

Lamb Chops with Minted Honey Marinade

WEEK 1   MAKES 2 SERVINGS

If cost is a concern, use lamb shoulder chops in this recipe rather than loin chops.

¼ cup fresh mint leaves
1 tablespoon Dijon-style mustard
1½ teaspoons *each* honey and
   champagne vinegar *or* red wine
   vinegar

2 loin lamb chops (5 ounces each)

In blender container combine mint, mustard, honey, and vinegar and process until smooth, scraping down sides of container as necessary. In glass or stainless-steel bowl (not aluminum*) arrange chops; add mint mixture and turn to coat. Cover with plastic wrap and refrigerate for at least 2 hours or overnight.

Spray rack in broiling pan with nonstick cooking spray; transfer chops to rack, reserving marinade. Broil chops until browned, 5 to 8 minutes; turn chops over, brush with reserved marinade, and broil 5 to 8 minutes longer or until done to taste. In small saucepan heat any remaining marinade.

To serve, arrange chops on serving platter and top with remaining marinade.

Each serving provides: 3 Protein Exchanges; 15 Optional Calories
Per serving: 210 calories; 26 g protein; 9 g fat; 6 g carbohydrate; 4 mg calcium;
   297 mg sodium; 80 mg cholesterol; dietary fiber data not available

*It's best to marinate in glass or stainless-steel containers; ingredients such as vinegar may react with aluminum, causing color and flavor changes in food.

Oriental Pork and Rice Salad

WEEK 2   MAKES 2 SERVINGS, ABOUT 1½ CUPS EACH

You can prepare the rice mixture and the dressing for this salad in advance. Keep the rice mixture in the refrigerator and the dressing at room temperature; add the dressing to the salad just before serving.

1 cup cooked long-grain rice
¼ pound boned cooked pork, cut into strips or cubes
½ cup *each* julienne-cut carrot, green bell pepper, and red bell pepper (matchstick pieces)
¼ cup *each* sliced scallions (green onions) and mushrooms

1 tablespoon *each* corn syrup, teriyaki sauce, and rice vinegar
1½ teaspoons *each* grated pared gingerroot and peanut *or* vegetable oil
⅓ teaspoon Chinese sesame oil
¼ teaspoon freshly ground pepper

In medium mixing bowl combine rice, pork, and vegetables; set aside. In blender container combine remaining ingredients and process until combined, scraping down sides of container as necessary. Pour dressing over salad and toss to combine. Serve immediately.

Each serving provides: 2 Protein Exchanges; 1 Bread Exchange; 2 Vegetable Exchanges; 1 Fat Exchange; 30 Optional Calories
Per serving: 356 calories; 22 g protein; 11 g fat; 42 g carbohydrate; 42 mg calcium; 412 mg sodium; 56 mg cholesterol; 2 g dietary fiber

Pork with Caraway Cream

WEEK 4   MAKES 2 SERVINGS

Use leftover cooked pork to make this creamy dish and serve it over noodles or fettuccine.

2 teaspoons margarine
2 tablespoons chopped shallot
   (or onion)
1 tablespoon all-purpose flour
¼ cup *each* dry white table wine and
   canned ready-to-serve chicken broth
1 teaspoon Dijon-style mustard

½ teaspoon caraway seed, crushed
⅛ teaspoon *each* salt and white pepper
3 tablespoons sour cream
6 ounces boned cooked pork, thinly
   sliced

In 10-inch nonstick skillet melt margarine; add shallot (or onion) and sauté until translucent, about 1 minute. Sprinkle with flour and stir quickly to combine; gradually stir in wine. Add broth and cook, stirring constantly, until mixture is smooth and slightly thickened, about 2 minutes. Reduce heat to lowest possible setting; add mustard, caraway seed, salt, and pepper and stir to combine. Continue cooking until flavors blend and sauce has thickened, 4 to 5 minutes. Stir in sour cream; add pork to skillet and cook until heated through, 1 to 2 minutes.

Each serving provides: 3 Protein Exchanges; ⅛ Vegetable Exchange; 1 Fat Exchange;
   105 Optional Calories
Per serving: 335 calories; 26 g protein; 20 g fat; 7 g carbohydrate; 44 mg calcium;
   457 mg sodium; 87 mg cholesterol; 0.2 g dietary fiber

Pork with Dijon Cream ◖

2 pork cutlets (¼ pound each)
2 teaspoons margarine
2 tablespoons finely chopped shallot
    (or onion)
1 garlic clove, minced
2 teaspoons all-purpose flour

½ cup canned ready-to-serve chicken
    broth
1 tablespoon Dijon-style mustard
2 tablespoons whipping cream

On rack in broiling pan broil pork 4 inches from heat source, turning once, until thoroughly cooked, 2 to 3 minutes on each side.

While pork is broiling, prepare sauce. In small saucepan melt margarine; add shallot (or onion) and garlic and sauté over medium heat until tender, 1 to 2 minutes. Sprinkle flour over garlic mixture and stir quickly to combine; continuing to stir, gradually add broth. Stir in mustard and cook, stirring occasionally, until mixture thickens, 4 to 5 minutes. Add pork to skillet and cook 3 minutes longer. Stir in cream and remove from heat. Arrange pork cutlets on serving platter and top with sauce.

Each serving provides: 3 Protein Exchanges; ⅛ Vegetable Exchange; 1 Fat Exchange;
    70 Optional Calories
Per serving: 301 calories; 26 g protein; 19 g fat; 6 g carbohydrate; 24 mg calcium;
    582 mg sodium; 97 mg cholesterol; 0.2 g dietary fiber

Ham Steaks with Cider-Pear Sauce ◐

WEEK 5   MAKES 2 SERVINGS

2 teaspoons reduced-calorie margarine
6 ounces "fully cooked" boneless
  smoked ham steak
1 small pear (about 5 ounces), cored,
  pared, and thinly sliced (⅛-inch-thick
  slices)
¼ cup port wine

⅔ cup unfermented apple cider
  (no sugar added)
1 teaspoon *each* cornstarch and
  Dijon-style mustard
½ teaspoon lemon juice

In 12-inch skillet melt margarine; add ham and cook over high heat, turning once, until browned on both sides, 2 to 3 minutes on each side. Transfer ham to plate; set aside and keep warm.

To same skillet add pear slices and sauté over medium heat, gently shaking pan occasionally, until slices begin to soften, about 1 minute. Add wine to skillet and cook 1 minute longer. In 1-cup liquid measure or small bowl combine remaining ingredients, stirring to dissolve cornstarch; add to pear mixture and cook, stirring constantly, until mixture thickens and is reduced by half, 2 to 3 minutes. Return ham to skillet and turn to coat with sauce. Transfer ham to serving platter and top with sauce.

Each serving provides: 3 Protein Exchanges; ½ Fat Exchange; 1½ Fruit Exchanges;
  55 Optional Calories
Per serving: 258 calories; 17 g protein; 7 g fat; 25 g carbohydrate; 21 mg calcium;
 1,336 mg sodium; 40 mg cholesterol; 2 g dietary fiber

Legumes

Think beans are boring? You won't once you've tried Creole Red Beans and Rice, Marinated Black Bean Salad, or Vegetarian Tamale Pie. Even if you're not a vegetarian, legumes are a wonderfully satisfying and healthful alternative to meat.

255

Spicy Black Bean Soup ⊜⊕

WEEK 4   MAKES 4 SERVINGS, ABOUT 1 CUP EACH

Soups are great when you want to warm up. This spicy pot of soup can be ready in about 20 minutes.

2 teaspoons olive *or* vegetable oil
½ cup chopped onion
1 garlic clove, minced
1 cup *each* water and canned
   ready-to-serve beef broth
8 ounces drained canned black (turtle)
   beans
2 tablespoons tomato paste

6 sun-dried tomato halves (not packed
   in oil), cut into matchstick pieces
1 teaspoon balsamic vinegar *or*
   red wine vinegar
¼ teaspoon *each* basil leaves, crushed
   red pepper, and salt

In 2-quart saucepan heat oil; add onion and garlic and sauté over medium heat, stirring occasionally, until onion is translucent, 2 to 3 minutes. Add water, broth, beans, and tomato paste. Bring to a boil and cook for 1 minute. Remove from heat and let cool slightly; transfer to work bowl of food processor and process until pureed. Return to saucepan; add remaining ingredients and cook over low heat, stirring occasionally, until mixture is heated through, about 5 minutes.

Each serving provides: 1 Protein Exchange; 1⅛ Vegetable Exchanges; ½ Fat Exchange;
   10 Optional Calories
Per serving: 123 calories; 6 g protein; 3 g fat; 19 g carbohydrate; 42 mg calcium;
   940 mg sodium (estimated); 0 mg cholesterol; 3 g dietary fiber

Variation: Spicy Bean and Tomato Soup —Substitute 3 large plum tomatoes, peeled, seeded, and chopped, for the sun-dried tomato halves.

Per serving: Reduce sodium to 415 mg

Black Beans and Rice with Cumin Vinaigrette

WEEK 3   MAKES 2 SERVINGS

Canned beans and leftover rice can be combined into a salad with a Latin flavor in almost no time.

6 ounces drained canned black (turtle) beans
1 cup cooked long-grain rice, chilled
½ cup diced red bell pepper
1 tablespoon *each* rice vinegar and water

2 teaspoons *each* chopped fresh cilantro (Chinese parsley) *or* parsley and olive oil
¼ teaspoon ground cumin
⅛ teaspoon *each* salt and pepper

In medium bowl combine beans, rice, and bell pepper, mixing well. Using a fork or wire whisk, in small mixing bowl beat together remaining ingredients; pour over rice mixture and toss to coat. Serve immediately or cover and refrigerate until chilled.

Each serving provides: 1½ Protein Exchanges; 1 Bread Exchange; ½ Vegetable Exchange; 1 Fat Exchange
Per serving: 257 calories; 8 g protein; 5 g fat; 44 g carbohydrate; 52 mg calcium; 427 mg sodium (estimated); 0 mg cholesterol; 5 g dietary fiber

Marinated Black Bean Salad ⊖ ◑

Using canned beans makes this recipe super-easy. You can put it together in minutes and have a wonderful dish to enjoy later.

8 ounces drained canned black (turtle)
  beans, rinsed
½ cup *each* chopped red onion,
  chopped celery, and diced tomato
1 tablespoon *each* red wine vinegar,
  lemon juice, and water
2 teaspoons olive oil

1 teaspoon chopped fresh cilantro
  (Chinese parsley) *or* parsley
1 small garlic clove, minced
½ teaspoon Dijon-style mustard
8 lettuce leaves
3 tablespoons sour cream

In medium mixing bowl (not aluminum*) combine all ingredients except lettuce and sour cream and mix well until thoroughly combined. Cover with plastic wrap and refrigerate until flavors blend, overnight or at least 3 hours.

To serve, line a chilled serving platter with lettuce leaves; spoon bean mixture onto center of lettuce liner and top with sour cream.

Each serving provides: 2 Protein Exchanges; 2½ Vegetable Exchanges; 1 Fat Exchange;
  50 Optional Calories
Per serving: 253 calories; 10 g protein; 10 g fat; 33 g carbohydrate; 121 mg calcium;
  466 mg sodium; 9 mg cholesterol; 6 g dietary fiber

*It's best to marinate in glass or stainless-steel containers; acidic ingredients such as lemon juice may react with aluminum, causing color and flavor changes in food.

Veal Sausage and White Bean Soup

WEEK 3   MAKES 4 SERVINGS

2 teaspoons olive *or* vegetable oil
½ cup chopped celery
¼ cup chopped onion
1 tablespoon minced shallot (optional)
1 garlic clove, minced
2 cups canned ready-to-serve chicken broth
12 ounces drained canned small white beans

1 cup water
2 ounces cooked veal sausage link, sliced
2 teaspoons chopped fresh Italian (flat-leaf) parsley
1 teaspoon chopped fresh sage *or* ¼ teaspoon dried
Dash *each* salt and pepper

In 4-quart saucepan heat oil; add celery, onion, shallot, if desired, and garlic and sauté over medium heat until onion is translucent, about 3 minutes. Add broth, beans, and water, and bring mixture to a boil. Reduce heat to low and let simmer for 5 minutes. Add remaining ingredients, stir to combine, and cook over medium heat, stirring occasionally, until sausage is heated through and flavors blend, about 10 minutes.

Each serving provides: 2 Protein Exchanges; ¼ Vegetable Exchange; ½ Fat Exchange; 20 Optional Calories
Per serving: 171 calories; 12 g protein; 5 g fat; 20 g carbohydrate; 81 mg calcium; 1,028 mg sodium (estimated); 14 mg cholesterol; 0.2 g dietary fiber (this figure does not include white beans; nutrition analysis not available)

White Bean and Cheddar Casserole ⓒⓘ

WEEK 3   MAKES 2 SERVINGS

2 teaspoons olive *or* vegetable oil
½ cup chopped onion
1 garlic clove, minced
2 cups canned Italian tomatoes (with liquid); drain, seed, and chop tomatoes, reserving liquid
2 teaspoons molasses
1 teaspoon red wine vinegar
¼ teaspoon ground nutmeg

⅛ teaspoon *each* salt and ground ginger
Dash *each* black pepper and ground red pepper
6 ounces drained canned white beans
1 ounce *each* day-old Italian bread, toasted and cut into cubes, and Cheddar cheese, shredded

In 2½-quart saucepan heat oil; add onion and garlic and sauté over medium heat, stirring occasionally, until onion is translucent, about 3 minutes. Add tomatoes and reserved liquid, molasses, vinegar, and seasonings and stir to combine. Reduce heat to low and let simmer for 5 minutes. Add beans, stir to combine, and let simmer until heated through, about 5 minutes.

In 1-quart flameproof casserole arrange bread cubes; spoon bean mixture over bread and sprinkle with cheese. Broil until cheese is melted and lightly browned, about 1 minute.

Each serving provides: 2 Protein Exchanges; ½ Bread Exchange; 2½ Vegetable Exchanges; 1 Fat Exchange; 20 Optional Calories
Per serving: 314 calories; 14 g protein; 10 g fat; 44 g carbohydrate; 261 mg calcium; 992 mg sodium (estimated); 15 mg cholesterol; 3 g dietary fiber (this figure does not include white beans; nutrition analysis not available)

Italian Cannellini Beans and Sausage

WEEK 3   MAKES 2 SERVINGS

This hot and hearty dinner can be ready to enjoy in just 15 minutes.

2 teaspoons olive *or* vegetable oil
5 ounces veal sausage links
½ cup diced onion
1 garlic clove, minced
1 cup drained canned Italian tomatoes,
 seeded and chopped

4 ounces drained canned white kidney
 (cannellini) beans
1 tablespoon chopped fresh basil
⅛ teaspoon salt
Dash pepper

In 10-inch nonstick skillet heat oil; add sausage and cook over medium-high heat, turning occasionally, until browned on all sides, 3 to 4 minutes. Remove from skillet and set aside.

In same skillet combine onion and garlic and sauté, stirring occasionally, until onion is translucent, 1 to 2 minutes. Add tomatoes, beans, and seasonings and stir to combine. Reduce heat to low and let simmer until flavors blend, 3 to 4 minutes. Thinly slice veal sausage, add to bean mixture, and cook until heated through, about 1 minute.

Each serving provides: 3 Protein Exchanges; 1½ Vegetable Exchanges; 1 Fat Exchange
Per serving: 277 calories; 22 g protein; 12 g fat; 20 g carbohydrate; 109 mg calcium;
 923 mg sodium (estimated); 57 mg cholesterol; 1 g dietary fiber

Latin-Style Beans, Beef, and Hominy ⓒ

WEEK 4   MAKES 4 SERVINGS

For a wonderful lunch or side dish on a cold winter day, try this satisfying stew. It takes only 10 minutes to combine; then just 30 minutes to cook.

2 teaspoons olive *or* vegetable oil
½ cup *each* diced onion and red
  or green bell pepper
1 small garlic clove, minced
2 cups water
4 ounces drained canned white kidney
  (cannellini) beans
1 cup drained canned whole yellow
  or white hominy
2 ounces cooked ground beef,
  crumbled

2 large plum tomatoes, blanched,
  peeled, seeded, and chopped
1 tablespoon chopped fresh cilantro
  (Chinese parsley) *or* parsley
1 packet instant beef broth and
  seasoning mix
⅛ teaspoon *each* salt, chili powder,
  and pepper

In 2-quart saucepan heat oil; add onion, bell pepper, and garlic and cook, stirring frequently, until vegetables are tender-crisp. Add remaining ingredients and bring to a boil. Reduce heat to low and let simmer until flavors blend, about 20 minutes.

Each serving provides: 1 Protein Exchange; ½ Bread Exchange; 1 Vegetable Exchange;
  ½ Fat Exchange; 3 Optional Calories
Per serving: 142 calories; 7 g protein; 6 g fat; 16 g carbohydrate; 28 mg calcium;
  575 mg sodium (estimated); 13 mg cholesterol; 2 g dietary fiber (this figure does not
  include hominy; nutrition analysis not available)

Mexican Beans on Rice Ⓒ

WEEK 3   MAKES 4 SERVINGS

1 tablespoon plus 1 teaspoon olive *or* vegetable oil
1 cup diced onions
½ cup *each* diced celery and red bell pepper
1 tablespoon minced cilantro (Chinese parsley) *or* parsley
1 teaspoon minced seeded hot chili *or* jalapeño pepper
1 large garlic clove, minced

2 cups canned Italian tomatoes (with liquid); drain and chop tomatoes, reserving liquid
14 ounces drained canned white kidney (cannellini) beans
2 cups cooked long-grain rice (hot)
1 ounce sharp Cheddar cheese, shredded
Garnish: fresh cilantro (Chinese parsley) *or* parsley leaves

In 2-quart saucepan heat oil; add onions, celery, bell pepper, minced cilantro (or parsley), chili pepper, and garlic and sauté until vegetables are tender-crisp, about 2 minutes. Add tomatoes and reserved liquid and stir to combine; cook over high heat until mixture comes to a boil. Reduce heat to low; add beans, stir to combine, and let simmer until flavors blend, about 20 minutes.

To serve, spoon rice onto serving platter; top with bean mixture, sprinkle with cheese, and garnish with cilantro (or parsley) leaves.

Each serving provides: 2 Protein Exchanges; 1 Bread Exchange; 2 Vegetable Exchanges; 1 Fat Exchange
Per serving: 335 calories; 13 g protein; 8 g fat; 54 g carbohydrate; 159 mg calcium; 595 mg sodium (estimated); 7 mg cholesterol; 6 g dietary fiber

Vegetarian Tamale Pie

WEEK 5   MAKES 4 SERVINGS

1 tablespoon plus 1 teaspoon olive
  or vegetable oil, divided
½ cup *each* chopped onion and green
  bell pepper
1 garlic clove, minced
12 ounces drained canned red kidney
  beans, slightly mashed
½ cup drained canned Italian tomatoes,
  diced
4 *each* pitted green and black olives,
  sliced

2 teaspoons chili powder
1 teaspoon chopped fresh cilantro
  (Chinese parsley) *or* parsley
2¼ ounces uncooked yellow cornmeal
3 tablespoons all-purpose flour
¼ teaspoon baking soda
½ cup buttermilk
1 egg
2 ounces Cheddar cheese, shredded

In 10-inch nonstick skillet heat 2 teaspoons oil; add onion, green
pepper, and garlic and sauté over medium-high heat until vegetables are tender, 2 to 3 minutes. Add beans, tomatoes, olives, chili
powder, and cilantro (or parsley) and cook, stirring frequently, until
flavors blend, 2 to 3 minutes. Spray four 1¾-cup flameproof casseroles with nonstick cooking spray; spoon ¼ of bean mixture
(about ½ cup) into each casserole and set aside.

Preheat oven to 400° F. In small mixing bowl combine cornmeal,
flour, and baking soda; set aside. In separate small mixing bowl beat
together buttermilk, egg, and remaining 2 teaspoons oil; stir into
flour mixture, mixing well. Pour ¼ of cornmeal mixture over each
portion of bean mixture and bake for 15 to 20 minutes (until a knife,
inserted into cornmeal mixture, comes out clean). Sprinkle each
portion of cornmeal mixture with ¼ of the cheese. Turn oven control
to broil and broil until cheese is melted and lightly browned, 1 to 2
minutes.

Each serving provides: 2 Protein Exchanges; 1 Bread Exchange; ¾ Vegetable Exchange;
  1 Fat Exchange; 45 Optional Calories
Per serving: 334 calories; 16 g protein; 13 g fat; 40 g carbohydrate; 212 mg calcium;
  654 mg sodium (estimated); 85 mg cholesterol; 5 g dietary fiber

Refried Beans Monterey

WEEK 4   MAKES 4 SERVINGS

2 teaspoons olive or vegetable oil
¼ cup finely chopped onion
1 tablespoon each seeded and
   chopped jalapeño pepper and
   chopped cilantro (Chinese parsley)
   or parsley
1 garlic clove, minced
6 ounces drained canned red kidney
   beans, mashed

1 ounce Monterey Jack cheese,
   shredded
2 flour or corn tortillas (6-inch diameter
   each), heated and cut into 6 wedges
   each

In 9-inch nonstick skillet heat oil; add onion, pepper, cilantro (or parsley), and garlic and sauté over medium-high heat, stirring frequently, until vegetables are tender, 1 to 2 minutes. Add beans and continue cooking, stirring frequently, until mixture is heated through, 2 to 3 minutes.

Spray a 1½-quart shallow flameproof casserole with nonstick cooking spray; spread bean mixture in casserole and sprinkle with cheese. Broil until cheese is melted, about 1 minute. Serve each portion with 3 tortilla wedges.

Each serving provides: 1 Protein Exchange; ½ Bread Exchange; ⅛ Vegetable Exchange;
   ½ Fat Exchange
Per serving with flour tortilla: 134 calories; 6 g protein; 6 g fat; 16 g carbohydrate;
   99 mg calcium; 255 mg sodium (estimated); 6 mg cholesterol; 2 g dietary fiber
With corn tortilla: 133 calories; 6 g protein; 5 g fat; 16 g carbohydrate; 100 mg calcium;
   212 mg sodium (estimated); 6 mg cholesterol; 2 g dietary fiber

Creole Red Beans and Rice

WEEK 3   **MAKES 2 SERVINGS**

1 teaspoon olive *or* vegetable oil
¼ cup *each* chopped celery, onion, and
  green bell pepper
1 ounce cooked smoked ham, diced
1 small garlic clove, minced
6 ounces drained canned red kidney
  beans
¼ cup water

½ bay leaf
½ teaspoon *each* chili powder and hot
  sauce
⅛ teaspoon *each* thyme leaves and
  oregano leaves
1 cup cooked long-grain rice (hot)

In 1½-quart saucepan heat oil; add celery, onion, pepper, ham, and garlic and sauté over medium heat, stirring frequently, until vegetables are tender-crisp. Stir in remaining ingredients except rice; bring to a boil. Reduce heat to low, cover, and let simmer until vegetables are tender and flavors blend, 10 to 15 minutes. Remove and discard bay leaf. Serve with rice.

Each serving provides: 2 Protein Exchanges; 1 Bread Exchange; ¾ Vegetable Exchange;
  ½ Fat Exchange
Per serving: 262 calories; 12 g protein; 4 g fat; 46 g carbohydrate; 72 mg calcium;
  547 mg sodium (estimated); 7 mg cholesterol; 4 g dietary fiber

Mexican Pizza ⒸⓄ

1 teaspoon olive *or* vegetable oil
¼ cup *each* chopped onion and green bell pepper
1 teaspoon chopped jalapeño pepper
4 ounces drained canned pink beans, mashed
½ cup seeded and diced tomato, divided
¼ cup water

2 corn tortillas (6-inch diameter each), heated
2 ounces Colby *or* Monterey Jack cheese
2 tablespoons sour cream
4 pitted black olives, sliced
2 tablespoons chopped scallion (green onion)

In 10-inch nonstick skillet heat oil; add onion, bell pepper, and jalapeño pepper and sauté, stirring frequently, until vegetables are softened, 1 to 2 minutes. Add beans, all but 2 tablespoons tomato, and all of the water; mix well and cook until mixture thickens, 3 to 4 minutes.

On baking sheet arrange tortillas in a single layer; spread half of the bean mixture over each tortilla and sprinkle each with 1 ounce cheese. Broil until cheese melts, 1 to 2 minutes. Top each with 1 tablespoon sour cream, half of the olive slices, 1 tablespoon scallion, and ½ of the reserved tomatoes.

Each serving provides: 2 Protein Exchanges; 1 Bread Exchange; 1⅛ Vegetable Exchanges; ½ Fat Exchange; 45 Optional Calories
Per serving with Colby cheese: 327 calories; 14 g protein; 17 g fat; 31 g carbohydrate; 296 mg calcium; 472 mg sodium (estimated); 33 mg cholesterol; 5 g dietary fiber
With Monterey Jack cheese: 321 calories; 14 g protein; 17 g fat; 30 g carbohydrate; 314 mg calcium; 453 mg sodium (estimated); 31 mg cholesterol; 5 g dietary fiber

Hummus Soup ◐

WEEK 3   MAKES 4 SERVINGS

8 ounces drained canned chick-peas
2 cups canned ready-to-serve chicken broth, divided
¼ cup tahini (sesame paste)

1 teaspoon Dijon-style mustard
½ teaspoon garlic powder
⅛ teaspoon white pepper

In blender container combine chick-peas, 1 cup broth, the tahini, mustard, and seasonings and process at high speed until pureed, about 2 minutes, scraping down sides of container as necessary. Transfer to 2½-quart saucepan; add remaining 1 cup broth and cook over medium heat, stirring frequently, until mixture is heated through, about 5 minutes *(do not boil)*.

Each serving provides: 1 Protein Exchange; 1 Bread Exchange; 1 Fat Exchange; 20 Optional Calories
Per serving: 178 calories; 7 g protein; 10 g fat; 16 g carbohydrate; 84 mg calcium; 751 mg sodium (estimated); 0 mg cholesterol; 1 g dietary fiber

Variation: Hummus Soup with Sesame Seed (Week 4) — Toast 1 teaspoon sesame seed; sprinkle an equal amount on each portion of soup. Increase Optional Calories to 25.

Per serving: 182 calories; 7 g protein; 11 g fat; 16 g carbohydrate; 92 mg calcium; 752 mg sodium (estimated); 0 mg cholesterol; 1 g dietary fiber

Bean Burgers ©

WEEK 3   MAKES 2 SERVINGS, 2 BURGERS EACH

1 tablespoon plus 1 teaspoon olive
   or vegetable oil, divided
¼ cup *each* minced onion, green bell
   pepper, carrot, and celery
6 ounces drained canned chick-peas
   or white kidney (cannellini) beans

1 egg, lightly beaten
⅓ cup plus 2 teaspoons seasoned
   dried bread crumbs

In 8-inch nonstick skillet heat 1 teaspoon oil; add onion, pepper, carrot, and celery and cook over medium heat, stirring occasionally, until vegetables are soft and moisture has evaporated, about 1 minute. Set aside and let cool slightly.

Using a fork, in medium mixing bowl mash chick-peas (or kidney beans); stir in egg. Add bread crumbs and vegetable mixture and mix until thoroughly combined. Shape into 4 equal patties; set on plate, cover, and chill for at least 20 minutes.

In same skillet heat remaining 1 tablespoon oil; add patties and cook over medium heat, turning once, until browned on both sides and heated throughout.

Each serving provides: 2 Protein Exchanges; 1 Bread Exchange; 1 Vegetable Exchange;
   2 Fat Exchanges
Per serving with chick-peas: 320 calories; 12 g protein; 14 g fat; 37 g carbohydrate;
   79 mg calcium; 941 mg sodium (estimated); 138 mg cholesterol; 2 g dietary fiber
With kidney beans: 312 calories; 13 g protein; 13 g fat; 37 g carbohydrate; 89 mg calcium;
   941 mg sodium (estimated); 138 mg cholesterol; 4 g dietary fiber

Greek Lentil Salad

When you don't have much time to prepare lunch, make this hearty and flavorful salad in advance, then cover and chill it. It will be ready when lunchtime arrives.

3 cups water
4½ ounces sorted uncooked lentils, rinsed
1 *each* medium red and yellow bell pepper
½ cup chopped scallions (green onions)
3 tablespoons red wine vinegar

2 tablespoons *each* drained capers and chopped fresh mint
1 tablespoon plus 1 teaspoon olive oil
1 tablespoon lemon juice
8 lettuce leaves
2 ounces feta cheese, crumbled

In 3-quart oauoopan bring water to a boil, add lentils, cover, and cook over high heat, stirring occasionally, until tender, 25 to 30 minutes.

While lentils are cooking, roast peppers. Preheat broiler. On baking sheet lined with heavy-duty foil broil peppers 3 inches from heat source, turning frequently, until charred on all sides; let stand until cool enough to handle, 15 to 20 minutes. Peel peppers; remove and discard stem ends and seeds. Cut peppers into strips and set aside.

Strain lentils' through sieve, reserving ¼ cup cooking liquid. Transfer to medium mixing bowl, stir in scallions, and set aside.

In small mixing bowl combine reserved cooking liquid, vinegar, capers, mint, oil, and lemon juice; pour over lentil mixture and mix well to thoroughly coat. Cover and chill in refrigerator, 1 to 2 hours.

To serve, line serving platter with lettuce leaves; spoon lentil mixture onto center of lettuce. Decoratively arrange pepper slices on lettuce and sprinkle feta cheese over salad.

Each serving provides: 2 Protein Exchanges; 1¾ Vegetable Exchanges; 1 Fat Exchange
Per serving: 203 calories; 12 g protein; 8 g fat; 23 g carbohydrate; 108 mg calcium;
    275 mg sodium; 13 mg cholesterol; 5 g dietary fiber

Peasant Lentil Soup

WEEK 5   MAKES 4 SERVINGS

In only 15 minutes you can have this hearty soup cooking on the stove.

2 teaspoons olive *or* vegetable oil
5 ounces veal sausage links
1 cup diced carrots
6 ounces diced pared all-purpose
　potato
½ cup diced onion
2 to 3 garlic cloves, minced
1½ quarts water
2 cups thoroughly washed and drained
　Swiss chard, chopped

3 ounces sorted uncooked lentils,
　rinsed
3 packets instant chicken broth and
　seasoning mix
1 tablespoon chopped fresh parsley
1 teaspoon paprika
1 bay leaf
⅛ teaspoon pepper

In 3-quart saucepan heat oil; add sausage and cook over medium-high heat, turning occasionally, until sausage is cooked through and browned on all sides, 3 to 4 minutes. Remove from saucepan and set aside.

In same saucepan combine carrots, potato, onion, and garlic and sauté, stirring occasionally, until onion is translucent, 1 to 2 minutes. Add water, Swiss chard, lentils, broth mix, parsley, paprika, bay leaf, and pepper and stir to combine. Reduce heat to medium-low, partially cover, and cook until lentils are tender, 40 to 45 minutes. Thinly slice sausage and add to soup; cook until heated through, 1 to 2 minutes. Remove and discard bay leaf before serving.

Each serving provides: 2 Protein Exchanges; ½ Bread Exchange; 1¾ Vegetable Exchanges;
　½ Fat Exchange; 10 Optional Calories
Per serving: 229 calories; 17 g protein; 6 g fat; 27 g carbohydrate; 49 mg calcium;
　1,180 mg sodium (estimated); 29 mg cholesterol; 4 g dietary fiber (this figure does not
　include Swiss chard; nutrition analysis not available)

Variation: Peasant Lentil Soup with Spinach (Week 3)—2 cups spinach leaves may be substituted for the Swiss chard.

Per serving: 232 calories; 17 g protein; 6 g fat; 28 g carbohydrate; 67 mg calcium;
　1,164 mg sodium (estimated); 29 mg cholesterol; 5 g dietary fiber

Skillet Lentils and Potatoes ⊝ ◑

WEEK 3   MAKES 4 SERVINGS

If you plan ahead and cook up some extra potatoes in advance, you can have this filling lunch or side dish on the table in about 25 minutes.

2 teaspoons olive *or* vegetable oil
6 ounces pared cooked all-purpose
   potato, diced
½ cup chopped onion
1 ounce finely chopped cooked
   smoked ham
1 garlic clove, minced

6 ounces drained canned lentils
¼ cup water
½ packet (about ½ teaspoon) instant
   vegetable broth and seasoning mix
1 bay leaf
1 teaspoon chopped fresh parsley

In 10-inch nonstick skillet heat oil; add potato, onion, ham, and garlic and sauté over medium-high heat, stirring occasionally, until vegetables are lightly browned, 2 to 3 minutes. Add remaining ingredients except parsley and mix well to combine; continue cooking until flavors blend and mixture is heated through, 4 to 5 minutes. Remove and discard bay leaf. Serve sprinkled with parsley.

Each serving provides: 1 Protein Exchange; ½ Bread Exchange; ¼ Vegetable Exchange;
   ½ Fat Exchange; 2 Optional Calories
Per serving: 123 calories; 6 g protein; 3 g fat; 19 g carbohydrate; 20 mg calcium;
   372 mg sodium (estimated); 3 mg cholesterol; 3 g dietary fiber

Lentil, Cheese, and Vegetable Soup Ⓒ

| WEEK 5 | MAKES 4 SERVINGS, ABOUT 1 CUP EACH |

1 tablespoon plus 1 teaspoon olive
   or vegetable oil
1 cup *each* julienne-cut carrots
   (matchstick pieces) and diced onions
1 garlic clove, minced
¼ teaspoon thyme leaves
1 bay leaf
1 quart water
3 ounces sorted uncooked lentils,
   rinsed

2 packets instant chicken broth and
   seasoning mix
4 cups thoroughly washed and drained
   Swiss chard, chopped
¼ pound Cheddar cheese, shredded
Dash *each* salt and pepper
Garnish: chopped fresh Italian
   (flat-leaf) parsley

In 2-quart saucepan heat oil; add carrots, onions, garlic, thyme, and bay leaf and sauté over medium heat, stirring constantly, until vegetables are tender-crisp, about 2 minutes. Add water, lentils, and broth mix and stir to combine; bring to a boil. Reduce heat to low and let simmer until lentils soften, about 15 minutes; stir in Swiss chard and cook until tender, about 10 minutes longer. Stir in cheese and let simmer, stirring occasionally, until cheese melts, about 5 minutes; season with salt and pepper. Remove and discard bay leaf. Serve garnished with parsley.

Each serving provides: 2 Protein Exchanges; 3 Vegetable Exchanges; 1 Fat Exchange;
   5 Optional Calories
Per serving: 268 calories; 15 g protein; 14 g fat; 21 g carbohydrate; 259 mg calcium;
   796 mg sodium; 30 mg cholesterol; 3 g dietary fiber (this figure does not include Swiss
   chard; nutrition analysis not available)

Vegetarian Lentil Patties-in-a-Pita

WEEK 5

MAKES 2 SERVINGS, 1 PATTY EACH

2 ounces drained canned lentils, mashed
3 tablespoons plain dried bread crumbs
2 tablespoons *each* cooked cracked wheat (bulgur) and chopped scallion (green onion)
1½ teaspoons *each* lemon juice and chopped fresh parsley

Dash *each* salt and pepper
1 teaspoon vegetable oil
2 pitas (1 ounce each), heated
1 serving (about 3 tablespoons) Dilled Tahini Dip (see page 385)
½ cup shredded lettuce
2 tomato slices

In medium mixing bowl combine lentils, bread crumbs, cracked wheat, scallion, lemon juice, parsley, salt, and pepper; mix well. Form mixture into 2 equal patties and arrange on nonstick baking sheet. Using a pastry brush, brush top side of each patty with ¼ teaspoon oil. Bake 15 minutes; turn patties over, brush with remaining oil, and continue to bake until patties are lightly browned, about 10 minutes longer.

To serve, using a sharp knife, cut halfway around edge of each pita; open to form pocket. Spread ½ of the Dilled Tahini Dip over each patty and place in a pita; top each patty with ¼ cup lettuce and 1 tomato slice and serve immediately.

Each serving (including Dilled Tahini Dip) provides: ½ Protein Exchange; 1½ Bread Exchanges; 1 Vegetable Exchange; ½ Fat Exchange; 55 Optional Calories
Per serving (including Dilled Tahini Dip): 232 calories; 9 g protein; 6 g fat; 37 g carbohydrate; 00 mg calcium; 431 mg sodium (estimated); 2 mg cholesterol; 2 g dietary fiber

Seasoned Tofu in Broth ☺

WEEK 1   MAKES 2 SERVINGS

1 packet instant chicken broth and
   seasoning mix, dissolved in 2 cups
   hot water, divided
1 tablespoon reduced-sodium soy
   sauce
½ small garlic clove, minced

Gingerroot
6 ounces firm-style tofu, cubed
½ cup thoroughly washed and drained
   spinach leaves, shredded

In medium bowl (not aluminum*) combine ¼ cup dissolved broth mix with the soy sauce, garlic, and ¼ teaspoon grated pared gingerroot; add tofu and let marinate for 20 minutes.

While tofu is marinating, in 1-quart saucepan combine remaining 1¾ cups dissolved broth mix and 1 slice pared gingerroot (¼ inch thick) and bring to a boil. Reduce heat to low and let simmer for 15 minutes; remove and discard gingerroot. Drain tofu and add to saucepan, discarding marinade; cook until tofu is heated through, about 10 minutes. Add spinach and let simmer until tender, 1 to 2 minutes longer.

Each serving provides: 1 Protein Exchange; ½ Vegetable Exchange; 5 Optional Calories
Per serving: 136 calories; 15 g protein; 7 g fat; 6 g carbohydrate; 191 mg calcium;
   818 mg sodium; 0 mg cholesterol; 0.4 g dietary fiber (this figure does not include tofu;
   nutrition analysis not available)

*It's best to marinate in glass or stainless-steel containers; ingredients such as soy sauce may react with aluminum, causing color and flavor changes in food.

Sesame-Tofu
Hors d'Oeuvres ◐ ◑

WEEK 4   MAKES 4 SERVINGS

Firm tofu, with its cheese-like texture and subtle flavor, is perfect with this delicious sweet sauce. Best of all, this hit-of-the-party hors d'oeuvre is a snap to make.

2 tablespoons teriyaki sauce
1 tablespoon *each* minced onion,
   minced pared gingerroot, and firmly
   packed dark brown sugar
2 garlic cloves, minced
1 teaspoon sesame seed

6 ounces firm-style tofu, cut into cubes
1 tablespoon plus 1 teaspoon peanut
   or vegetable oil
2 tablespoons chopped scallion
   (green onion)

In medium bowl (not aluminum*) combine all ingredients except tofu, oil, and scallion; add tofu, stir to coat, and let marinate for 15 minutes.

Drain tofu, reserving marinade. In 9-inch nonstick skillet heat oil; add tofu and sauté over medium heat, stirring occasionally, until browned, 2 to 3 minutes. Pour in reserved marinade and bring mixture to a boil. Reduce heat to low and cook, stirring frequently, until mixture thickens slightly, 1 to 2 minutes. Carefully remove tofu from liquid and transfer to serving platter; transfer liquid to heat-proof bowl, sprinkle with scallion, and serve as dipping sauce for tofu.

Each serving provides: ½ Protein Exchange; 1 Fat Exchange; 20 Optional Calories
Per serving: 131 calories; 8 g protein; 9 g fat; 8 g carbohydrate; 105 mg calcium;
   353 mg sodium; 0 mg cholesterol; 0.1 g dietary fiber (this figure does not include tofu;
   nutrition analysis not available)

*It's best to marinate in glass or stainless-steel containers; ingredients such as teriyaki sauce may react with aluminum, causing color and flavor changes in food.

Tofu Tostadas ⊂◐

Start a Mexican dinner with these authentic-tasting tostadas, or serve them as a light lunch.

3 ounces firm-style tofu, diced
2 tablespoons *each* diced scallion
  (green onion), red bell pepper, green
  bell pepper, and tomato
2 pimiento-stuffed green olives, sliced
1½ teaspoons *each* chopped hot *or*
  mild chili pepper, chopped cilantro
  (Chinese parsley) *or* parsley, and
  lime juice (no sugar added)
1 teaspoon olive *or* vegetable oil

1 garlic clove, chopped
¼ teaspoon salt
Dash pepper
2 tostada shells
1 ounce Monterey Jack cheese,
  shredded
1 tablespoon sour cream
Garnish: cilantro (Chinese parsley)
  or parsley sprigs

In medium mixing bowl combine all ingredients except tostada shells, cheese, sour cream, and cilantro (or parsley); stir to combine and set aside. On nonstick baking sheet arrange tostada shells and broil until they begin to brown, about 1 minute. Top each shell with ½ of the tofu mixture; sprinkle each with ½ ounce cheese and broil just until cheese melts, about 1 minute.

To serve, transfer tostadas to serving platter and serve with sour cream on the side. Garnish platter with cilantro (or parsley).

Each serving provides: 1 Protein Exchange; 1 Bread Exchange; ½ Vegetable Exchange;
  ½ Fat Exchange; 20 Optional Calories
Per serving: 223 calories; 12 g protein; 15 g fat; 11 g carbohydrate; 215 mg calcium;
  509 mg sodium; 16 mg cholesterol; 1 g dietary fiber (this figure does not include tofu;
  nutrition analysis not available)

Tofu Cheesecake

WEEK 5   MAKES 8 SERVINGS

The flavor and texture of tofu make it a perfect ingredient in this wonderful dessert. If you've never tried it, you're in for a real treat. If you make the crust earlier in the day than you make the filling, be sure to preheat the oven before beginning to prepare filling.

16 graham squares (2½-inch squares), made into crumbs
1 tablespoon plus 1 teaspoon unsweetened cocoa
⅓ cup reduced-calorie margarine (tub)
¾ pound firm-style tofu, cut into ½-inch cubes
½ cup part-skim ricotta cheese

2 eggs
¼ cup granulated sugar
2 tablespoons orange juice (no sugar added)
1½ teaspoons grated orange peel
1 teaspoon vanilla extract
1½ ounces mini chocolate chips

Preheat oven to 350° F. To prepare crust, in medium mixing bowl combine graham cracker crumbs and cocoa; with pastry blender or 2 knives used scissors-fashion, cut in margarine until mixture resembles coarse crumbs. Using the back of a spoon, press crumb mixture over bottom and up sides of 9-inch pie plate. Bake until crust is crisp, about 10 minutes; remove to wire rack and let cool. Leave oven on while preparing filling.

To prepare filling, in blender container combine remaining ingredients except chocolate chips and process at high speed until puréed, scraping down sides of container as necessary; add chocolate chips and stir to combine. Pour tofu mixture into cooled crust and bake for 40 minutes (until a knife, inserted in center, comes out clean). Remove pie plate to wire rack and let cool. Serve immediately or cover and refrigerate until ready to serve.

Each serving provides: 1 Protein Exchange; 1 Bread Exchange; 1 Fat Exchange; 65 Optional Calories
Per serving: 249 calories; 12 g protein; 13 g fat; 24 g carbohydrate; 155 mg calcium; 221 mg sodium; 74 mg cholesterol; 1 g dietary fiber (this figure does not include tofu; nutrition analysis not available)

Lemon-Berry Tofu Pudding ☻☽

WEEK 2   MAKES 2 SERVINGS

6 ounces firm-style tofu
1 cup strawberries
1 tablespoon plus 1 teaspoon reduced-
    calorie strawberry spread (16 calories
    per 2 teaspoons)
1 tablespoon lemon juice

½ teaspoon vanilla extract
½ cup blueberries
2 tablespoons thawed frozen dairy
    whipped topping

In work bowl of food processor or blender container combine all ingredients except blueberries and whipped topping and process until smooth, scraping down sides of container as necessary.

Into each of 2 dessert dishes spoon half of the tofu mixture; top each portion with ¼ cup blueberries and 1 tablespoon whipped topping. Serve immediately or cover with plastic wrap and refrigerate until ready to serve.

Each serving provides: 1 Protein Exchange; 1 Fruit Exchange; 30 Optional Calories
Per serving: 200 calories; 14 g protein; 9 g fat; 20 g carbohydrate; 188 mg calcium;
    21 mg sodium; 0 mg cholesterol; 3 g dietary fiber (this figure does not include tofu;
    nutrition analysis not available)

The Bread Exchange

Act 5: Bravo for Bread

As the curtain goes up on Act 5, we find a cast of crusty characters masquerading under the banner of the Bread Exchange. Bread, muffins, biscuits, pancakes, cereal, potatoes, and pasta all join in the costumed chorus. There's so much to sing about — Raisin Crumb Cake, Savory Bread Pudding, and Buckwheat Pancakes are but a few of our soloists.

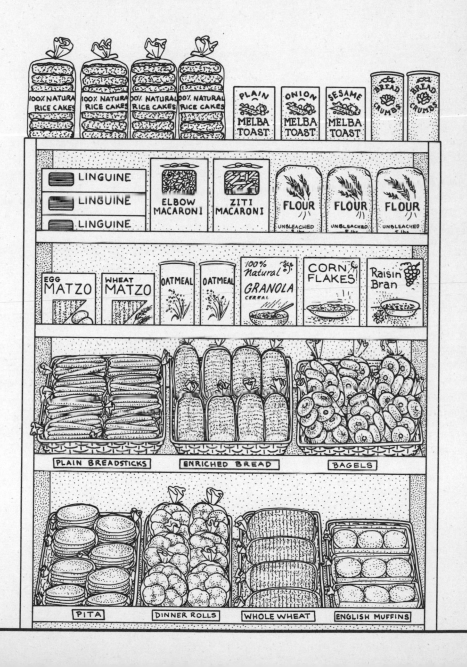

Daily Exchanges

	WEEK 1	WEEK 2	WEEK 3	WEEK 4	WEEK 5
Women	2	2 to 3	2 to 3	3	3
Men and Youths	4	4 to 5	4 to 5	5	5

Bread Exchange Notes

• Items from the Bread Exchange supply B vitamins, carbohydrate, iron, and fiber.

• Breads may contain up to 80 calories per Exchange. You may select 2 slices of thin-sliced, high-fiber, diet, or low-calorie bread as 1 Bread Exchange if 2 slices are no more than 80 calories.

• Bread and pasta should be made with enriched or whole-grain flour; white rice should be enriched. Enriched products contain added vitamins and minerals (thiamin, niacin, riboflavin, and iron) to restore the nutrients lost during milling and processing. Whole-grain products contain the inner parts of the seed and kernel, which provide good sources of vitamins and minerals.

• Mixed vegetables that contain a starchy vegetable (such as corn, parsnips, peas, water chestnuts, etc.) should be considered a Bread Exchange; ½ cup is 1 Exchange.

• Use ¾ ounce uncooked weight as 1 Exchange for grain selections (except barley, buckwheat groats, cracked wheat, and rice; for these, use 1 ounce). Bear in mind that uncooked weight may not yield the indicated cooked amount; this is due to the cooking method used, length of cooking time, and other variables. For most items the nutritional difference is negligible. For very small macaroni products (pastina, orzo, tubettini, etc.), use only the uncooked weight, then cook according to package directions.

• Three-fourths ounce cold cereal or ½ cup cooked hot cereal (¾ ounce uncooked) is 1 Bread Exchange. You may combine different varieties of cereal.

• Presweetened cereals are not permitted. Cereals may contain up to 110 calories per ounce and up to 8.5 grams of sucrose and other related sugars per ounce. Some cereals with fruit contain 110 calories per ounce but may have a slightly higher sugar content due to the fruit (for example, bran flakes cereal with raisins); this is permitted.

• You may prepare popcorn in a hot-air popper or by following package directions. Whichever you choose, 1 Exchange is 2 cups popped or 1 ounce unpopped.

Bread Exchange Lists

Week 1

Selections	One Exchange
Biscuit, refrigerated (ready-to-bake)	1 (1 ounce unbaked *or* ¾ ounce baked)
Bran, all varieties	¾ ounce dry
Bread Crumbs, dried (plain *or* seasoned)	3 tablespoons
Bread, cocktail (party-style)	2 slices (¾ ounce)
Bread, enriched *or* whole-grain (any type)	1 slice (1 ounce)
Bread, reduced-calorie	2 slices
Cereal, cold (not presweetened)	¾ ounce
Cereal, hot	¾ ounce dry *or* ½ cup cooked
Cornflake Crumbs	¾ ounce (5 tablespoons)
Flour, enriched *or* whole-grain *or* self-rising (sifted *or* unsifted)	3 tablespoons
Frankfurter Roll	½ (1 ounce)
Hamburger Roll	½ (1 ounce)
Matzo, egg, regular, *or* whole wheat	½ board (about ½ ounce)
Matzo Cake Meal	3 tablespoons
Matzo Farfel	½ ounce (about ¼ cup)
Matzo Meal	3 tablespoons
Melba Toast, all varieties	6 rounds *or* 4 slices
Pita	1 ounce
Roll, any type	1 ounce

Week 2

You may use all of the items listed under Week 1 and may add the following to your Exchange List:

Selections	One Exchange
Bagel, small	½ (1 ounce)
English Muffin	½ (1 ounce)

Pasta, enriched *or* whole-grain (macaroni, noodles, spaghetti, etc.)	½ cup cooked *or* ¾ ounce uncooked
Potato Flakes (instant mashed potatoes)	⅓ cup flakes
Potato, sweet *or* white	3 ounces
Rice, enriched, brown, *or* wild	½ cup cooked *or* 1 ounce uncooked
Rice Cakes, any type	2
Yam	3 ounces

Week 3

You may use all of the items listed under Weeks 1 and 2 and may add the following to your Exchange List:

Selections	One Exchange
Breadsticks	¾ ounce
Dry Beans, Lentils, Peas	2 ounces cooked *or* ¾ ounce dry
Graham Crackers (cinnamon, honey, *or* plain)	2 (2½-inch squares)
Plantain, peeled	3 ounces
Popcorn, plain	2 cups popped *or* 1 ounce unpopped

Week 4

You may use all of the items listed under Weeks 1, 2, and 3 and may add the following to your Exchange List:

Selections	One Exchange
Cellophane Noodles	½ cup cooked
Corn	
Baby (ears)	1 cup (about 4 ounces)
Cream-style, canned *or* homemade (without sugar and/or cream)	½ cup
Ear	1 small (approximately 5 inches long)
Whole-kernel, canned, fresh, *or* frozen	½ cup
Hominy, grits *or* whole	½ cup cooked *or* ¾ ounce uncooked
Peas, green	½ cup
Saltines	6
Succotash	½ cup

Selections	One Exchange
Taco Shell	1
Tortilla, any type	1 (6-inch diameter)
Tostada Shell	1

Week 5

You may use all of the items listed under Weeks 1, 2, 3, and 4 and may add the following to your Exchange List:

Selections	One Exchange
Barley	½ cup cooked (about 3 ounces) *or* ¾ ounce uncooked
Buckwheat Groats (kasha)	½ cup cooked *or* 1 ounce uncooked
Chestnuts	6 small
Cornmeal	½ cup cooked *or* ¾ ounce (2 tablespoons) uncooked
Cornmeal Mix (self-rising)	¾ ounce uncooked
Couscous	½ cup cooked *or* ¾ ounce uncooked
Cracked Wheat (bulgur)	½ cup cooked *or* 1 ounce uncooked
Crispbreads	¾ ounce
Croutons, any type	½ ounce
Flatbreads	¾ ounce
Lima Beans, green	½ cup
Millet	⅓ cup cooked *or* ¾ ounce uncooked
Oyster Crackers	20
Parsnips	½ cup
Squash, winter	
Acorn (table queen)	½ cup *or* 4 ounces
Banana	½ cup *or* 4 ounces
Buttercup	½ cup *or* 4 ounces
Butternut	½ cup *or* 4 ounces
Calabaza	½ cup *or* 4 ounces
Cushaw	½ cup *or* 4 ounces
Des Moines	½ cup *or* 4 ounces
Gold Nugget	½ cup *or* 4 ounces
Hubbard	½ cup *or* 4 ounces
Peppercorn	½ cup *or* 4 ounces
Water Chestnuts	3 ounces
Wonton Skins (wrappers)	5 skins (3 x 3-inch squares)
Zwieback	2

Crunchy Oven-Fried French Toast ◑

WEEK 3   MAKES 2 SERVINGS

Make your own cornflake crumbs by processing cornflake cereal in a blender or food processor.

2 teaspoons margarine, melted
2 eggs
2 tablespoons half-and-half (blend of milk and cream)
1 teaspoon vanilla extract
¾ ounce cornflake crumbs
1 teaspoon *each* granulated sugar and firmly packed light brown sugar

½ teaspoon ground cinnamon
4 slices day-old Italian bread (½ ounce each)
2 tablespoons reduced-calorie pancake syrup (60 calories per fluid ounce)

Preheat oven to 450° F. Using a pastry brush, brush margarine over bottom of 8 x 8 x 2-inch baking pan; set aside.

In medium mixing bowl beat together eggs, half-and-half, and vanilla. On sheet of wax paper or a paper plate combine cornflake crumbs, sugars, and cinnamon. Dip 1 slice of bread into egg mixture, than lightly into crumb mixture, coating both sides; repeat procedure with remaining bread, being sure to use all of egg and crumb mixture. Arrange bread slices in a single layer in prepared pan and bake, turning once, until crisp and lightly browned, about 10 minutes on each side. Serve with syrup.

Each serving provides: 1 Protein Exchange; 1½ Bread Exchanges; 1 Fat Exchange; 75 Optional Calories
Per serving: 307 calories; 10 g protein; 11 g fat; 39 g carbohydrate; 59 mg calcium; 418 mg sodium; 280 mg cholesterol; 0.9 g dietary fiber

French Toast with Cran-Apple Topping ☾ ◑

WEEK 5   MAKES 2 SERVINGS

2 teaspoons margarine
1 small apple (about 4 ounces), cored, pared, and cut into ½-inch pieces
½ cup fresh *or* thawed frozen cranberries (no sugar added)
2 tablespoons plus 2 teaspoons apple juice *or* unfermented apple cider (no sugar added)
1 tablespoon firmly packed dark brown sugar

½ teaspoon vanilla extract
1 egg
¼ cup evaporated skimmed milk
½ teaspoon ground cinnamon
4 slices reduced-calorie white bread* (40 calories per slice)

In 1-quart saucepan melt margarine; add apple, cranberries, apple juice (or cider), sugar, and vanilla and cook over high heat until mixture comes to a boil. Reduce heat to medium-low and let simmer until mixture is syrupy, about 10 minutes.

While fruit mixture simmers prepare French toast. In shallow bowl beat together egg, milk, and cinnamon; set aside. Spray 10-inch nonstick skillet with nonstick cooking spray and heat over medium-high heat. Dip bread slices into egg mixture, coating both sides; add to skillet and pour an equal amount of any remaining egg mixture over each slice. Cook, turning once, until golden brown on each side.

To serve, cut each slice of French toast in half diagonally, making 8 triangles. Arrange on serving platter and top with cranberry-apple mixture.

Each serving provides: ½ Protein Exchange; 1 Bread Exchange; 1 Fat Exchange; 1 Fruit Exchange; ¼ Milk Exchange; 30 Optional Calories
Per serving: 260 calories; 10 g protein; 7 g fat; 43 g carbohydrate; 166 mg calcium; 309 mg sodium; 138 mg cholesterol; 2 g dietary fiber (this figure does not include cranberries; nutrition analysis not available)

*Reduced-calorie wheat bread may be substituted for the white bread

Open-Face Strawberry-Cheese Sandwiches ©◐

WEEK 4   MAKES 2 SERVINGS

These attractive sandwiches are a great addition to a weekend brunch or an afternoon tea.

¼ cup whipped cream cheese
1 tablespoon reduced-calorie
   strawberry spread (16 calories per
  2 teaspoons), melted

2 slices reduced-calorie pumpernickel
  bread (40 calories per slice)

In medium mixing bowl combine cream cheese and strawberry spread, mixing thoroughly. Onto each slice of bread spread half the cream cheese mixture; cut each slice of bread diagonally in half making 4 triangles. Arrange on serving platter; serve immediately or cover with plastic wrap and refrigerate until ready to serve.

Each serving provides: ½ Bread Exchange; 80 Optional Calories
Per serving: 116 calories; 3 g protein; 6 g fat; 13 g carbohydrate; 33 mg calcium;
  165 mg sodium; 19 mg cholesterol; 1 g dietary fiber

Cinnamon Monkey Bread

WEEK 1   MAKES 10 SERVINGS

3 tablespoons plus 1 teaspoon
   margarine, melted, divided
¼ cup granulated sugar
1 teaspoon ground cinnamon

10-ounce package ready-to-bake
   refrigerated buttermilk flaky biscuits
   (10 biscuits)

Using a pastry brush, brush some of the margarine over bottom and up sides of 7⅜ x 3⅝ x 2¼-inch nonstick loaf pan; set aside.

Preheat oven to 350°F. In small bowl combine sugar and cinnamon; stir to combine and set aside. Cut each biscuit into quarters; dip each quarter into remaining margarine, then into sugar mixture, turning to lightly coat and using all of the margarine and sugar mixture. Layer biscuit quarters in loaf pan and bake until loaf is browned, 30 to 35 minutes. Invert pan onto serving platter and let loaf stand in pan for 1 minute; carefully remove pan from loaf and serve warm.

Each serving provides: 1 Bread Exchange; 1 Fat Exchange; 25 Optional Calories
Per serving: 139 calories; 2 g protein; 7 g fat; 18 g carbohydrate; 4 mg calcium;
  340 mg sodium; 0 mg cholesterol; dietary fiber data not available

Spoon Bread

WEEK 5   MAKES 4 SERVINGS

4½ ounces uncooked white cornmeal   ¼ teaspoon baking soda
1 cup boiling water   4 eggs, beaten
¼ cup whipped butter
¾ cup buttermilk

Preheat oven to 375° F. In medium mixing bowl combine cornmeal, water, and butter; let stand for 5 minutes. In 1-cup liquid measure combine buttermilk and baking soda. Add buttermilk mixture and eggs to cornmeal mixture and stir to thoroughly combine.

    Spray 8 x 8 x 2-inch nonstick baking pan with nonstick cooking spray; pour cornmeal mixture into pan and bake until set and lightly browned, about 30 minutes. Remove from oven and let stand for 10 minutes before serving.

Each serving provides: 1 Protein Exchange; 1½ Bread Exchanges; ¼ Milk Exchange;
   50 Optional Calories
Per serving: 264 calories; 10 g protein; 12 g fat; 28 g carbohydrate; 85 mg calcium;
   227 mg sodium; 291 mg cholesterol; dietary fiber data not available

Banana Bread Pudding ⊙

WEEK 5   MAKES 6 SERVINGS

Bored with breakfast? Prepare this recipe in advance and in the morning heat bread pudding in your microwave oven for about 1 minute.

12 slices 2-day-old reduced-calorie wheat bread (40 calories per slice), cut into 1-inch cubes
1 cup skim *or* nonfat milk
¼ cup evaporated skimmed milk
3 very ripe medium bananas (about 6 ounces each), peeled

2 eggs
⅓ cup cottage cheese
2 tablespoons honey
½ teaspoon *each* ground cinnamon and vanilla extract

In medium mixing bowl combine bread cubes and milks and let stand until bread is well moistened, about 5 minutes.

Preheat oven to 375°F. In blender container combine 2 bananas with the eggs, cottage cheese, honey, cinnamon, and vanilla. Squeeze any excess milk mixture from soaked bread into blender and process banana mixture at medium speed until pureed, about 2 minutes, scraping down sides of container as necessary; add to bread mixture in bowl. Slice remaining banana; add to bread mixture and stir to combine.

Spray 8 x 8 x 2-inch baking dish with nonstick cooking spray; turn banana mixture into dish. Set baking dish in 13 x 9 x 2-inch baking pan and pour boiling water into pan to a depth of about 1 inch; bake for 45 minutes (until a knife, inserted in center, comes out clean). Remove baking pan from oven and baking dish from water bath; let cool for 10 minutes and serve warm, or cool completely, cover, and refrigerate until chilled.

Each serving provides: ½ Protein Exchange; 1 Bread Exchange; 1 Fruit Exchange; ¼ Milk Exchange; 20 Optional Calories
Per serving: 216 calories; 10 g protein; 3 g fat; 41 g carbohydrate; 143 mg calcium; 294 mg sodium; 94 mg cholesterol; 0.8 g dietary fiber

Savory Bread Pudding

1 teaspoon margarine
¼ cup *each* chopped onion and sliced
   mushrooms
½ small garlic clove, minced
1 ounce Canadian-style bacon, diced
1½ teaspoons chopped fresh parsley
Dash *each* salt and white pepper

2 slices white bread, cut into cubes
¾ ounce *each* Cheddar and Monterey
   Jack cheeses, shredded
½ cup low-fat milk (1% milk fat)
1 egg
2 tablespoons part-skim ricotta cheese

Preheat oven to 350°F. In 9-inch nonstick skillet melt margarine; add onion, mushrooms, and garlic and sauté over medium-high heat until vegetables are tender, 1 to 2 minutes. Add bacon, parsley, salt, and pepper and stir to combine. Into each of two 10-ounce custard cups spoon half of the bacon mixture; add half of the bread cubes, half of the Cheddar, and half of the Monterey Jack cheese to each cup and stir to combine. Set aside.

In blender container combine milk, egg, and ricotta cheese and process until smooth, scraping down sides of container as necessary. Pour half of the milk mixture into each cup and bake for 30 to 40 minutes (until lightly browned and a knife, inserted in pudding, comes out clean).

Each serving provides: 2 Protein Exchanges; 1 Bread Exchange; ½ Vegetable Exchange;
   ½ Fat Exchange; ¼ Milk Exchange; 5 Optional Calories
Per serving: 283 calories; 18 g protein; 15 g fat; 19 g carbohydrate; 317 mg calcium;
   618 mg sodium; 172 mg cholesterol; 0.8 g dietary fiber

Toasted Cinnamon Sticks

WEEK 1   MAKES 2 SERVINGS, 4 STICKS EACH

A sweet snack that is ready in only 15 minutes.

2 slices white *or* raisin bread   **1 teaspoon granulated sugar**
2 teaspoons margarine, melted   **¼ teaspoon ground cinnamon**

Preheat oven to 400°F. On nonstick baking sheet arrange bread slices and, using pastry brush, brush each side of each slice of bread with ½ teaspoon margarine. Cut each slice of bread into four equal strips; set aside. In cup or small bowl combine sugar and cinnamon; sprinkle half of the sugar mixture over bread strips. Bake for 7 minutes; turn bread strips over. Sprinkle with remaining sugar mixture and bake until bread is crisp and browned, about 3 minutes longer. Serve immediately.

Each serving provides: 1 Bread Exchange; 1 Fat Exchange; 10 Optional Calories
Per serving with white bread: 108 calories; 2 g protein; 5 g fat; 14 g carbohydrate;
   25 mg calcium; 166 mg sodium; 0.7 mg cholesterol; 0.4 g dietary fiber
With raisin bread: 108 calories; 2 g protein; 5 g fat; 16 g carbohydrate; 23 mg calcium;
   136 mg sodium; 0.8 mg cholesterol; dietary fiber data not available

Variation: Syrupy Cinnamon Sticks—Serve each portion with 1 tablespoon reduced-calorie pancake syrup (60 calories per fluid ounce) for dipping. Increase Optional Calories to 40.

Per serving with white bread: 137 calories; 2 g protein; 5 g fat; 22 g carbohydrate;
   25 mg calcium; 166 mg sodium; 0.7 mg cholesterol; 0.4 g dietary fiber
With raisin bread: 138 calories; 2 g protein; 5 g fat; 23 g carbohydrate; 23 mg calcium;
   136 mg sodium; 0.8 mg cholesterol; dietary fiber data not available

Spicy Salad Croutons

WEEK 1   MAKES 4 SERVINGS

Bread that is getting stale makes great croutons.

1 tablespoon plus 1 teaspoon vegetable
   or peanut oil
¼ teaspoon *each* garlic powder, ground
   cumin, and curry powder

2 ounces day-old Italian bread, cut into
   cubes

Preheat oven to 450°F. In small mixing bowl combine oil and seasonings; add bread cubes and toss to coat. On nonstick baking sheet arrange bread cubes; drizzle with any oil mixture remaining in bowl. Bake, turning occasionally, until bread cubes are golden brown, about 5 minutes.

Each serving provides: ½ Bread Exchange; 1 Fat Exchange
Per serving: 81 calories; 1 g protein; 5 g fat; 8 g carbohydrate; 4 mg calcium;
   83 mg sodium; 0.1 mg cholesterol; 0.4 g dietary fiber

Tomato-Garlic Toasts

WEEK 1   MAKES 4 SERVINGS

The no-cook sauce in this recipe is the perfect solution when an overabundance of fresh garden tomatoes is taking over your refrigerator.

5 large plum tomatoes, diced
2 tablespoons *each* chopped fresh basil
   and olive oil
½ small garlic clove, mashed

Dash *each* salt and pepper
4 ounces Italian bread, diagonally cut
   into 4 equal slices and toasted

In small mixing bowl combine all ingredients except bread. Arrange bread slices on individual serving plates and top each with ¼ of tomato mixture (about 3 tablespoons).

Each serving provides: 1 Bread Exchange; 1¼ Vegetable Exchanges; 1½ Fat Exchanges
Per serving: 152 calories; 3 g protein; 7g fat; 19 g carbohydrate; 22 mg calcium;
   204 mg sodium; 0.3 mg cholesterol; 1 g dietary fiber

Barley Pilaf ◑

Save time by cooking the barley, according to package directions, in advance.

1 teaspoon margarine
2 tablespoons *each* finely chopped carrot, celery, and thoroughly washed leek (white portion and some green)
½ garlic clove, minced

1 cup cooked barley
¼ cup canned ready-to-serve beef broth
Dash *each* salt (optional) and white pepper

In 8-inch nonstick skillet melt margarine; add carrot, celery, leek, and garlic and sauté over medium-high heat, stirring frequently, until celery is softened, 2 to 3 minutes. Add remaining ingredients and stir to combine; continue cooking until carrot is tender and liquid is absorbed, 3 to 4 minutes.

Each serving provides: 1 Bread Exchange; ¼ Vegetable Exchange; ½ Fat Exchange;
    5 Optional Calories
Per serving with salt: 130 calories; 4 g protein; 2 g fat; 24 g carbohydrate; 17 mg calcium;
    204 mg sodium; 0 mg cholesterol; 3 g dietary fiber
Without salt: reduce sodium to 138 mg

Barley Salad Vinaigrette

WEEK 5   MAKES 4 SERVINGS

2 cups cooked pearl barley, chilled
½ cup seeded and diced cucumber
¼ cup *each* diced red bell pepper and
   diagonally sliced scallions (green
   onions)
2 tablespoons chopped radishes
1 tablespoon *each* chopped fresh
   parsley and dill

2 tablespoons red wine vinegar
1 tablespoon plus 1 teaspoon olive oil
1 tablespoon water
½ teaspoon Dijon-style mustard
¼ teaspoon salt
⅛ teaspoon pepper
4 cups shredded lettuce

In medium mixing bowl combine barley, cucumber, bell pepper, scallions, radishes, parsley, and dill; set aside. In small bowl combine remaining ingredients except lettuce, stirring well. Pour over barley mixture and toss well to coat.

To serve, line serving platter with lettuce and top with barley mixture.

Each serving provides: 1 Bread Exchange; 2½ Vegetable Exchanges; 1 Fat Exchange
Per serving: 159 calories; 4 g protein; 5 g fat; 25 g carbohydrate; 57 mg calcium;
   164 mg sodium; 0 mg cholesterol; 4 g dietary fiber

Autumn Oatmeal ◐

WEEK 5   MAKES 2 SERVINGS

1 teaspoon margarine
1 small apple (about ¼ pound), cored, pared, and diced
⅔ cup water
⅓ cup unfermented apple cider (no sugar added)
1½ ounces uncooked old-fashioned oats
2 tablespoons golden raisins

1 teaspoon *each* granulated sugar and firmly packed light brown sugar
¼ teaspoon ground cinnamon
⅛ teaspoon *each* ground nutmeg and mace
2 tablespoons half-and-half (blend of milk and cream)

In 2-quart saucepan melt margarine; add apple and sauté over medium-high heat until lightly browned and softened, 1 to 2 minutes. Remove from saucepan and set aside.

In same pan combine water and cider, cover, and bring to a boil. Stir oats and raisins into liquid and cook, uncovered, stirring occasionally, until mixture thickens and oats are cooked through, about 5 minutes. Stir apple mixture into oatmeal mixture.

While oatmeal is cooking, in small bowl combine sugars and spices. To serve, spoon oatmeal into 2 serving bowls; sprinkle each portion with half of the sugar mixture, then top with 1 tablespoon half-and-half.

Each serving provides: 1 Bread Exchange; ½ Fat Exchange; 1½ Fruit Exchanges; 45 Optional Calories
Per serving: 212 calories; 4 g protein; 5 g fat; 38 g carbohydrate; 43 mg calcium; 32 mg sodium; 6 mg cholesterol; 1 g dietary fiber

Granola ◑

WEEK 5   MAKES 4 SERVINGS, ABOUT ½ CUP EACH

**3 ounces *each* mixed dried fruit and
uncooked old-fashioned oats
1 tablespoon *each* sunflower seed and
shredded coconut
1 teaspoon wheat germ**

**1 tablespoon plus 1 teaspoon *each*
honey and safflower *or* vegetable oil
¼ teaspoon vanilla extract
Dash ground cinnamon**

Preheat oven to 325° F. In medium mixing bowl combine dried fruit, oats, sunflower seed, coconut, and wheat germ; set aside.

In small saucepan combine remaining ingredients and cook over medium heat, stirring occasionally, until heated through, 1 to 2 minutes. Drizzle honey mixture evenly over oat mixture and mix until oat mixture is lightly coated. On nonstick baking sheet spread oat mixture in an even layer and bake, stirring occasionally, until lightly browned, 15 to 20 minutes.

Each serving provides: 1 Bread Exchange; 1 Fat Exchange; 1 Fruit Exchange;
45 Optional Calories
Per serving: 217 calories; 5 g protein; 8 g fat; 35 g carbohydrate; 22 mg calcium;
8 mg sodium; 0 mg cholesterol; 1 g dietary fiber

Buckwheat Pancakes

MAKES 4 SERVINGS, 2 PANCAKES EACH

½ cup all-purpose flour
¼ cup buckwheat flour
¾ teaspoon baking soda
¾ cup buttermilk
1 egg

2 teaspoons molasses
2 teaspoons margarine, melted, divided
¼ cup reduced-calorie pancake syrup
(60 calories per fluid ounce)

In medium mixing bowl combine flours and baking soda; set aside. Using a wire whisk, in small mixing bowl combine buttermilk, egg, and molasses and beat until thoroughly combined; add to flour mixture, stirring until slightly lumpy.

Brush 12-inch skillet or griddle with half the margarine and heat. Using half of batter, drop batter into hot skillet (or griddle), forming 4 pancakes, each 4 inches in diameter. Cook over medium heat until bubbles appear on surface and bottom is golden brown, 2 to 3 minutes; using pancake turner, turn pancakes over and cook until the other side is browned. Remove pancakes to plate and keep warm. Repeat procedure, brushing pan with remaining margarine and making 4 more pancakes. Serve each portion of pancakes topped with 1 tablespoon syrup.

Each serving provides: 1 Bread Exchange; ½ Fat Exchange; ¼ Milk Exchange;
  60 Optional Calories
Per serving: 170 calories; 5 g protein; 4 g fat; 28 g carbohydrate; 76 mg calcium;
  243 mg sodium; 70 mg cholesterol; 0.5 g dietary fiber

Hominy Chowder ⓒ

1 tablespoon plus 1 teaspoon olive *or* vegetable oil

1 cup *each* diced onions and celery

½ cup *each* diced red and green bell pepper

1 tablespoon seeded minced chili *or* jalapeño pepper

2 cups water

6 ounces pared all-purpose potato, cut into cubes

1 cup drained canned whole-kernel corn

2 packets instant chicken broth and seasoning mix

1 cup *each* drained canned yellow and white whole hominy*

Garnish: ½ medium jalapeño pepper, seeded and sliced

In 3-quart saucepan heat oil; add onions, celery, and peppers and cook over medium heat, stirring occasionally, until tender-crisp, 3 to 5 minutes. Add water, potato, corn, and broth mix; stir to combine and bring mixture to a full boil. Reduce heat to low and let simmer until flavors blend, about 15 minutes. Stir in hominy and cook until heated through, about 3 minutes. Transfer to soup tureen or serving bowl and garnish with jalapeño pepper.

Each serving provides: 2 Bread Exchanges; 1½ Vegetable Exchanges; 1 Fat Exchange; 5 Optional Calories
Per serving: 200 calories; 5 g protein; 6 g fat; 35 g carbohydrate; 30 mg calcium; 847 mg sodium; 0 mg cholesterol; 2 g dietary fiber

*2 cups of either yellow or white whole hominy may be used.

Polenta with Gorgonzola and Roasted Peppers

WEEK 5   MAKES 4 SERVINGS

2 medium red bell peppers	1 ounce grated Parmesan cheese
3 cups water	2 teaspoons olive oil
3 ounces uncooked yellow cornmeal	1 small garlic clove, sliced
1 teaspoon salt	4 basil leaves
1 tablespoon whipped butter	3 ounces Gorgonzola cheese, crumbled

Preheat broiler. On baking sheet lined with heavy-duty foil broil bell peppers 3 inches from heat source, turning frequently, until charred on all sides; let stand until cool enough to handle, 15 to 20 minutes.

While bell peppers are cooling prepare polenta. In 1-quart saucepan bring water to a boil; stir in cornmeal and salt and cook over high heat, stirring constantly at a full boil, until mixture is thick and smooth and leaves the sides of the pan, about 20 minutes.

Preheat oven to 400° F. Grease 8 x 8 x 2-inch square pan or 7-inch round pan with butter. Stir Parmesan cheese into cornmeal mixture; spread cornmeal mixture in prepared pan and bake until golden, about 20 minutes.

Over small bowl to catch juice peel cooled bell peppers; remove and discard stem ends and seeds. Cut bell peppers into strips and add to juice in bowl; add oil, garlic, and basil and stir to combine.

To serve, turn oven off and sprinkle polenta with Gorgonzola cheese. Let stand in warm oven until cheese begins to melt, about 5 minutes. Serve with bell pepper mixture.

Each serving provides: 1 Protein Exchange; 1 Bread Exchange; 1 Vegetable Exchange; ½ Fat Exchange; 15 Optional Calories
Per serving: 227 calories; 10 g protein; 12 g fat; 20 g carbohydrate; 222 mg calcium; 995 mg sodium; 25 mg cholesterol; 1 g dietary fiber

Buttered Fettuccine-
Spinach Toss ◐

WEEK 5	MAKES 2 SERVINGS

To add an unusual touch to this dish, substitute 1 cup oyster mushrooms, cut into matchstick pieces, or sliced regular mushrooms, in place of the shiitake mushrooms.

1 tablespoon *each* olive oil and
   whipped butter
2 cups spinach leaves, trimmed,
   thoroughly washed, drained, and
   chopped
1 cup sliced shiitake mushrooms

4 small plum tomatoes, blanched,
   peeled, seeded, and diced
1 large garlic clove, minced
½ cup canned ready-to-serve chicken
   broth
2 cups cooked fettuccine (hot)

In 10-inch nonstick skillet combine oil and butter and heat until butter is melted; add spinach, mushrooms, tomatoes, and garlic and sauté over high heat until mushrooms are lightly browned, 2 to 3 minutes. Add broth and stir to combine. Reduce heat to low and cook until flavors blend, 3 to 4 minutes. Add fettuccine to skillet and, using 2 forks, toss to combine.

Each serving provides: 2 Bread Exchanges; 4 Vegetable Exchanges; 1½ Fat Exchanges;
   35 Optional Calories
Per serving: 286 calories; 8 g protein; 11 g fat; 40 g carbohydrate; 78 mg calcium;
   333 mg sodium; 8 mg cholesterol; 5 g dietary fiber

Serving Suggestion: Add 1 tablespoon grated Parmesan cheese along with the fettuccine to skillet. Increase Optional Calories to 50.

Per serving: 297 calories; 9 g protein; 12 g fat; 40 g carbohydrate; 112 mg calcium;
   380 mg sodium; 10 mg cholesterol; 5 g dietary fiber

Variation: Fettuccine-Spinach Toss (Week 2)—Omit butter from recipe and proceed as directed. Decrease Optional Calories to 10.

Per serving: 261 calories; 8 g protein; 8 g fat; 40 g carbohydrate; 77 mg calcium;
   304 mg sodium; 0 mg cholesterol; 5 g dietary fiber
With Parmesan cheese: 272 calories; 9 g protein; 9 g fat; 40 g carbohydrate; 111 mg calcium;
   351 mg sodium; 2 mg cholesterol; 5 g dietary fiber

Cold Sesame Noodles

WEEK 5   MAKES 2 SERVINGS

Immediately after blanching the vegetables, plunge them into cold water, then drain. This will stop the cooking process and chill the vegetables so that they are just the right temperature for this recipe.

1 cup cooked fettuccine, chilled
½ cup *each* julienne-cut carrot (matchstick pieces), blanched, and julienne-cut zucchini (matchstick pieces)
¼ cup *each* julienne-cut red and yellow bell pepper (matchstick pieces), blanched
1½ ounces drained canned water chestnuts, sliced
2 cherry tomatoes, cut into quarters
1 tablespoon *each* sliced scallion (green onion) and sherry wine vinegar *or* rice wine vinegar

1½ teaspoons *each* vegetable *or* peanut oil, reduced-sodium soy sauce, and water
1 teaspoon sesame seed, lightly toasted
½ teaspoon Chinese sesame oil
1 garlic clove, minced
¼ teaspoon powdered mustard
Dash white pepper
8 romaine lettuce leaves

In medium bowl combine fettuccine, carrot, zucchini, bell peppers, water chestnuts, cherry tomatoes, and scallion; toss to combine. In small mixing bowl combine remaining ingredients except lettuce and, using a wire whisk, beat until thoroughly combined; pour over noodle mixture and toss to coat. Serve immediately or cover and refrigerate until ready to serve.

To serve, arrange lettuce leaves on serving platter and top with fettuccine mixture.

Each serving provides: 1 Bread Exchange; 2¾ Vegetable Exchanges; 1 Fat Exchange; 30 Optional Calories
Per serving: 210 calories; 6 g protein; 7 g fat; 32 g carbohydrate; 68 mg calcium; 180 mg sodium; 25 mg cholesterol; 2 g dietary fiber

Noodles Romanoff

WEEK 4   MAKES 2 SERVINGS

2 teaspoons margarine, divided
½ cup sliced mushrooms
1 small garlic clove, minced
1 cup cooked noodles
¼ cup sour cream

2 teaspoons chopped fresh parsley
Dash *each* salt and pepper
1 tablespoon grated Parmesan cheese

Preheat oven to 350° F. In 8-inch nonstick skillet melt 1 teaspoon margarine; add mushrooms and garlic and sauté over high heat, stirring frequently, until mushrooms are lightly browned, 2 to 3 minutes. Transfer to medium mixing bowl; add remaining ingredients except cheese and stir well to thoroughly combine.

In small metal measuring cup, or other small flameproof container, melt remaining teaspoon margarine; spread over bottom and sides of shallow 2-cup casserole. Transfer noodle mixture to prepared casserole and spread in an even layer; sprinkle with cheese. Bake until noodle mixture is heated through and topping is lightly browned, 15 to 20 minutes.

Each serving provides: 1 Bread Exchange; ½ Vegetable Exchange; 1 Fat Exchange;
  80 Optional Calories
Per serving: 213 calories; 6 g protein; 12 g fat; 21 g carbohydrate; 82 mg calcium;
  175 mg sodium; 39 mg cholesterol; 0.5 g dietary fiber

Pasta with Eggplant-Prosciutto Sauce

WEEK 2   MAKES 4 SERVINGS

Our recipe calls for cooking eggplant in a skillet, but if you own a microwave oven this step can be done successfully in this handy piece of equipment. We've topped spinach bow-tie macaroni with this flavorful sauce, but it works well on any pasta.

2 teaspoons olive *or* vegetable oil
2 cups diced pared eggplant
1 cup low-fat milk (2% milk fat)
2 teaspoons margarine
1 cup *each* sliced onions and red
   or green bell peppers
1 small garlic clove, minced

¼ pound prosciutto (Italian-style
   ham), chopped
Dash *each* ground nutmeg and pepper
2 cups cooked spinach bow-tie
   macaroni (hot)
Garnish: Italian (flat-leaf) parsley

In 10-inch nonstick skillet heat oil; add eggplant and stir to combine. Cover and cook over medium heat until eggplant softens, 5 to 7 minutes. Transfer to work bowl of food processor and process until pureed. Transfer to medium mixing bowl; stir in milk and set aside.

In same skillet melt margarine; add onions, bell peppers, and garlic and sauté until tender-crisp, 2 to 3 minutes. Stir in eggplant mixture and cook over low heat until heated through, 1 to 2 minutes. Add prosciutto and seasonings and stir to combine. To serve, arrange pasta on serving platter; top with eggplant mixture and sprinkle with parsley.

Each serving provides: 1 Protein Exchange; 1 Bread Exchange; 2 Vegetable Exchanges;
   1 Fat Exchange; ¼ Milk Exchange; 10 Optional Calories
Per serving: 223 calories; 12 g protein; 8 g fat; 25 g carbohydrate; 112 mg calcium;
   399 mg sodium; 40 mg cholesterol; 2 g dietary fiber

Fettuccine with Chick-Peas and Eggplant

WEEK 3   MAKES 2 SERVINGS

This flavorful side dish or appetizer is a delicious addition to any Italian dinner.

2 teaspoons olive *or* vegetable oil
2 cups cubed pared eggplant (½-inch cubes)
2 garlic cloves, minced
1 cup canned ready-to-serve chicken broth
8 sun-dried tomato halves (not packed in oil), cut into matchstick pieces

2 ounces drained canned chick-peas
Dash pepper
1½ cups cooked fettuccine (hot)
1 tablespoon grated Parmesan cheese
2 teaspoons drained capers

In 10-inch nonstick skillet heat oil; add eggplant and garlic and sauté over medium-high heat, stirring frequently, until eggplant is lightly browned, 2 to 3 minutes. Add remaining ingredients except fettuccine, cheese, and capers and cook until eggplant is cooked through and flavors blend, 3 to 4 minutes. Add remaining ingredients to skillet and, using 2 forks, toss well to combine.

Each serving provides: ½ Protein Exchange; 1½ Bread Exchanges; 4 Vegetable Exchanges; 1 Fat Exchange; 35 Optional Calories
Per serving: 338 calories; 13 g protein; 8 g fat; 59 g carbohydrate; 122 mg calcium; 763 mg sodium (estimated); 2 mg cholesterol; 7 g dietary fiber

Pasta Mediterranean ◐

WEEK 5   MAKES 2 SERVINGS

2 teaspoons olive *or* vegetable oil
½ cup sliced leeks (white portion and some green)
2 garlic cloves, minced
1½ cups canned Italian tomatoes, seeded and diced
¼ cup dry red table wine
6 Gaeta olives,* cut into halves and pitted

1 tablespoon drained capers
¼ teaspoon salt
Dash pepper
2 cups cooked penne *or* ziti macaroni (hot)
2 teaspoons grated Parmesan cheese
Garnish: fresh basil leaves

In 10-inch nonstick skillet heat oil; add leeks and garlic and sauté over medium-high heat, stirring frequently, until leeks are softened, about 1 minute. Add tomatoes and stir to combine; cook, stirring frequently, for 3 minutes. Add wine, olives, capers, salt, and pepper and stir to combine; cover and cook, stirring occasionally, until mixture thickens and flavors blend, 10 to 15 minutes. Add pasta and stir well to thoroughly combine.

To serve, transfer pasta to serving bowl; sprinkle with Parmesan cheese and garnish with basil.

Each serving provides: 2 Bread Exchanges; 2 Vegetable Exchanges; 1 Fat Exchange; 55 Optional Calories
Per serving: 300 calories; 8 g protein; 8 g fat; 46 g carbohydrate; 118 mg calcium; 794 mg sodium; 1 mg cholesterol; 3 g dietary fiber

*Calamata olives may be substituted for the Gaeta olives.

Pasta-Radicchio Sauté

WEEK 2   MAKES 2 SERVINGS

1 teaspoon olive *or* vegetable oil
1 tablespoon minced shallot *or* onion
½ cup *each* shredded radicchio (red chicory leaves) *or* red cabbage, shredded spinach leaves, thoroughly washed and drained, and canned ready-to-serve chicken broth
2 tablespoons dry white table wine

1 teaspoon unsalted margarine
1½ cups cooked whole wheat *or* white linguine (hot)
1 tablespoon chopped fresh Italian (flat-leaf) parsley
¼ teaspoon oregano leaves
2 teaspoons grated Parmesan cheese

In 10-inch nonstick skillet heat oil; add shallot (or onion) and sauté over medium heat, stirring frequently, until translucent, about 1 minute. Add radicchio (or red cabbage) and spinach and sauté until spinach is wilted, about 3 minutes. Add broth and wine and cook over high heat until mixture comes to a boil; continue cooking until liquid is reduced to just less than ½ cup, about 2 minutes. Stir in margarine and cook, stirring constantly, until margarine is melted. Add linguine, parsley, and oregano and toss to coat. Serve sprinkled with Parmesan cheese.

Each serving provides: 1½ Bread Exchanges; 1 Vegetable Exchange; 1 Fat Exchange; 35 Optional Calories
Per serving with radicchio and whole wheat linguine: 194 calories; 8 g protein; 6 g fat; 26 g carbohydrate; 96 mg calcium; 316 mg sodium; 1 mg cholesterol; 1 g dietary fiber
With red cabbage and whole wheat linguine: 188 calories; 8 g protein; 6 g fat; 25 g carbohydrate; 60 mg calcium; 297 mg sodium; 1 mg cholesterol; 0.7 g dietary fiber
With radicchio and white linguine: 199 calories; 7 g protein; 6 g fat; 28 g carbohydrate; 99 mg calcium; 316 mg sodium; 1 mg cholesterol; 2 g dietary fiber
With red cabbage and white linguine: 193 calories; 6 g protein; 6 g fat; 27 g carbohydrate; 63 mg calcium; 298 mg sodium; 1 mg cholesterol; 2 g dietary fiber

Pasta with Salmon Cream Sauce

WEEK 2   MAKES 2 SERVINGS

1 teaspoon margarine
½ cup sliced red onion
1 teaspoon all-purpose flour
½ cup low-fat milk (2% milk fat)
1 tablespoon plus 1½ teaspoons
  each prepared horseradish and
  lemon juice
2 teaspoons reduced-calorie
  mayonnaise

2 large plum tomatoes, blanched,
  peeled, seeded, and diced
2 ounces smoked salmon (lox), diced
2 cups cooked linguine (hot)
2 tablespoons sliced fresh chives

In 9-inch nonstick skillet melt margarine; add onion and sauté until tender-crisp, 1 to 2 minutes. Sprinkle flour over onion and stir quickly to combine; continuing to stir, cook 1 minute longer. Remove from heat and gradually stir in milk. Return to low heat and cook, stirring constantly, until mixture thickens slightly. Stir in horseradish, lemon juice, and mayonnaise. Stir in remaining ingredients, except pasta and chives, and cook until thoroughly heated, about 15 minutes.

   To serve, onto each of 2 serving plates arrange 1 cup linguine; top each with half of the salmon mixture and 1 tablespoon chives.

Each serving provides: 1 Protein Exchange; 2 Bread Exchanges; 1½ Vegetable Exchanges;
  1 Fat Exchange; ¼ Milk Exchange; 15 Optional Calories
Per serving: 285 calories; 13 g protein; 6 g fat; 43 g carbohydrate; 114 mg calcium;
  332 mg sodium; 13 mg cholesterol; 2 g dietary fiber

Quick Noodle-Beef Soup ⓒ ⓘ

WEEK 2   MAKES 2 SERVINGS, ABOUT 2 CUPS EACH

We've added roast beef to this hearty soup, but leftover sliced steak can be substituted too.

2 teaspoons margarine
½ cup diced onion
¼ cup *each* diced celery and carrot
3 cups water
2 packets instant beef broth and
　seasoning mix

1½ ounces uncooked broad noodles
2 ounces roast beef, cut into thin strips
Garnish: 2 teaspoons chopped fresh
　parsley

In 2-quart saucepan melt margarine; add onion, celery, and carrot and sauté over medium heat, stirring frequently, until tender-crisp, about 3 minutes. Add water and broth mix and stir to combine; cook over high heat until mixture comes to a boil. Reduce heat to low; stir in noodles and let simmer for 10 minutes. Stir in beef and cook until heated through, 2 to 3 minutes. Serve sprinkled with parsley.

Each serving provides: 1 Protein Exchange; 1 Bread Exchange; 1 Vegetable Exchange;
　1 Fat Exchange; 10 Optional Calories
Per serving: 201 calories; 13 g protein; 7 g fat; 21 g carbohydrate; 29 mg calcium;
　1,013 mg sodium; 43 mg cholesterol; 1 g dietary fiber

Pasta with Veal Sausage Bolognese

WEEK 3   MAKES 2 SERVINGS

A flavorful meat sauce that can be prepared up to the point of adding the half-and-half and then frozen. To serve, heat thawed sauce and stir in half-and-half when sauce is almost heated through.

1¼ cups canned Italian tomatoes (with liquid), divided
1 teaspoon olive *or* vegetable oil
3 ounces veal sausage, remove and discard casing
¼ cup chopped onion
1 garlic clove, minced

1 tablespoon chopped fresh basil
1½ teaspoons chopped fresh parsley
Dash pepper
2 tablespoons half-and-half (blend of milk and cream)
1½ cups cooked rigatoni (hot)

In blender container process 1 cup tomatoes with the liquid until pureed; chop remaining ¼ cup tomatoes and set aside.

In 10-inch nonstick skillet heat oil; add sausage and sauté over medium-high heat, stirring frequently, until sausage is browned, 2 to 3 minutes. Add onion and garlic and cook, stirring frequently, until onion is softened, about 1 minute longer. Add pureed and chopped tomatoes and seasonings and stir to combine. Reduce heat to low, cover, and cook, stirring occasionally, until flavors blend, 25 to 30 minutes. Stir in half-and-half and continue cooking until heated through, 2 to 3 minutes. Add rigatoni and mix thoroughly to combine.

Each serving provides: 1 Protein Exchange; 1½ Bread Exchanges;
    1½ Vegetable Exchanges; ½ Fat Exchange; 25 Optional Calories
Per serving: 263 calories; 14 g protein; 8 g fat; 34 g carbohydrate; 88 mg calcium;
    620 mg sodium (estimated); 34 mg cholesterol; 2 g dietary fiber

Variation: Pasta with Turkey Sausage Bolognese — Substitute turkey sausage for the veal sausage.

Per serving: 261 calories; 12 g protein; 9 g fat; 34 g carbohydrate; 90 mg calcium;
    447 mg sodium; 29 mg cholesterol; 2 g dietary fiber (this figure does not include turkey
    sausage; nutrition analysis not available)

Honey-Poached Pear Fans

Buttered Fettuccine-Spinach Toss

Caesar Salad
Steak au Poivre Vert

Tofu Tostadas

Halibut Steaks in Vegetable-Wine Sauce

Buttermilk-Raisin Scones
French Toast with Cran-Apple Topping
Peaches and Cream Muffins
Orange Breakfast Loaf

Meringues with Raspberry Sauce

Spinach and Walnut-Stuffed Shells

WEEK 8   MAKES 8 SERVINGS, 2 SHELLS EACH

1 tablespoon plus 1 teaspoon olive
   or vegetable oil
½ cup minced onion
1 small garlic clove, minced
1 ounce ground walnuts
1 package frozen chopped spinach
   (10 ounces), cooked according
   to package directions and drained
16 uncooked jumbo macaroni shells
   (3 ounces), cooked according to
   package directions and drained

1 tablespoon plus 1 teaspoon margarine
1 tablespoon all-purpose flour
2 cups skim or nonfat milk
2 ounces grated Parmesan cheese
Dash grated nutmeg

In 10-inch nonstick skillet heat oil; add onion and garlic and sauté over medium-high heat until translucent, about 1 minute. Reduce heat to medium; stir in walnuts and cook 1 minute longer. Remove from heat and stir in spinach. Spoon ¹⁄₁₆ of spinach mixture into each shell; put shells in shallow casserole that is large enough to hold them in a single layer and set aside.

Preheat oven to 350° F. Wipe skillet clean and melt margarine over medium heat; sprinkle with flour and stir quickly to combine. Continuing to stir, cook for 1 minute. Remove from heat and gradually stir in milk. Return to low heat and stir in cheese; continuing to stir, cook until mixture thickens slightly, about 1 minute. Pour over shells in casserole, sprinkle with nutmeg, and bake until bubbly and hot, 10 to 15 minutes.

Each serving provides: ½ Protein Exchange; ½ Bread Exchange; ½ Vegetable Exchange;
   1 Fat Exchange; ¼ Milk Exchange; 15 Optional Calories
Per serving: 168 calories; 8 g protein; 9 g fat; 15 g carbohydrate; 222 mg calcium;
   213 mg sodium; 7 mg cholesterol; 1 g dietary fiber

Orange-Raisin Rice ◑

WEEK 5　　　　　　　　　　　　　　　　　　MAKES 2 SERVINGS

Wild or brown rice becomes a special side dish when simmered with raisins and orange juice.

1 teaspoon margarine
2 tablespoons chopped scallion
　(green onion)
½ cup *each* orange juice (no sugar
　added) and water
2 tablespoons golden raisins
1 tablespoon chopped fresh parsley

½ packet (about ½ teaspoon) instant
　chicken broth and seasoning mix
⅛ teaspoon grated orange peel
Dash *each* salt and pepper
2 ounces uncooked wild *or* brown rice

In small saucepan melt margarine; add scallion and sauté over high heat, stirring frequently, until softened, about 1 minute; add remaining ingredients except rice. Cover and bring to a boil; stir in rice. Reduce heat to low, cover, and let simmer until rice is tender and liquid is absorbed, 15 to 20 minutes.

Each serving provides: 1 Bread Exchange; ⅛ Vegetable Exchange; ½ Fat Exchange;
　1 Fruit Exchange; 3 Optional Calories
Per serving with wild rice: 177 calories; 5 g protein; 2 g fat; 36 g carbohydrate;
　24 mg calcium; 340 mg sodium; 0 mg cholesterol; 1 g dietary fiber (this figure does not
　include wild rice; nutrition analysis not available)
With brown rice: 179 calories; 3 g protein; 3 g fat; 37 g carbohydrate; 27 mg calcium;
　341 mg sodium; 0 mg cholesterol; 3 g dietary fiber

Rice Pilaf

WEEK 8   MAKES 4 SERVINGS

2 teaspoons margarine
½ cup *each* diced onion and sliced
  mushrooms
¼ cup diced celery
½ cup frozen peas
3 ounces uncooked long-grain regular
  rice
1 packet instant chicken broth and
  seasoning mix

1¼ cups boiling water
½ ounce pignolias (pine nuts), toasted
2 tablespoons grated Parmesan cheese
1 tablespoon chopped fresh parsley
Dash *each* salt and pepper

In 4-quart saucepan melt margarine; add onion, mushrooms, and
celery and sauté over medium heat until onion is translucent, 3 to 4
minutes. Add peas, rice, and broth mix and sauté 1 minute longer;
add water and bring mixture to a boil. Reduce heat to low, cover,
and let simmer until rice is fluffy, about 20 minutes. Stir in remaining
ingredients and serve immediately.

Each serving provides: 1 Bread Exchange; ½ Vegetable Exchange; ½ Fat Exchange;
  45 Optional Calories
Per serving: 150 calories; 5 g protein; 5 g fat; 23 g carbohydrate; 55 mg calcium;
  378 mg sodium; 2 mg cholesterol; 1 g dietary fiber (this figure does not include pignolias;
  nutrition analysis not available)

Rice Stroganoff 🌓

WEEK 4   MAKES 4 SERVINGS

2 teaspoons margarine
1 cup sliced mushrooms
¼ cup sliced scallions (green onions)
1 garlic clove, minced
¾ cup canned ready-to-serve chicken broth
¼ cup dry white table wine

1 tablespoon chopped fresh parsley
⅛ teaspoon salt
Dash white pepper
4 ounces uncooked regular long-grain rice
¼ cup sour cream

In 2-quart saucepan melt margarine; add mushrooms, scallions, and garlic and sauté over medium heat until mushrooms are just tender, 1 to 2 minutes. Add remaining ingredients except rice and sour cream and bring mixture to a boil; add rice and stir to combine. Reduce heat to low, cover, and cook until liquid is absorbed and rice is tender, 10 to 15 minutes. Stir in sour cream and serve immediately.

Each serving provides: 1 Bread Exchange; ½ Vegetable Exchange; ½ Fat Exchange; 55 Optional Calories
Per serving: 174 calories; 3 g protein; 6 g fat; 25 g carbohydrate; 33 mg calcium; 291 mg sodium; 6 mg cholesterol; 0.9 g dietary fiber

Country Corn Pudding ©

WEEK 4	MAKES 2 SERVINGS

2 teaspoons margarine
1 tablespoon chopped scallion
  (green onion)
1 tablespoon plus 1½ teaspoons
  all-purpose flour
½ cup low-fat milk (1% milk fat)
2 tablespoons plus 2 teaspoons instant
  nonfat dry milk powder

¾ cup canned cream-style corn
1 egg, beaten
1½ teaspoons granulated sugar
Dash *each* salt and white pepper

In 1-quart saucepan melt margarine; add scallion and sauté over medium-high heat, stirring frequently, until softened, about 1 minute. Sprinkle flour over scallion and stir quickly to combine; cook, stirring constantly, for 1 minute. Continuing to stir, gradually add low-fat milk and milk powder. Reduce heat to low and cook, stirring frequently, until mixture thickens, about 5 minutes. Remove from heat and let cool.

Preheat oven to 350° F. Spray two 10-ounce custard cups with nonstick cooking spray. Stir remaining ingredients into scallion mixture; pour half of mixture into each prepared cup. Bake for 45 to 50 minutes (until a knife, inserted in center, comes out clean). Serve warm.

Each serving provides: ½ Protein Exchange; 1 Bread Exchange, 1 Fat Exchange;
  ½ Milk Exchange; 20 Optional Calories
Per serving: 223 calories; 9 g protein; 8 g fat; 31 g carbohydrate; 167 mg calcium;
  481 mg sodium; 140 mg cholesterol; 0.3 g dietary fiber

Pennsylvania Dutch Corn Chowder ℂ

WEEK 6   MAKES 4 SERVINGS, ABOUT 1¼ CUPS EACH

Canned cream-style corn and whole-kernel corn come together in this hearty soup.

2 teaspoons margarine
¼ cup chopped scallions (green onions)
2 tablespoons all-purpose flour
2 cups *each* low-fat milk (1% milk fat) and water
2 packets instant chicken broth and seasoning mix
6 ounces diced pared all-purpose potato

½ cup *each* canned cream-style and whole-kernel corn
4 slices crisp bacon, crumbled
1 tablespoon chopped fresh parsley
⅛ teaspoon white pepper
Dash salt

In 3- or 4-quart saucepan melt margarine; add scallions and sauté over high heat until softened, 1 to 2 minutes. Sprinkle with flour and stir quickly to combine; continuing to stir, gradually add milk. Add water and broth mix, stirring to dissolve broth mix. Reduce heat to low, add remaining ingredients, and stir to combine. Cook, stirring frequently, until mixture thickens and potato is tender, 25 to 30 minutes.

Each serving provides: 1 Bread Exchange; ⅛ Vegetable Exchange; ½ Fat Exchange; ½ Milk Exchange; 75 Optional Calories
Per serving: 200 calories; 9 g protein; 7 g fat; 27 g carbohydrate; 162 mg calcium; 807 mg sodium; 10 mg cholesterol; 2 g dietary fiber

Summer Corn and Vegetable Salad

WEEK 4   MAKES 4 SERVINGS

Fresh corn kernels right off the cob are wonderful in this summertime specialty.

4 cups whole green beans, cut into 3-inch pieces and blanched
2 cups *each* whole-kernel corn, blanched, and green *or* red bell pepper strips (3 x ¼-inch strips)
1 cup thinly sliced red onion (separated into rings)
1 tablespoon minced hot *or* mild chili pepper

1 small garlic clove, minced
3 tablespoons freshly squeezed lime juice
2 tablespoons chopped fresh cilantro (Chinese parsley) *or* parsley
1 tablespoon plus 1 teaspoon olive oil
1 tablespoon white wine vinegar
1 teaspoon honey, warmed

In large mixing bowl combine green beans, corn, bell pepper, onion, chili pepper, and garlic; set aside. In cup or small bowl combine remaining ingredients; pour over green bean mixture and toss to thoroughly coat.

Each serving provides: 1 Bread Exchange; 3½ Vegetable Exchanges; 1 Fat Exchange; 5 Optional Calories
Per serving: 183 calories; 5 g protein; 6 g fat; 34 g carbohydrate; 60 mg calcium; 12 mg sodium; 0 mg cholesterol; 5 g dietary fiber

Turkey-Corn Chowder Ⓒ

WEEK 4

MAKES 4 SERVINGS, ABOUT 2 CUPS EACH

1 tablespoon plus 1 teaspoon
reduced-calorie margarine (tub)
1 cup *each* diced carrots, onions,
celery, red *or* green bell peppers, and
seeded plum tomatoes
1 quart water
9 ounces pared all-purpose potatoes,
cut into cubes

2 packets instant chicken broth and
seasoning mix
1½ cups frozen whole-kernel corn
¼ pound skinned and boned cooked
turkey, diced

In 3-quart saucepan melt margarine; add vegetables and sauté until carrots are tender-crisp, about 5 minutes. Add water, potatoes, and broth mix; stir to combine and bring to a full boil. Reduce heat to medium and cook until potatoes are tender, about 10 minutes. Add corn and turkey and cook until heated through, about 5 minutes.

Each serving provides: 1 Protein Exchange; 1½ Bread Exchanges;
2½ Vegetable Exchanges; ½ Fat Exchange; 5 Optional Calories
Per serving: 221 calories; 14 g protein; 4 g fat; 36 g carbohydrate; 49 mg calcium;
605 mg sodium; 22 mg cholesterol; 4 g dietary fiber

Minestrone Salad

WEEK 4   MAKES 2 SERVINGS

2 medium tomatoes, blanched, peeled, seeded, and chopped
½ cup *each* diced carrot, blanched, diced celery, diced zucchini, and chilled cooked small macaroni shells
¼ cup blanched frozen peas
1 ounce *each* minced prosclutto (Italian-style ham) and drained rinsed canned chick-peas
2 tablespoons finely diced red onion

1 small garlic clove, minced
2 tablespoons canned ready-to-serve chicken broth
1 tablespoon chopped fresh Italian (flat-leaf) parsley
2 teaspoons *each* olive oil and red wine vinegar
½ teaspoon Italian seasoning
2 teaspoons grated Parmesan cheese

In medium bowl combine tomatoes, carrot, celery, zucchini, macaroni, peas, ham, chick-peas, onion, and garlic. In small mixing bowl, using a wire whisk, combine remaining ingredients except cheese and beat until combined; pour over vegetable mixture and toss well to coat. Serve sprinkled with Parmesan cheese.

Each serving provides: ½ Protein Exchange; 1 Bread Exchange; 3½ Vegetable Exchanges; 1 Fat Exchange; 15 Optional Calories
Per serving: 195 calories; 9 g protein; 7 g fat; 26 g carbohydrate; 76 mg calcium; 389 mg sodium (estimated); 9 mg cholesterol; 3 g dietary fiber

Quick Pea Soup with Shrimp

WEEK 4   MAKES 4 SERVINGS, ABOUT 1 CUP EACH

3 cups water
6 ounces sliced pared all-purpose
  potato
1 cup frozen peas
½ cup chopped onions
2 tablespoons *each* chopped fresh basil
  and Italian (flat-leaf) parsley
1 packet instant chicken broth and
  seasoning mix

½ small garlic clove
¼ teaspoon salt
Dash white pepper
5 ounces shelled and deveined small
  shrimp, cut lengthwise into halves
1 tablespoon plus 1 teaspoon sour
  cream
Garnish: 4 parsley sprigs

In 2-quart saucepan combine water and potato and bring to a boil; add remaining ingredients except shrimp, sour cream, and garnish and cook over medium heat until potato is soft, about 15 minutes. Remove from heat and let cool slightly.

Pour into blender container and process at low speed until pureed; pour soup back into saucepan. Stir in shrimp and cook over low heat until shrimp turn pink, 3 to 4 minutes.

To serve, ladle soup into 4 bowls and top each portion with 1 teaspoon sour cream; garnish with parsley.

Each serving provides: 1 Protein Exchange; 1 Bread Exchange; ¼ Vegetable Exchange;
  15 Optional Calories
Per serving: 120 calories; 11 g protein; 2 g fat; 15 g carbohydrate; 56 mg calcium;
  482 mg sodium; 56 mg cholesterol; 2 g dietary fiber

Succotash ☺◑

WEEK 5   MAKES 2 SERVINGS

This colorful side dish is ready in only 15 minutes.

½ cup *each* frozen whole-kernel corn
   and green lima beans
2 tablespoons water
2 teaspoons margarine
¼ teaspoon granulated sugar

⅛ teaspoon salt
1 tablespoon half-and-half (blend
   of milk and cream)
Dash pepper

In small saucepan combine all ingredients except half-and-half and pepper and cook over high heat until mixture comes to a boil. Reduce heat to low, cover, and let simmer until vegetables are tender, about 15 minutes. Remove from heat and stir in half-and-half and pepper.

Each serving provides: 1 Bread Exchange; 1 Fat Exchange; 15 Optional Calories
Per serving: 124 calories; 4 g protein; 5 g fat; 17 g carbohydrate; 22 mg calcium;
   211 mg sodium; 3 mg cholesterol; 6 g dietary fiber

Creamy Herb Potatoes

WEEK 4	MAKES 2 SERVINGS

Try this recipe with any leftover cooked all-purpose potatoes.

1 teaspoon margarine
2 tablespoons minced onion
9 ounces pared cooked all-purpose
  potatoes, diced
3 tablespoons sour cream
2 tablespoons low-fat milk (1% milk fat)

1½ teaspoons *each* chopped fresh dill
  and chives
1 teaspoon pickle relish
⅛ teaspoon salt
Dash white pepper

In 9-inch nonstick skillet melt margarine; add onion and sauté over medium heat until softened, 1 to 2 minutes. Add potatoes and sauté, stirring frequently, until heated through, 2 to 3 minutes. In small mixing bowl combine remaining ingredients; pour into skillet and stir well to combine. Cook until mixture thickens and flavors blend, 3 to 5 minutes. Serve immediately.

Each serving provides: 1½ Bread Exchanges; ⅛ Vegetable Exchange; ½ Fat Exchange;
  60 Optional Calories
Per serving: 178 calories; 4 g protein; 7 g fat; 26 g carbohydrate; 62 mg calcium;
  206 mg sodium; 10 mg cholesterol; 3 g dietary fiber

Creamy Minted Potatoes

WEEK 3   MAKES 4 SERVINGS

2 teaspoons vegetable oil
¾ pound new potatoes, scrubbed and
   cut into halves
½ cup sliced onion
⅛ teaspoon salt
Dash pepper

¼ cup canned ready-to-serve chicken
   broth
2 tablespoons half-and-half (blend
   of milk and cream)
1 tablespoon chopped fresh mint
2 teaspoons Dijon-style mustard

Preheat oven to 450° F. Pour oil into 8 x 8 x 2-inch baking dish; add
potatoes, onion, salt, and pepper and mix well until potatoes and
onion slices are thoroughly coated with oil. Bake, stirring occasionally, until potatoes are browned and fork-tender, 15 to 20 minutes. In
1-cup liquid measure combine remaining ingredients; pour over
potato mixture and stir to combine. Continue baking until liquid
thickens and is slightly reduced, about 5 minutes longer. Stir potatoes and transfer to serving bowl.

Each serving provides: 1 Bread Exchange; ¼ Vegetable Exchange; ½ Fat Exchange;
   15 Optional Calories
Per serving: 109 calories; 2 g protein; 4 g fat; 18 g carbohydrate; 20 mg calcium;
   216 mg sodium; 3 mg cholesterol; 2 g dietary fiber

Golden Potato Bake Ⓒ

⅓ cup sour cream
2 tablespoons half-and-half (blend
 of milk and cream)
2 ounces Cheddar cheese, shredded
¼ cup chopped scallions (green onions)
1 teaspoon chopped fresh parsley
Dash white pepper

¾ pound pared cooked all-purpose
 potatoes, grated
2 teaspoons margarine, melted
1 tablespoon plain dried bread crumbs
1 teaspoon grated Parmesan cheese

Preheat oven to 450° F. In small saucepan combine sour cream and half-and-half and cook over medium heat until heated through *(do not boil).* Stir in Cheddar cheese, scallions, parsley, and pepper and continue cooking, stirring frequently, until cheese melts. In medium mixing bowl combine potatoes and cheese mixture and mix well.

Spread margarine over bottom of 9-inch pie pan; turn potato mixture into pie pan and spread evenly over bottom of pan. In cup or small bowl combine bread crumbs and Parmesan cheese; sprinkle over potato mixture. Bake until potato mixture is heated through, 20 to 25 minutes. Turn oven control to broil and broil until topping is lightly browned, 1 to 2 minutes.

Each serving provides: ½ Protein Exchange; 1 Bread Exchange; ⅛ Vegetable Exchange;
 ½ Fat Exchange; 65 Optional Calories
Per serving: 202 calories; 7 g protein; 12 g fat; 18 g carbohydrate; 151 mg calcium;
 148 mg sodium; 26 mg cholesterol; 2 g dietary fiber

Harvest Home Fries

WEEK 5   MAKES 4 SERVINGS

1 tablespoon plus 1 teaspoon vegetable
   oil, divided
15 ounces pared all-purpose potatoes,
   thinly sliced, divided
1 small pear (about 5 ounces), cored
   and thinly sliced
1 small apple (about ¼ pound), cored
   and thinly sliced
6 small chestnuts, roasted, peeled, and
   sliced

¼ cup canned ready-to-serve chicken
   broth
2 teaspoons chopped fresh parsley
½ teaspoon rosemary leaves
⅛ teaspoon salt
Dash white pepper

In 12-inch nonstick skillet heat 2 teaspoons oil; arrange half of the
potato slices in a single layer over bottom of pan and cook over
high heat, turning occasionally, until potatoes are lightly browned,
2 to 3 minutes. Transfer potatoes to a plate and set aside. Repeat
procedure using remaining 2 teaspoons oil and potatoes; set aside.

   To same skillet add pear, apple, and chestnuts and sauté until
lightly browned, 1 to 2 minutes. Return potatoes to skillet; add
remaining ingredients and stir to combine. Cook over medium heat
until potatoes are tender and liquid is absorbed, 5 to 7 minutes.

Each serving provides: 1½ Bread Exchanges; 1 Fat Exchange; ½ Fruit Exchange;
   3 Optional Calories
Per serving: 180 calories; 3 g protein; 5 g fat; 32 g carbohydrate; 19 mg calcium;
   141 mg sodium; 0 mg cholesterol; 3 g dietary fiber (this figure does not include
   chestnuts; nutrition analysis not available)

New Potato Salad with Mint and Peas

WEEK 4   MAKES 4 SERVINGS

Fresh mint and peas are new additions to our homemade potato salad.

¼ cup *each* sliced scallions (green onions), sour cream, and buttermilk
2 tablespoons plus 2 teaspoons reduced-calorie mayonnaise
2 tablespoons chopped fresh mint
½ teaspoon salt

Dash white pepper
15 ounces cooked new potatoes, sliced and chilled
½ cup cooked tiny peas, chilled

In medium mixing bowl stir together scallions, sour cream, buttermilk, mayonnaise, mint, salt, and pepper. Add potatoes and peas and mix until thoroughly combined. Cover with plastic wrap and refrigerate for at least 30 minutes to allow flavors to blend.

Each serving provides: 1½ Bread Exchanges; ⅛ Vegetable Exchange; 1 Fat Exchange; 40 Optional Calories
Per serving: 173 calories; 4 g protein; 6 g fat; 26 g carbohydrate; 54 mg calcium; 410 mg sodium; 10 mg cholesterol; 3 g dietary fiber

Stuffed Sweet Potato Surprise

WEEK 4 · MAKES 2 SERVINGS, 1 STUFFED POTATO SHELL EACH

If you own a microwave oven you can save time by using it to bake the sweet potato; be sure to follow manufacturer's directions for baking.

1 sweet potato (9 ounces), scrubbed
   and cut in half lengthwise
2 tablespoons sour cream
1 tablespoon maple syrup

1 teaspoon margarine
1 ounce cooked smoked ham, diced
1 tablespoon finely chopped onion

Preheat oven to 425° F. Spray nonstick baking sheet with nonstick cooking spray; arrange potato halves cut side down on baking sheet. Bake until potatoes are fork-tender, 30 to 40 minutes.

In small bowl combine sour cream and syrup; mix well and set aside. In small nonstick skillet melt margarine; add ham and onion and sauté over high heat until onion is lightly browned and tender, 1 to 2 minutes. Set aside.

Using a spoon, scoop pulp from each potato half into a bowl, leaving ⅛-inch-thick shells; reserve shells. Add ham mixture to potato pulp and, using a fork or potato masher, mash until smooth. Spoon half of potato mixture into each reserved shell; transfer stuffed shells to baking sheet and broil until heated through and lightly browned, 1 to 2 minutes. To serve, top each stuffed shell with half of the sour cream mixture.

Each serving provides: ½ Protein Exchange; 1½ Bread Exchanges; ½ Fat Exchange; 65 Optional Calories
Per serving: 227 calories; 5 g protein; 6 g fat; 38 g carbohydrate; 58 mg calcium; 250 mg sodium; 13 mg cholesterol; 3 g dietary fiber

Vinaigrette Potato Salad

This versatile salad is good served warm or chilled.

9 ounces pared cooked new potatoes,
 diced (½-inch pieces)
¼ cup finely diced celery
1 tablespoon *each* finely diced shallot
 or onion and finely diced dill pickle

2 teaspoons *each* red wine vinegar,
 olive oil, and water
1 teaspoon prepared mustard
Dash *each* salt and pepper

In salad bowl combine potatoes, celery, shallot (or onion), and pickle, tossing to combine. In small mixing bowl combine remaining ingredients and, using a wire whisk, beat until thoroughly combined; pour over potato mixture and toss to coat. Serve immediately or cover with plastic wrap and refrigerate until ready to serve.

Each serving provides: 1½ Bread Exchanges; ¼ Vegetable Exchange; 1 Fat Exchange
Per serving: 150 calories; 3 g protein; 5 g fat; 25 g carbohydrate; 20 mg calcium;
 189 mg sodium; 0 mg cholesterol; 3 g dietary fiber

Sweet Potato-Cider Bake

WEEK 5   MAKES 4 SERVINGS

You can use your microwave oven to do the final baking of the sweet potato mixture until it is heated through.

1 pound 2 ounces pared sweet potatoes, diced (¼-inch pieces)
1⅓ cups unfermented apple cider (no sugar added)
2 tablespoons plus 2 teaspoons reduced-calorie margarine (tub)

2 tablespoons evaporated skimmed milk
¼ teaspoon ground nutmeg
1 whole clove
1 tablespoon firmly packed dark brown sugar

In 4-quart saucepan combine all ingredients except sugar and cook over high heat until liquid begins to boil. Reduce heat to medium-low, cover, and let simmer until sweet potatoes are tender, about 20 minutes. Remove from heat and let cool for 2 minutes. Remove and discard clove. Using potato masher, mash sweet potato mixture.

Preheat oven to 350° F. Spray 8 x 8 x 2-inch baking dish with non-stick cooking spray; spread sweet potato mixture in baking dish and sprinkle with sugar. Bake until heated through, about 20 minutes.

Each serving provides: 1½ Bread Exchanges; 1 Fat Exchange; 1 Fruit Exchange; 20 Optional Calories
Per serving: 226 calories; 3 g protein; 5 g fat; 45 g carbohydrate; 60 mg calcium; 109 mg sodium; 0.3 mg cholesterol; 3 g dietary fiber

Sweet Potato-Ham Biscuits

WEEK 5   MAKES 6 SERVINGS, 2 BISCUITS EACH

1 cup plus 2 tablespoons all-purpose
  flour, divided
2 teaspoons double-acting baking
  powder
½ teaspoon baking soda
1 tablespoon granulated sugar
2 tablespoons *each* margarine and
  whipped butter

3 ounces *each* cooked smoked ham,
  finely chopped, and drained canned
  sweet potatoes
½ cup buttermilk
2 tablespoons honey

Into medium mixing bowl sift together 1 cup flour, the baking powder, and baking soda; stir in sugar. With a pastry blender, or two knives used scissors-fashion, cut in margarine and butter until mixture resembles coarse crumbs; stir in ham and set aside.

Preheat oven to 425° F. In small mixing bowl combine potatoes and buttermilk and mash until smooth. Add to flour mixture and stir until thoroughly combined and mixture forms dough; turn dough out onto work surface and knead lightly until smooth. Using remaining 2 tablespoons flour, flour work surface. Using rolling pin, roll dough into a circle about ¼ inch thick. Using 2½-inch-diameter cookie cutter, cut dough into 12 circles, rerolling scraps of dough when necessary and using all of dough; transfer to nonstick baking sheet and bake until biscuits are puffed and lightly browned, 10 to 15 minutes. Transfer biscuits to serving platter and, using a pastry brush, brush each biscuit with ½ teaspoon honey. Serve warm.

Each serving provides: ½ Protein Exchange; 1 Bread Exchange; 1 Fat Exchange;
  70 Optional Calories
Per serving: 207 calories; 6 g protein; 7 g fat; 30 g carbohydrate; 105 mg calcium;
  507 mg sodium; 13 mg cholesterol; 1 g dietary fiber

Sweet Potato Praline Bake

WEEK 8   MAKES 4 SERVINGS

Turn leftover sweet potatoes or yams into this special side dish.

¾ pound pared cooked sweet potatoes
   or yams, mashed
2 eggs, beaten
1 tablespoon plus 1 teaspoon
   margarine
3 gingersnap cookies (½ ounce),
   crushed

½ ounce ground pecans
1 tablespoon *each* firmly packed light
   brown sugar and whipped butter,
   melted

Preheat oven to 400° F. In medium mixing bowl combine potatoes (or yams), eggs, and margarine. Spray 1-quart casserole with non-stick cooking spray and spread potato mixture in casserole. Bake for 15 minutes.

In small bowl combine remaining ingredients; sprinkle over potato mixture and continue baking until pecan mixture is golden brown, 5 to 10 minutes longer. Serve warm.

Each serving provides: ½ Protein Exchange; 1 Bread Exchange; 1 Fat Exchange;
   75 Optional Calories
Per serving: 227 calories; 5 g protein; 11 g fat; 28 g carbohydrate; 41 mg calcium;
   126 mg sodium; 142 mg cholesterol; 2 g dietary fiber

Squash and Turnip Soufflé

¾ pound diced pared butternut squash (½-inch pieces), boiled until tender, then drained

2 cups diced pared turnips (½-inch pieces), boiled until tender, then drained

2 tablespoons reduced-calorie margarine (tub)

3 eggs, separated
3 tablespoons all-purpose flour
Salt
Dash pepper

Preheat oven to 450° F. In work bowl of food processor combine squash, turnips, and margarine and, using an on-off motion, process until pureed; transfer to medium mixing bowl. Stir in egg yolks, flour, ¼ teaspoon salt, and the pepper; set aside.

Using electric mixer, in medium mixing bowl combine egg whites and dash salt, beating until soft peaks form; fold into squash mixture. Spray 1½-quart soufflé dish with nonstick cooking spray; carefully turn squash mixture into dish. Bake until golden brown and puffed, about 30 minutes. Serve immediately.

Each serving provides: ½ Protein Exchange; 1 Bread Exchange; 1 Vegetable Exchange; ½ Fat Exchange; 30 Optional Calories
Per serving: 162 calories; 7 g protein; 7 g fat; 19 g carbohydrate; 84 mg calcium; 327 mg sodium; 206 mg cholesterol; 2 g dietary fiber (this figure does not include butternut squash; nutrition analysis not available)

Applesauce-Rye Muffins

WEEK 5   MAKES 12 SERVINGS, 1 MUFFIN EACH

Prepare these muffins ahead and freeze them; then just thaw at room temperature and, if desired, heat in a toaster oven and serve warm.

1½ cups all-purpose flour
¾ cup rye flour
2 teaspoons double-acting baking
    powder
1 teaspoon ground cinnamon
½ teaspoon baking soda

1½ cups applesauce (no sugar added)
¼ cup firmly packed light brown sugar
1 egg
2 tablespoons vegetable oil
3 ounces mixed dried fruit, diced

Preheat oven to 375° F. In medium mixing bowl combine flours, baking powder, cinnamon, and baking soda; stir well. Using a wire whisk, in separate medium mixing bowl beat together applesauce, sugar, egg, and oil; stir into flour mixture along with dried fruit, combining thoroughly. Spray twelve 2½-inch-diameter nonstick muffin-pan cups with nonstick cooking spray; fill each cup with an equal amount of batter (each will be about ⅔ full). Bake for 20 to 25 minutes (until muffins are lightly browned and a toothpick, inserted in center, comes out dry). Transfer muffins from pan to wire rack to cool.

Each serving provides: 1 Bread Exchange; ½ Fat Exchange; ½ Fruit Exchange;
    30 Optional Calories
Per serving: 151 calories; 3 g protein; 3 g fat; 29 g carbohydrate; 52 mg calcium;
    115 mg sodium; 23 mg cholesterol; 1 g dietary fiber

Brown Bread Muffins

WEEK 5   MAKES 8 SERVINGS, 1 MUFFIN EACH

These muffins may be frozen; to serve, thaw at room temperature. Enjoy muffins warm or at room temperature.

½ cup plus 1 tablespoon *each* rye and
  whole wheat flour
1½ ounces uncooked yellow cornmeal
½ cup golden raisins
1 teaspoon baking soda
½ cup buttermilk

¼ cup dark molasses
1 egg
2 tablespoons plus 2 teaspoons
  vegetable oil

Preheat oven to 400° F. In medium mixing bowl combine flours and cornmeal; in small bowl combine raisins with 2 tablespoons flour mixture, tossing to coat. Set aside. Add baking soda to flour mixture and stir to combine. In small mixing bowl combine buttermilk, molasses, egg, and oil; using electric mixer at medium speed, beat until combined. Add to flour mixture and mix well. Stir in raisin mixture. Spray eight 2½-inch-diameter muffin-pan cups with non-stick cooking spray; fill each cup with an equal amount of batter and partially fill remaining cups with water (this will prevent pan from burning and/or warping). Bake for 15 to 20 minutes (until muffins are lightly browned and a toothpick, inserted in center, comes out dry). Remove muffins to wire rack to cool.

Each serving provides: 1 Bread Exchange; 1 Fat Exchange; ½ Fruit Exchange;
  45 Optional Calories
Per serving: 174 calories; 4 g protein; 6 g fat; 28 g carbohydrate; 102 mg calcium;
  139 mg sodium; 35 mg cholesterol; 1 g dietary fiber

Cheese and Rice Muffins

WEEK 3   MAKES 12 SERVINGS, 1 MUFFIN EACH

These wonderful muffins offer a new way to use leftover cooked rice.

1¾ cups less 1 tablespoon all-purpose
  flour
¼ pound extra-sharp Cheddar cheese,
  shredded
½ cup chopped scallions (green
  onions)
1 tablespoon double-acting baking
  powder

1 cup whole milk
¼ cup vegetable oil
2 eggs
1½ cups cooked long-grain rice

Preheat oven to 425° F. In medium mixing bowl combine flour, cheese, scallions, and baking powder; set aside. Using a fork or wire whisk, in separate medium mixing bowl combine milk and oil; add eggs and beat until combined. Stir into flour mixture; fold in rice *(mixture will be lumpy; do not beat or overmix)*. Spray twelve 2½-inch-diameter muffin-pan cups with nonstick cooking spray. Fill each with an equal amount of batter (each will be about ⅔ full). Bake for 15 minutes (until muffins are golden brown and a toothpick, inserted in center, comes out dry). Transfer muffins to wire rack and let cool.

Each serving provides: ½ Protein Exchange; 1 Bread Exchange; 1 Fat Exchange;
  15 Optional Calories
Per serving: 197 calories; 6 g protein; 9 g fat; 21 g carbohydrate; 158 mg calcium;
  187 mg sodium; 58 mg cholesterol; 1 g dietary fiber

Pinwheel Pizza Muffins

WEEK 4   MAKES 10 SERVINGS, 1 MUFFIN EACH

1 refrigerated all-ready pizza crust
   dough (10 ounces)
2 tablespoons tomato sauce
3 ounces mozzarella cheese, shredded

2 ounces grated Parmesan cheese
½ teaspoon Italian seasoning

Preheat oven to 425° F. Spray rolling pin with nonstick cooking spray and roll pizza dough into a 12 x 8-inch rectangle, about ⅛ inch thick; using pastry brush, brush dough with tomato sauce. Sprinkle with cheeses and seasoning. Starting from wide end, roll dough jelly-roll fashion to enclose filling. Cut roll crosswise into 10 equal slices.

Spray ten 2½-inch-diameter muffin-pan cups with nonstick cooking spray; place 1 slice of roll into each sprayed cup and partially fill remaining cups with water (this will prevent pan from burning and/or warping). Bake until puffed and golden brown, 20 to 25 minutes. Remove pan from oven and carefully drain off water (remember it will be boiling hot). Invert muffins onto serving platter and serve immediately.

Each serving provides: ½ Protein Exchange; 1 Bread Exchange; 2 Optional Calories
Per serving: 123 calories; 6 g protein; 4 g fat; 13 g carbohydrate; 122 mg calcium;
  293 mg sodium; 11 mg cholesterol; dietary fiber data not available

Banana Brown Betty ⊙

WEEK 1   MAKES 6 SERVINGS

6 slices cinnamon-raisin bread, made
  into crumbs
¼ cup reduced-calorie margarine (tub),
  melted
3 tablespoons granulated sugar
½ teaspoon ground cinnamon
¼ teaspoon ground nutmeg

1 pound 2 ounces bananas, peeled and
  sliced
2 tablespoons *each* reduced-calorie
  orange marmalade (16 calories per
  2 teaspoons) and hot water
1 tablespoon lemon juice

Preheat oven to 350° F. In medium mixing bowl combine bread crumbs, margarine, sugar, cinnamon, and nutmeg and mix until well combined. Spray 8 x 8 x 2-inch baking dish with nonstick cooking spray; sprinkle half of the crumb mixture evenly over bottom of dish. Arrange banana slices evenly over crumb mixture; sprinkle with remaining crumb mixture and set aside.

Using a wire whisk or fork, in small mixing bowl combine remaining ingredients; pour evenly over crumb mixture in dish. Bake until golden brown, about 30 minutes.

Each serving provides: 1 Bread Exchange; 1 Fat Exchange; 1 Fruit Exchange;
  40 Optional Calories
Per serving: 185 calories; 2 g protein; 5 g fat; 35 g carbohydrate; 24 mg calcium;
  172 mg sodium, 0.8 mg cholesterol; 0.8 g dietary fiber (this figure does not include raisin
  bread; nutrition analysis not available)

Buttermilk-Raisin Scones

WEEK 5   MAKES 12 SERVINGS

2¼ cups all-purpose flour, sifted
2 teaspoons double-acting baking
  powder
1 teaspoon baking soda
¼ cup chilled margarine
¾ cup *each* buttermilk, divided, and
  dark raisins, plumped and drained*

1 egg, beaten
2 teaspoons firmly packed light brown
  sugar, sifted

Spray 10-inch pie plate or round cake pan with nonstick cooking spray; set aside.

Preheat oven to 375° F. In large mixing bowl combine flour, baking powder, and baking soda. With pastry blender, or 2 knives used scissors-fashion, cut in margarine until mixture resembles coarse meal; add all but 1 tablespoon of the buttermilk along with the raisins and egg and stir to form dough. Knead mixture in bowl until smooth and elastic, about 5 minutes. Transfer dough to prepared pan and spread over bottom to sides of pan; brush surface with reserved 1 tablespoon milk and sprinkle with sugar. Using a sharp knife and cutting no more than ¼ inch deep, score surface of dough to form 12 equal wedges. Bake until golden, 30 to 35 minutes. Set pan on wire rack and let cool for 5 minutes; invert scones onto rack and let cool completely.

Each serving provides: 1 Bread Exchange; 1 Fat Exchange; ½ Fruit Exchange;
  15 Optional Calories
Per serving: 162 calories; 4 g protein; 5 g fat; 27 g carbohydrate; 66 mg calcium;
  208 mg sodium; 23 mg cholesterol; 1 g dietary fiber

*This recipe calls for plumping raisins. To do this rapidly and easily, in a microwave-safe bowl combine raisins with water to cover and microwave on High for less than 1 minute.

Lemon Tea Loaf ☾

WEEK 5   MAKES 12 SERVINGS

Individual slices of this loaf may be wrapped in plastic freezer wrap and frozen for later use; thaw at room temperature.

2¼ cups all-purpose flour
2 teaspoons double-acting baking
  powder
2 tablespoons grated lemon peel
¾ cup granulated sugar
½ cup whipped butter

2 eggs
¼ cup margarine
⅓ cup whole milk
Garnish: 6 thin lemon slices

Preheat oven to 350° F. Spray 9 x 5-inch loaf pan with nonstick cooking spray, set aside. Into medium mixing bowl sift together flour and baking powder; stir in lemon peel and set aside.

In large mixing bowl combine sugar, butter, eggs, and margarine and, using electric mixer at medium speed, beat until combined; increase speed to high and beat until mixture is light and fluffy and double in volume. Add flour mixture alternately with milk, beating at low speed until batter is smooth. Transfer batter to prepared pan and bake for 50 to 55 minutes (until browned and a cake tester, inserted in center, comes out clean). Let cake cool in pan for 5 minutes; invert cake onto wire rack and let cool completely. To serve, garnish with lemon slices and cut into 12 equal slices.

Each serving provides: 1 Bread Exchange; 1 Fat Exchange; 110 Optional Calories
Per serving: 220 calories; 4 g protein; 9 g fat; 31 g carbohydrate; 56 mg calcium;
  170 mg sodium; 57 mg cholesterol; 0.8 g dietary fiber

Oatmeal Wafers Ⓒ

WEEK 5   MAKES 12 SERVINGS, 2 WAFERS EACH

Paired with a glass of skim milk these buttery cookies make a satisfying snack.

4½ ounces uncooked old-fashioned
   oats
½ cup firmly packed light brown sugar
1 teaspoon baking soda

½ cup whipped butter, melted
1 egg, beaten

Preheat oven to 350° F. In medium mixing bowl combine oats, sugar, and baking soda, mixing until blended. Add butter and egg and stir until combined.

Using half of dough, drop dough by teaspoonfuls onto nonstick cookie sheet, forming 12 equal cookies and leaving about 1 inch between each. Bake until edges of cookies are lightly browned, 8 to 10 minutes. Using a spatula, carefully remove cookies to wire rack to cool (wafers will harden as they cool). Using a cooled cookie sheet, repeat procedure 1 more time, making 12 more cookies.

Each serving provides: ½ Bread Exchange; 80 Optional Calories
Per serving: 116 calories; 2 g protein; 5 g fat; 16 g carbohydrate; 17 mg calcium;
   116 mg sodium; 33 mg cholesterol; dietary fiber data not available

Orange Breakfast Loaf

WEEK 4 MAKES 10 SERVINGS

2 tablespoons granulated sugar
1 tablespoon firmly packed light brown
  sugar
1 teaspoon grated orange peel, divided
1 tablespoon plus 2 teaspoons
  margarine, melted, divided
10-ounce package ready-to-bake
  refrigerated buttermilk flaky biscuits
  (10 biscuits)

3 tablespoons whipped cream cheese
1 tablespoon plus 1 teaspoon
  confectioners' sugar, sifted
1 tablespoon orange juice (no sugar
  added)

Preheat oven to 350° F. In small bowl combine granulated sugar, brown sugar, and ½ teaspoon orange peel; set aside. Set aside and reserve 1 teaspoon margarine; separate biscuits and brush top of each with an equal amount of remaining margarine. Sprinkle top of each biscuit with an equal amount of the brown sugar mixture (about 1 teaspoon). Arrange biscuits into a loaf by holding 1 biscuit on its side and gently pressing the sugared side against the un-sugared side of another biscuit; repeat procedure, using all of the biscuits. Carefully transfer loaf to a 7⅜ x 3⅝ x 2¼-inch nonstick loaf pan and brush top with reserved teaspoon margarine. Bake until loaf is lightly browned, about 35 minutes. Transfer loaf from pan to wire rack and let cool slightly, about 5 minutes.

While loaf is cooling, in small mixing bowl combine cream cheese, confectioners' sugar, orange juice, and remaining ½ tea-spoon orange peel, mixing until smooth. Pour sugar mixture along center of warm loaf.

Each serving provides: 1 Bread Exchange; ½ Fat Exchange; 35 Optional Calories
Per serving: 131 calories; 2 g protein; 6 g fat; 18 g carbohydrate; 4 mg calcium;
  329 mg sodium; 3 mg cholesterol; dietary fiber data not available

Orange-Iced Chiffon Cake

WEEK 1   MAKES 12 SERVINGS

Slices of this cake may be wrapped in individual plastic freezer bags and frozen for future use as a quick dessert; thaw at room temperature.

2¼ cups cake flour
1¼ cups granulated sugar, divided
1 tablespoon double-acting baking
   powder
½ cup vegetable oil
6 eggs, separated

2 tablespoons grated orange peel
1 cup orange juice (no sugar added),
   divided
2 egg whites
½ teaspoon cream of tartar
1 small navel orange (about 6 ounces)

Preheat oven to 325° F. Into large mixing bowl sift together flour, 1 cup sugar, and the baking powder; add oil, egg yolks, and orange peel and, using electric mixer at low speed, beat until combined. Increase speed to medium and beat in ¾ cup orange juice; set aside.

In separate large mixing bowl, using clean beaters, beat the 8 egg whites with cream of tartar until stiff but not dry. Fold ¼ of the flour mixture into beaten whites; then fold beaten whites into remaining flour mixture. Spray 10-inch nonstick tube pan with nonstick cooking spray. Transfer batter to prepared pan and bake for 50 minutes (until cake is golden and a cake tester, inserted in center, comes out clean). Let cake cool in pan for 5 minutes. Remove cake from pan and let cool completely on wire rack.

In small saucepan combine remaining ¼ cup sugar and orange juice and cook, stirring constantly with a wire whisk, until mixture comes to a boil. Continue cooking, stirring constantly, until sugar is dissolved and mixture thickens slightly, about 2 minutes.

Set cake on 12-inch diameter cake plate and drizzle orange juice mixture over cake. Thinly slice orange; cut each slice in half. Fold each orange slice in half making a loop and arrange loops around outside edge of cake plate.

Each serving provides: ½ Protein Exchange; 1 Bread Exchange; 2 Fat Exchanges;
   120 Optional Calories
Per serving: 299 calories; 5 g protein; 12 g fat; 42 g carbohydrate; 79 mg calcium;
   150 mg sodium; 137 mg cholesterol; 1 g dietary fiber

Variation: Orange Chiffon Cake—Omit orange juice icing and orange slices from recipe. Decrease Optional Calories to 90.

Per serving: 276 calories; 5 g protein; 12 g fat; 37 g carbohydrate; 74 mg calcium;
   150 mg sodium; 137 mg cholesterol; 0.4 g dietary fiber

Quick Apricot "Danish"

WEEK 5   MAKES 10 SERVINGS, 1 "DANISH" EACH

¼ cup reduced-calorie apricot spread
  (16 calories per 2 teaspoons)
2 tablespoons golden raisins, chopped
4 dried apricot halves, chopped
1 tablespoon granulated sugar

10-ounce package ready-to-bake
  refrigerated buttermilk flaky biscuits
  (10 biscuits)
2 tablespoons confectioners' sugar
1 to 2 teaspoons water

Preheat oven to 400° F. In small mixing bowl combine apricot spread, raisins, apricots, and granulated sugar and mix well; set aside.

Separate biscuits and set upright on nonstick baking sheet; using thumb, firmly press center of each biscuit making an indentation about 1 inch in diameter. Spoon an equal amount of apricot mixture (about 1 teaspoon) into each indentation. Bake until biscuits are lightly browned, 10 to 12 minutes. Transfer biscuits to wire rack.

In cup or small bowl combine confectioners' sugar and water, *adding water 1 teaspoon at a time* and stirring constantly until mixture is smooth and syrupy. Drizzle an equal amount (about ½ teaspoon) of sugar mixture over each biscuit.

Each serving provides: 1 Bread Exchange; 40 Optional Calories
Per serving: 114 calories; 2 g protein; 4 g fat; 20 g carbohydrate; 2 mg calcium;
  296 mg sodium; 0 mg cholesterol; 2 g dietary fiber

Quick Butter Coffeecake

2¼ cups all-purpose flour
½ cup granulated sugar, divided
2 teaspoons double-acting baking
   powder
1 cup whole milk

½ cup whipped butter, melted, divided
1 egg, beaten
1 teaspoon *each* vanilla extract
   and ground cinnamon

Preheat oven to 350° F. Spray 13 x 9 x 2-inch baking pan with nonstick cooking spray; set aside. In large mixing bowl combine flour, ⅓ cup sugar, and the baking powder; set aside. Using a wire whisk, in small mixing bowl beat together milk, ⅓ cup melted butter, the egg, and vanilla. Pour into flour mixture and, using an electric mixer, beat until mixture is smooth. Pour into prepared pan and smooth surface; brush with remaining melted butter. In small bowl combine remaining 2 tablespoons plus 2 teaspoons sugar with the cinnamon and sprinkle evenly over batter. Bake for 35 to 45 minutes (until golden brown and a toothpick, inserted in center, comes out dry). Set pan on wire rack and let cool completely.

Each serving provides: 1 Bread Exchange; 90 Optional Calories
Per serving: 172 calories; 4 g protein; 5 g fat; 28 g carbohydrate; 69 mg calcium;
   126 mg sodium; 36 mg cholesterol; 0.8 g dietary fiber

Raisin Crumb Cake

WEEK 5   MAKES 12 SERVINGS

Here's a buttery coffee cake that will become a family favorite. Leftovers freeze well; thaw at room temperature.

2¼ cups cake flour, sifted, divided
½ cup granulated sugar, divided
2 teaspoons double-acting baking
   powder
1 cup skim *or* nonfat milk
½ cup whipped butter, melted, divided
1 egg, lightly beaten

1 teaspoon vanilla extract
¾ cup golden raisins, plumped and
   drained
1 teaspoon ground cinnamon

Preheat oven to 350° F. Spray 13 x 9 x 2-inch baking pan with nonstick cooking spray. Line pan with sheet of wax paper and spray again with cooking spray; set aside.

In large mixing bowl combine 1¾ cups flour, ¼ cup sugar, and the baking powder. In small mixing bowl combine milk, ¼ cup plus 1 tablespoon butter, and the egg and extract, stirring to combine; pour into dry ingredients and, using electric mixer at medium speed, beat until blended. Stir in raisins. Spread batter evenly in prepared pan; set aside.

Using a fork, in small mixing bowl combine remaining ½ cup flour, ¼ cup sugar, 3 tablespoons butter, and the cinnamon and stir until mixture is crumbly. Sprinkle crumb mixture evenly over batter and bake for 25 to 30 minutes (until cake is lightly browned and a cake tester, inserted in center, comes out clean). Let cake cool in pan for 10 minutes. Using a spatula lift cake from pan and slide onto wire rack; let cool completely. To serve, cut into 12 equal pieces.

Each serving provides: 1 Bread Exchange; ½ Fruit Exchange; 85 Optional Calories
Per serving: 190 calories; 3 g protein; 5 g fat; 34 g carbohydrate; 75 mg calcium;
  128 mg sodium; 34 mg cholesterol; 1 g dietary fiber

Quick Fruit 'n' Cheese "Danish" ◒◐

WEEK 4   MAKES 2 SERVINGS, 1 "DANISH" EACH

2 ready-to-bake refrigerated buttermilk flaky biscuits (1 ounce each)*
2 teaspoons whipped cream cheese
1 teaspoon reduced-calorie raspberry spread (16 calories per 2 teaspoons)

¼ to ½ teaspoon water
1 tablespoon confectioners' sugar

Preheat oven to 375° F. Separate each biscuit into 2 thin layers of dough. Onto center of each of 2 layers of dough spoon 1 teaspoon cream cheese, then top each with a remaining layer of dough, making two "Danish"; pinch edges of dough together to seal. Using finger, gently press center of each "Danish," making an indentation in each biscuit; spoon ½ teaspoon raspberry spread into each indentation. Arrange "Danish" on nonstick baking sheet and bake until lightly browned, 15 to 20 minutes. Transfer to wire rack and let cool.

In cup or small bowl gradually add water to sugar, stirring until mixture is smooth and thoroughly combined and forms an icing. Drizzle ½ of sugar mixture over each cooled "Danish" and let stand until mixture hardens.

Each serving provides: 1 Bread Exchange; 45 Optional Calories
Per serving: 114 calories; 2 g protein; 5 g fat; 17 g carbohydrate; 2 mg calcium;
   307 mg sodium; 3 mg cholesterol; dietary fiber data not available

*Keep biscuits refrigerated until ready to use. Separate dough into layers as soon as it is removed from the refrigerator; it will be difficult to work with if allowed to come to room temperature.

Walnut Marble Cake

WEEK 8   MAKES 12 SERVINGS

¾ cup granulated sugar, divided
2 ounces ground walnuts
1 tablespoon ground cinnamon
2¼ cups cake flour
1 tablespoon double-acting baking
  powder

½ cup whipped butter
¼ cup margarine
1½ cups plain low-fat yogurt
2 eggs
2 teaspoons vanilla extract

Spray 10-inch fluted or plain tube pan with nonstick cooking spray; set aside. In small mixing bowl combine 2 tablespoons sugar with the nuts and cinnamon; set aside. Onto sheet of wax paper or a paper plate sift together cake flour and baking powder; set aside.

Preheat oven to 350° F. In large mixing bowl combine butter, margarine, and remaining sugar and, using electric mixer at medium speed, beat until mixture is light and fluffy. Beat in yogurt, eggs, and vanilla, beating until blended. Stir in flour mixture. Spread half of the batter in prepared pan, then sprinkle with nut mixture. Spread remaining batter over nuts and, using a knife, cut through batter several times to swirl. Bake 35 to 45 minutes (until golden brown and a toothpick, inserted in center, comes out clean). Let cake cool in pan for 5 minutes. Transfer cake from pan to wire rack and let cool completely.

Each serving provides: ½ Protein Exchange; 1 Bread Exchange, 1 Fat Exchange;
  ¼ Milk Exchange; 105 Optional Calories
Per serving: 263 calories; 5 g protein; 12 g fat; 34 g carbohydrate; 127 mg calcium;
  223 mg sodium; 58 mg cholesterol; 0.7 g dietary fiber

The Milk Exchange

Act 6: Mad About Milk

Yes, the milk train does stop here and it's loaded with delicious things to eat and drink. As the curtain goes up on Act 6 you'll see an enchanted dairyland where Gingered Custard, Tropical Yogurt Snack, and Tangy Colada Shake are yours for the asking.

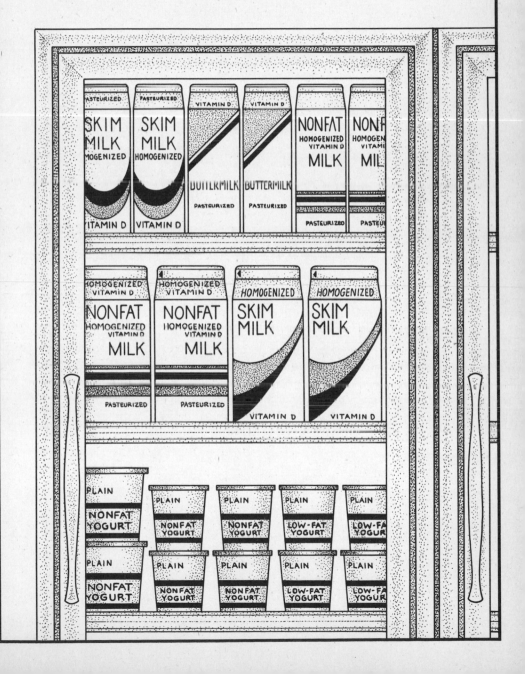

Daily Exchanges

	WEEKS 1 AND 2	WEEKS 3, 4, AND 5
Women and Men	2 Exchanges	2 Exchanges
Youths	3 Exchanges	3 to 4 Exchanges

Milk Exchange Notes

• Items from the Milk Exchange supply calcium, an essential nutrient that performs many functions in addition to maintaining bone integrity. Milk products also provide protein, riboflavin, phosphorus, and vitamins A and D.

• Use skim milk containing up to 90 calories per cup.

• Reduced-calorie flavored milk beverages or puddings that contain at least 6 grams of protein and 200 milligrams of calcium may be used to fulfill the Daily Totals for Milk. Products that contain 4 to 5 grams of protein and 150 to 200 milligrams of calcium must be limited to no more than 1 Milk Exchange per day.

Milk Exchange Lists

Weeks 1, 2, 3, and 4

Selections	One Exchange
Buttermilk	¾ cup
Flavored Milk Beverages, reduced-calorie	1 serving
Flavored Milk Puddings, reduced-calorie	½ cup prepared
Milk, instant nonfat dry	⅓ cup powder
Milk, skim *or* nonfat	1 cup
Yogurt, plain	
low-fat	½ cup
nonfat	¾ cup

Week 5

You may use all of the items listed under Weeks 1, 2, 3, and 4 and may add the following to your Exchange List:

Selections	One Exchange
Milk, evaporated skimmed	½ cup

Week 5

You may use all of the items listed under Weeks 1, 2, 3, and 4 and may add the following to your Exchange List:

Selections	*One Exchange*
Milk, evaporated skimmed	½ cup

Cream of Wild Mushroom Soup

WEEK 2   MAKES 4 SERVINGS, ABOUT 1 CUP EACH

Ready in less than 30 minutes, this elegant soup tastes as if it took all day to prepare.

1 tablespoon plus 1 teaspoon
   reduced-calorie margarine (tub)
2 cups sliced shiitake mushrooms*
1 cup quartered mushrooms
¼ cup chopped thoroughly washed
   leeks (white portion and some green)
1 garlic clove, minced
3 tablespoons all-purpose flour
2 cups *each* low-fat milk (1% milk fat)
   and water

2 tablespoons dry sherry
1 tablespoon chopped fresh parsley
2 packets instant chicken broth and
   seasoning mix
¼ teaspoon thyme leaves
Dash white pepper

In 3-quart saucepan melt margarine; add mushrooms, leeks, and garlic and sauté over medium-high heat, stirring occasionally, until mushrooms are tender-crisp, 2 to 3 minutes. Sprinkle flour over vegetables and stir quickly to combine. Continuing to stir, gradually add milk and water; add remaining ingredients and stir to combine. Reduce heat to medium-low and simmer until flavors blend and soup is thickened, 20 to 25 minutes.

Each serving provides: 1½ Vegetable Exchanges; ½ Fat Exchange; ½ Milk Exchange;
   45 Optional Calories
Per serving: 120 calories; 6 g protein; 4 g fat; 15 g carbohydrate; 162 mg calcium;
   601 mg sodium; 5 mg cholesterol; 2 g dietary fiber

*Regular mushrooms may be substituted for the shiitake mushrooms.

Buttermilk-Blue Cheese Dressing

WEEK 1	MAKES 12 SERVINGS, ¼ CUP EACH

This dressing will keep for about 1 week in the refrigerator.

2¼ cups buttermilk
½ cup reduced-calorie mayonnaise
3 ounces blue cheese, crumbled*

1 tablespoon *each* chopped fresh
   parsley and basil
¼ teaspoon white pepper

In blender container combine buttermilk and mayonnaise and process until thoroughly combined; stir in remaining ingredients. Transfer to bowl or jar that has a tight-fitting cover; refrigerate until ready to use. Just before serving, stir well.

Each serving provides: 1 Fat Exchange; ¼ Milk Exchange; 20 Optional Calories
Per serving: 71 calories; 3 g protein; 5 g fat; 3 g carbohydrate; 93 mg calcium;
   222 mg sodium; 10 mg cholesterol; trace dietary fiber

*The cheese will crumble more easily if it is well chilled.

Creamy Onion Dressing

WEEK 3	MAKES 4 SERVINGS, ABOUT ¼ CUP EACH

½ cup *each* plain low-fat yogurt and
   part-skim ricotta cheese
1 tablespoon minced onion

¼ teaspoon *each* Italian seasoning
   and salt
Dash pepper

In blender container combine yogurt and cheese and process until smooth, scraping down sides of container as necessary. Transfer to small bowl; add remaining ingredients and stir to combine. Cover with plastic wrap or transfer to jar with tight-fitting cover; refrigerate until ready to serve. Just before serving, stir well.

Each serving provides: ½ Protein Exchange; ¼ Milk Exchange
Per serving: 62 calories; 5 g protein; 3 g fat; 4 g carbohydrate; 137 mg calcium;
   194 mg sodium; 11 mg cholesterol; trace dietary fiber

Gingered Custard ©

This recipe will be ready for the oven in only 5 minutes.

1 cup *each* evaporated skimmed milk
   and low-fat milk (1% milk fat)
⅓ cup nonfat dry milk powder
2 eggs

3 tablespoons granulated sugar
½ teaspoon *each* ground ginger and
   vanilla *or* brandy extract

Preheat oven to 350° F. Using a wire whisk, in medium mixing bowl combine all ingredients and beat until combined. Spray four 6-ounce custard cups with nonstick cooking spray and pour ¼ of milk mixture into each cup; set cups in 8 x 8 x 2-inch baking pan and pour hot water into pan to a depth of about 1 inch. Bake for 50 minutes (until a knife, inserted in center, comes out clean). Remove baking pan from oven and cups from water bath; let cool. Cover with plastic wrap and refrigerate until ready to serve.

Each serving provides: ½ Protein Exchange; 1 Milk Exchange; 50 Optional Calories
Per serving: 173 calories; 12 g protein; 4 g fat; 23 g carbohydrate; 343 mg calcium;
   169 mg sodium; 143 mg cholesterol; 0 g dietary fiber

Pudding Cake Roll

WEEK 1   MAKES 8 SERVINGS

A glamorous cake that is out of the oven in 10 minutes.

¾ cup cake flour
1 teaspoon double-acting baking powder
4 eggs
⅓ cup granulated sugar
2 cups skim *or* nonfat milk

1 envelope (four ½-cup servings) reduced-calorie vanilla instant pudding mix
1 tablespoon confectioners' sugar, sifted
Garnish: grated lemon peel

Preheat oven to 400° F. Spray 15 x 10½ x 1-inch jelly-roll pan with nonstick cooking spray. Line pan with sheet of wax paper and spray again; set aside. Onto sheet of wax paper or a paper plate sift together flour and baking powder; set aside.

Using electric mixer at high speed, in large mixing bowl beat eggs until frothy; gradually beat in sugar, beating until thick and lemon colored and double in volume, about 2 minutes. Fold in flour mixture. Spread batter evenly in paper-lined pan and bake for 10 minutes (until cake springs back when lightly touched with fingers). Turn cake onto a linen towel; remove and discard wax paper. Starting at narrow end, roll cake with towel; set on wire rack and let cool.

Using 2 cups milk, prepare pudding according to package directions. Unroll cooled cake, remove towel, and spread pudding over surface of cake, leaving a ½-inch border. Reroll cake and place, seam-side down, on serving platter. Sprinkle with confectioners' sugar. Loosely cover with plastic wrap and refrigerate until chilled, about 30 minutes; garnish with lemon peel.

Each serving provides: ½ Protein Exchange; ½ Bread Exchange; ½ Milk Exchange; 50 Optional Calories
Per serving: 150 calories; 6 g protein; 3 g fat; 24 g carbohydrate; 118 mg calcium; 285 mg sodium; 138 mg cholesterol; 0.2 g dietary fiber

Raspberry and Pudding Treat

WEEK 2   MAKES 4 SERVINGS

1 cup thawed frozen raspberries
   (no sugar added)
¾ cup boiling water
1 envelope (four ½-cup servings)
   low-calorie raspberry-flavored
   gelatin (8 calories per ½ cup)
Ice cubes
½ cup cold water

2 cups skim or nonfat milk
1 envelope (four ½-cup servings)
   reduced-calorie vanilla instant
   pudding mix
¼ cup thawed frozen dairy whipped
   topping

Into each of four 8-ounce dessert dishes arrange ¼ of the raspberries; set aside. In medium heatproof bowl combine boiling water
and gelatin and stir until gelatin is completely dissolved. Add ice
cubes to cold water to measure 1¼ cups; add to gelatin mixture and
stir until mixture is slightly thickened. Remove any unmelted ice.
Pour ¼ of gelatin mixture over raspberries in each dessert dish.
Cover and refrigerate until partially set, about 20 minutes.

Using 2 cups milk, prepare pudding according to package directions; carefully pour ¼ of pudding over gelatin in each dessert dish.
Cover and refrigerate until chilled, about 30 minutes longer. To
serve, top each portion with ¼ of the whipped topping.

Each serving provides: ½ Fruit Exchange; 1 Milk Exchange; 20 Optional Calories
Per serving: 105 calories; 6 g protein; 1 g fat, 17 g carbohydrate; 159 mg calcium;
   459 mg sodium; 2 mg cholesterol; 1 g dietary fiber

Sweet Semolina Pudding

WEEK 5   MAKES 4 SERVINGS

Although this delightful pudding needs to chill in the refrigerator for at least 1 hour, it will only take 10 to 15 minutes to prepare. Enjoy it as an evening snack with a cup of coffee or tea.

2 cups low-fat milk (1% milk fat)
½ cup evaporated skimmed milk
⅓ cup instant nonfat dry milk powder
¼ cup granulated sugar
1 tablespoon cornstarch
1 teaspoon vanilla extract
¼ teaspoon *each* grated lemon peel,
   ground nutmeg, and ground
   cinnamon

1 teaspoon unflavored gelatin
2 eggs
1 cup cooked couscous (semolina)
¼ cup golden raisins

In 2-quart saucepan combine milks, sugar, cornstarch, vanilla, lemon peel, and spices, stirring to dissolve cornstarch; sprinkle gelatin over milk mixture and let stand to soften. Cook over medium heat, stirring frequently with a wire whisk, until mixture thickens, 3 to 4 minutes *(do not boil).* In small mixing bowl lightly beat eggs. Stir ½ cup milk mixture into eggs; slowly stir egg mixture into remaining milk mixture in saucepan. Add couscous and raisins; stir to combine and cook until heated through, about 1 minute.

Into each of four 10-ounce custard cups pour ¼ of milk mixture. Cover with plastic wrap and refrigerate until set, overnight or at least 1 hour.

Each serving provides: ½ Protein Exchange; ½ Bread Exchange; ½ Fruit Exchange;
   1 Milk Exchange; 80 Optional Calories
Per serving: 263 calories; 14 g protein; 4 g fat; 42 g carbohydrate; 336 mg calcium;
   165 mg sodium; 144 mg cholesterol; 1 g dietary fiber

Serving Suggestion: Top each pudding with 1 tablespoon thawed frozen dairy whipped topping. Increase Optional Calories to 90.

Per serving: 275 calories; 14 g protein; 5 g fat; 43 g carbohydrate; 336 mg calcium;
   170 mg sodium; 144 mg cholesterol; 1 g dietary fiber

Vanilla Pudding Surprise

WEEK 4   MAKES 2 SERVINGS

Instant pudding is the secret to having this luscious dessert on the table in about 15 minutes.

2 cups skim *or* nonfat milk
1 envelope (four ½-cup servings)
   reduced-calorie vanilla instant
   pudding mix
¼ cup *each* thawed frozen dairy
   whipped topping, divided, and sour
   cream

1 tablespoon granulated sugar
½ teaspoon grated lemon peel, divided
½ cup blueberries (reserve 6 berries
   for garnish)

Using 2 cups milk, prepare pudding according to package directions but do not chill; set aside. In medium mixing bowl combine 2 tablespoons whipped topping, the sour cream, sugar, and ¼ teaspoon lemon peel, stirring well to thoroughly combine. Stir in blueberries.

Into each of two 10-ounce parfait glasses spoon ¼ of the pudding, then top each with half of the blueberry mixture and the remaining pudding. Top each parfait with 1 tablespoon of the remaining whipped topping and 3 reserved berries; sprinkle evenly with remaining ¼ teaspoon lemon peel. Serve immediately or refrigerate until ready to serve.

Each serving provides: ½ Fruit Exchange; 2 Milk Exchanges; 120 Optional Calories
Per serving: 269 calories; 10 g protein; 9 g fat; 39 g carbohydrate; 341 mg calcium;
   815 mg sodium; 18 mg cholesterol; 1 g dietary fiber

Vanilla Cream Pudding with Fruit ◑

WEEK 5   MAKES 4 SERVINGS

1 cup strawberries, sliced (reserve
 4 whole berries for garnish)
6 ounces kiwi fruit, pared and sliced
 (reserve 6 slices for garnish)
½ cup raspberries (reserve 4 berries
 for garnish)
1 cup skim *or* nonfat milk

1 envelope (four ½-cup servings)
 reduced-calorie vanilla instant
 pudding mix
½ cup plain low-fat yogurt
½ teaspoon vanilla extract
1 teaspoon grated orange peel
4 mint sprigs

In small mixing bowl combine fruits and toss to combine; set aside. In blender container combine milk, pudding mix, yogurt, and vanilla and process until smooth, scraping down sides of container as necessary.

Into each of 4 dessert dishes evenly divide ⅓ of the pudding mixture and top with ½ of the fruit mixture. Repeat layers ending with pudding mixture. Top each portion with 1 reserved strawberry, 1 raspberry, and 1½ slices kiwi fruit. Garnish each portion with ¼ of the orange peel and a mint sprig. Serve immediately or cover and refrigerate until ready to serve.

Each serving provides: 1 Fruit Exchange; 1 Milk Exchange
Per serving: 110 calories; 4 g protein; 1 g fat; 22 g carbohydrate; 147 mg calcium;
 384 mg sodium; 3 mg cholesterol; 1 g dietary fiber

Applesauce-Yogurt Dessert ◐

WEEK 5   MAKES 2 SERVINGS

½ cup applesauce (no sugar added)
¼ teaspoon ground cinnamon
½ cup plain low-fat yogurt
1 teaspoon firmly packed light brown
  sugar

¼ teaspoon vanilla extract
2 tablespoons golden raisins, chopped
1 teaspoon wheat germ

In small bowl combine applesauce and cinnamon, mixing well; set aside. In separate small bowl combine yogurt, sugar, and vanilla, mixing well; set aside. In third small bowl combine raisins and wheat germ, set aside.

Into each of two 6-ounce parfait glasses or dessert dishes spoon half of the applesauce mixture; top each with half of the yogurt mixture and then with half of the raisin mixture. Serve immediately or cover with plastic wrap and refrigerate until ready to serve.

Each serving provides: 1 Fruit Exchange; ½ Milk Exchange; 15 Optional Calories
Per serving: 105 calories; 4 g protein; 1 g fat; 21 g carbohydrate; 116 mg calcium;
  43 mg sodium; 3 mg cholesterol; 1 g dietary fiber

Berry-Yogurt Parfait ◑

Graham cracker crumbs combine with margarine to form a crunchy addition to these easy-to-make parfaits. To turn graham crackers into crumbs in seconds, process in a food processor or blender.

4 cinnamon graham crackers (2½-inch
 squares), made into crumbs
2 teaspoons margarine, melted
½ cup plain low-fat yogurt
1 teaspoon *each* granulated sugar and
 raspberry-flavored syrup

½ cup blueberries
2 tablespoons thawed frozen dairy
 whipped topping

In small mixing bowl combine graham cracker crumbs and margarine, mixing thoroughly until crumbs are moistened; set aside. In separate small mixing bowl combine yogurt, sugar, and syrup and mix well.

Into each of two 8-ounce parfait glasses spoon 1 tablespoon crumb mixture; top each with ¼ of the yogurt mixture (about 2 tablespoons) and ¼ cup blueberries. Sprinkle 2 teaspoons crumb mixture evenly into each glass; top each with half of the remaining yogurt mixture and then sprinkle each with half of the remaining crumb mixture. Top each portion with 1 tablespoon whipped topping.

Each serving provides: 1 Bread Exchange; 1 Fat Exchange; ½ Fruit Exchange;
 ½ Milk Exchange; 35 Optional Calories
Per serving: 173 calories; 4 g protein; 7 g fat; 25 g carbohydrate; 113 mg calcium;
 186 mg sodium; 3 mg cholesterol; 3 g dietary fiber

Creamy Yogurt Topping

WEEK 3   MAKES 4 SERVINGS, ABOUT ¼ CUP EACH

A wonderful treat when served over fresh fruit.

½ cup *each* plain low-fat yogurt and
   part-skim ricotta cheese
1 tablespoon granulated sugar
   or maple syrup

⅛ teaspoon *each* ground cinnamon
   and vanilla extract

In blender container combine yogurt and cheese and process until smooth, scraping down sides of container as necessary. Transfer to small bowl; add remaining ingredients and stir to combine. Serve immediately or cover with plastic wrap and refrigerate until ready to serve.

Each serving provides: ½ Protein Exchange; ¼ Milk Exchange; 15 Optional Calories
Per serving with sugar: 73 calories; 5 g protein; 3 g fat; 7 g carbohydrate; 136 mg calcium;
   58 mg sodium; 11 mg cholesterol; 0 g dietary fiber
With maple syrup: 73 calories; 5 g protein; 3 g fat; 7 g carbohydrate; 142 mg calcium;
   59 mg sodium; 11 mg cholesterol; 0 g dietary fiber

Tropical Yogurt Snack

½ medium banana (about 3 ounces), peeled
1 teaspoon lemon juice
1 cup plain low-fat yogurt
2 teaspoons firmly packed light brown sugar

1 kiwi fruit (about 3 ounces), pared
2 tablespoons shredded coconut, toasted, divided

In small mixing bowl combine banana and lemon juice and, using tines of fork, mash until smooth. Stir in yogurt and sugar, mixing well. Cut kiwi crosswise making 2 thin slices; set aside. Dice remaining kiwi and stir into yogurt mixture. Add 1 tablespoon plus 1 teaspoon coconut to yogurt mixture and stir to combine.

Into each of two 8-ounce dessert dishes or wineglasses spoon half of the yogurt mixture. Cut each reserved slice of kiwi fruit in half and arrange 2 halves on each dessert; sprinkle each with 1 teaspoon of remaining coconut. Serve immediately or cover with plastic wrap and refrigerate until ready to serve.

Each serving provides: 1 Fruit Exchange; 1 Milk Exchange; 50 Optional Calories
Per serving: 160 calories; 7 g protein; 4 g fat; 27 g carbohydrate; 224 mg calcium; 95 mg sodium; 7 mg cholesterol; 1 g dietary fiber (this figure does not include kiwi fruit; nutrition analysis not available)

Banana-Buttermilk Shake

WEEK 5   MAKES 1 SERVING

½ cup buttermilk
¼ cup evaporated skimmed milk
½ medium banana (about 3 ounces),
   peeled and cut into pieces
1 teaspoon granulated sugar

½ teaspoon vanilla extract
Ground cinnamon
1 tablespoon thawed frozen dairy
   whipped topping

In blender container combine milks, banana, sugar, vanilla, and ¼ teaspoon cinnamon and process at high speed until thoroughly combined and smooth, about 1 minute. Pour into 12-ounce glass; top with whipped topping and, if desired, sprinkle with a dash ground cinnamon. Serve immediately.

Each serving provides: 1 Fruit Exchange; 1 Milk Exchange; 50 Optional Calories
Per serving: 188 calories; 9 g protein; 2 g fat; 33 g carbohydrate; 337 mg calcium;
   208 mg sodium; 7 mg cholesterol; 0.8 g dietary fiber

Choc-a-Nut-Drink

WEEK 8   MAKES 2 SERVINGS, ABOUT 1 CUP EACH

1 cup *each* freshly brewed coffee and
   low-fat milk (2% milk fat)
2 tablespoons hazelnut liqueur

1½ teaspoons *each* unsweetened
   cocoa and granulated sugar
Ice cubes

In a pitcher combine all ingredients except ice cubes, stirring until cocoa and sugar are dissolved. Fill two 10-ounce glasses with ice cubes; pour half of the mixture into each glass and serve.

Each serving provides: ½ Milk Exchange; 90 Optional Calories
Per serving: 120 calories; 4 g protein; 3 g fat; 15 g carbohydrate; 153 mg calcium;
   63 mg sodium; 10 mg cholesterol; dietary fiber data not available

Cocoa-Rum Warmer

WEEK 5   MAKES 2 SERVINGS

1 cup skim *or* nonfat milk
½ cup evaporated skimmed milk
¼ cup dark rum
2 teaspoons unsweetened cocoa
1 teaspoon *each* instant coffee powder
   and granulated sugar

¼ teaspoon ground cinnamon
2 tablespoons thawed frozen dairy
   whipped topping

In 1-quart saucepan combine milks and rum and cook over medium heat for 3 minutes; add cocoa, coffee, sugar, and cinnamon and cook, stirring, until cocoa and sugar are dissolved and mixture is heated through, about 1 minute *(do not boil)*. Into two 8-ounce mugs pour half of the milk mixture; top each with 1 tablespoon whipped topping. Serve immediately.

Each serving provides: 1 Milk Exchange; 105 Optional Calories
Per serving: 183 calories; 9 g protein; 2 g fat; 18 g carbohydrate; 342 mg calcium;
   143 mg sodium; 5 mg cholesterol; dietary fiber data not available

Coffee Cream

WEEK 8   MAKES 2 SERVINGS, ABOUT ½ CUP EACH

1 cup low-fat milk (2% milk fat)
2 tablespoons coffee liqueur

1 teaspoon granulated sugar

Chill two 6-ounce glasses. In 2-cup liquid measure or small bowl combine all ingredients, stirring until sugar is dissolved. Pour into chilled glasses.

Each serving provides: ½ Milk Exchange; 80 Optional Calories
Per serving: 110 calories; 4 g protein; 2 g fat; 12 g carbohydrate; 149 mg calcium;
   61 mg sodium; 10 mg cholesterol; 0 g dietary fiber

New York Egg Cream

WEEK 1	MAKES 1 SERVING

An old-fashioned soda fountain favorite that you can make yourself.

1 tablespoon chocolate syrup   **½ cup chilled seltzer**
¼ cup skim *or* nonfat milk

Pour chocolate syrup into 8-ounce glass. Using a long-handled spoon, stir in milk. Quickly stir in seltzer and serve immediately.

Each serving provides: ¼ Milk Exchange; 60 Optional Calories
Per serving: 62 calories; 2 g protein; 0.3 g fat; 14 g carbohydrate; 78 mg calcium;
    50 mg sodium; 1 mg cholesterol; 0 g dietary fiber

Tangy Colada Shake

WEEK 5	MAKES 2 SERVINGS

¾ cup buttermilk   **2 tablespoons shredded coconut**
½ cup canned crushed pineapple   **¼ teaspoon vanilla extract**
**   (no sugar added)**   **4 to 6 ice cubes**
⅓ cup pineapple juice (no sugar added)
¼ cup thawed frozen dairy whipped
**   topping**

Chill two 10-ounce glasses. In blender container combine all ingredients except ice cubes and process until smooth; with motor running add ice cubes, 1 at a time, processing after each addition until mixture is smooth and frothy. Pour half of mixture into each chilled glass.

Each serving provides: 1 Fruit Exchange; ½ Milk Exchange; 55 Optional Calories
Per serving: 145 calories; 4 g protein; 4 g fat; 24 g carbohydrate; 123 mg calcium;
    119 mg sodium; 4 mg cholesterol; 0.8 g dietary fiber

Options

Finale: Exercising Your Options

Our last act brings our entire cast onstage for an inside look at a world most dieters only dream about. Welcome to Options, where you can indulge yourself in some of the most delectable culinary creations, like Chocolate Cream Log and Hollandaise Sauce, safe in the knowledge that you will continue to lose weight. Once you've studied the "script," put on your own production — then sit back and enjoy the cheers and applause.

Notes on Options Lists

For enjoyment and variety, turn to Options. This wide array of flavorful items can turn reduced-calorie eating into a taste adventure.

The Options Lists are divided into the following categories: 10-Calorie Foods; 50-Calorie Foods; 100-Calorie Foods; 150-Calorie Foods; Combination Foods; Diet Foods; and Additional Items (Beverages and Seasonings/Condiments).

Combination Foods add variety to your diet and give you more options in planning menus. Combination Foods are *more* than just a pure Exchange; they are a combination of an Exchange plus Optional Calories, as in low-fat milk (Milk Exchange plus Optional Calories). Or, they are a combination of two different Exchanges, as in peanut butter (Protein Exchange and Fat Exchange).

Each week on the Food Plan, the Options Lists grow in the number and variety of foods, and you get more Optional Calories, too. A glance at the chart below will give you an idea of how it works:

	WEEK 1	WEEK 2	WEEK 3	WEEK 4	WEEK 5
Weekly Total	up to 150	up to 200	up to 300	up to 400	up to 500

• Spend your Optional Calories wisely. You may put them in a "bank account" and spend them little by little throughout the week, or you may "cash" them in and spend them all at once. If all your Optional Calories are not spent within the one week time frame, they cannot be carried over or "saved" from week to week.

• In calculating the Optional Calories for recipes, calories have been rounded to the nearest 5 (for example, round 7.5 or 8 calories to 10 calories; round 11 or 12 calories to 10; 12.5 or 13 calories to 15, etc.). Additionally, Exchange Information in recipes has been given in whole and half Exchanges for items from the Fruit, Bread, Fat, and Protein Exchanges; whole, half, and quarter Exchanges for items from the Milk Exchange; and no less than ⅛ Exchange for Vegetable Exchanges. When recipe Exchanges result in other than the above fractions, the foods involved have been calculated as Optional Calories, using the following caloric values:

EXCHANGES	OPTIONAL CALORIES PER EXCHANGE
Fruit	60
Fat	40
Protein	70
Bread	80
Milk	90

Therefore, if a recipe provides (per serving):	Count as:
⅛ Bread Exchange	80 calories per Bread Exchange ÷ 8 = 10 Optional Calories
¼ Fat Exchange	40 calories per Fat Exchange ÷ 4 = 10 Optional Calories
¼ Fruit Exchange	60 calories per Fruit Exchange ÷ 4 = 15 Optional Calories

• Bouillon cubes and broth and seasoning mixes may contain up to 12 calories per serving.

• You may prepare homemade broth by boiling meat, fish, or skinned poultry or game in water, with or without vegetables. Refrigerate the liquid until the fat congeals on top, then remove and discard congealed fat (this step is not necessary for fish broth).

• All varieties of flour and cornstarch are permitted; they need not be enriched.

• Check labels of diet foods carefully for calorie count; do not use if label does not indicate calories. An item is permitted as a diet food if it falls within one of the following categories and the label indicates that it is calorie-reduced, low-calorie, low-fat, low-sugar, reduced-calorie, reduced-sugar, or sugar-free:

Beverages, carbonated *or* noncarbonated
Gelatin, flavored
Gum
Hard Candy
Jams, Jellies, *or* Preserves
Ketchup
Mints
Salad Dressings
Syrups
Toppings

You may use diet foods that contain sucrose, fructose, or sorbitol as long as they meet the above guidelines.

• Coffees and teas may contain only those ingredients that are not restricted (for example, seasonings, condiments, flavorings, or extracts).

• We strongly recommend that you drink 6 to 8 glasses of water or mineral water daily.

• All seasonings and condiments are permitted except those containing added fat and/or sugar. You may use all types of dehydrated vegetable flakes as a seasoning except potato flakes; potato flakes are listed under the Bread Exchange.

Week 1 — Up to 150 calories weekly
10-Calorie Foods

Selections	Amounts
Arrowroot	1 teaspoon
Bouillon	1 cube *or* 1 teaspoon
Bran, all varieties	1 tablespoon
Bread Crumbs, dried (plain *or* seasoned)	1 teaspoon
Broth and Seasoning Mix, instant	1 packet *or* ¾ cup prepared
Broth *or* Consommé, canned *or* fat-free homemade	¼ cup
Carob Powder, unsweetened	2 teaspoons
Cheese	
Cottage	2 teaspoons
Hard, grated	1 teaspoon
Ricotta, part-skim	1 teaspoon
Chewing Gum	1 stick *or* piece
Cocoa, unsweetened	2 teaspoons
Cereal Beverage Powder *or* Coffee Substitute	1 teaspoon
Cornstarch	1 teaspoon
Creamer, nondairy (liquid *or* powder)	1 teaspoon
Egg White	½
Flour	1 teaspoon
Fructose	½ teaspoon
Honey	½ teaspoon

Selections	Amounts
Ketchup	2 teaspoons
Matzo Cake Meal	1 teaspoon
Matzo Meal	1 teaspoon
Molasses	½ teaspoon
Potato Starch	1 teaspoon
Sugar, all varieties	½ teaspoon
Syrup	½ teaspoon
Toppings	½ teaspoon
Wheat Germ	1 teaspoon

50-Calorie Foods

Selections	Amounts
Jams, Jellies, *or* Preserves	1 tablespoon

Diet Foods

Check labels for calories.

Combination Foods

Selections	Amounts	Exchange Information
Milk, low-fat (1% fat)	1 cup	1 Milk Exchange; 20 Optional Calories

Week 2—Up to 200 calories weekly

You may use all of the items listed under Week 1 and may add the following to your Options Lists:

10-Calorie Foods

Selections	Amounts
Bacon Bits, imitation	1 teaspoon
Wine	
light	1 tablespoon
regular, dry	2 teaspoons

50-Calorie Foods

Selections	Amounts
Whipped Topping, dairy *or* nondairy	¼ cup prepared

100-Calorie Foods

Selections	Amounts
Beer	
light	12 fluid ounces (1½ cups)
regular	8 fluid ounces (1 cup)
Champagne	4 fluid ounces (½ cup)
Wine	
light	6 fluid ounces (¾ cup)
regular, dry	4 fluid ounces (½ cup)

Combination Foods

Selections	Amounts	Exchange Information
Milk, low-fat (2% fat)	1 cup	1 Milk Exchange; 40 Optional Calories

Week 3 — Up to 300 calories weekly

You may use all of the items listed under Weeks 1 and 2 and may add the following to your Options Lists:

10-Calorie Foods

Selections	Amounts
Maraschino Cherry	1
Relish, any type	1 teaspoon

50-Calorie Foods

Selections	Amounts
Half-and-Half	2 tablespoons

Combination Foods

Selections	Amounts	Exchange Information
Baked Beans, without meat	4 ounces	1 Bread Exchange; 45 Optional Calories
Biscuit, any type	1 (2-inch diameter)	1 Bread Exchange; 1 Fat Exchange
Milk, whole	1 cup	1 Milk Exchange; 60 Optional Calories
Peanut Butter	1 tablespoon	1 Protein Exchange; 1 Fat Exchange
Tahini	1 tablespoon	1 Protein Exchange; 1 Fat Exchange

Week 4 — Up to 400 calories weekly

You may use all of the items listed under Weeks 1, 2, and 3 and may add the following to your Options Lists:

10-Calorie Foods

Selections	Amounts
Coconut (sweetened *or* unsweetened), shredded	1 teaspoon
Seeds (caraway, poppy, pumpkin, sesame, *or* sunflower)	½ teaspoon
Tapioca, uncooked	1 teaspoon

50-Calorie Foods

Selections	Amounts
Tomato Paste	¼ cup
Tomato Puree *or* Sauce	½ cup

100-Calorie Foods

Selections	Amounts
Cream Cheese	2 tablespoons
Cream Cheese, whipped	3 tablespoons
Sour Cream	3 tablespoons

Combination Foods

Selections	Amounts	Exchange Information
Coleslaw	½ cup	1 Vegetable Exchange; 2 Fat Exchanges
Crackers, any type	1 ounce	1 Bread Exchange; 60 Optional Calories
Croissant, plain	1 (1½ ounces)	1 Bread Exchange; 100 Optional Calories
Muffin, any type	1 (2 ounces)	2 Bread Exchanges; 1 Fat Exchange

Week 5 — Up to 500 calories weekly

You may use all of the items listed under Weeks 1, 2, 3, and 4 and may add the following to your Options Lists:

10-Calorie Foods

Selections	Amounts
Anchovies	2 fillets *or* 1 teaspoon mashed
Black Bean Sauce	1 teaspoon
Clam Juice	¼ cup
Concentrated Yeast Extract	1 teaspoon
Hoisin Sauce	1 teaspoon
Miso (fermented soybean paste)	1 teaspoon
Olives, any type	2
Oyster Sauce	1 teaspoon

50-Calorie Foods

Selections	Amounts
Cream, any type	1 tablespoon
Sauce: barbecue, chili, seafood cocktail, *or* steak	3 tablespoons
Tartar Sauce	2 teaspoons
Whipped Cream, aerosol instant	¼ cup

100-Calorie Foods

Selections	Amounts
Avocado	¼ (2 ounces with skin)
Butter	1 tablespoon
Butter, whipped	2 tablespoons
Gelatin, fruit-flavored	½ cup (prepared)
Neufchâtel Cheese	2 tablespoons
Wine, dessert	2 fluid ounces
Yogurt Drinks	4 fluid ounces (½ cup)

150-Calorie Foods

Selections	Amounts
Chocolate, any type	1 ounce
Cookies, any type	2 medium (1 ounce)
Amaretti Cookies	4 (1 ounce)
Chocolate-Coated Graham Crackers	2 (2-inch square)
Chocolate Wafers	4 (1 ounce)
Gingerbread Cookies	2 medium (1 ounce)
Gingersnap Cookies	6 (1 ounce)
Vanilla Wafers	6 (1 ounce)
Frozen Tofu, soft-serve	4 ounces
Frozen Yogurt, soft-serve	4 ounces
Fudge	1 ounce
Gin	2 fluid ounces
Rum	2 fluid ounces
Sherbet, any flavor	½ cup
Scotch	2 fluid ounces
Sorbet, any flavor	½ cup
Sprinkles, any type	3 tablespoons
Tequila	2 fluid ounces
Vodka	2 fluid ounces
Whiskey	2 fluid ounces

Combination Foods

Selections	Amounts	Exchange Information
Granola, any type	1 ounce	1 Bread Exchange; 60 Optional Calories
Pretzels (3-ring)	5 (1 ounce)	1 Bread Exchange; 30 Optional Calories

Week 6

You may use all of the items listed under Weeks 1, 2, 3, 4, and 5 and may add the following to your Options Lists:

Selections	Amounts	Exchange Information
Bacon, crisp	2 slices	85 Optional Calories
Sausage (brown-and-serve)	2 links (1 ounce)	1 Protein Exchange; 70 Optional Calories
Soda, any flavor	8 fluid ounces	100 Optional Calories

Week 8

You may use all of the items listed under all previous weeks and may add the following to your Options Lists:

Selections	Amounts	Exchange Information
Almonds	11 nuts (½ ounce shelled)	1 Protein Exchange; 1 Fat Exchange
Angel Food Cake	(1/12 of 9-inch cake)	½ Bread Exchange; 120 Optional Calories
Brandy	2 fluid ounces	150 Optional Calories
Brazil Nuts	4 nuts (½ ounce shelled)	1 Protein Exchange; 1 Fat Exchange
Cashews	7 large nuts (½ ounce shelled)	1 Protein Exchange; 40 Optional Calories
Cognac	2 fluid ounces	150 Optional Calories
Hazelnuts	10 nuts (½ ounce shelled)	1 Protein Exchange; 1 Fat Exchange
Liqueurs (any type)	1 fluid ounce	100 Optional Calories
Macadamia Nuts	6 nuts (½ ounce shelled)	1 Protein Exchange; 40 Optional Calories
Marshmallows	2 medium (½ ounce)	50 Optional Calories
Peanuts	7 nuts (½ ounce shelled)	1 Protein Exchange; 1 Fat Exchange
Pecans	12 halves (½ ounce shelled)	1 Protein Exchange; 1 Fat Exchange

Selections	Amounts	Exchange Information
Pignolias (pine nuts)	(½ ounce)	1 Protein Exchange; 1 Fat Exchange
Pistachios	12 nuts (½ ounce shelled)	1 Protein Exchange; 1 Fat Exchange
Pound Cake	1 slice (2 ounces)	1 Bread Exchange; 175 Optional Calories
Walnuts	13 halves (½ ounce shelled)	1 Protein Exchange; 1 Fat Exchange

Additional Items

The following items may be consumed in all weeks in reasonable amounts:

Beverages

Club Soda
Coffee
Mineral Water, flavored and
  unflavored

Seltzer, flavored and
  unflavored
Tea
Water

Seasonings/Condiments

Aromatic Bitters
Baking Powder
Baking Soda
Browning Sauce
Capers
Cream of Tartar
Dehydrated Vegetable Flakes
Extracts
Flavorings
Gelatin, unflavored
Herbs
Horseradish
Hot Sauce (pepper sauce)
Lemon Juice
Lime Juice (no sugar added)
Mustard

Nonstick Cooking Spray
Nori Sheets (dried seaweed)
Pectin
Pepper
Picante Sauce
Rennin Tablets
Salt
Seaweed
Soy Sauce
Spices
Sugar Substitutes
Tamari
Teriyaki Sauce
Vinegar, all types
Worcestershire Sauce
Yeast

Crab-Stuffed Mushrooms

WEEK 4   MAKES 4 SERVINGS, 4 MUSHROOMS EACH

1 tablespoon plus 1 teaspoon margarine
¼ cup chopped scallions (green onions)
1 garlic clove, minced
5 ounces thawed and well-drained
   frozen crabmeat
2 tablespoons dry vermouth
1 tablespoon lemon juice
2 ounces round buttery crackers, made
   into fine crumbs

3 tablespoons sour cream
Dash pepper
16 large mushroom caps
1 ounce Monterey Jack cheese,
   shredded

Preheat oven to 450° F. In 12-inch nonstick skillet melt margarine; add scallions and garlic and sauté over medium-high heat until softened, about 1 minute. Add crabmeat, vermouth, and lemon juice and cook until crabmeat is heated through, 2 to 3 minutes. Transfer to medium mixing bowl; add remaining ingredients except mushroom caps and cheese and mix well until thoroughly combined. Fill each mushroom cap with a rounded tablespoon of crabmeat mixture and set on nonstick baking sheet. Sprinkle an equal amount of cheese over stuffing portion of each mushroom and bake until cheese is melted and mushrooms are fork-tender, 12 to 15 minutes.

Each serving provides: 1½ Protein Exchanges; ½ Bread Exchange; 2¼ Vegetable
   Exchanges; 1 Fat Exchange; 90 Optional Calories
Per serving: 223 calories; 12 g protein; 13 g fat; 15 g carbohydrate; 134 mg calcium;
   312 mg sodium; 46 mg cholesterol; 2 g dietary fiber

Cheddar-Bacon Puffs

**2 ready-to-bake refrigerated buttermilk
   flaky biscuits (1 ounce each)***
**2 slices crisp bacon, each cut into
   4 equal pieces**

½ ounce Cheddar cheese, shredded
2 teaspoons chopped fresh chives

Preheat oven to 375° F. Carefully separate each biscuit into 4 thin layers. Onto center of each layer of dough arrange 1 piece of bacon, ⅛ of the cheese (about 1½ teaspoons), and ¼ teaspoon chives; gather together edges of dough and twist to enclose filling, forming 8 puffs. Spray eight 2½-inch-diameter muffin-pan cups with nonstick cooking spray; set puffs seam-side down in sprayed cups and partially fill remaining cups with water (this will prevent pan from burning and/or warping). Bake until biscuits are puffed and lightly browned, 10 to 15 minutes.

Each serving provides: 1 Bread Exchange; 60 Optional Calories
Per serving: 150 calories; 5 g protein; 9 g fat; 13 g carbohydrate; 53 mg calcium;
   441 mg sodium; 13 mg cholesterol; trace dietary fiber

*Keep biscuits refrigerated until ready to use. Separate dough into layers as soon as biscuits are removed from refrigerator; they will be difficult to work with if allowed to come to room temperature.

Sardine Canapés ⊙ ◐

WEEK 4   MAKES 2 SERVINGS, 4 CANAPÉS EACH

8 round buttery crackers (1 ounce)
1 large plum tomato, sliced crosswise
   into 8 slices
8 canned sardines (¼ ounce each),
   packed in oil, drained

¼ cup thinly sliced red onion, separated
   into rings
1 tablespoon plus 1 teaspoon mustard
Garnish: dill sprigs

Arrange crackers on serving platter; top each with 1 tomato slice, 1 sardine, ⅛ of the onion rings, and ½ teaspoon mustard. Garnish each canapé with a dill sprig.

Each serving provides: 1 Protein Exchange; ½ Bread Exchange; ¾ Vegetable Exchange;
   30 Optional Calories
Per serving: 148 calories; 9 g protein; 8 g fat; 12 g carbohydrate; 144 mg calcium;
   396 mg sodium; 40 mg cholesterol; 0.4 g dietary fiber

Dilled Tahini Dip ◐

WEEK 4   MAKES 4 SERVINGS, ABOUT 3 TABLESPOONS EACH

This exotic dip is wonderful spread on pita breads or used as a dip with assorted vegetables.

½ cup plain low-fat yogurt
2 tablespoons tahini (sesame paste)
1 tablespoon sour cream

1 teaspoon *each* lemon juice and
   chopped fresh dill
½ teaspoon granulated sugar

In small mixing bowl combine all ingredients, mixing well until thoroughly combined. Cover with plastic wrap and refrigerate until flavors blend, about 30 minutes.

Each serving provides: ½ Protein Exchange; ½ Fat Exchange; ¼ Milk Exchange;
   10 Optional Calories
Per serving: 73 calories; 3 g protein; 5 g fat; 4 g carbohydrate; 89 mg calcium;
   31 mg sodium; 3 mg cholesterol; dietary fiber data not available

Smoked Salmon
Corn Muffins ◑

WEEK 4	MAKES 2 SERVINGS, 2 MUFFIN HALVES EACH

2 corn muffins (2 ounces each)
2 ounces smoked salmon (lox), chopped
3 tablespoons whipped cream cheese

1 tablespoon minced onion
2 teaspoons drained capers
¼ teaspoon lemon juice

Preheat oven to 350° F. Cut a thin slice from top of each muffin so muffin is flat on top, reserving slices for garnish. Cut each muffin in half horizontally; separate muffin halves and turn top halves over so they are sitting on their tops. Using a fork, in small mixing bowl combine remaining ingredients, mixing well. Onto cut-side of each muffin half spread ¼ of salmon mixture. Spray 8 x 8 x 2-inch baking dish with nonstick cooking spray and arrange muffin halves salmon-mixture-side up in pan. Bake until warm, about 15 minutes. Cut each reserved muffin slice in half and arrange each on a muffin half. Serve immediately.

Each serving provides: 1 Protein Exchange; 2 Bread Exchanges; 1 Fat Exchange; 50 Optional Calories
Per serving: 261 calories; 10 g protein; 12 g fat; 28 g carbohydrate; 73 mg calcium; 621 mg sodium; 50 mg cholesterol; trace dietary fiber

Spinach-Bacon Pesto

WEEK 8   MAKES 8 SERVINGS, ABOUT ¼ CUP EACH

Enjoy this flavorful mixture as a dip or tossed with hot cooked pasta.

4 cups firmly packed spinach leaves, trimmed, thoroughly washed, and drained
1 ounce shelled walnuts
4 slices crisp bacon
3 tablespoons freshly squeezed lemon juice
2 tablespoons plus 2 teaspoons olive oil

1 small garlic clove
1 teaspoon grated lemon peel
½ teaspoon salt
¼ teaspoon *each* basil leaves and white pepper
4 ounces grated Parmesan cheese

In work bowl of food processor combine all ingredients except cheese and process until smooth, scraping down sides of container as necessary. Transfer mixture to bowl; stir in cheese. Cover with plastic wrap and refrigerate until ready to serve. Serve at room temperature.

Each serving provides: ½ Protein Exchange; 1 Vegetable Exchange; 1 Fat Exchange; 50 Optional Calories
Per serving: 155 calories; 8 g protein; 13 g fat; 3 g carbohydrate; 233 mg calcium; 476 mg sodium; 14 mg cholesterol; 1 g dietary fiber

Banana-Peanut Breakfast Shake

WEEK 3   MAKES 1 SERVING

¾ cup buttermilk
½ medium banana (about 3 ounces),
   peeled and sliced
1 tablespoon creamy peanut butter

2 teaspoons honey
½ teaspoon wheat germ
3 to 4 ice cubes

In blender container combine all ingredients except ice cubes and process at high speed until smooth; with motor running add ice cubes, 1 at a time, processing after each addition until mixture is smooth and frothy. Pour into a 12-ounce glass and serve immediately.

Each serving provides: 1 Protein Exchange; 1 Fat Exchange; 1 Fruit Exchange;
   1 Milk Exchange; 45 Optional Calories
Per serving: 269 calories; 12 g protein; 10 g fat; 37 g carbohydrate; 223 mg calcium;
   270 mg sodium; 7 mg cholesterol; 2 g dietary fiber

German Apple-Sausage Pancake ⊝

WEEK 6   MAKES 2 SERVINGS, ½ PANCAKE EACH

½ cup all-purpose flour
2 teaspoons granulated sugar, divided
¼ teaspoon baking soda
¾ cup buttermilk
2 eggs, separated
⅛ teaspoon cream of tartar
1 small apple (about ¼ pound), cored,
   pared, and thinly sliced

2 brown-and-serve sausage links
   (1 ounce), cooked and cut
   lengthwise into halves
½ teaspoon apple pie spice

Preheat oven to 375° F. In medium mixing bowl combine flour, 1 teaspoon sugar, and the baking soda; set aside. In small mixing bowl beat together buttermilk and egg yolks; set aside. In separate small mixing bowl, using electric mixer at high speed, beat egg whites until foamy; add cream of tartar and continue beating until whites are stiff but not dry. Stir buttermilk mixture into dry ingredients, stirring until smooth; fold in beaten whites.

Spray 9-inch pie plate with nonstick cooking spray; spread batter evenly over bottom of pie plate. Decoratively arrange apple slices and sausage halves over batter. In cup or small bowl combine remaining teaspoon sugar with the apple pie spice; sprinkle over pancake. Bake for 15 to 20 minutes (until pancake is lightly browned and a cake tester, inserted in center, comes out clean).

Each serving provides: 1½ Protein Exchanges; 1 Bread Exchange; ½ Fruit Exchange;
   ½ Milk Exchange; 85 Optional Calories
Per serving: 331 calories; 14 g protein; 12 g fat; 41 g carbohydrate; 148 mg calcium;
   381 mg sodium; 287 mg cholesterol; 2 g dietary fiber

Variation: German Pancake with Syrup—Drizzle 2 tablespoons reduced-calorie pancake syrup (60 calories per fluid ounce) over cooked pancake. Increase Optional Calories to 115.

Per serving: 391 calories; 14 g protein; 12 g fat; 56 g carbohydrate; 148 mg calcium;
   381 mg sodium; 287 mg cholesterol; 2 g dietary fiber

Avocado and Roquefort Salad ◑

To keep the unused portion of avocado from turning brown, sprinkle it with lemon juice.

¼ avocado (2 ounces), pared and diced
1 tablespoon plus 1 teaspoon lemon
  juice, divided
1 small orange (about 6 ounces)
1 tablespoon *each* chopped fresh mint
  and raspberry *or* seasoned rice
  vinegar

2 teaspoons olive oil
12 lettuce leaves
1 ounce Roquefort cheese, crumbled

In small bowl combine avocado and 1 teaspoon lemon juice, tossing to coat; set aside. Over bowl to catch juice, remove skin and membranes from orange and section orange; set sections aside. Add remaining tablespoon lemon juice, the mint, vinegar, and oil to juice from orange, mixing well; set aside.

Line chilled serving platter with lettuce leaves. Decoratively arrange avocado and orange sections on platter and sprinkle with Roquefort cheese. Stir orange juice mixture again and pour over salad.

Each serving provides: ½ Protein Exchange; 1½ Vegetable Exchanges; 1 Fat Exchange; ½ Fruit Exchange; 50 Optional Calories
Per serving: 170 calories; 5 g protein; 13 g fat; 12 g carbohydrate; 158 mg calcium; 265 mg sodium; 13 mg cholesterol; 2 g dietary fiber

Variation: Avocado Salad with Goat Cheese—One ounce goat cheese may be substituted for the Roquefort cheese.

Per serving: 169 calories; 4 g protein; 12 g fat; 13 g carbohydrate; 86 mg calcium; 96 mg sodium; 13 mg cholesterol; 2 g dietary fiber (this figure does not include goat cheese; nutrition analysis not available)

Brussels Sprouts 'n' Bacon Sauté ⓒ Ⓞ

WEEK 6   MAKES 2 SERVINGS

You'll be out of the kitchen in no time when you cook the brussels sprouts and the bacon for this recipe in advance.

2 teaspoons margarine
½ cup diced onion
2 cups cooked brussels sprouts

3 slices crisp bacon, crumbled
⅛ teaspoon *each* salt and pepper

In 10-inch nonstick skillet melt margarine; add onion and sauté over medium-high heat until tender, about 1 minute. Add remaining ingredients and cook, stirring frequently, until brussels sprouts are heated through, 3 to 4 minutes.

Each serving provides: 2½ Vegetable Exchanges; 1 Fat Exchange; 65 Optional Calories
Per serving: 163 calories; 7 g protein; 9 g fat; 17 g carbohydrate; 70 mg calcium;
    368 mg sodium; 8 mg cholesterol; 3 g dietary fiber

Elegant Ham 'n' Cheese Sandwich ◑

WEEK 8   MAKES 2 SERVINGS

Delicious for brunch.

1 croissant (1½ ounces)
2 teaspoons margarine
2 ounces thinly sliced cooked smoked
  ham
1 small apple (about 4 ounces), cored,
  pared, and thinly sliced

1 teaspoon maple syrup
2 ounces Brie cheese (rind removed),
  thinly sliced
½ ounce sliced almonds, toasted

Using a serrated knife, cut croissant in half horizontally. Arrange croissant halves cut-side up on baking sheet or toaster oven tray and broil (or toast) until lightly browned, about 1 minute. Set aside.

In 10-inch nonstick skillet melt margarine; add ham and sauté over medium-high heat until lightly browned, 1 to 2 minutes. Top each croissant half with 1 ounce ham; set aside. To same skillet add apple and sauté until apple is tender, 2 to 3 minutes; drizzle maple syrup over apple and sauté just until heated through, about 30 seconds. Spoon half of the apple slices over each portion ham and then top each with 1 ounce Brie. Broil or top-brown in toaster oven until cheese melts, about 1 minute.

To serve, transfer croissant halves to 2 serving plates and top each portion with ¼ ounce almonds.

Each serving provides: 2½ Protein Exchanges; ½ Bread Exchange; 1½ Fat Exchanges;
  ½ Fruit Exchange; 60 Optional Calories
Per serving: 333 calories; 15 g protein; 22 g fat; 20 g carbohydrate; 89 mg calcium;
  744 mg sodium; 42 mg cholesterol; 1 g dietary fiber

Cashew Butter

WEEK 8   MAKES 8 SERVINGS, ABOUT 1 TABLESPOON PLUS 1 TEASPOON EACH

Serve with sautéed or grilled pork or chicken. Butter will keep for about 2 weeks in the refrigerator.

½ cup whipped butter, softened   1 garlic clove, minced
1 ounce roasted cashews, ground
1 tablespoon minced Italian (flat-leaf)
   parsley

In blender container combine all ingredients and process until smooth, scraping down sides of container as necessary. Transfer to resealable plastic container and refrigerate until ready to serve.

Each serving provides: 80 Optional Calories
Per serving: 72 calories; 0.6 g protein; 7 g fat; 1 g carbohydrate; 5 mg calcium;
   59 mg sodium; 16 mg cholesterol; trace dietary fiber

Caper and Anchovy Butter

WEEK 5   MAKES 8 SERVINGS, ABOUT 1 TABLESPOON EACH

Add pizzazz to broiled fish with this zesty butter. Prepare it up to 1 week in advance to have on hand all week long.

½ cup whipped butter, softened   2 drained canned anchovy fillets
2 tablespoons *each* drained capers
   and lemon juice

In blender container combine all ingredients and process until combined, scraping down sides of container as necessary. Transfer to resealable plastic container and refrigerate until ready to use.

Each serving provides: 50 Optional Calories
Per serving: 54 calories; 0.4 g protein; 6 g fat; 0.2 g carbohydrate; 4 mg calcium;
   151 mg sodium; 16 mg cholesterol; dietary fiber data not available

Ginger Butter

WEEK 5   MAKES 6 SERVINGS, ABOUT 2 TABLESPOONS EACH

Spice up grilled pork or chicken with this tasty butter. It will keep in the refrigerator for up to 2 weeks.

½ cup whipped butter, softened
1 tablespoon *each* grated pared
   gingerroot, dark corn syrup, and
   teriyaki sauce

½ teaspoon grated orange peel

In blender container combine all ingredients and process until combined, scraping down sides of container as necessary. Transfer to resealable plastic container and refrigerate until ready to use.

Each serving provides: 75 Optional Calories
Per serving: 81 calories; 0.3 g protein; 8 g fat; 3 g carbohydrate; 5 mg calcium;
   195 mg sodium; 21 mg cholesterol; 0 g dietary fiber

Lime Butter

WEEK 5   YIELDS ½ CUP

This delightful butter, which can be made up to 1 week in advance, goes well with cooked seafood, fish, or chicken.

¼ cup *each* whipped butter and freshly
   squeezed lime juice
1 tablespoon chopped Italian (flat-leaf)
   parsley

Dash *each* salt and white pepper

In blender container combine butter and lime juice and process until combined, scraping down sides of container as necessary; stir in remaining ingredients. Transfer to resealable plastic container and refrigerate until ready to use.

Each 2-tablespoon serving provides: 50 Optional Calories
Per serving: 55 calories; 0.1 g protein; 6 g fat; 1 g carbohydrate; 5 mg calcium;
   92 mg sodium; 16 mg cholesterol; trace dietary fiber
Each 1-tablespoon serving provides: 25 Optional Calories
Per serving: 28 calories; 0.07 g protein; 3 g fat; 0.7 g carbohydrate; 2 mg calcium;
   46 mg sodium; 8 mg cholesterol; trace dietary fiber

Pistachio Cream

WEEK 8	MAKES 8 SERVINGS, ABOUT 1 TABLESPOON EACH

Serve as a topping for fresh fruit.

½ cup thawed frozen dairy whipped
    topping
1 tablespoon sour cream

½ ounce finely ground pistachio nuts

Using a wire whisk or fork, in small mixing bowl combine topping and sour cream; stir in nuts. Cover with plastic wrap and refrigerate until flavors blend, about 1 hour.

Each serving provides: 30 Optional Calories
Per serving: 26 calories; 0.4 g protein; 2 g fat; 2 g carbohydrate; 4 mg calcium;
    6 mg sodium; 0.8 mg cholesterol; dietary fiber data not available

Hollandaise Sauce   ◐◑

WEEK 5	MAKES 4 SERVINGS, ABOUT 3 TABLESPOONS EACH

2 eggs
2 tablespoons *each* freshly squeezed
    lemon juice and butter, cut into small
    pieces

¼ teaspoon salt
Dash *each* ground red pepper and
    powdered mustard

In blender container combine eggs and lemon juice and process until combined; add butter, 1 piece at a time, and continue processing until blended, scraping down sides of container as necessary. Add seasonings and process to combine. Transfer to small saucepan and cook over low heat, stirring constantly, until mixture is smooth and thickened, about 5 minutes.

Each serving provides: ½ Protein Exchange; 50 Optional Calories
Per serving: 92 calories; 3 g protein; 9 g fat; 1 g carbohydrate; 17 mg calcium;
    228 mg sodium; 153 mg cholesterol; 0 g dietary fiber

Horseradish-Caper Sauce

MAKES 12 SERVINGS, ABOUT 1 TABLESPOON EACH

A perfect accompaniment for cold sliced meats, fish, or poultry.
This sauce will keep in the refrigerator for about 2 weeks.

⅓ cup plus 2 teaspoons sour cream   **1 tablespoon prepared horseradish**
¼ cup drained capers

In small bowl combine all ingredients, stirring until combined. Cover with plastic wrap or transfer to jar with tight-fitting cover and refrigerate until ready to serve. Just before serving, stir well.

Each serving provides: 15 Optional Calories
Per serving: 16 calories; 0.2 g protein; 2 g fat; 0.4 g carbohydrate; 9 mg calcium;
    78 mg sodium; 3 mg cholesterol; dietary fiber data not available

Pignolias, Capers, and Tomato Sauce

WEEK 8   MAKES 8 SERVINGS, ABOUT ½ CUP EACH

You can keep this delicious sauce in your refrigerator for up to 4 days. Or measure the sauce into plastic freezer bags or freezer containers, label with date and amount, and keep frozen for up to 2 months.

2 tablespoons plus 2 teaspoons olive
   or vegetable oil
1 cup diced onions
2 small garlic cloves, minced
1 quart canned Italian tomatoes (with
   liquid), seeded and chopped
2 ounces pignolias (pine nuts), toasted

¼ cup *each* chopped fresh basil, Italian
   (flat-leaf) parsley, and drained capers
2 bay leaves
1 teaspoon salt
Dash pepper

In 3-quart saucepan heat oil; add onions and garlic and sauté over medium heat until onions are translucent. Add remaining ingredients; stir to combine and bring to a boil. Reduce heat and let simmer until flavors blend and raw tomato taste is cooked out, 20 to 25 minutes. Discard bay leaves before serving.

Each serving provides: ½ Protein Exchange; 1¼ Vegetable Exchanges; 1½ Fat Exchanges
Per serving: 111 calories; 3 g protein; 8 g fat; 8 g carbohydrate; 57 mg calcium;
   582 mg sodium; 0 mg cholesterol; 1 g dietary fiber (this figure does not include pignolias
   and capers; nutrition analysis not available)

Peanut-Cocoa Cookies

WEEK 3   MAKES 4 SERVINGS, 3 COOKIES EACH

⅓ cup plus 2 teaspoons *each* whole
 wheat and all-purpose flour
1 tablespoon unsweetened cocoa
1 teaspoon baking powder
3 tablespoons chunky peanut butter
1 tablespoon margarine

2 tablespoons *each* granulated sugar
 and firmly packed dark brown sugar
1 egg
¼ teaspoon vanilla extract

Preheat oven to 350° F. In small mixing bowl combine flours, cocoa, and baking powder; set aside. Using a fork, in medium mixing bowl combine peanut butter and margarine until combined; add sugars and, using electric mixer at medium speed, beat until thoroughly combined and mixture is light and fluffy. Add egg and vanilla and beat until combined. Add flour mixture and beat until combined.

Divide dough into 12 equal portions and, using hands, shape each portion into a ball; arrange balls on nonstick cookie sheet, leaving a space of about 1 inch between each. Using the tines of a fork, slightly press each cookie to flatten, then press down in opposite direction to create a checkerboard pattern. Bake until cookies are firm to the touch, about 15 minutes. Transfer to wire rack and let cool.

Each serving provides: 1 Protein Exchange; 1 Bread Exchange; 1½ Fat Exchanges;
    65 Optional Calories
Per serving: 251 calories; 8 g protein; 11 g fat; 32 g carbohydrate; 79 mg calcium;
    209 mg sodium; 69 mg cholesterol; 1 g dietary fiber

Lemon-Nut Cookies

WEEK 8   MAKES 12 SERVINGS, 2 COOKIES EACH

½ cup reduced-calorie margarine (tub)
⅓ cup granulated sugar
1½ teaspoons grated lemon peel
1 cup plus 2 tablespoons all-purpose
   flour

1 teaspoon double-acting baking
   powder
1½ ounces finely chopped walnuts

Using electric mixer at medium speed, in medium mixing bowl beat together margarine and sugar until fluffy; beat in lemon peel. In small mixing bowl combine flour and baking powder; add to margarine mixture and stir well to form dough. Form dough into a log. On sheet of wax paper spread nuts; roll log in nuts. Wrap log in wax paper, then in plastic wrap, and refrigerate until chilled, at least 1 hour.

Preheat oven to 375° F. Cut log crosswise into 24 equal pieces and arrange on nonstick cookie sheet. Bake cookies until golden, about 15 minutes. Transfer to wire rack and let cool.

Each serving provides: ½ Bread Exchange; 1 Fat Exchange; 55 Optional Calories
Per serving: 120 calories; 2 g protein; 6 g fat; 15 g carbohydrate; 23 mg calcium;
   116 mg sodium; 0 mg cholesterol; 0.6 g dietary fiber

Fresh Fruit Ambrosia

WEEK 8   MAKES 4 SERVINGS

1 small orange (about 6 ounces)
1 cup fresh pineapple chunks, divided
20 small red seedless grapes, halved
½ ounce miniature marshmallows
2 teaspoons shredded coconut

⅔ cup cottage cheese
2 tablespoons sour cream
¼ ounce chopped walnuts

Over small bowl to catch juice, remove skin and membranes from orange and reserve juice; section orange. In medium mixing bowl combine orange sections, ½ cup pineapple, the grapes, marshmallows, and coconut; stir to combine and set aside. In blender container combine remaining ½ cup pineapple, the reserved orange juice, the cottage cheese, and sour cream and process until pureed, scraping down sides of container as necessary. Pour over fruit mixture and stir to coat. Cover with plastic wrap and refrigerate until ready to serve.

To serve, sprinkle with walnuts.

Each serving provides: ½ Protein Exchange; 1 Fruit Exchange; 50 Optional Calories
Per serving: 121 calories; 5 g protein; 5 g fat; 16 g carbohydrate; 50 mg calcium;
  150 mg sodium; 8 mg cholesterol; 1 g dietary fiber

Raspberry Peaches

WEEK 8   MAKES 8 SERVINGS

1 cup fresh *or* frozen thawed
   raspberries (no sugar added)
1½ pounds peaches, blanched, peeled,
   pitted, and sliced

2 tablespoons *each* granulated sugar,
   lemon juice, whipped butter, and
   raspberry liqueur

In work bowl of food processor process raspberries until pureed.
Set sieve over small mixing bowl and press puree through sieve into
bowl, discarding seeds.

In medium mixing bowl combine peaches, sugar, and lemon
juice, tossing to combine. In 8-inch nonstick skillet melt butter; add
peach mixture and sauté until sugar is dissolved, about 1 minute.
Pour in raspberry puree and liqueur and stir to combine; reduce
heat to low and cook until thoroughly heated, 2 to 3 minutes.
Remove peach mixture from skillet. Place in serving bowl; cover
and refrigerate until chilled, about 1 hour.

Each serving provides: 1 Fruit Exchange; 40 Optional Calories
Per serving: 71 calories; 1 g protein; 2 g fat; 13 g carbohydrate; 7 mg calcium;
   15 mg sodium; 4 mg cholesterol; 1 g dietary fiber

Serving Suggestion: Top each portion with 1 tablespoon thawed
frozen dairy whipped topping. Increase Optional Calories to 55.

Per serving: 83 calories; 1 g protein; 3 g fat; 14 g carbohydrate; 7 mg calcium;
   20 mg sodium; 4 mg cholesterol; 1 g dietary fiber

Chocolate-Dipped
Strawberries ◑

WEEK 5	MAKES 4 SERVINGS, ABOUT 2 STRAWBERRIES EACH

Prepare this recipe on the day you plan to serve it.

2 ounces semisweet chocolate chips
5 ounces strawberries, about 8 berries (with hulls attached)

Place chocolate in 1-cup heat-resistant glass liquid measure and microwave on High (100% power)* until chocolate begins to melt, for 30 seconds;† stir to combine. Microwave on High (100% power) until chocolate is completely melted and smooth, 30 seconds longer;† stir to combine.

Line a plate with a sheet of wax paper and set aside. Holding 1 berry by the hull dip berry about halfway into the melted chocolate; set on wax-paper-lined plate. Repeat procedure with remaining berries and chocolate. Place plate of berries in refrigerator and chill until chocolate hardens, about 20 minutes. Transfer berries to serving platter and serve immediately or cover loosely with plastic wrap and keep in refrigerator until ready to serve.

Each serving provides: 90 Optional Calories
Per serving: 82 calories; 1 g protein; 5 g fat; 10 g carbohydrate; 9 mg calcium;
    1 mg sodium; 0 mg cholesterol; 1 g dietary fiber

*Chocolate can be melted in the top half of a double boiler. In double boiler cook chocolate over hot *(not boiling)* water, stirring frequently, until chocolate is melted and smooth, 2 to 3 minutes. When melting chocolate, it should not come in contact with water or steam; moisture will cause it to harden.
†Cooking time may be different in your microwave oven. To ensure good results, be sure to check for doneness while cooking.

Quick Strawberry Shortcakes ⊖ ⊕

WEEK 8   MAKES 4 SERVINGS, 1 SHORTCAKE EACH

Take a shortcake shortcut by using thawed frozen pound cake.

4 round slices pound cake (1 ounce each), lightly toasted
2 cups strawberries, sliced

¼ cup thawed frozen dairy whipped topping
Garnish: 4 mint sprigs

Onto each of 4 individual plates arrange 1 slice of pound cake; decoratively arrange ¼ of the strawberries on each slice of cake, overlapping slices slightly. Using a pastry bag fitted with a star tip, pipe ¼ of the whipped topping onto center of each shortcake. Garnish each serving with a mint sprig.

Each serving provides: ½ Bread Exchange; ½ Fruit Exchange; 100 Optional Calories
Per serving: 151 calories; 2 g protein; 8 g fat; 20 g carbohydrate; 21 mg calcium;
    102 mg sodium; 0 mg cholesterol; 1 g dietary fiber

Baked Alaska Cream Loaf

Always an impressive dessert, with our recipe it is also easy to prepare using the frozen pound cake that is usually available in the freezer section of the supermarket.

**1 frozen pound cake loaf (10¾ ounces),   2 egg whites (at room temperature)
   slightly thawed*   2 tablespoons granulated sugar
1 cup ice milk (any flavor), softened**

Place 15 x 10-inch sheet of foil on baking sheet; set aside. Using a sharp knife, cut cake horizontally into 3 equal layers and set bottom layer on foil, cut-side up. Spread ½ cup ice milk over cake; top with second cake layer and spread with remaining ½ cup ice milk. Set remaining cake layer over ice milk and wrap loaf in foil. Transfer baking sheet with loaf to freezer and freeze until ice milk is solid, about 4 hours (loaf may be frozen for up to 1 week).

To serve, preheat oven to 450° F. Using electric mixer at medium speed, in medium mixing bowl beat egg whites until soft peaks form; gradually add sugar and continue beating until stiff peaks form. Remove loaf from freezer and remove and discard foil. Place loaf on chilled baking sheet and spread meringue over top and sides of loaf. Bake until meringue is lightly browned, 5 to 10 minutes. Serve immediately.

Each serving provides: ½ Bread Exchange; 135 Optional Calories
Per serving: 156 calories; 3 g protein; 7 g fat; 20 g carbohydrate; 29 mg calcium;
   124 mg sodium; 2 mg cholesterol; 0 g dietary fiber

*Freshly baked pound cake may be used in this recipe. Partially freeze prior to slicing.

Chocolate Cream Log

WEEK 8 · MAKES 8 SERVINGS

¾ cup cake flour
2 tablespoons unsweetened cocoa
1 teaspoon double-acting baking
    powder
4 eggs
⅓ cup granulated sugar

2 cups vanilla ice milk, softened
¾ cup thawed frozen dairy whipped
    topping
1 tablespoon chocolate syrup

Preheat oven to 400° F. Spray 15 x 10 x 1-inch jelly-roll pan with nonstick cooking spray. Line pan with sheet of wax paper and spray again; set aside.

On separate sheet of wax paper or a paper plate sift together flour, cocoa, and baking powder; set aside. Using electric mixer on high speed, in large mixing bowl beat eggs until combined; gradually add sugar, beating until mixture is thick and lemon colored and double in volume, 5 to 7 minutes. Fold in sifted ingredients. Spread batter evenly in prepared pan and bake until golden, about 10 minutes (top should spring back when lightly touched with finger).

Remove cake from oven and turn cake onto a towel; remove and discard wax paper. Starting at narrow end, roll cake with towel; set on wire rack and let cool.

Unroll cooled cake, remove towel, and spread ice milk over cake surface, leaving ½-inch edge on all sides of cake; reroll cake and place, seam-side down, on serving platter. Spread whipped topping over top and sides of log; drizzle with syrup. Cover log loosely with plastic wrap and freeze until firm, about 1 hour. To serve, cut into 8 equal slices.

Each serving provides: ½ Protein Exchange; ½ Bread Exchange, 130 Optional Calories
Per serving: 198 calories; 6 g protein; 6 g fat; 30 g carbohydrate; 101 mg calcium;
    132 mg sodium; 143 mg cholesterol; 0.2 g dietary fiber

Coffee-Nut-Flavored Mousse

WEEK 8   MAKES 4 SERVINGS

4 eggs, separated
2 tablespoons granulated sugar
¼ cup coffee-flavored liqueur
2 tablespoons hazelnut-flavored liqueur

1 teaspoon unflavored gelatin
2 tablespoons half-and-half (blend
  of milk and cream)

In top half of double boiler combine egg yolks and sugar and cook over medium heat, stirring constantly with a wire whisk, until mixture is thick and lemon colored, 2 to 3 minutes. In 1-cup liquid measure combine liqueurs; sprinkle gelatin over liqueurs and let stand to soften. Stir liqueur mixture to combine; stir into yolk mixture and cook, stirring constantly, until gelatin is completely dissolved. Stir in half-and-half and, continuing to stir, cook until mixture is heated through, 1 to 2 minutes. Transfer to large mixing bowl and set aside.

Using electric mixer at high speed, in large mixing bowl beat egg whites until stiff but not dry. Gently fold beaten whites into yolk mixture until thoroughly combined. Into each of four dessert dishes pour ¼ of mousse mixture; cover with plastic wrap and refrigerate until set, about 30 minutes.

Each serving provides: 1 Protein Exchange; 120 Optional Calories
Per serving: 177 calories; 7 g protein; 6 g fat; 14 g carbohydrate; 36 mg calcium;
  73 mg sodium; 277 mg cholesterol; 0 g dietary fiber

Nutty Chocolate Pudding

WEEK 3   MAKES 4 SERVINGS

2 tablespoons *each* half-and-half
(blend of milk and cream) and
creamy peanut butter
1 cup thawed frozen dairy whipped
topping

2 cups skim *or* nonfat milk
1 envelope (four ½-cup servings)
reduced-calorie chocolate instant
pudding mix

In medium mixing bowl combine half-and-half and peanut butter; mix well until peanut butter is smooth and mixture is well combined. Stir in whipped topping; set aside.

Using 2 cups milk, prepare pudding according to package directions. Into each of 4 dessert dishes spoon ¼ of the pudding; top each with ¼ of the peanut butter mixture (about ¼ cup). Cover with plastic wrap and refrigerate until pudding is firm and chilled, about 1 hour.

Each serving provides: ½ Protein Exchange; ½ Fat Exchange; 1 Milk Exchange;
65 Optional Calories
Per serving: 183 calories; 7 g protein; 10 g fat; 20 g carbohydrate; 165 mg calcium;
471 mg sodium; 5 mg cholesterol; 0.6 g dietary fiber

Quick Pots de Crème ☾◐

Instant pudding is the secret for turning out our version of this classic dessert that is ready in only 10 minutes.

1 cup low-fat milk (1% milk fat)
1 envelope (four ½-cup servings)
    reduced-calorie chocolate instant
    pudding mix
½ cup *each* thawed frozen dairy
    whipped topping, divided, and
    evaporated skimmed milk

2 teaspoons vanilla extract
1 tablespoon chocolate syrup

Using a wire whisk, in medium mixing bowl combine low-fat milk, pudding mix, ⅓ cup whipped topping, the evaporated skimmed milk, and vanilla, beating until blended and smooth.

Into each of 4 dessert dishes pour ¼ of pudding mixture; top each with ¼ of the remaining whipped topping and ¼ of the chocolate syrup. Serve immediately or cover and refrigerate until ready to serve.

Each serving provides: 1 Milk Exchange; 45 Optional Calories
Per serving: 127 calories; 5 g protein; 3 g fat; 20 g carbohydrate; 172 mg calcium;
    428 mg sodium; 4 mg cholesterol; dietary fiber data not available

Hot Citrus Tea ⊖ ⊕

WEEK 1	MAKES 4 SERVINGS, ABOUT 1 CUP EACH

1 quart plus 2 tablespoons water,
  divided
2 tablespoons granulated sugar
1 tablespoon *each* orange juice
  (no sugar added) and lemon juice

One 2-inch cinnamon stick
2 tea bags

In 1½-quart saucepan bring 1 quart water to a boil. In small saucepan combine remaining 2 tablespoons water, the sugar, juices, and cinnamon stick and cook, stirring constantly, until sugar is dissolved and mixture comes to a boil. Reduce heat to low and let simmer for 2 minutes. Place tea bags in teapot and pour boiling water over bags; set aside to steep for 5 minutes. Remove and discard tea bags. Remove cinnamon stick and pour juice mixture into teapot; stir to combine.

Each serving provides: 30 Optional Calories
Per serving: 29 calories; 0.05 g protein; trace fat; 8 g carbohydrate; 8 mg calcium;
  5 mg sodium; 0 mg cholesterol; 0 g dietary fiber

White Sangria ◑

MAKES 8 SERVINGS, ABOUT ½ CUP EACH

2 cups lemon-flavored club soda, chilled

1½ cups dry white table wine, chilled

1 cup orange juice (no sugar added), chilled

¼ cup *each* orange liqueur, vodka, and freshly squeezed lime juice

1 tablespoon superfine sugar*

1 small orange (about 6 ounces), cut into 8 slices

1 small apple (about 4 ounces), cored and cut into 8 wedges

1 lemon, cut into 8 slices

Ice cubes

In 2-quart pitcher or punch bowl combine club soda, wine, orange juice, liqueur, vodka, lime juice, and sugar, stirring until sugar is dissolved. Add fruits and stir well to combine.

To serve, fill eight 12-ounce glasses with ice cubes; transfer 1 orange slice, 1 apple wedge, and 1 lemon slice from punch to each glass and then pour in ½ cup sangria.

Each serving provides: ½ Fruit Exchange; 85 Optional Calories
Per serving: 106 calories; 1 g protein; 0.1 g fat; 13 g carbohydrate; 23 mg calcium;
   3 mg sodium; 0 mg cholesterol; 1 g dietary fiber

*If superfine sugar is not available, process granulated sugar in blender container until superfine.

Appendix

Dry and Liquid Measure Equivalents

Teaspoons	Tablespoons	Cups	Fluid Ounces
3 teaspoons	1 tablespoon		½ fluid ounce
6 teaspoons	2 tablespoons	⅛ cup	1 fluid ounce
8 teaspoons	2 tablespoons plus 2 teaspoons	⅙ cup	
12 teaspoons	4 tablespoons	¼ cup	2 fluid ounces
15 teaspoons	5 tablespoons	⅓ cup less 1 teaspoon	
16 teaspoons	5 tablespoons plus 1 teaspoon	⅓ cup	
18 teaspoons	6 tablespoons	⅓ cup plus 2 teaspoons	3 fluid ounces
24 teaspoons	8 tablespoons	½ cup	4 fluid ounces
30 teaspoons	10 tablespoons	½ cup plus 2 tablespoons	5 fluid ounces
32 teaspoons	10 tablespoons plus 2 teaspoons	⅔ cup	
36 teaspoons	12 tablespoons	¾ cup	6 fluid ounces
42 teaspoons	14 tablespoons	1 cup less 2 tablespoons	7 fluid ounces
45 teaspoons	15 tablespoons	1 cup less 1 tablespoon	
48 teaspoons	16 tablespoons	1 cup	8 fluid ounces

Note: Measurements of less than ⅛ teaspoon are considered a Dash or a Pinch.

411

Goal Weights
Women

Height Range Without Shoes	Age in Years				
	18	19–20	21–22	23–24	25 & Over
Ft. Inches	Weight in Pounds Without Shoes				
4 6(54)	83– 99	84–101	85–103	86–104	88–106
4 7(55)	84–100	85–102	86–104	88–105	90–107
4 8(56)	86–101	87–103	88–105	90–106	92–108
4 9(57)	89–102	90–104	91–106	92–108	94–110
4 10(58)	91–105	92–106	93–109	94–111	96–113
4 11(59)	93–109	94–111	95–113	96–114	99–116
5 0(60)	96–112	97–113	98–115	100–117	102–119
5 1(61)	100–116	101–117	102–119	103–121	105–122
5 2(62)	104–119	105–121	106–123	107–125	108–126
5 3(63)	106–125	107–126	108–127	109–129	111–130
5 4(64)	109–130	110–131	111–132	112–134	114–135
5 5(65)	112–133	113–134	114–136	116–138	118–139
5 6(66)	116–137	117–138	118–140	120–142	122–143
5 7(67)	121–140	122–142	123–144	124–146	126–147
5 8(68)	123–144	124–146	126–148	128–150	130–151
5 9(69)	130–148	131–150	132–152	133–154	134–155
5 10(70)	134–151	135–154	136–156	137–158	138–159
5 11(71)	138–155	139–158	140–160	141–162	142–163
6 0(72)	142–160	143–162	144–164	145–166	146–167
6 1(73)	146–164	147–166	148–168	149–170	150–171
6 2(74)	150–168	151–170	152–172	153–174	154–175

Goal Weights
Men

Height Range Without Shoes	Age in Years				
	18	19–20	21–22	23–24	25 & Over
Ft. Inches	Weight in Pounds Without Shoes				
5 0(60)	109–122	110–133	112–135	114–137	115–138
5 1(61)	112–126	113–136	115–138	117–140	118–141
5 2(62)	115–130	116–139	118–140	120–142	121–144
5 3(63)	118–135	119–143	121–145	123–147	124–148
5 4(64)	120–145	122–147	124–149	126–151	127–152
5 5(65)	124–149	125–151	127–153	129–155	130–156
5 6(66)	128–154	129–156	131–158	133–160	134–161
5 7(67)	132–159	133–161	134–163	136–165	138–166
5 8(68)	135–163	136–165	138–167	140–169	142–170
5 9(69)	140–165	141–169	142–171	144–173	146–174
5 10(70)	143–170	144–173	146–175	148–178	150–179
5 11(71)	147–177	148–179	150–181	152–183	154–184
6 0(72)	151–180	152–184	154–186	156–188	158–189
6 1(73)	155–187	156–189	158–190	160–193	162–194
6 2(74)	160–192	161–194	163–196	165–198	167–199
6 3(75)	165–198	166–199	168–201	170–203	172–204
6 4(76)	170–202	171–204	173–206	175–208	177–209

Goal Weights
Girls

Height Range Without Shoes	Age in Years							
	10	11	12	13	14	15	16	17
Ft. Inches	Weight in Pounds Without Shoes							
3 11(47)	48– 55							
4 0(48)	49– 58	51– 61						
4 1(49)	50– 61	52– 65	53– 69					
4 2(50)	51– 64	53– 67	55– 71	60– 73				
4 3(51)	54– 67	55– 70	57– 73	62– 76	63– 84			
4 4(52)	58– 70	59– 73	60– 76	64– 79	67– 88	77– 91		
4 5(53)	59– 73	62– 76	63– 79	66– 82	71– 90	78– 93	79– 94	80– 96
4 6(54)	62– 75	65– 77	66– 81	68– 85	74– 91	79– 94	80– 95	82– 98
4 7(55)	64– 77	68– 78	69– 84	70– 88	76– 92	80– 95	81– 96	83– 99
4 8(56)	66– 79	71– 80	72– 87	73– 91	78– 94	81– 96	82– 97	85–100
4 9(57)	68– 83	74– 84	75– 90	76– 94	81– 97	84– 99	85–100	88–101
4 10(58)	70– 86	76– 87	77– 93	79– 97	84–100	87–102	88–103	90–104
4 11(59)	75– 89	78– 90	80– 96	82–100	87–103	90–105	91–106	92–108
5 0(60)	80– 92	81– 93	82– 98	86–103	90–106	93–108	94–110	95–111
5 1(61)	82– 95	84– 97	86–101	88–106	94–109	97–111	98–112	99–113
5 2(62)	84– 98	86–102	89–104	92–109	98–112	101–115	102–117	103–118
5 3(63)	87–101	89–104	92–106	96–112	101–115	103–122	104–123	105–124
5 4(64)	90–103	93–106	97–109	100–115	104–118	106–124	107–126	108–128
5 5(65)	94–105	98–108	102–111	104–118	107–121	109–126	110–129	111–131
5 6(66)		103–111	106–116	108–121	111–124	113–131	114–132	115–134
5 7(67)		107–114	110–120	112–124	116–127	118–134	119–135	120–137
5 8(68)			114–124	117–127	119–130	120–135	121–138	122–140
5 9(69)			118–127	122–130	124–133	126–141	128–142	129–144
5 10(70)				127–134	128–137	130–143	132–146	133–148
5 11(71)				132–138	133–141	135–146	136–150	137–152
6 0(72)					136–145	138–148	140–151	141–156
6 1(73)					140–150	142–155	144–158	145–160

Goal Weights
Boys

Height Range Without Shoes	Age in Years							
	10	11	12	13	14	15	16	17
Ft. Inches	Weight in Pounds Without Shoes							
3 11(47)	48– 52							
4 0(48)	50– 55	51– 57						
4 1(49)	52– 57	53– 58						
4 2(50)	54– 59	55– 60	56– 62					
4 3(51)	58– 62	59– 63	60– 64					
4 4(52)	60– 65	61– 66	62– 67					
4 5(53)	63– 68	64– 69	65– 70	66– 71				
4 6(54)	65– 71	66– 72	67– 73	68– 75				
4 7(55)	70– 75	71– 76	72– 77	73– 79	74– 80			
4 8(56)	75– 80	76– 81	77– 83	78– 85	79– 87			
4 9(57)	79– 82	80– 84	81– 86	83– 89	84– 90	86– 95		
4 10(58)	82– 86	83– 87	84– 88	88– 93	89– 94	92–100	95–108	
4 11(59)	86– 90	87– 91	88– 92	93– 97	94– 98	96–104	98–110	101–114
5 0(60)	90– 94	91– 95	92– 96	96–101	98–103	100–108	102–113	105–117
5 1(61)	93– 97	95– 99	96–100	100–105	101–108	103–112	106–116	108–120
5 2(62)	97–101	99–103	100–104	104–109	106–113	108–116	110–120	112–123
5 3(63)	100–104	102–106	104–108	107–113	111–118	113–120	114–123	117–126
5 4(64)	102–107	104–109	108–112	111–117	114–121	116–123	118–127	119–130
5 5(65)	105–110	107–112	112–116	115–121	117–125	119–127	122–130	123–133
5 6(66)		111–116	116–120	118–125	121–129	123–131	126–133	127–137
5 7(67)		115–120	119–124	121–130	125–133	128–134	130–136	131–141
5 8(68)			122–128	124–133	129–137	132–138	133–140	134–145
5 9(69)			125–132	127–136	133–141	136–142	138–144	139–149
5 10(70)				130–140	137–145	140–149	141–155	142–160
5 11(71)				135–144	141–149	144–155	145–160	146–168
6 0(72)					146–153	148–156	149–163	150–170
6 1(73)					150–157	152–163	153–166	154–175
6 2(74)						157–165	158–170	159–182
6 3(75)						162–175	163–180	164–190
6 4(76)						167–185	168–191	169–195

Index

A

E

F

G

German Apple-Sausage Pancake, 389
German Pancake with Syrup
    (variation), 389
Ginger Butter, 394
Gingered Citrus Carrots, 110
Gingered Custard, 357
Gingered Salmon, 197
Girls, weight and height tables, 414
Glazed Onions with Cranberries, 128
Goat cheese
    Avocado Salad with Goat Cheese
        (variation), 390
    Mediterranean Cucumber Salad, 113
Golden Potato Bake, 326
Gorgonzola cheese
    Broccoli, Potato, and Cheese Soup,
        105
    Cheese-Filled Cucumber Cups, 178
    Four-Cheese Omelet, 182
    Gratin of Leeks and Gorgonzola, 121
    Pears with Gorgonzola and Port, 86
    Polenta with Gorgonzola and
        Roasted Peppers, 302
Granola, 299
Grapefruit
    Citrus Sauce, 78
Grapes
    Fresh Fruit Ambrosia, 400
    Grapes Brûlée, 77
Gratin of Leeks and Gorgonzola, 121
Greek Lentil Salad, 271
Green beans
    Green Bean and Mushroom Salad,
        120
    Green Beans Sauté, 119
    Summer Corn and Vegetable Salad,
        319
Green peppers see Peppers
Grilled Cheese and Turkey Club
    Sandwich, 235
Grilled Chicken with Dijon
    Mayonnaise, 221
Grilled Chicken with Tomato Butter, 219
Grilled Oriental Chicken Salad, 220
Gruyère cheese
    Broccoli-Cheese Soup, 168
    Cheese Crisps, 180
    Fennel Salad, 118
    Fennel Salad with Yogurt Dressing
        (variation), 118
    Four-Cheese Omelet, 182
    Scallop and Crab Gratin, 212
    Tomato-Cheese Tarts, 173

H

Halibut Steaks in Vegetable-Wine
    Sauce, 195
Ham
    Buttery Eggs and Prosciutto Toasts
        (variation), 162
    Cheese 'n' Ham-Topped Biscuits, 175
    Chicken, Prosciutto, and Eggplant
        Bake, 224
    Chicken Zaragoza, 232
    Chunky Cheese Salad, 177
    Creole Red Beans and Rice, 267
    Eggs and Prosciutto Toasts, 162
    Elegant Ham 'n' Cheese Sandwich,
        392
    Ham Steaks with Cider-Pear Sauce,
        254
    Minestrone Salad, 321
    Open-Face Turkey Sandwich with
        Brie Sauce, 234
    Pasta with Eggplant-Prosciutto
        Sauce, 306
    Portuguese Clams with Sausage and
        Ham (variation), 205
    Pumpkin Chowder with Ham
        (variation), 131
    Skillet Lentils and Potatoes, 273
    Smoked Ham Calzones (variation),
        169
    Stuffed Sweet Potato Surprise, 329
    Sweet Potato-Ham Biscuits, 332
    Veal España, 248
Harvest Home Fries, 327
Height and weight tables, 412–415
Herb-Cheese Spread, 166
High-Fiber Apple Muffins, 64
Hollandaise Sauce, 395
Hominy Chowder, 301
Honey-Poached Pear Fans, 84
Honeydew
    Compote of Spiced Fresh Fruit, 76
Hors d'Oeuvres see Appetizers and
    hors d'oeuvres
Horseradish-Caper Sauce, 396
Hot Citrus Tea, 409
Hummus Soup, 269

P